by Jesse Feiler

Swift™ For Dummies®

Published by: **John Wiley & Sons, Inc.,** 111 River Street, Hoboken, NJ 07030-5774, www.wiley.com

Copyright © 2015 by John Wiley & Sons, Inc., Hoboken, New Jersey

Media and software compilation copyright © 2015 by John Wiley & Sons, Inc. All rights reserved.

Published simultaneously in Canada

No part of this publication may be reproduced, stored in a retrieval system or transmitted in any form or by any means, electronic, mechanical, photocopying, recording, scanning or otherwise, except as permitted under Sections 107 or 108 of the 1976 United States Copyright Act, without the prior written permission of the Publisher. Requests to the Publisher for permission should be addressed to the Permissions Department, John Wiley & Sons, Inc., 111 River Street, Hoboken, NJ 07030, (201) 748-6011, fax (201) 748-6008, or online at www.wiley.com/go/permissions.

Trademarks: Wiley, For Dummies, the Dummies Man logo, Dummies.com, Making Everything Easier, and related trade dress are trademarks or registered trademarks of John Wiley & Sons, Inc. and may not be used without written permission. Swift is a trademark of Apple, Inc. All other trademarks are the property of their respective owners. John Wiley & Sons, Inc. is not associated with any product or vendor mentioned in this book. *Swift For Dummies®* is an independent publication and has not been authorized, sponsored, or otherwise approved by Apple, Inc.

LIMIT OF LIABILITY/DISCLAIMER OF WARRANTY: THE PUBLISHER AND THE AUTHOR MAKE NO REPRESENTATIONS OR WARRANTIES WITH RESPECT TO THE ACCURACY OR COMPLETENESS OF THE CONTENTS OF THIS WORK AND SPECIFICALLY DISCLAIM ALL WARRANTIES, INCLUDING WITHOUT LIMITATION WARRANTIES OF FITNESS FOR A PARTICULAR PURPOSE. NO WARRANTY MAY BE CREATED OR EXTENDED BY SALES OR PROMOTIONAL MATERIALS. THE ADVICE AND STRATEGIES CONTAINED HEREIN MAY NOT BE SUITABLE FOR EVERY SITUATION. THIS WORK IS SOLD WITH THE UNDERSTANDING THAT THE PUBLISHER IS NOT ENGAGED IN RENDERING LEGAL, ACCOUNTING, OR OTHER PROFESSIONAL SERVICES. IF PROFESSIONAL ASSISTANCE IS REQUIRED, THE SERVICES OF A COMPETENT PROFESSIONAL PERSON SHOULD BE SOUGHT. NEITHER THE PUBLISHER NOR THE AUTHOR SHALL BE LIABLE FOR DAMAGES ARISING HEREFROM. THE FACT THAT AN ORGANIZATION OR WEBSITE IS REFERRED TO IN THIS WORK AS A CITATION AND/OR A POTENTIAL SOURCE OF FURTHER INFORMATION DOES NOT MEAN THAT THE AUTHOR OR THE PUBLISHER ENDORSES THE INFORMATION THE ORGANIZATION OR WEBSITE MAY PROVIDE OR RECOMMENDATIONS IT MAY MAKE. FURTHER, READERS SHOULD BE AWARE THAT INTERNET WEBSITES LISTED IN THIS WORK MAY HAVE CHANGED OR DISAPPEARED BETWEEN WHEN THIS WORK WAS WRITTEN AND WHEN IT IS READ.

For general information on our other products and services, please contact our Customer Care Department within the U.S. at 877-762-2974, outside the U.S. at 317-572-3993, or fax 317-572-4002. For technical support, please visit www.wiley.com/techsupport.

Wiley publishes in a variety of print and electronic formats and by print-on-demand. Some material included with standard print versions of this book may not be included in e-books or in print-on-demand. If this book refers to media such as a CD or DVD that is not included in the version you purchased, you may download this material at http://booksupport.wiley.com. For more information about Wiley products, visit www.wiley.com.

Library of Congress Control Number: 2014954655

ISBN 978-1-119-02222-0 (pbk); ISBN 978-1-119-02224-4(ebk); ISBN 978-1-119-02223-7 (ebk)

Manufactured in the United States of America

10 9 8 7 6 5 4 3 2 1

Contents at a Glance

Table of Contents

Introduction

In June of 2014, one of the highlights of Apple's Worldwide Developers Conference (WWDC) was the announcement — a surprise to many attendees, including the multitudes of developers watching the videos around the world — of the development of a new language aimed at developers to use with iOS and OS X devices. Called Swift, it was presented as the language of the future for Apple's developers, but it was made very clear that it would cooperate with the existing basic development language — Objective-C. (In describing the ways Swift and Objective-C would interact, Apple repeatedly used the phrase "mix and match" — not only in the presentations at WWDC, but in other venues as well.)

Think about that date— Swift has only been around since June 2014: We're all beginners with Swift.

About This Book

Swift For Dummies is a beginner's introduction to Apple's new programming language. The book gets you started developing with Swift. You'll quickly see how to create projects in Swift from the built-in templates that are part of the Xcode development tool. From there, you delve into the features of the language, from the basic to the advanced. Some of these features are unique to Swift whereas other, possibly more familiar features were inherited from other programming languages.

Before we get started with Swift, consider these two points:

- **Apple has done this before, and they know how to do it.** On both the hardware and software sides, Apple has successfully managed transitions to new technologies. Developers have sometimes cheered, sometimes booed, and even sometimes not even noticed much difference, but nonetheless, Apple has managed to bring them along to a new technology that makes their lives easier and improves things for users.
- **The languages are only part of the development environment for Apple.** When you develop apps for iOS or OS X, you use the Xcode development tool (technically an Integrated Development Environment, or IDE), the Cocoa or Cocoa Touch frameworks, and a programming language — either Objective-C or Swift. What differentiates the iOS and OS X development environment from most others is that the language is only one-third of the overall environment, as well as the fact that a single company (Apple) controls all of that environment.

Conventions Used in This Book

Cocoa is the framework you use for developing Mac apps; Cocoa Touch is the framework for iOS apps. Both have a common heritage and many similar classes. In general, classes that start with `NS` are Cocoa classes, and classes that start with `UI` are Cocoa Touch classes. Many Cocoa `NS` classes are also used in Cocoa Touch, so you'll find both types of classes in many of your apps and in the sample code and templates.

Code examples in this book appear in a `monospaced` font so that they stand out a bit better. Some non-syntax components appear in an italicized monospaced font. (Thus, `weatherConditions` might be a variable, but *variable* could be any variable you want to use.)

Like many languages, including Objective-C, Swift is case-sensitive, so please enter the code that appears in this book *exactly* as it appears in the text. I also use the standard Cocoa naming conventions — such as capitalizing class names and leaving the names of methods and instance variables lowercase.

Note that all URLs in this book appear in a monospaced font as well. In accordance with common usage, most URLs in this book include the subdomain (such as `www`) at the beginning of many URLs except for addresses that don't require that component (such as `developer.apple.com`).

If you're ever uncertain about anything in the code, you can always look at the source code on my website at `www.northcountryconsulting.com` or the *For Dummies* website at `www.dummies.com`. From time to time, I'll provide updates for the code there and post other things you might find useful.

Foolish Assumptions

This book makes few assumptions about readers because Swift programmers come from many backgrounds and with varying degrees of proficiency in various languages. As to the future, however, there's one simple assumption: You want to create apps based on the Cocoa and Cocoa Touch frameworks, and you want to do it in the simplest way possible.

Fittingly, then, this book is aimed at Cocoa and Cocoa Touch developers at all stages of expertise, from those who've developed a multitude of App Store apps to those who have only thought about developing an app . . . someday.

I also assume you have some Mac or iOS experience. If you have never used a Mac or iOS device, you may find it hard to follow this book. I explain advanced technical terms as they arise, but my assumption is that you know, for example, what Settings (on iOS devices) and System Preferences (on Macs are), and that similar concepts are familiar to you.

You must have access to a Mac that can run the current version of Xcode (a free download from `developer.apple.com`). Without Xcode and the Mac to run it on, you can't experiment with the sample code.

Note that Xcode runs only on Macintosh computers running Mac OS X v10.9.4 (Mavericks) or later on a 64-bit Intel-based Mac.

Additionally, you must have Internet access. It's very important to stress, however, that I don't mean "always-on" Internet access. I only mean that you must at least have limited Internet access — so you can access the App Store, for example, and connect with Apple's `developer.apple.com` to download software and upload apps.

Perhaps the most foolish assumption of all may be your own: that you can't learn Swift or the Cocoa and Cocoa Touch frameworks. You can, and this book is designed to help you. Bear in mind that app development is not easy: If it were, the App Store would have far more than just over a million apps. It's not easy, but you can do it.

Icons Used in This Book

This icon indicates a useful pointer that you shouldn't skip.

REMEMBER

This icon represents a friendly reminder. It describes a vital point that you should keep in mind while proceeding through a particular section of the chapter.

This icon signifies that the accompanying explanation may be informative (dare we say interesting?), but it isn't essential to understanding Swift. Feel free to skip past these tidbits if you like (though skipping while learning may be tricky).

This icon alerts you to potential problems that you may encounter along the way. Read and obey these blurbs to avoid trouble.

Beyond the Book

A lot of extra content that you won't find in this book is available at `www.dummies.com`. Go online to find the following:

- **Source code for the examples in this book at**

  ```
  www.dummies.com/extras/swift
  ```

  This book contains a lot of code, and you might not want to type it. In fact, it's probably better if you don't type this code manually. Fortunately, you can find the source code for this book on the Dummies.com website at `www.dummies.com/extras/swift`. The source code is organized by chapter. The best way to work with a chapter is to download all the source code for it at one time.

- **Online articles covering additional topics at**

  ```
  www.dummies.com/extras/swift
  ```

  Here you'll find out how to know whether to use a type, collection, flow control, or function to implement an action; how to initialize stored properties in a class or structure; and how to let Xcode create actions and outlets for you.

  Ongoing discussions at `developer.apple.com` (for registered developers only) and at my website (`www.northcountryconsulting.com`) provide even more information.

- **The Cheat Sheet for this book is at**

  ```
  www.dummies.com/cheatsheet/swift
  ```

  Here you'll find an examination of the anatomy of a Swift class, the best way to update Xcode for a new Swift release, and advice about working with both Swift and Objective-C.

- **Updates to this book, if we have any, are also available at**

  ```
  www.dummies.com/extras/swift
  ```

Where to Go from Here

It's time to start your Swift adventure! If you're new to programming, start with Chapter 1 and progress through the book at a pace that allows you to absorb as much of the material as possible. If you're in an absolute rush to get going with Swift as quickly as possible, you could possibly skip to Chapter 2 with the understanding that you may find some topics a bit confusing later.

Part I
Getting Started with Swift

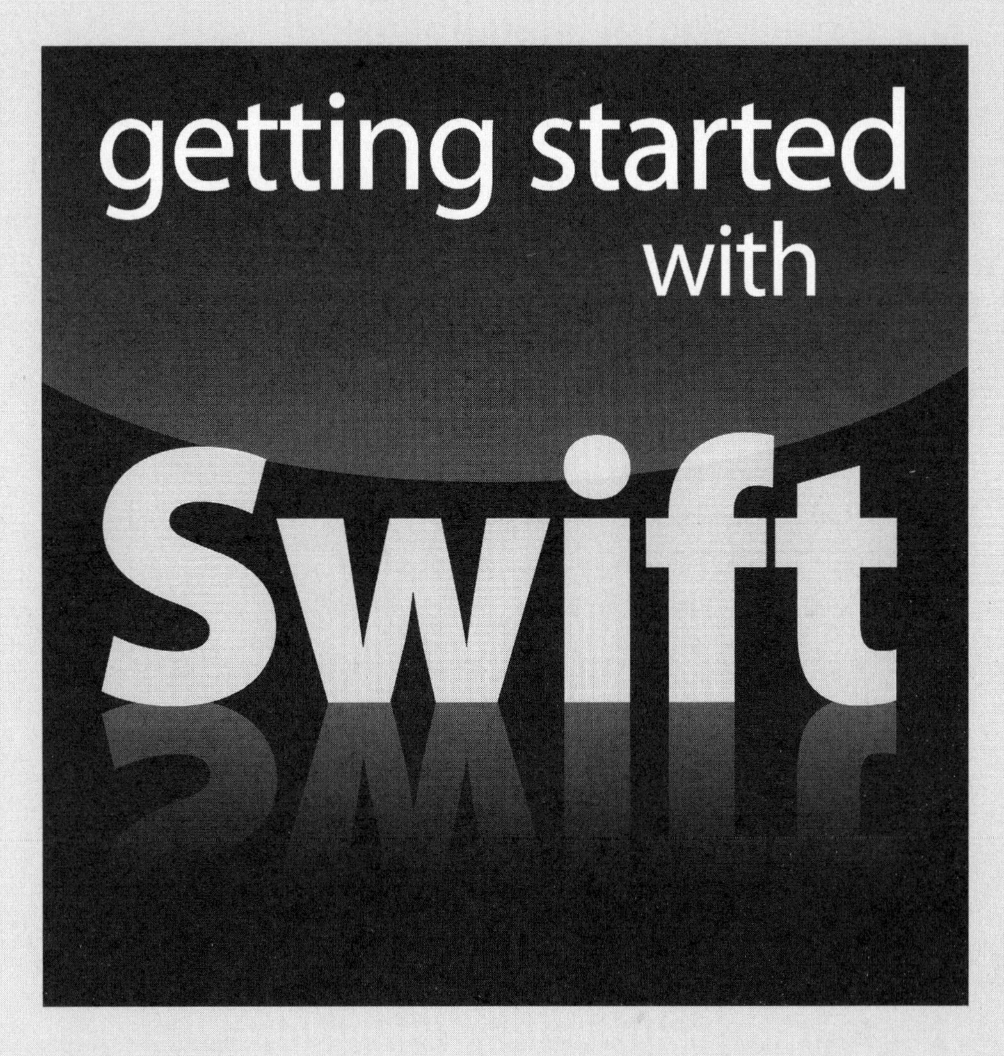

Visit `www.dummies.com` for great *For Dummies* content online.

In this part . . .

- Set up an Xcode Swift project.
- Find out how to use a playground.
- Explore the Xcode editing tools.
- Write your first Swift app.

Chapter 1

Setting Up an Xcode Swift Project

In This Chapter

- Introducing Swift
- Setting up your computer for Swift
- Defining your development preferences
- Creating and exploring your first project

Swift is Apple's new language for developers to use with iOS and OS X devices. As such, it is the successor to Apple's existing iOS/OS X development language, Objective-C, but Swift has been designed to cooperate with and work alongside Objective-C, so this should be a slow transition to power.

Some Swift beginners come to the language with proficiency in other languages, ranging from C and its offshoots such as C++ and Objective-C, to newer languages such as Ruby, Python, and Java, as well as scripting languages such as PHP and JavaScript.

Whether you're just starting out as an Apple developer or are an experienced developer who wants to add Swift to your skills, this chapter helps you get started. There's one very important point to remember: As of this writing, the iOS API (application programming interface) and SDK (software development kit) are less than ten years old. (They were launched in early 2008, six months after the launch of iPhone.) The early years of iOS development were an exciting period as the pieces of today's hardware and software environment fell into place. Only as thousands of developers and millions of users started actually using these devices and the languages that support them did some issues — bugs as well as great enhancements — begin to take shape.

Arguably, it took several years for the SDK to reach maturity. Many developers (including your humble author) believe that it was only with the release of iOS 4 in 2010 that the platform more or less stabilized as the operating system we recognize today. This was the first version to be called "iOS" rather than "iPhone OS," and, with the release of iOS 4.2.1 in the fall of 2010, it was the first to support both iPhone and iPad. The first version of multitasking was present, and preparations were made for iCloud that was first released in iOS 5.

If you haven't looked at iOS since that time, a lot has changed. The release of Swift and iOS 8 is a good opportunity to look around and get up to date with iOS (and, for that matter, OS X). This chapter helps you do that.

In this book, you'll occasionally find warnings like this one about serious issues you should avoid. The warnings are used sparingly, so pay attention to them when they appear. The focus in this book is on getting you up and running as a Swift developer. That involves giving you the information you need as well as helping you along the way with encouragement and, from time to time, reminding you that you're not the first person to learn Swift. Others have been there before, and, in most cases, others (most definitely including the author) have encountered the problems you may be facing. There are a multitude of warnings in this chapter. This isn't intended to scare you off: Rather, it's designed to help you over that first hump of becoming a Swift developer. After you have your first clean compile and have finished a build of a project (in the section, "Planning Your Environment," later in this chapter), you'll be on your way.

Looking Ahead to the End

As you make progress in Swift, this book helps you build an app — a real, live app — based on one of the built-in Xcode templates. *Sure,* you're probably thinking, *that's just what I need — another "Hello World" app.*

Actually, no. There's no "Hello World" here. Instead, the app you'll be building, called Locatapp, is a full-fledged Swift app created using the Master-Detail Application template that's built into Xcode, and it uses Cocoa Touch and a number of its frameworks to do its work. Locatapp uses location services on Cocoa Touch and the iOS mobile devices to find your location, as you see in Figure 1-1.

If you prefer, you can download Locatapp from this book's companion website, as described in the Introduction, but be warned — some of the details of registering as a developer described later in this chapter are needed to get Locatapp to run on your own device.

The pulsing blue dot shows your current location. Locatapp lets you store other locations you've visited. The latitude and longitude values of locations that have been visited are shown in the list at the left of Figure 1-1. Tap one

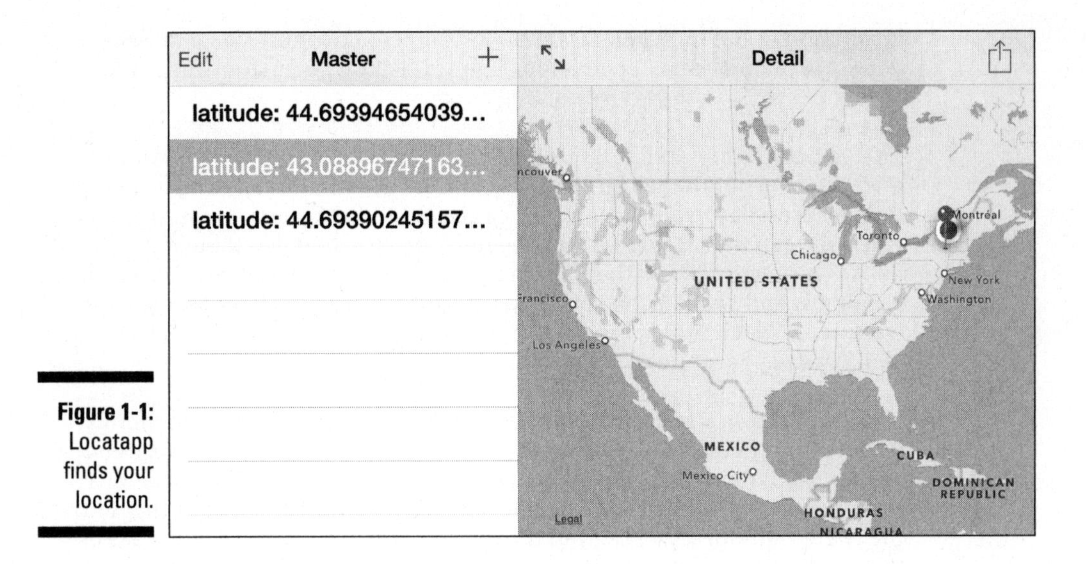

Figure 1-1: Locatapp finds your location.

of them, and you'll see a map with your current location and with the tapped location indicated by a red pin.

You can zoom in on the map (see Figure 1-2). This zoom-in functionality is all built into MapKit and the device so you don't have to write any code. As you zoom in, you can see that the two locations shown in Figure 1-1 are actually over 100 miles apart. The annotation for Current Location is also part of the framework.

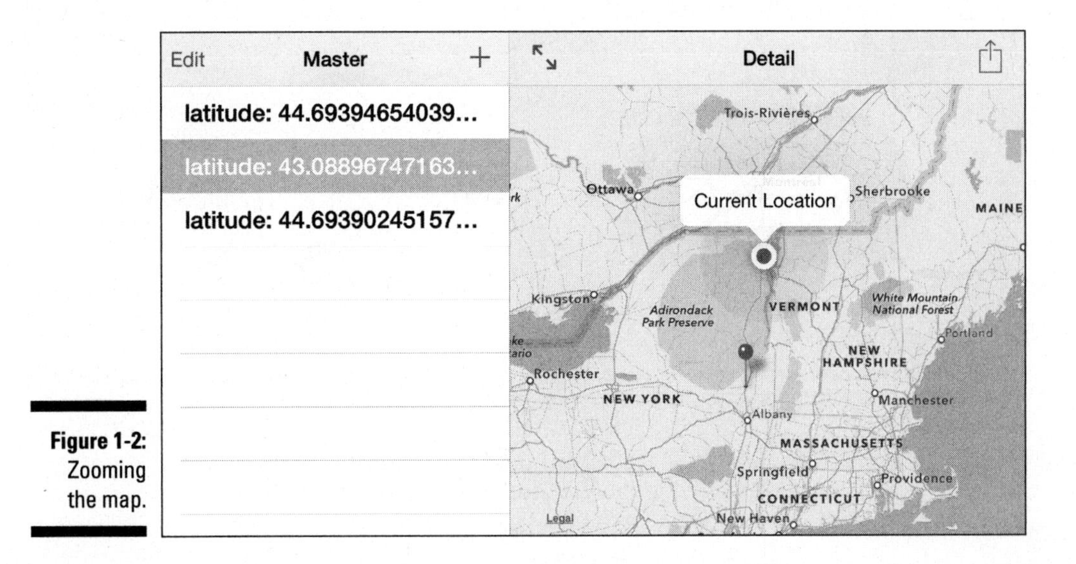

Figure 1-2: Zooming the map.

In addition to the built-in annotation for Current Location, you can write your own annotations in Locatapp. Figure 1-3 shows a custom annotation that you'll write in the course of this book.

That action button at the right of the bar in the interface (the box with the arrow poking out of the top) is an interface element you can drag from the Xcode library into your user interface (called a *storyboard*). What happens when you tap that action button depends on a method you'll build in this book. This method uses the built-in actions such as Messages, Mail, Twitter, Facebook, and so forth, as shown in Figure 1-4. (Yes, you'll write this code, but Cocoa Touch writes the supporting code to interact with Messages, Mail, Twitter, Facebook, and more.)

Figure 1-5 shows a tweet you can construct in your app. Users can modify it (note that there are 57 characters left), but you write the code for the message and to insert the map coordinates. Note, too, that the image of a web page is part of the tweet. You'll see how to automatically put that into the tweet. Although you can tap the image of the web page all you want in this book, in Locatapp, tapping that image will take you to the web page in Safari.

I'm sure you'll like Locatapp and enjoy thinking of ways you can build on it.

As I like to say, "Goodbye, 'Hello World.'"

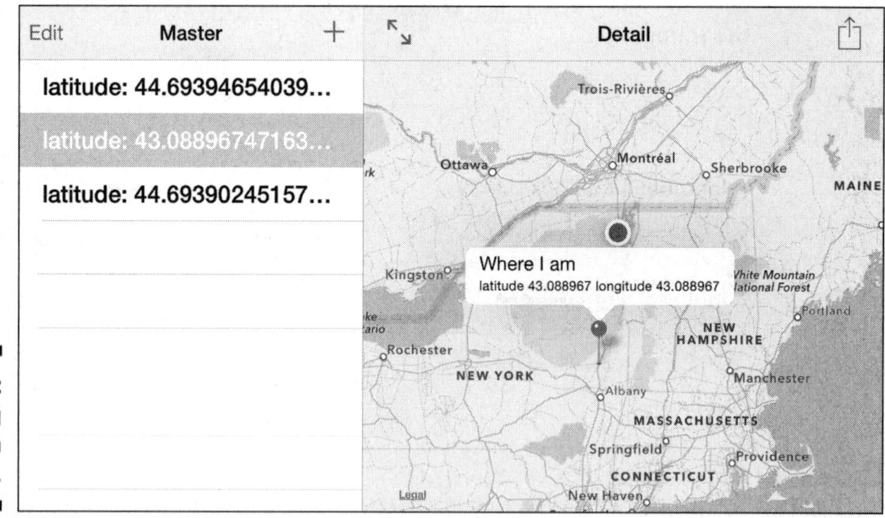

Figure 1-3: Writing your own annotations.

Figure 1-4: Implementing an action button.

Figure 1-5: Constructing social media messages from your code.

Working with Swift

Apple has two annual calendars of events. Each is highlighted by one or more major announcements with periodic updates throughout the year. For consumers and end users, the annual calendar focuses on the releases of new and updated devices. As is true throughout the world of electronics, a large portion of annual sales occur during the summer and fall ("back-to-school") and during the year-end holiday season.

On the software side, there is a related peak period. It's no accident that Apple, Google, and Microsoft all hold conferences for their developers in May and June. Typically, they unveil the new features in their operating systems at that time, allowing developers a few months to work with those features before the peak period of hardware sales.

In June of 2014, one of the highlights of Apple's Worldwide Developers Conference (WWDC) was the announcement — a surprise to many attendees — of a new development language for iOS and OS X devices. Called Swift, it was presented as the language of the future for Apple's developers, but it was made very clear that it would co-operate with the existing basic development language — Objective-C.

This book gets you started developing with Swift. You'll quickly see how to create projects in Swift from the built-in templates that are part of the Xcode development tool. From there, you'll delve into features of the languages ranging from the basics to the advanced features that are unique to Swift as well as some features of Swift that may be familiar to you from other modern programming languages.

Swift and Objective-C are the languages most often used in building apps for iOS and OS X. Combined with the Cocoa (OS X) and Cocoa Touch (iOS) frameworks and Xcode, these languages allow you to develop just about anything you can dream of. It is hard to find an app that can't be written with these tools: OS X and iOS apps as well as other Apple products such as Pages, Keynote, and Numbers are developed using Xcode and the Cocoa frameworks. Most of the language work for these products is in Objective-C or Swift, although some sections are still in C++. Apps developed with these technologies are *native* apps.

If you don't want to go the native route, you can consider using other (non-Apple) frameworks. Three widely used frameworks are Titanium Appcelerator, PhoneGap, and HTML5, which is frequently used as a development tool without being a framework. In the world of Titanium Appcelerator, you typically write in JavaScript, whereas in PhoneGap you use Javascript, HTML, and CSS. HTML5, of course, is itself a language, which you can use in conjunction with JavaScript as well as other languages.

The advantages of using these non-native frameworks center around two features:

- With these frameworks, the development process may be faster than the native-app framework.
- Using these frameworks can help you develop cross-platform apps.

The biggest disadvantage is that non-native frameworks are third-party tools and as such aren't guaranteed to support new (or even all current) features of Apple's operating systems and hardware.

The cost of developing a native app for iOS, OS X, Android, or even Windows is likely to be significantly higher than that of using one of the tools listed here. Before making a decision, you may want to explore tools such as FileMaker (a wholly-owned subsidiary of Apple), which is designed for use by non-programmers. Originally a database application, FileMaker now has become a key tool for people who may never write a line of code in their life but are comfortable (and happy!) spending their time analyzing data and the processes that use it. Give FileMaker a look — particularly if your app idea is data-related.

In terms of cost and difficulty, FileMaker is likely to be your best choice; Titanium Appcelerator, PhoneGap, and HTML5 the second-best; and native app development with Swift or Objective-C (or both) the third. In terms of flexibility, however, this order would be reversed — the native apps are the most flexible, and tools like FileMaker are the least.

If your goal is to "get an app deployed by next Tuesday," FileMaker may be your best bet (if it can be done at all). On the other hand, if your goal is to build something that will last or — perhaps more importantly — something that will develop your skills and expertise in this rapidly-growing mobile world, native apps with iOS and OS X are usually the way to go.

Getting the Developer Tools

The tools you need to develop with Swift for iOS or OS X are simple:

- **A Mac:** Any current Mac has enough processor power and memory to build apps. As of this writing, you must be running Mavericks (OS X 10.9) or Yosemite (OS X 10.10).
- **Xcode:** Xcode is the integrated development environment (IDE) for building OS X and iOS apps. You can download it for free from the Mac App Store.

These are the essentials: They're really all you need. However, a few additional tools can be very helpful — even necessary for some developers — but if you don't have them, don't worry about it. There are some workarounds and compromises if you're missing these tools. They include:

- **An iOS device (if you're developing for the iOS platform):** It's possible to develop an iOS app with no hands-on experience, but the results will show, particularly when you get reviews in the App Store along the lines of, "Hasn't the developer ever tried to use an iPhone?" Writing an app based on an understanding of iOS devices gained from articles and advertising is very difficult. It's much easier if you have access to the real thing. The one exception to this is when you're working on only a component of a larger app, one that doesn't involve the user interface.

- **Internet access:** If you only have intermittent Internet access, you can still develop, but with limitations. Certain tasks, such as getting your app into the App Store, require Internet access.
- **Plenty of disk space and a robust backup mechanism, such as Time Machine:** "Plenty of disk space" can mean a large internal disk, one or more external disks connected to your Mac, or cloud-based storage. The backup mechanism is important because you need to be confident that all of your project's files are properly backed up and can be restored, if necessary.

The Apple developer discussion boards (Apple Developer Forums, located at `https://devforums.apple.com`) provide a valuable resource, as I describe in the following section. Every few months, a plea for help shows up on those boards that goes something like this: "How do I get my app into the App Store? I've written it and now I have to get it into the App Store." (Such questions pop up in other places on the Internet as well.) Native apps need to be written in Swift or Objective-C, and they must abide by the rules of the App Store and the Mac App Store. Make certain you understand this before you start work. Writing an app in Java, HTML5, JavaScript, Objective-C without the Cocoa or Cocoa Touch framework, or even COBOL counts only as a personal experiment with a user interface; your app can't be moved into the App Store. You may be able to distribute it as an app-like website, but not as a native app. Along those lines, the various commercial app development frameworks and services may or may not be useful to you.

Setting Up Your Mac

This section provides a quick overview of setting up your Mac for development in general and for Swift in particular. The basic steps are included here, and, as you'll see, each one can open a variety of doors to additional steps and information.

Registering as a developer

The basic developer tools are free, and you can start work immediately, but Apple requires that you register as a developer at `developer.apple.com` before you can access many of the tools and features that you'll need, particularly for testing. More and more of the developer website is available without logging in, but some of the key features require registration.

Not only do you need to register, but in some areas of developer.apple.com, you need to sign a non-disclosure agreement. You will be invited to join a developer program, which may entail an annual fee (see the upcoming section, "Choosing your program," for more on this), but if you're on a limited budget or just exploring, you can get quite a long way by saying "No, Thanks" to the offers. Rejecting offers like these and surveying the site is a good way to get your feet wet and get a good general understanding of the environment — although it does not let you submit your apps to the App Store.

The rules and policies of Apple's developer programs change from time to time and from country to country. Look at developer.apple.com for the latest definitive information. Be particularly careful of web postings you find that may be from the past. Always check the posting date from any articles you rely on — and that includes articles from Apple on developer.apple.com. You can usually find this date at the bottom of an article.

Preparing your credentials

For basic registration, you need to identify yourself to Apple. The standard way of doing this is to provide an Apple ID. Your Apple ID is not confidential, but your password is. Go to appleid.apple.com to register or to manage your Apple ID (including changing your password, if you want).

You may have more than one Apple ID (and you may need to have more than one, in some cases). Some developers have separate Apple IDs for personal use in addition to ones used for development. You may have a different Apple ID for developing apps than you have for developing iBooks — in fact, at the moment, this is a requirement.

For more on this, see the section, "Planning Your Environment," later in this chapter.

Choosing your program

Apple offers a number of different developer programs in which you can enroll. The simplest one is an individual program, which, at the moment, costs $99 a year, with separate programs for iOS and OS X. Thus, if you register for both, you'll pay $198 a year.

You can also register as a business. This registration allows you to build teams of individual developers and share code among yourselves as you develop apps.

There are also programs for educational institutions. Make certain that you have an Apple ID that you will use for your development, and then choose your program. If you are working for a business or are enrolled in a school, check to see if you are eligible to join a program there: It may save you some money.

Planning Your Environment

Your development environment is centered around a Mac with Xcode installed on it, but you can use several Macs for development. Each one should have Xcode on it (see further topics in this section for a discussion of multiple versions of Xcode). Because Xcode is free, it's easy to install it on a number of Macs. In fact, if you have access to a shared computer lab (perhaps at school), Xcode may be a component that is part of the lab.

There are no special settings to use Xcode with Swift, except to choose Swift (rather than Objective-C) from the pop-up menu when creating a new project or file. You also need to download the latest Swift documentation and SDK, but this is part of the standard installation process. If you are working with an old version of Xcode, you may be better off downloading and installing a new version of Xcode from scratch and proceeding from there. Your older Xcode projects should be able to be opened (and automatically converted if necessary) by the new Xcode.

Using source control

Source control is built into Xcode with both Git and Subversion. Because of its architecture, Git is more closely integrated into Xcode than Subversion. If you use one of these tools, you can easily store your source code in a repository. If you make a practice of committing changes to your source code repository on a regular basis (at the end of each work session perhaps, or when a significant milestone has been achieved), you'll know that you can download the project on demand.

Using source control means that no matter which Mac you find yourself using, as long as you have a network (or Internet) connection, you can check out the latest copy of the project (or a branch thereof), make your changes, and then check your files back in. And the next time you want to work on it, just check out the project on another computer and keep going.

Source code control

Whether you're working on a single-developer app or a multiple-developer project of a large-scale system (think of the iOS and OS X operating systems), managing your source code is essential. This management, known as *source code control*, is sometimes referred to as *source control* or *revision control*.

For individual developers, source code control begins by having good, routine backups, often by using Time Machine. The next phase usually is an ad hoc and idiosyncratic process: creating a folder for each day's or week's work and then copying it over to a new folder on the following day or week. Together with Time Machine, which helps ensure the preservation of the various physical files, these folders provide you with a periodic backup of the entire project. (This is necessary because there are rare occasions when Time Machine's backups won't let you easily restore all of the files in a project to a specific time. This happens particularly when you use Xcode's default file locations).

Source control products such as Git and Subversion (both free, open-source projects) let you manage changes to your files. Whereas Time Machine and a file/folder structure focus on the files, source control focuses on the evolution of your app. You can define branches of code, and branches of branches, and you can identify these branches by name — "Implement Multi-User Preferences" for example — rather than just by date and time. The source control product keeps track of the date and time for you.

Both Git and Subversion are designed to allow multiple people to update a project (called a *repository*, or *repo* in these contexts). By keeping track of multiple branches and multiple people, you have an orderly process that lets you follow the development of a project.

When you start to work on a project, you *check it out* from the repository (with a check-out message you provide). When you're done, you either *drop it* (in the case of an experiment that fails), or *commit it* back to the project (with an explanatory message).

In addition to following the development, you can manage the project's development as you merge branches into one another, drop others, and generally prune your development tree."

A key part of source control is the ability for multiple users (or even a single user) to check code in and out either as part of an existing branch or a new one. If you think that your little experimental project is too small for source control, you may want to think again. Because you may eventually work on (or even manage) larger projects, you should get used to the source control process. Further, even if you're just one person, source control is a good way to manage your development over time. When a bug appears and you have to return to something you wrote a year ago, source control — particularly with the check-out messages you provide — can be a critical part of your troubleshooting and problem-solving process.

Using GitHub

Your environment may include a shared source code repository that you can use, or you can create your own environment on a remote server such as `www.github.com`, which uses Git to manage the files you add to Github. The cost is not great, and it allows you (and perhaps your colleagues) to work together on a project on various Macs. When you're confident that your source control is working properly (and, more important, when you understand *how* to use it properly), you can forget about keeping files and folders labeled "Thursday version before restructure" and "Friday version after restructure." If you haven't used source control, now is a good time to get familiar with it.

Organizing files

If you're using Git or Subversion (or another source control tool), you can cross "Organizing files" off your to-do list right now. Xcode manages files within the project folder for you, and the source control software manages changes to those files using its repository. (Preferably this repository won't be on your own disk.)

The only thing you have to do is to trust Xcode and your source control software. If all of your files are within a single project folder (which is the Xcode default), just leave them there. Don't move them around or rename them.

Preparing for environmental changes

During your development process, it is very likely that there will be changes to your environment. In addition to the changes you make to your project, there are likely to be other changes you should prepare for. The most important are the new releases of Xcode, OS X, and iOS.

Review the releases of these products over the last year on `https://developer.apple.com/downloads`, and you may see a pattern. (Note that this address may change. In addition, access to this site may be available only to registered developers.) At this writing, the release cycle is as follows:

- **Early June:** Apple's Worldwide Developer Conference (WWDC) provides updates of upcoming releases. It typically has previews and demonstrations of new operating systems and their features. It doesn't normally have product announcements. Developer previews of iOS and OS X may be distributed to attendees as well as to registered developers.
- **Summer:** Updates to developer previews are distributed to developers and sometimes to users who want to beta test software.
- **Early fall:** New devices (often iPhones) are announced and the new iOS is made final.
- **Late fall:** Other iOS devices are announced along with new Macs. A new OS X is made final and released.

- **Winter and spring:** Quiet on the developer software front (but pretty busy behind the scenes at Apple). This is the time to follow the Apple developer discussion boards closely and to file bug reports and requests (for registered developers only at this time).

As new releases of the OS X operating system and Xcode (including new SDKs for iOS and OS X) ship to developers over the summer and fall, you need to decide if you will install them and which version(s) you will support. You don't have to make this decision now, but you should think about how you will handle these updates.

If you can, you may want to have one complete development environment for current production (including your own personal software, emails, and documents) and a separate one for testing and development.

My development environment

Every developer has a different environment, although it can change from time to time (depending on what they're working on and where they're working). I've sometimes been asked what I recommend, and my answer is that I can only tell people what I use. So here's that answer. Remember, this is only the environment that works for me.

My primary device is a Mac Pro with a Thunderbolt screen. I like the speed and expandability of the Mac Pro and the size of the display. This is not the cheapest alternative, but because I spend almost all of my working time every day at the computer, it's worth it to me. The Mac Pro is backed up via Time Machine to an external disk.

If I wanted a less expensive primary device, I would use an iMac. Many developers use an iMac, and you don't even need the top-of-the-line model.

In addition to my Mac Pro, I have a 2TB disk configured as a RAID disk (that is, two 1TB disks that mirror one another). It is connected to a UPS so that a power failure is unlikely to damage the files (although that has happened). This disk is connected to an Airport base station so I can access the files from my desktop as well as remotely over the Internet. I use this disk for backup copies of everything I'm working on.

I have a stack of MacBook Pro computers on my desk. At the moment, the stack consists of four computers dating back several years. The most recent is on top, and I move files to it as needed when I head out for a meeting, conference, or even time off(!). The other Mac Book Pro models are kept in chronological order. I don't use them for storing archival versions of files — that's what the shared disk is for. I use them for old versions of the operating system. On each one, I have several user accounts for different types of projects.

I could achieve many of the same results by partitioning disks, but my preference is not to partition disks because every once in a while I wind up with a project that really needs an enormous amount of disk space.

That's how I work. If any of those ideas are useful to you, feel free to make them your own.

Getting Started with Swift

It's very difficult to discuss any computer language in the abstract, so in this book, I provide an example application that you can use to follow along with the syntax discussions. (I show this earlier in this chapter — in Figures 1-1 through 1-5.) The various files for this application are discussed over the course of many chapters. You can download these files from this book's companion website, as described in the Introduction. (Not every chapter has code from the example. This is because my priority here is to describe Swift and, strictly speaking, exploring the use of the Cocoa and Cocoa Touch frameworks is beyond this scope. However, by experimenting with Swift features that you may one day use in your own apps, you can better understand how the language works with the frameworks.

The example application uses a built-in Xcode template called *Master-Detail Application* for iOS. This template has some additions that allow you to access social media and the location tools with the features built into iOS.

This section has two components:

- Installing Xcode and setting your preferences.
- Creating your own project to use.

As noted, you can download sample code for many of the chapters in this book. You must create the two components listed here before your downloaded code can work, so you'll see the steps involved here.

Installing Xcode and setting preferences

Begin by registering as a developer and downloading Xcode from the Mac App Store, as described earlier in this chapter. If you've already done these things and you're eager to get started, feel free to skip ahead — to the "Creating your project" section, later in this chapter — but be aware that setting up your preferences as described in this section can be useful. It takes only a few minutes to familiarize yourself with the Xcode preferences. Whether or not you use the default settings, just knowing which settings are available can save you hours and hours of time. If you're trying to figure out how to do something — such as how to make your version of the example look like the version in this book — these settings can be a help.

It's easy to find helpful tips about adjusting your settings and preferences on the web, but be aware that these may be out of date. Over time, Apple has refined Xcode, so some of the features in the version you downloaded may be new or may be accessible in a new way.

Here follows a step-by-step tour of the major preferences in Xcode. Work through each step to familiarize yourself with the various settings, or come back later on to look at specific settings. In each of the step lists that follow, I've assumed that you've set up your environment as described earlier in this chapter.

Obtaining your developer account

It's not essential to use a developer account at the beginning, but, considering the fact that registration can be free, it's a good idea to have one so that you can use it when you need it. Here are the steps to follow to get a developer account:

1. **Launch Xcode.**
2. **Choose Xcode⇨Preferences.**
3. **Select the Accounts tab.**
4. **Using the + at the bottom left of the window, add a new account for an Apple ID that you've registered on `developer.apple.com`.**

   This can be a free registration or one of the paid programs.
5. **Enter the appropriate Apple ID and password along with a description of the account.**

   For the description, use the Apple ID or a few words that identify the account, such as "School" or "Freelance gig for GUKL."
6. **Verify that the information for the account is shown in the main section of the lower-right, as shown in Figure 1-6.**

   Any source code repositories you've set up will also be shown in this window. You can return to this window to add repositories or additional developer accounts.

Setting preferences with Fonts & Colors and Text Editing

Some developers may prefer to write code in dark text on a white background, and some prefer light text on a black background. This has nothing to do with anything except your preferences (and the lighting in your room). Xcode allows you to control these settings to make your code look the way you want. It has a variety of defaults, but you can create new settings as well as modify existing ones.

These preferences are applied to each file you work on, inasmuch as that's possible. Some preferences (such as spacing and indentation) rely on spaces within the file, and changing the preference settings affects new code you type in, so changing them in the middle of editing a file has the potential to make the spacing a bit erratic. (That's one reason why developers tend to set them and leave them alone after that.) Other preferences (such as syntax color highlighting) reflect the preferences only and do change in the files when you change the preference.

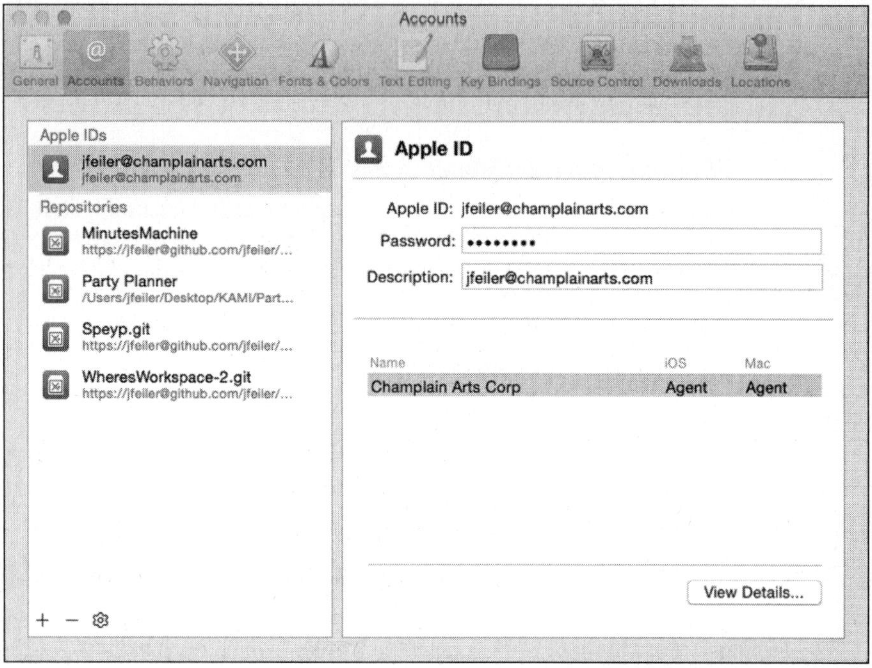

Figure 1-6: Setting your developer account.

In all cases, your preferences or the code-formatting settings you make won't affect the syntax. Changing, say, the font of the code can neither fix a syntax error or cause one. Even if this appears to be happening, something else is at work.

To change text styles, follow these steps:

1. **Choose the Fonts & Colors tab. (See Figure 1-7.)**
2. **In the right pane, each type of syntax element appears in the color assigned to it in the source editor and in the console. Use the tabs at the top of this pane to switch.**
3. **In the left pane, choose from a variety of styles.**

   Note that the colors and also the sizes vary.
4. **Adjust the color for any selected style by clicking the Background, Selection, Cursor, or Invisibles color wells at the bottom.**

   Clicking these brings up a color picker you can use to modify that color.
5. **To select a new font and size, click the Font field.**

   This opens the Font window.

Figure 1-7: Setting fonts and colors.

6. Use + at the bottom left to add a new style.

You can provide a title for the new style, as well as set colors and fonts.

To experiment with these settings, begin by creating a new style (as shown in step 6) before you modify the existing styles.

Use the Text Editing tab to set editing and indentation preferences. The editing preferences are shown in Figure 1-8. Most of the checkboxes are self-explanatory, but a few might benefit from some elaboration:

- **Code Completion:** This setting activates Xcode's autocomplete feature. As you type, Xcode will offer to complete words and will automatically track parentheses and braces (or "brackets" if you prefer that word).
- **Automatically Trim Trailing Whitespace:** This setting removes spaces at the end of a line (unless they are inside quotation marks). This can slightly reduce the size of your source code file, but it also can make it easier to copy your code and paste it elsewhere.
- **Convert Existing Files on Save:** This option applies your settings to old files when you save the files.

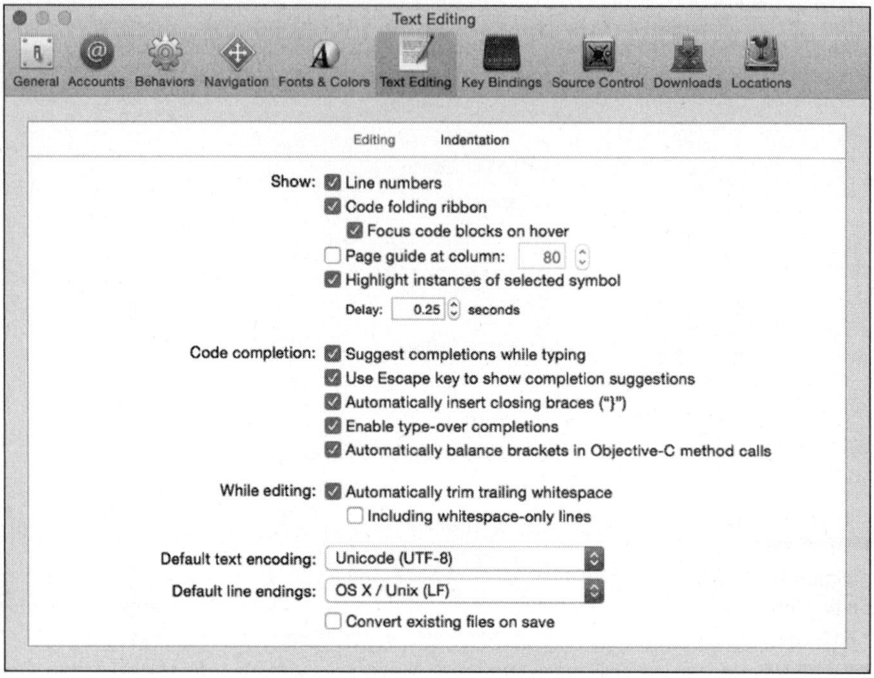

Figure 1-8: Setting general editing preferences.

Xcode automatically manages your code's indentation using the settings shown in Figure 1-9. The settings for indentation allow you to choose between using tabs and spaces for the indentations. If you commonly copy your code and paste it into other editors (perhaps into a word processor), indenting with spaces may make that operation easier.

Perhaps the most important point to make about the indentation settings is that they're not merely cosmetic. With Xcode managing the indentations, you have immediate feedback of certain syntax errors. If your code isn't aligned or indented properly, chances are you've missed (or added) an extra parenthesis or bracket or `end` or `begin` (and so on).

Setting behaviors

Figure 1-10 shows you some of the settings in the Behaviors tab. For each of the events at the left, you can choose the various actions shown at the right. As an example, among these settings is the one that, by default, makes the Debug area appear below the Editing area when you run an app in Xcode. (This is true whether you run it with a tethered device such as your iPhone or on iOS Simulator which is built into Xcode and lets you test your code without using a device.)

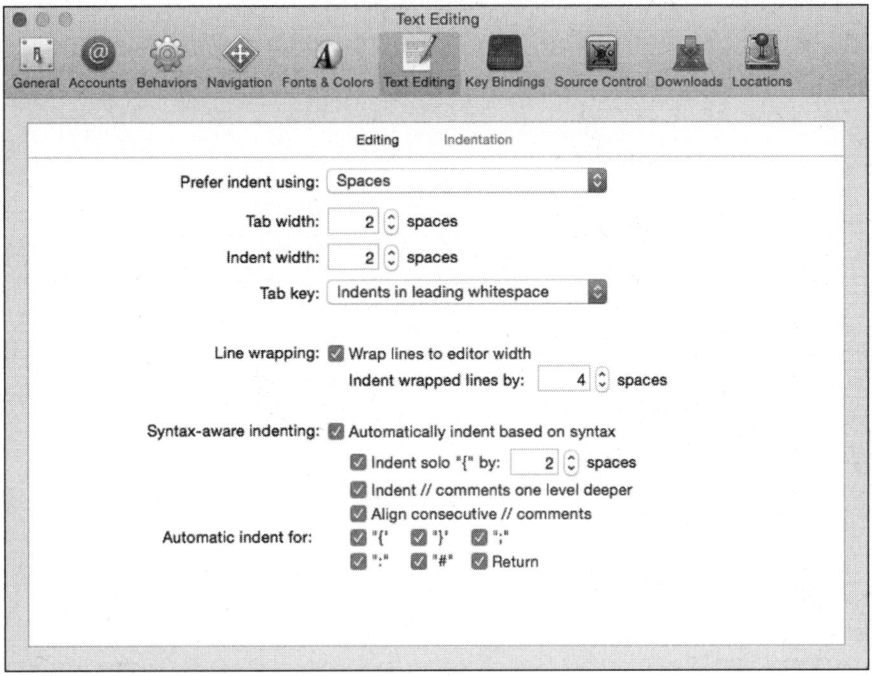

Figure 1-9: Setting indentation preferences.

Judging from comments on blogs and websites, I'd say that the settings in this tab are among those that developers most want to change (or stop). If you wonder why Xcode does certain things (or doesn't do others), take a look at the settings on the Behaviors tab.

Setting navigation preferences

The Nagivation tab (see Figure 1-11) lets you set preferences for the way windows behave and appear. If you find yourself constantly changing the appearance of your Xcode workspace window (particularly when using the Assistant), you can make those changes once and for all in navigation preferences.

Downloading new components

The Downloads tab, shown in Figure 1-12, is where you download more components, SDKs, and document libraries for Xcode. When you install Xcode, it comes with the current documentation and components (and, sometimes — if you've downloaded it from a preview section of the Developer site — with beta versions of the next releases). If you are supporting previous SDKs, you may need to download them and their related documentation manually: This is where you do that. (Many developers follow Apple's lead and design apps to support both the current operating system and one prior. Typically the current system's SDKs are downloaded with Xcode, and the first prior may also be there. You'll need to manually download others if you want to support them.)

Figure 1-10: Setting behaviors for Xcode events.

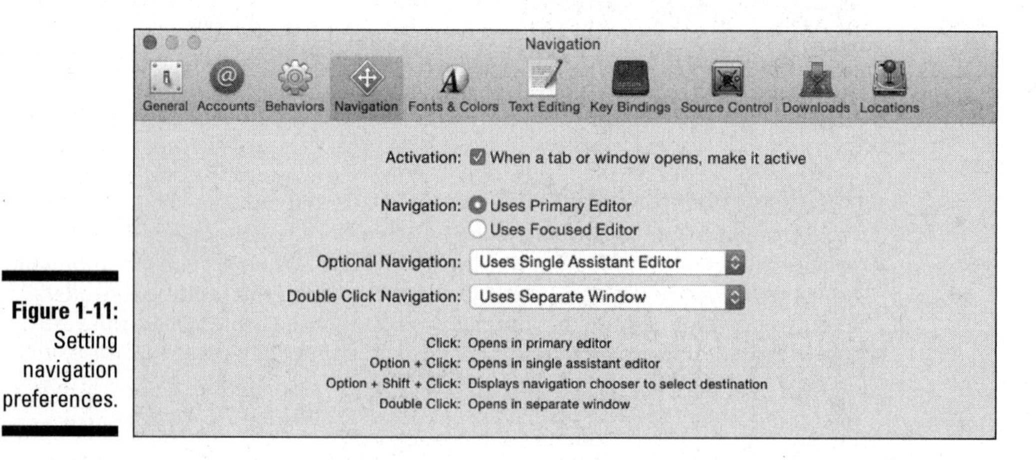

Figure 1-11: Setting navigation preferences.

Figure 1-12: Downloading new components and documentation to Xcode.

Downloading new components and documentation requires an Internet connection. After the materials have been downloaded, you can disconnect from the Internet for further work.

Setting file locations

The last item in this very quick overview of Xcode settings is the Locations tab, shown in Figure 1-13.

The Locations tab on Preferences lets you set and change the locations for the various files that Xcode uses in building your projects. You can change these locations, if you know what you're doing, but be careful: The most frequent case in which you need to know where those files are is if you want to go beyond the Clean command for your project. Clean (Command-Shift-Key or Product⇨Clean) cleans most of the build product results from your project. Removing or moving files in the directories shown in Figure 1-13 can cause Xcode to lose track of them and, before you know it, you can't build your app any more. So be careful.

A more thorough cleaning comes from Window⇨Organizer and the Projects tab where you can delete the derived data from wherever it happens to be (that is, from the location shown in the Locations tab). These two commands (Clean and Delete Derived Data) are safer than just deleting the files from disk. Doing that can have nasty side effects as noted in this section.

Figure 1-13: Working with file locations.

Creating your project

The project used for examples in this book, Locatapp, is based on the iOS Master-Detail Application template built into Xcode. In this section I give you an overview of the steps you must follow to create your own version of that template to experiment with.

You can download a complete project folder from this book's companion website, as described in the Introduction. There you'll find separate folders for the various chapters in which the example is used.

The following steps show you how to create your own project. You can follow these same basic steps to create any new project in Xcode:

1. **Click File⇨New⇨Project or Command-Shift-N.**

   Click Next.

2. **From the sheet that appears, choose Master-Detail Application in the iOS/Applcation section.**

   Click Next.

3. **In the Options window (see Figure 1-14), enter the product name (Locatapp if you're duplicating the example in this book).**
4. **Add your organization name.**

   You can use spaces and special characters in the name.

Figure 1-14: Setting options for the project.

5. **Enter an organization identifier.**

   This is typically a reverse domain name as in `com.apple` or `org.unicef`. The style is used in Java and is based on the idea that if your domain name is unique on the Internet (and it is), the reverse domain name will also be unique, and yet it can't easily be confused with an actual Internet address.

   Note that the bundle identifier will automatically be created from the organization identifier and the product name. Spaces and special characters will automatically be replaced by a hyphen.

6. **Set the language to Swift.**

   The alternative is Objective-C. If you want to create an Objective-C project, you're reading the wrong book! It is important to note that projects in either Objective-C or Swift can contain files in the other language — so, strictly speaking, there's no such thing as a Swift project or an Objective-C project.

7. **Set Devices to Universal.**

   You could also choose to target only an iPhone or iPad.

8. **Check the checkbox for Core Data.**

   Core Data is the technology to create and use a persistent store. It is independent of the specific data store technology, but in iOS apps, the built-in SQLite library is frequently used (it's the default). On OS X, SQLite can be used, but XML is also a supported choice.

9. **Click Next.**

10. **Select a location for your new project, as shown in Figure 1-15.**

    Note that you can use the button in the lower-left to create a new folder for the project; however, any new project is automatically placed in its own new folder, so the New Folder button is generally superfluous.

11. **(Optional) Implement source control by checking the Source Control checkbox.**

    If you use source control, choose a repository on your Mac or any other known repository. (Known repositories are defined in the Xcode Account preferences, as shown previously in Figure 1-6.)

12. **Open the Add To pop-up menu to choose a project or workspace to add this new project to.**

    If you're a beginner with Xcode (or even a moderately advanced user), leave the default setting — don't add to any project or workspace.

13. **Click Create.**

    That's it! You've created your first project, and you're ready to explore it.

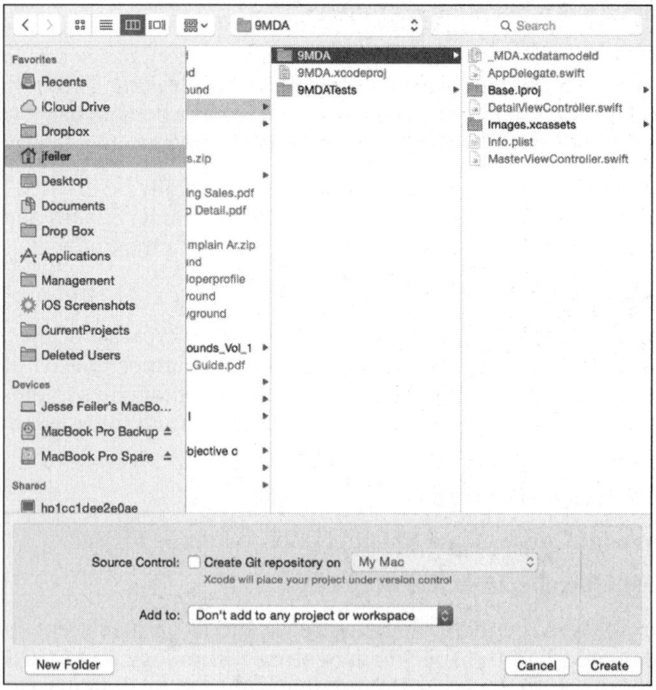

Figure 1-15: Choosing a location for the project.

This is a high-level overview of working with Xcode and creating a project so that we can get into the details of using Swift as quickly as possible.

It's always a good idea to make a duplicate of your project folder as a backup. An easy and safe way to do this is to locate the folder in the Finder (in the location you chose in Figure 1-15). With the folder selected, use File⇨Compress or Control-Compress to create a Zip archive. That way you'll have a duplicate, but because it's hidden inside a Zip archive, you won't be able to accidentally modify it.

Exploring Your Project

This section helps you walk through the project you've just created. Here you make a single change — you replace a view from the template with a map view that you'll later use in your code.

Touring your new project

To look over the details of your new project, follow these steps:

1. **Display the project navigator and the editing area as you see in Figure 1-16.**

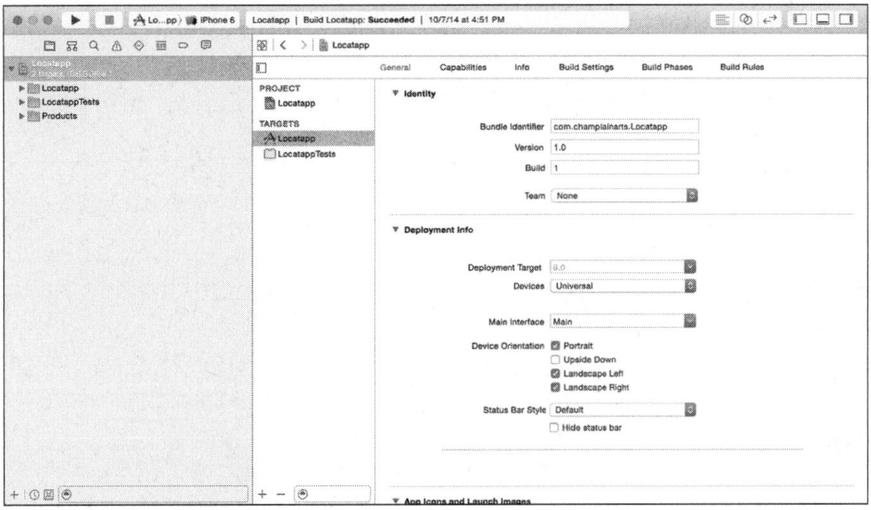

Figure 1-16: Checking out the project settings.

2. **Select the project — it's at the top of the project navigator.**

   You may need to open it with the disclosure triangle to the left of the project.

   At the left of the editing area you'll see each project and its targets. You can display and hide this section with the button just above it.

3. **In the General tab, make sure the bundle identifier is correct.**
4. **If you'll be using a development team, set it in the Team drop-down menu, as shown in Figure 1-17.**

   You can add this later or change it as you work. You don't need it for now, but it you have one set up in the Account tab of Preferences, you might as well use it.

5. **Check the device orientations and update them if you want.**

   If you want to change them later on, make certain to clean the project and delete intermediate files as described in the section, "Setting file locations," earlier in this chapter.

6. **Click the Capabilities tab to see the Cocoa and Cocoa Touch capabilities you can use, as shown in Figure 1-18.**

   This list grows over time as Apple adds new devices and features. Many of these capabilities rely on using a team with the appropriate permissions and provisioning profiles. Don't worry: If you need additional capabilities, they and the provisioning information will be provided in new releases of Xcode (possibly in beta versions downloadable from `developer.apple.com`).

Figure 1-17: Setting the team.

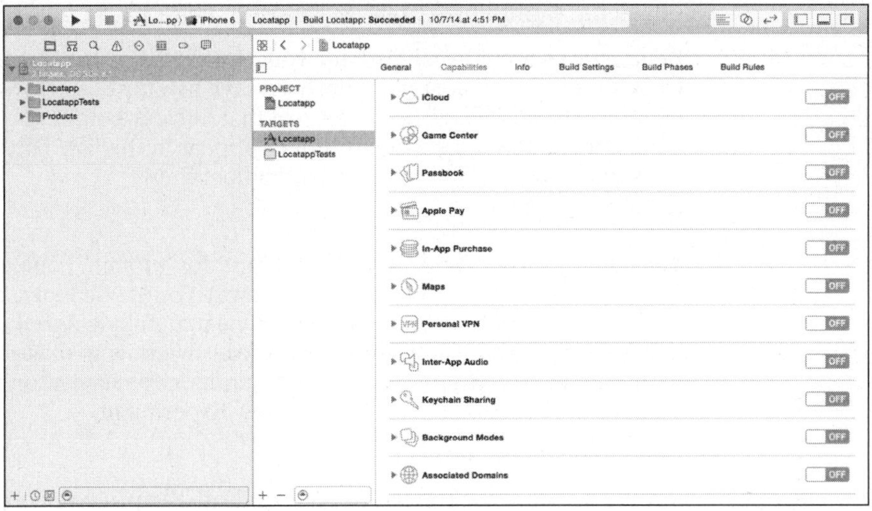

Figure 1-18: Reviewing capabilities.

7. **Open at the Info tab to see your target's property list. (See Figure 1-19.)**

   This is where you can change the bundle name that the user sees or the bundle identifier. The bundle identifier may need to be shared if you are using iCloud. Here's where you change it if necessary. (The bundle is the internal identifier for your app; it's separate from the app's name. There's more about bundles on `developer.apple.com`: Use the search tool there to find a number of references and documents.)

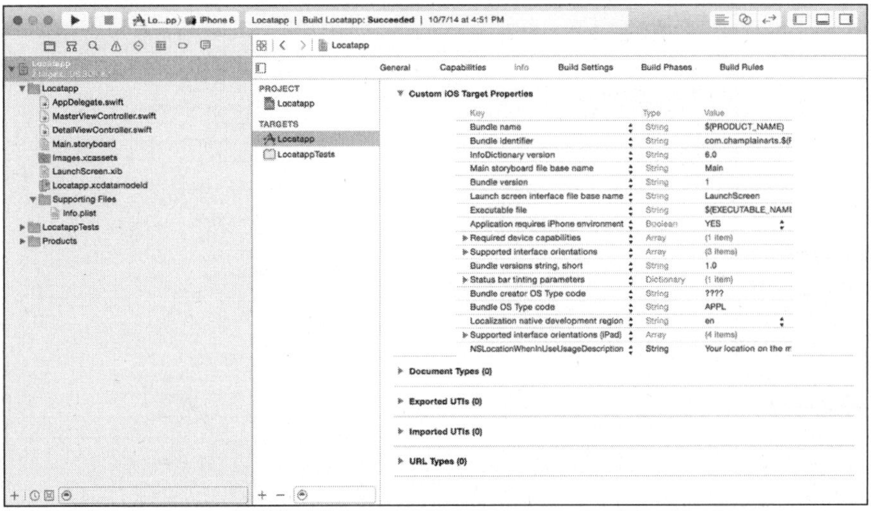

Figure 1-19: Reviewing the target's property list.

8. **Check the Build Phases tab, as shown in Figure 1-20.**

   Build phases are normally set for you as you add or remove files to or from the project. If at some point you have mysterious errors, you can check the Build Phases tab to ensure that all your source files are being included and that no extraneous ones appear in the list. You can use the + and – buttons below the lists to adjust them.

9. **Explore your Swift files.**

   You can look over these at this point, but don't touch. Look at the text fonts and coloring. If you don't like the way your code looks, adjust those preferences until the code looks meaningfully colored and indented. You may also want to resize your window to make lines wrap better. Remember that you can show and hide the navigator and utilities areas at the left and right of the window. Experiment!

10. **Build and run the project.**

    Use the arrow at the top left to build and run the project. You can choose to run it in iOS Simulator or in a tethered device. For now, however, try using one of iOS Simulator options (it doesn't matter which one).

11. **Make certain you see the launch image, as shown in Figure 1-21.**

    If you used a different name for your app, you'll see it on the launch screen instead of Locatapp.

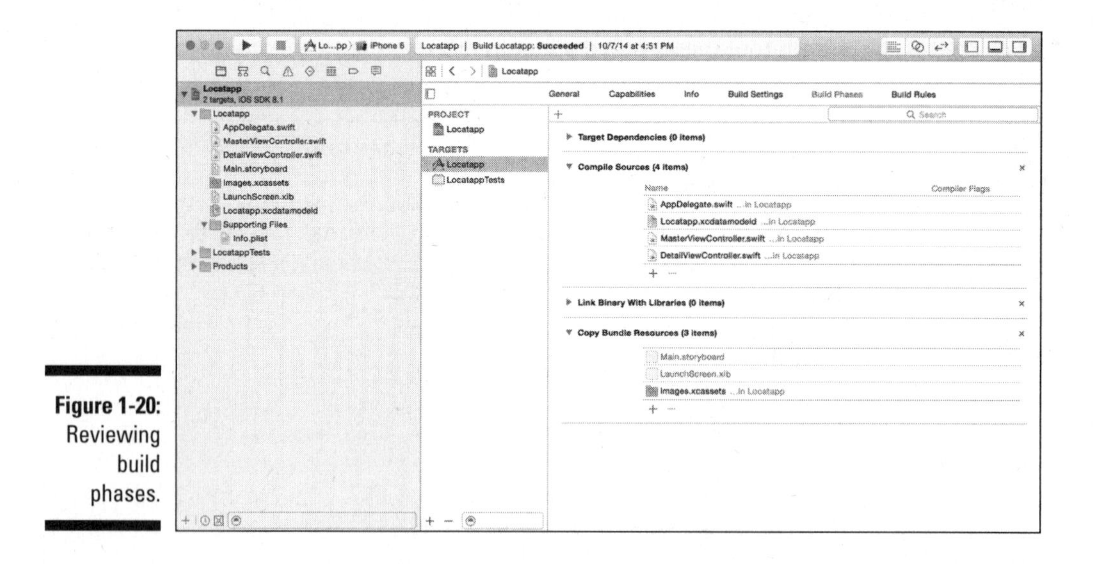

Figure 1-20: Reviewing build phases.

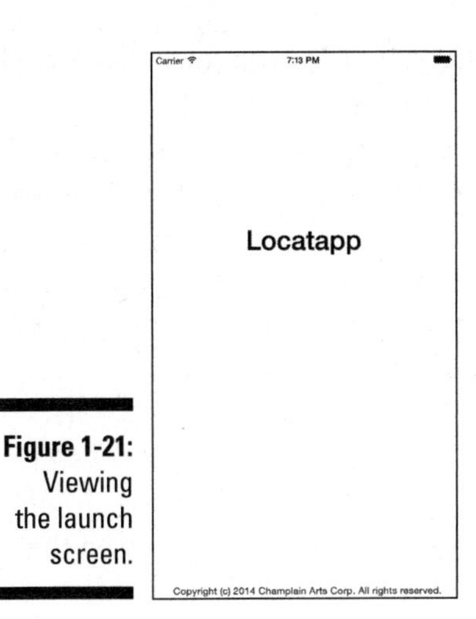

Figure 1-21: Viewing the launch screen.

Adding a map to the project's interface

A lot of your work in app development has nothing to do with Swift, Objective-C, or any other language. Much of it has to do with the user interface that you build and, with many of the templates built into Xcode, with modifying the basic template.

The example app, Locatapp, is a case in point. The Master-Detail Application template on which it's based lets you add data elements to a list (in the master detail list). Each element (called an `Event`) consists of a timestamp. In addition to creating new data elements, you can also delete existing ones. You can select any of the data elements and see the details in a detail view.

For Locatapp, you must modify the template so that instead of creating data elements with timestamps in them, you create data elements with a location (latitude and longitude) in them. By doing this, instead of selecting an `Event` from the master detail list and seeing its details in a detail view, you can select a `Location` from the master detail list and show its location on the map.

To prepare for this, you must change the detail view controller so that instead of text it displays a map on which you can place pins marking locations. The following steps show you how to replace the detail view with a map view:

1. **Open `LaunchScreen.xib`, the user interface file for the launch image (the editor is called Interface Builder).**

   As you see in Figure 1-22, in addition to the project navigator at the left, you also have a document outline at the left of the Interface Builder editor.

You show and hide the document outline with the small icon at the bottom left of the canvas view (with the word Locatapp in large letters).

2. **With the document outline open, click on the copyright notice in the canvas. Note that the copyright notice is highlighted in the document outline automatically.**

   You may have to open some disclosure triangles to do this.

   In Figure 1-22, the copyright notice at the bottom of the canvas is highlighted as is its representation in the document outline.

   The L in the document outline indicates that this is a label object. The handles around the copyright notice in the canvas indicate that it can be moved and resized there.

   Note that at any given moment, you may see some objects only on the canvas (the editing area) or only in the document outline.

3. **Repeat the process by selecting an element in the document outline and watching it become highlighted on the canvas.**

   Try this with the label (marked with an L) for the Locatapp title.

4. **Select `Main.storyboard` in the project navigator.**

   This is the primary user interface element.

5. **Open disclosure triangles as necessary to reveal the `Detail` view controller (a yellow circle) and a view labeled `View` within it, as shown in Figure 1-23.**

   Within `View`, you'll see a label with the text "Detail view content goes here" and a `Constraints` folder.

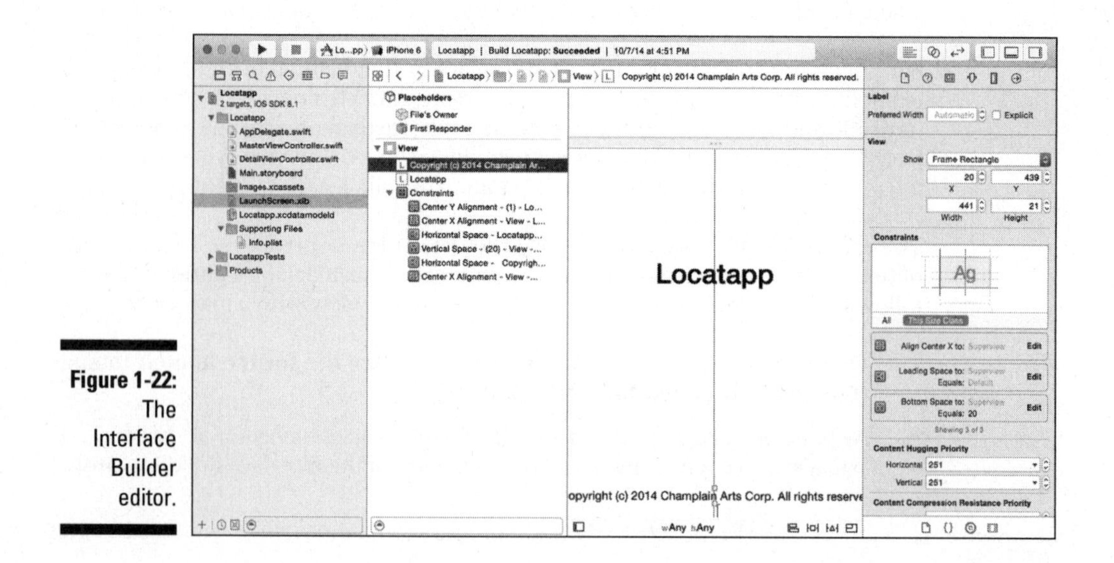

Figure 1-22: The Interface Builder editor.

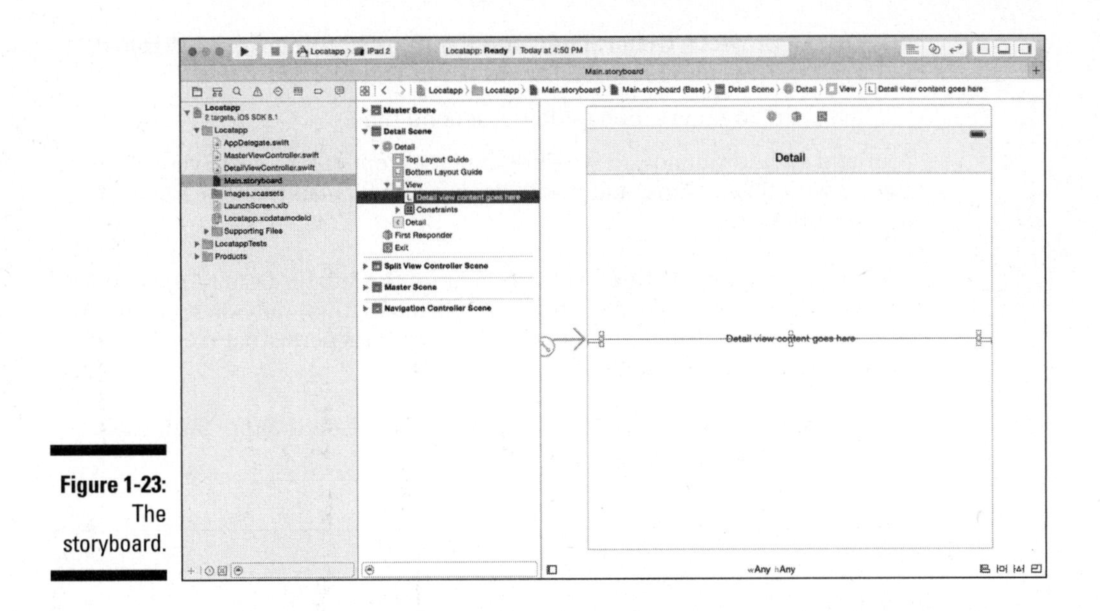

Figure 1-23: The storyboard.

6. **Open the library at the bottom of the utilities area, and drag a MapKit View into the document outline.**

   Place it on top of `View`. Make certain that it replaces `View` and is not placed within the `View` folder. The layout guides may disappear. The document outline should look like the one in Figure 1-24.

   You can display the Identity inspector in the utilities area, as in Figure 1-24, but you don't need to make any other changes at this point.

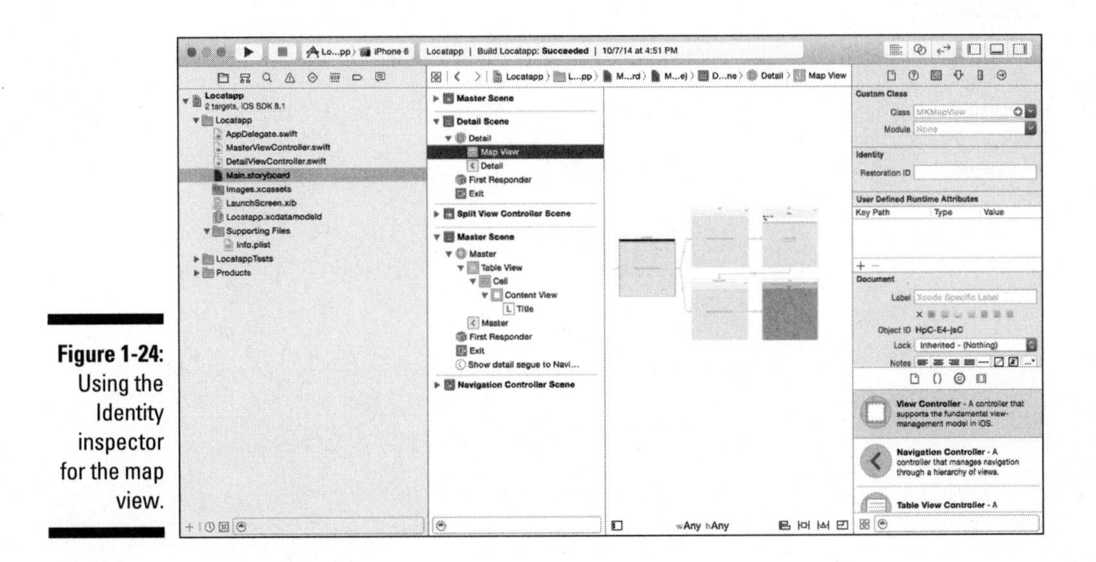

Figure 1-24: Using the Identity inspector for the map view.

7. **On the project's General tab, add the `MapKit` framework to Linked Frameworks and Libraries, as shown in Figure 1-25.**

   If it's already there, don't add it a second time.

Your app should run now. It won't do much except create new Event objects with timestamps, and it will display a blank map that's ready for you to work with it.

You now have a bare-bones Swift app built on the Master-Detail Application template. As you explore the project, you'll see that not only do you have an interface, but you also are running with a Core Data persistent store that's implemented with the built-in SQLite library.

Not bad for a few keystrokes! Now it's time to move on to more Swift tools before delving into the language itself.

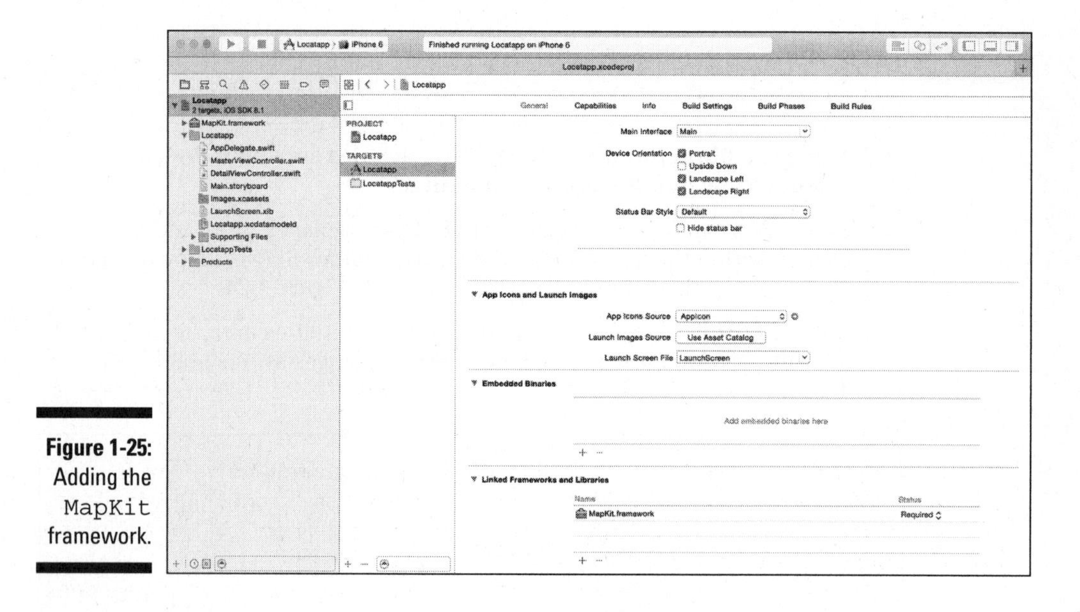

Figure 1-25: Adding the `MapKit` framework.

Chapter 2

Playing in the Playground

In This Chapter

- Trying out code in a playground
- Spotting syntax errors in a playground
- Observing values as code runs

One of the important features of Swift and Xcode 6 is the *playground,* a tool that you can use to experiment with syntax and code to get immediate response. You'll use playgrounds frequently in the exercises in this book to explore snippets of syntax.

You can build a playground for a section of code that you want to test repeatedly, but you can also create a playground to test code on the fly. When your test is complete, you can keep the playground or just throw the playground away.

This chapter provides an overview of playgrounds. Stepping through the examples in this chapter can help you get the hang of playgrounds and allow you to explore some basic Swift snippets.

Some of the snippets in this chapter have syntax errors in them. This is deliberate. The purpose of this is to demonstrate the way Xcode deals with typos. Somewhere in the universe there may be a place where software engineers always write error-free code, but Planet Earth apparently isn't it. It's easy to introduce errors — by, say, reversing the order of key-value items in your code (a problem made easier by the fact that Objective-C has a syntax element that lets you specify key-value properties in a value-key sequence and another syntax element that lets you specify key-value properties in a key-value sequence).

Creating a Playground

Playgrounds are part of Xcode. You can use and reuse a single playground as a scratchpad or you can create a variety of unique playgrounds to test various features of your app. The choice is yours.

In my case, I keep my playgrounds in a Playgrounds folder on my desktop. At the root level of this folder I keep a few playgrounds lying around. I commonly use the convention of adding "Junk" to the name of any playground or file I don't want to keep, and I can always find a few "Junk" playgrounds in that folder. Within Playgrounds, I also keep a folder or two for current projects. On occasion I've created a Playgrounds folder within a project folder, but the desktop folder works better for me — in my view, playgrounds are just scratchpads, and are more related to the computer I'm using than to the project I'm working on. (For similar reasons, I tend not to include playgrounds among the project files I share with colleagues. Who shares scratchpads?) I prefer to place playgrounds where they won't get stored in Git, and this suggests to me the desktop folder. However, this is just me. You should use whatever is easiest for you.

Here are the steps to create a playground:

1. **Click File⇨New⇨Playground (or just click Shift-Option-⌘-N).**

   The sheet shown in Figure 2-1 appears.

2. **Name your playground and choose iOS or OS X as the platform.**

3. **On the next screen, choose the location for your playground.**

   As noted earlier, you can place your playgrounds in a standard location (like my Playgrounds folder) or you can place them within your specific project folders (or anywhere else you like).

   That's all there is to creating a playground. Figure 2-2 shows a playground created for iOS. Note that if you have created a playground for OS X, the only difference is that it will import `Cocoa` rather than `UIKit`.

Choose options for your new file:

Name MyPlayground

Platform: iOS

Cancel

Previous

Figure 2-1: Creating a playground.

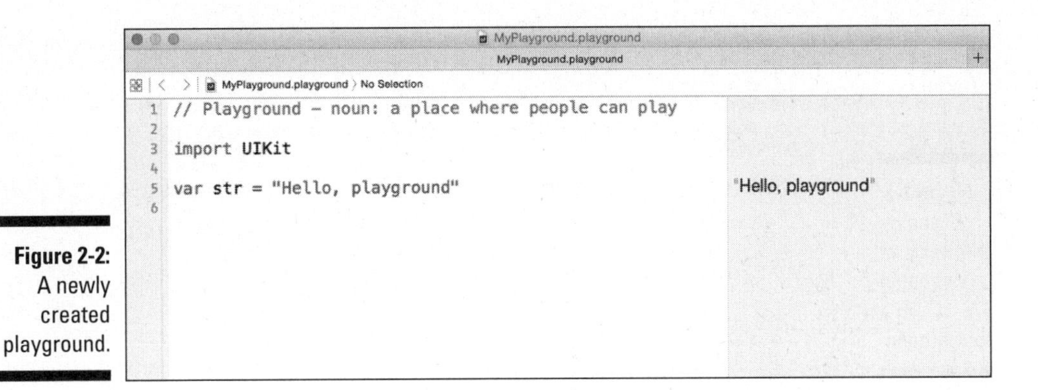

Figure 2-2: A newly created playground.

The basic playground that you create has a comment at the top and a single import statement. Following that is a line of Swift code:

```
var str = "Hello, playground"
```

Note that in the panel to the right of the code, the value of `str` appears. This is the value as it was set in the main body of the playground. This will be very important as you move through this chapter.

Using a Playground

You may not have explored any Swift syntax yet, but you can still experiment with it. In the following sections, I show you how to test the results of a line of code in a playground, and then how to check the syntax of your code within a playground.

Testing a line of code

The results of any code you type into the playground can be seen more or less instantly. To illustrate, begin with the playground I created in the previous section, the one shown in Figure 2-2. Then change the value of `str` with these steps:

1. **Add a line to change the value of `str` to "Another String" as shown in Figure 2-3.**
2. **Look at the sidebar to see the new value.**

   The original value of `str`, "Hello, playground," is now changed to "Another String."

```
MyPlayground.playground — Edited
MyPlayground.playground
MyPlayground.playground > No Selection
1 // Playground - noun: a place where people can play
2
3 import UIKit
4
5 var str = "Hello, playground"                    "Hello, playground"
6
7 str = "Another String"                           "Another String"
```

Figure 2-3: Changing the value of a variable in a playground.

This is the pattern for using playgrounds in Swift: Just type something in the playground and see the new result in the sidebar. The result in the sidebar may or may not be what you were looking for, but you can still respond accordingly, as follows:

- If the value is what you expect, you're done (and you're successful!).
- If nothing changes in the sidebar (that is, if no value appears or if the original value there remains unchanged), check for a syntax error. If the playground can't interpret your code, it's not going to execute it.
- If you see the wrong result, check your code. A flaw in logic may have given you the wrong answer.

Depending on your Mac's processor speed, the other apps or processes you have running, and the complexity of your code, there may be a delay while Swift parses and then executes the code. At least in early versions of playgrounds in Xcode 6, some developers reported that it was sometimes necessary to give the playground a little nudge. Changing your code a little (such as deleting a word or two and then adding it back in) may cause the parser to be reinvigorated.

Checking syntax

One of the best things to do with a playground is to check Swift syntax quickly. Here's an example of that kind of use. (Note that it involves a deliberate typo.)

This is a demonstration of playgrounds, so don't worry too much about the syntax here. The Swift syntax (good and bad) shown here will be discussed more fully in Chapter 6.

Swift is *type-safe*, which means that it requires you to explicitly do your own type conversions. How do you convert an integer to a string? This is a simple task, but if you're familiar with several languages, it's easy to forget which language uses which syntax. In such cases, a playground can be very useful: You just open a playground and try a variety of syntax approaches until you get the answer you want. The following steps show you how:

1. **Create a playground.**
2. **Open the Assistant (the two overlapping circles at the top right of the window shown in Figure 2-4).**

   Listing 2-1 shows the completed code you create in your playground.

   This opens a second pane in the playground, just as it does in Xcode editing windows. If you don't see the overlapping circles shown at the top right of Figure 2-4, choose View➪Show Toolbar.
3. **In the main pane (the leftmost pane), type in your first guess at the code.**

   After the `import` line and the `var` line, shown previously in Figure 2-3, I entered:

   ```
   str = (String)1
   ```

   If the syntax is incorrect, the playground shows you the errors, as in Figure 2-4. Note that in addition to the errors shown on the right, Xcode offers a Fix-It solution. If your syntax is incorrect, the suggested Fix-It

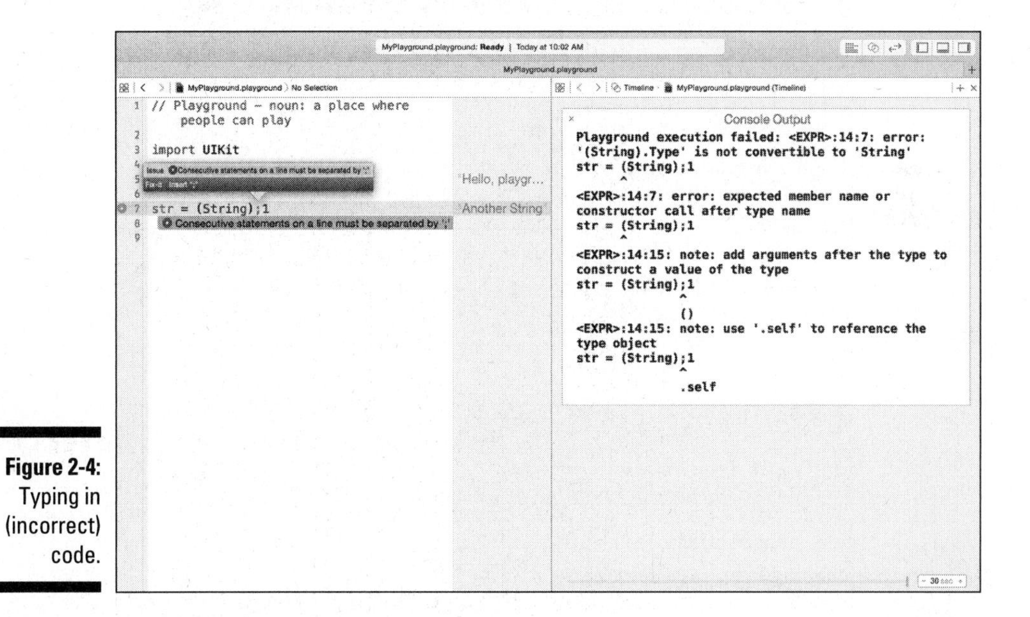

Figure 2-4: Typing in (incorrect) code.

Listing 2-1: Testing a Playground

```
// Playground - noun: a place where people can play
import UIKit
var str = String(1)
var str2: Int = 1
```

may be wrong (as it is in this case). However, the errors displayed in Console Output at the right of the window show you the actual error: It's in the conversion to `String`:

```
str = (String)1
```

4. **Type in the correct code:**

```
str = String(1)
```

5. **Check the right-hand sidebar to see the result.**

   The value shown, "1," is correct. This is the correct number, and the quotes correctly indicate that the value is a string, as shown in Figure 2-5.

6. **Verify the result by adding another line.**

   Here I made the conversion from string to integer by adding

```
var str2: Int = 1
```

   Check the result in the sidebar, as shown in Figure 2-6.

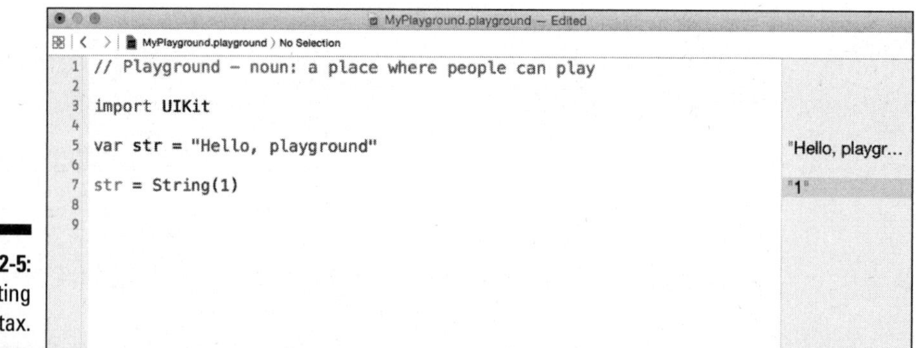

Figure 2-5: Testing syntax.

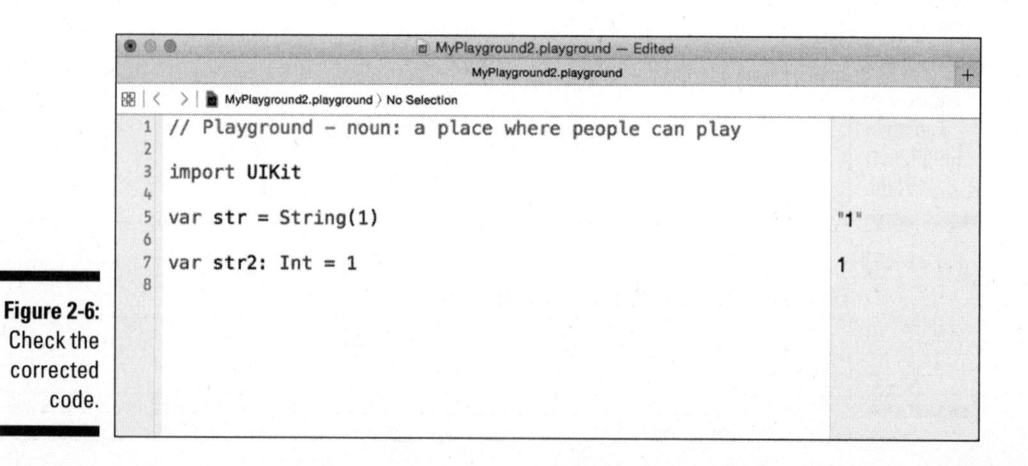

Figure 2-6: Check the corrected code.

Note that this new value is an `Int` and not a `String`, which you can tell by the absence of quotes.

Using the Timeline in the Playground

Figure 2-7 shows another example of using a playground. In this case, I tested a `for` loop. Note that the number of times the loop has iterated appears at the right instead of the values.

You can track value inside a loop. In Figure 2-8, I've changed the loop so that a local variable is set to the value of the counter. Because a value was set in

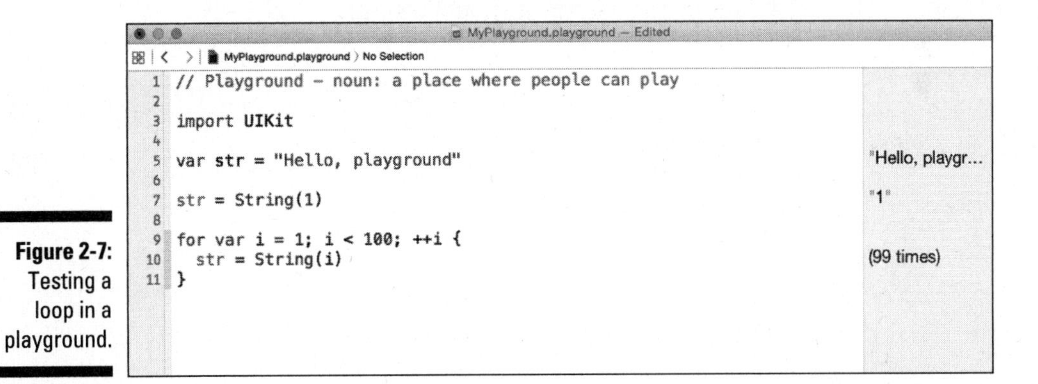

Figure 2-7: Testing a loop in a playground.

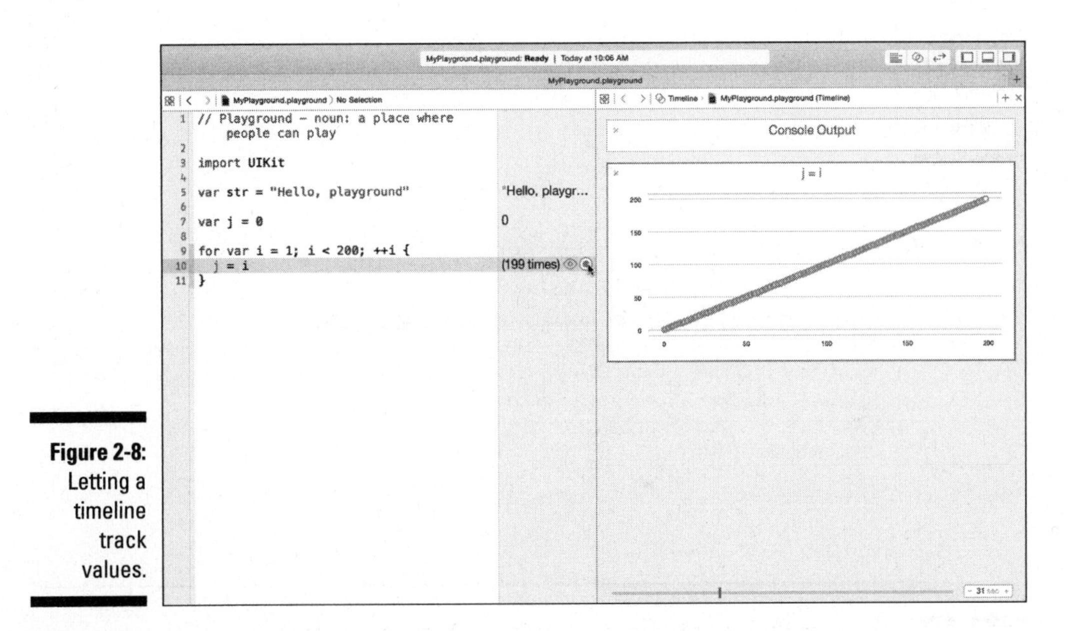

Figure 2-8: Letting a timeline track values.

that way, clicking the bull's-eye icon at the left of the Assistant window, as in Figure 2-8, shows you the value as the loop executes.

What you see at the right of Figure 2-8 is a timeline — a playground feature that graphs your output automatically. The value of *j* is plotted on the vertical axis, and the value of *i* is plotted on the horizontal axis. (The notations at the top of the graph show these legends. Because *i* and *j* are the same value, this may not be obvious.)

At the bottom of the right pane, dragging the blue line back and forth, as in Figure 2-9, allows you to check specific values. Note that its value — that is, the value of *j* where you have positioned the indicator — is shown in the small box at the lower-right.

Listing 2-2 shows the code as it should be now.

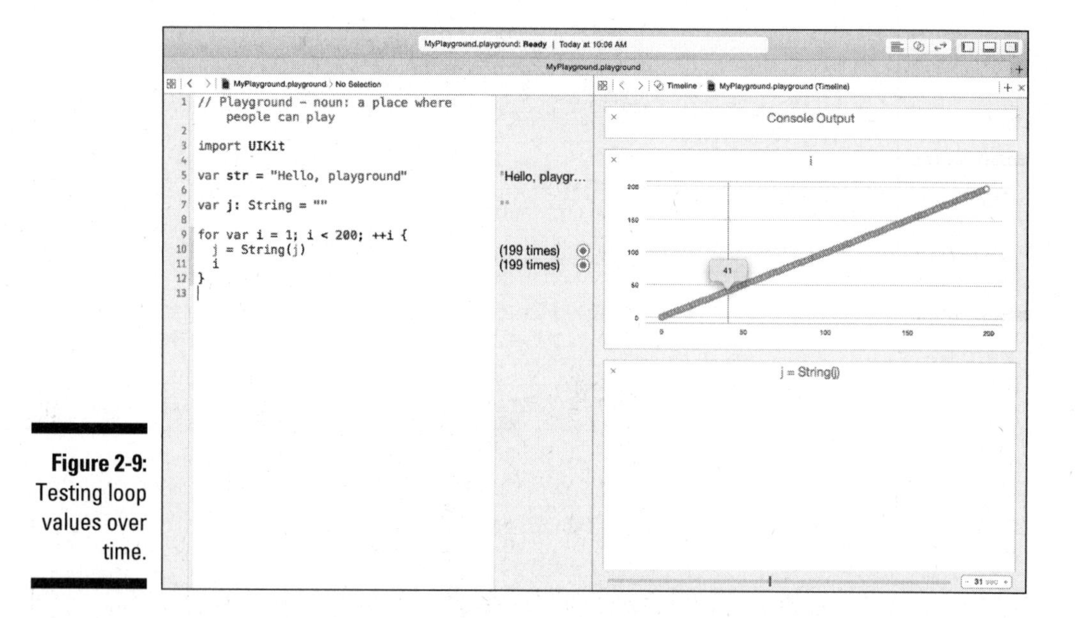

Figure 2-9: Testing loop values over time.

Listing 2-2: Testing a Playground and a Timeline

```
// Playground - noun: a place where people can play
import UIKit
var str = String(1)
var str2: Int = 1
var j = 0
for var i = 1; i < 200; i++ {
  j = i * 4
}
```

Chapter 3

Using the Xcode Editing Tools

In This Chapter

- Working with Xcode editing tools
- Using code completion features
- Correcting code with Fix-It
- Using code snippets

In Chapter 1, I show you how to get started with an Xcode Swift project. As you can see in that chapter, a great deal of your Swift Xcode development involves the graphical user interface of Xcode. A lot of the work — particularly at the beginning of a project — is graphical or involves checkboxes.

In Chapter 2, I show you how to write and test code — particularly small snippets of code — in a playground. This helps you learn Swift syntax and allows you to test out code fragments before you type them (or copy-and-paste them) into your project files.

Now, in this chapter, I introduce Xcode's editing tools. Here, you'll write code in the way you may have written it in your beginning programming class in school (that is, typing in code rather than drawing the interface and using Xcode checkboxes and other graphical elements to construct your app visually). The focus in this chapter is on the Xcode tools that assist you with writing code. Much of what Xcode does for you in regard to typing and editing text is made possible by the fact that it observes every keystroke and keeps track of the syntax of the terms you type (or copy-and-paste).

With the tools and techniques you find in these first three chapters, you can create your first Swift app — the Locatapp example app used throughout this book. (In case you haven't seen it yet, you can look at Figures 1-1 through 1-5 in Chapter 1 to see where you're headed.)

Getting Started with Editing Tools

The editing tools and techniques described in this chapter help you code with Swift and build your apps. Many of these editing tools apply both to Xcode itself as well as to the playgrounds that you create with Xcode. The examples here focus on the editing process; you'll use these tools as you write and edit the code in the rest of the chapters in this book.

In my discussions of these various editing tools, I include examples of Swift syntax, some of which are deliberately incorrect so that you can use the appropriate editing-correction features. The syntax itself is discussed in the later chapters of this book.

Completing Code with Code Completion

As noted previously, Xcode "watches" your keystrokes, which enables it to suggest code as you type. This feature is called *code completion*, and it's a great time-saver. Here are some examples of its use, along with some things to watch out for — just as you can sometimes make mistakes, so can Xcode's code completion!

Code completion is the name of the technology. In the user interface of Xcode, however, it's referred to as Fix-It.

As you may recall from Chapter 1, to create a new project, first launch Xcode and choose File⇨New⇨Project, select a template, and choose a name and location for your new project.

Similarly, as I show in Chapter 2, you can create a new playground by: launching Xcode, choosing File⇨New⇨Playground, selecting Swift as your language, and entering a name and location for the playground.

Using basic code completion

The following steps take you through your first demonstration of code completion. This demonstration uses a playground:

1. **Create a playground, as shown in Figure 3-1.**

   You can base it on iOS or OS X. The figures in this chapter happen to show iOS.

   You can delete the initial text if you want. Playgrounds begin with a comment, an `import` statement, and a string variable set to "Hello, playground." Leave those or not, as you wish.

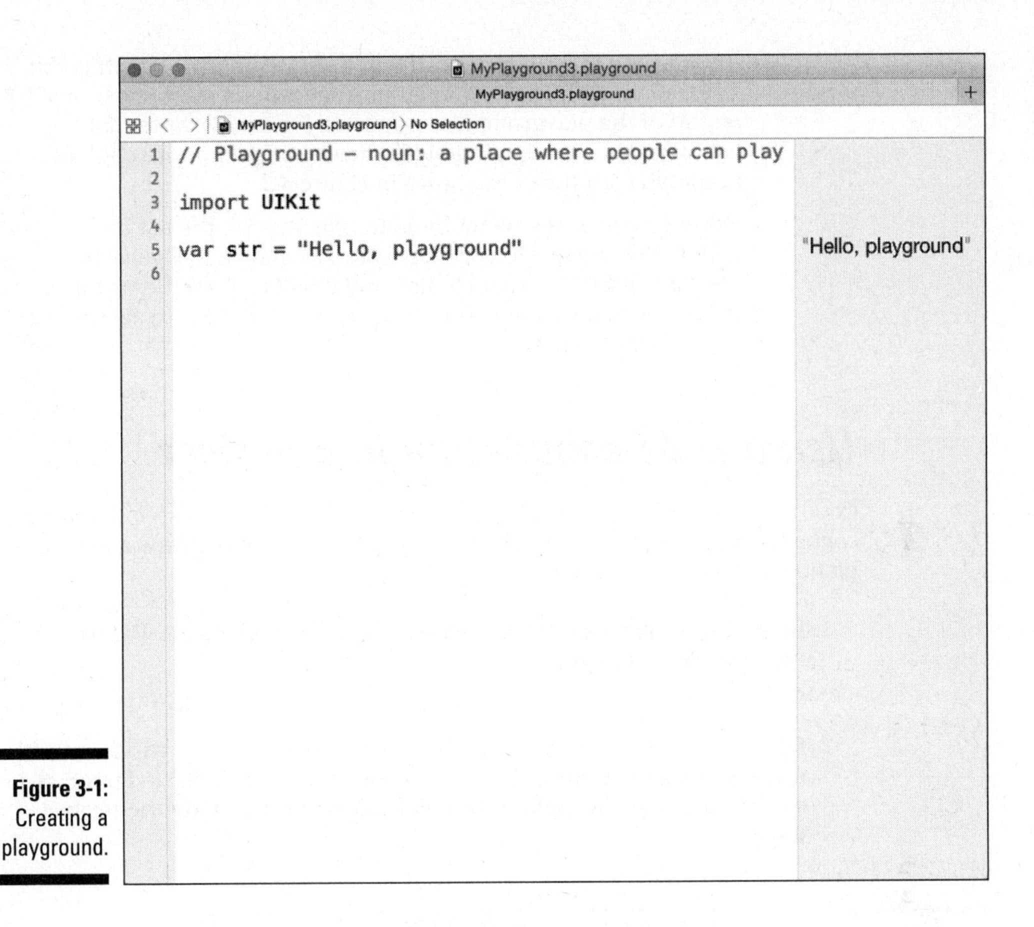

Figure 3-1: Creating a playground.

2. **Begin typing in the code to create a variable — `var myVar: String`. Slowly type `var myVar: S`.**

   Go slowly to allow code completion to do its work (not because code completion needs a long time to work, but because going slowly will give you a sense of how long the process takes on your Mac with your specific configuration). Shortly after you type the `S`, you'll see that the rest of the word `String` is filled in using gray text. Depending on your preferences, the `S` may be blue (the default value) or some other color, whereas the suggested completion (`String`) is gray.

3. **From here, you can do any of three things:**

   - *Accept the completion:* If the suggested completion (`String`) is what you want, press Return and the suggestion is accepted. The gray of `String` changes to the same color as the initial `S`.

- *Hesitate:* On the other hand, if you hesitate before accepting the suggestion, additional completion suggestions will appear in a list on top of the playground, as shown in Figure 3-2. Note that the list of additional completions is scrollable: A lot more choices are available than the ones shown in Figure 3-2.
- *Continue typing:* If you continue to type `Strin`, the list of completion suggestions gets shorter, as shown in Figure 3-3. Click a suggestion from the list, and it will replace the text in the playground. At any time, you can press Return to accept the suggested completion.

Using code completion in a project

Code completion doesn't just look at what you're typing; it also looks at the *context* of what you're typing. The following steps show you how code completion interprets according to context:

1. **Begin by creating a new project based on the iOS Master-Detail Application template.**

   If you need a refresher, refer back to "Creating your project" in Chapter 1.

2. **Open the project navigator at the left of the workspace window (if it's not already open) either by using View⇨Show Project Navigator, ⌘-1, or the button at the right of the toolbar to show or hide the project navigator.**

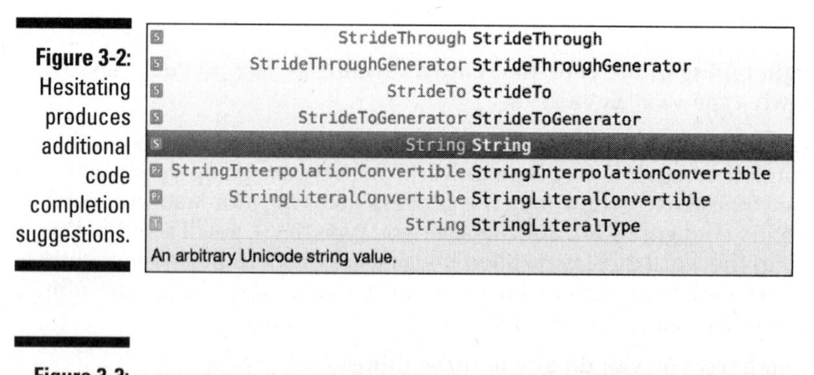

Figure 3-2: Hesitating produces additional code completion suggestions.

String String
StringInterpolationConvertible StringInterpolationConvertible
StringLiteralConvertible StringLiteralConvertible
String StringLiteralType
An arbitrary Unicode string value.

Figure 3-3: As you type, the list of suggested completions gets shorter.

3. **If necessary, open the project folder in the project navigator.**
4. **If necessary, open the project group (it has a folder icon, but it's a group).**
5. **Scroll to the top of the `AppDelegate.swift` file, as shown in Figure 3-4.**
6. **Just below the `var window: UIWindow?` line, begin typing in the code to create a variable — `var myVar: String` — much as you did in the preceding section.**

   A list of code completion suggestions appears, as shown in Figure 3-5. Notice that this list isn't the same as the list you generated in the previous section. New choices — `UnsafeMutablePointer<StringPtr>` and `UnsafeMutablePointer<UInt8>` — now appear in the list. These completions in the Xcode environment are possible because of the syntax that surrounds them.

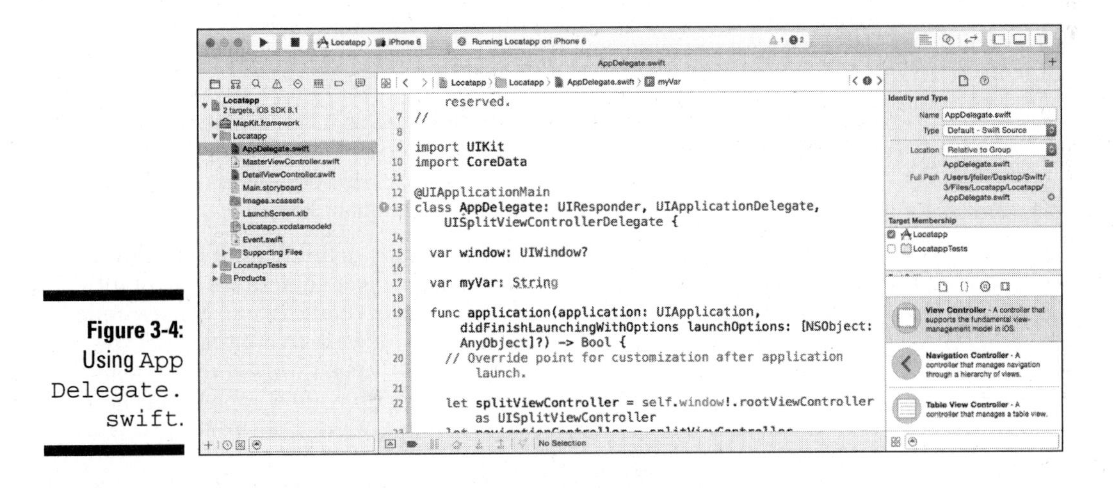

Figure 3-4: Using `AppDelegate.swift`.

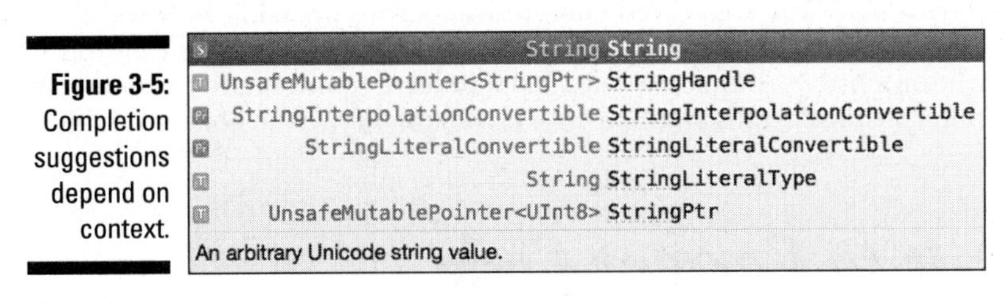

Figure 3-5: Completion suggestions depend on context.

Working with code completion

Code completion changes and evolves over time. Even if you've used it before, you may find it has features that weren't available when you first learned it. To get the most out of it, try some of these tips:

- **Pay attention to the color of the text as you type:** Versions of this book that are in color (mostly eBook editions) use the Presentation style in Xcode Preferences (the Font & Colors pane). Settle on a style you like and stick with it so that you can recognize when the coloring changes. If the coloring looks wrong, Xcode is probably not recognizing your syntax — the most common reason for this is that you've entered a typo. For example, if you type **`myVar: S`** instead of **`var myVar:S`**, the `S` will remain uncolored (black by default).
- **To regenerate the code completion suggestions, use Delete to backspace to a point in your code before the first letter that seems colored correctly:** For example, if you want to regenerate the suggestions for `S`, back up to the space before it and retype **`S`**.
- **Consider using code completion even if you're a fast typist:** If you type quickly, you may not think you need code completion — but don't be so sure. Not only does it save you keystrokes, it also completes the code accurately, and fast typists can always make mistakes.
- **Remember that code completion is accurate — but it's not infallible:** Code completion doesn't make mistakes, and yet sometimes its completions are wrong. Take the preceding example: Omitting `var` causes code completion to misbehave with `String`. If you were to continue on, the compiler would issue an error on `String` — even though the problem is the absence of `var`, not `String`. So although code completion is context-sensitive and doesn't make typos, simple errors can still throw it off-track.
- **Always look at the suggested completion before pressing Return:** Most of the time it's either correct or it's an obvious misinterpretation of your intentions. But sometimes, you do have to intervene to correct a misinterpretation, and in those cases, you must type the code yourself.

Using Fix-It to Correct Code

Fix-It is related to code completion in that it relies on the background processing of the text that you type, but it goes beyond just correcting typos. (As noted previously, Fix-It is the user interface name for code completion.)

Figure 3-6 uses the Master-Detail Application template to demonstrate this. (As mentioned earlier, use a copy of the project for these exercises, not the one you're planning to use for the rest of this book's examples.)

Earlier in this chapter I showed you how code completion can help you complete the code when you type `var myVar: S`. However, after you've typed (and completed) `var myVar: String`, you still have a syntax error.

An error message appears on the class declaration. The text is shown at the right ("Class 'AppDelegate' has no initializers"), and the red circle in the gutter indicates an error. (See Figure 3-6.)

This red circle — really a red doughnut — won't always accompany your error. Some error messages display a small red stop sign in the gutter instead. The red doughnut indicates that Fix-It is available. Click the doughnut to add a suggested Fix-It, as shown in Figure 3-6. Press Return and Xcode implements the Fix-It.

In this case, the error is the missing initializer for the class. That's all well and good, but if you're a beginning Swift developer, what do you do about it?

The Fix-It provides the solution. Swift requires that every variable and constant have an initial value. Unlike some other languages (including Objective-C), you cannot have a declared constant or variable that has no value. It has to have some value. Thus, to adhere to the Swift rules, you can

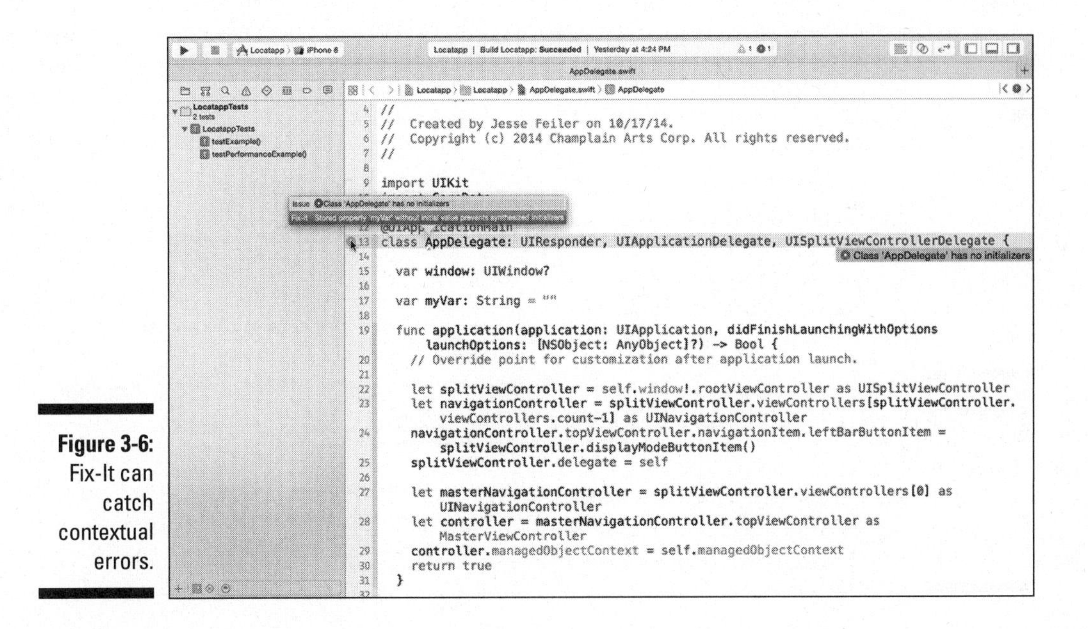

Figure 3-6: Fix-It can catch contextual errors.

get rid of the error message about the lack of an initializer by setting `myVar` to a blank string. It's only a blank string, true, but it's *something*. By using it, you don't have an uninitialized variable, and your error goes away.

Figure 3-7 shows the Fix-It and its solution.

Fix-It is very powerful. Consider, for example, that instead of `var myVar: String` you had entered the following line of code:

```
var myVar: Double
```

This new code gives you the same Fix-It message. However, the Fix-It solution would be different:

```
var myVar: Double = 0.0
```

Fix-It can not only recognize that `myVar` is uninitialized, but it can also provide an initialization that is the correct type. It gives you a solution that's syntactically (and contextually) correct.

Note, however, that even a syntactically and contextually correct solution may not be right. The best initialization value for your needs might actually be `"No Data"` (for the string) or `163.24` (for the double). Nevertheless, you are far ahead when you use Fix-It in a case like this — particularly because the solution of providing an initializer does not require creating a separate

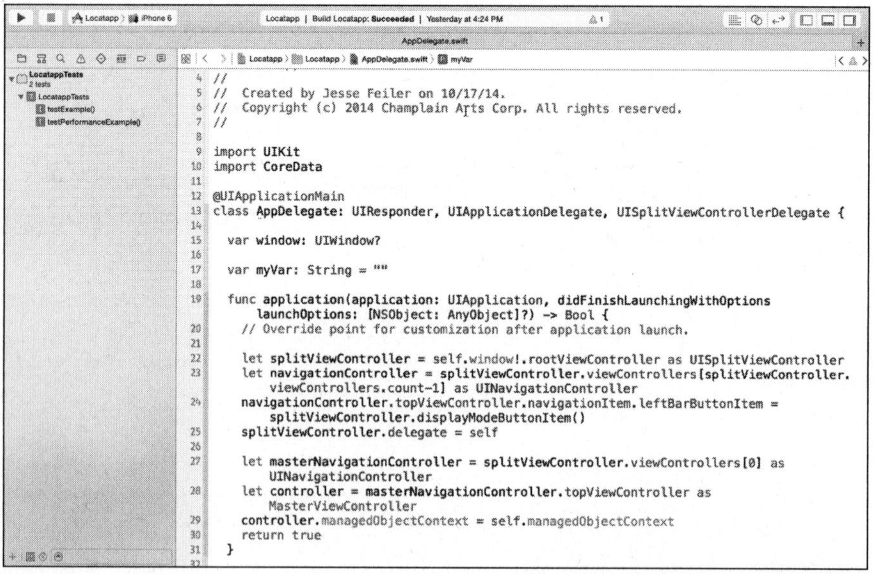
Locatapp | Build Locatapp: Succeeded | Yesterday at 4:24 PM
AppDelegate.swift
//
// Created by Jesse Feiler on 10/17/14.
// Copyright (c) 2014 Champlain Arts Corp. All rights reserved.
//
import UIKit
import CoreData
@UIApplicationMain
class AppDelegate: UIResponder, UIApplicationDelegate, UISplitViewControllerDelegate {
var window: UIWindow?
var myVar: String = ""
func application(application: UIApplication, didFinishLaunchingWithOptions launchOptions: [NSObject: AnyObject]?) -> Bool {
// Override point for customization after application launch.
let splitViewController = self.window!.rootViewController as UISplitViewController
let navigationController = splitViewController.viewControllers[splitViewController.viewControllers.count-1] as UINavigationController
navigationController.topViewController.navigationItem.leftBarButtonItem = splitViewController.displayModeButtonItem()
splitViewController.delegate = self
let masterNavigationController = splitViewController.viewControllers[0] as UINavigationController
let controller = masterNavigationController.topViewController as MasterViewController
controller.managedObjectContext = self.managedObjectContext
return true
}

Figure 3-7: Fix-It corrections can go beyond typos.

initializer function. The error message is correct (and creating an initializer called `init` could solve the problem), but there is this simpler solution: Just set a default value to the variable.

Folding and Unfolding Code

As you browse through your code in Xcode or in a playground, you can hone in on areas you're concerned with by *folding* and *unfolding* the sections of code you're not interested in at the moment. Folding and unfolding affects the display only: The code is still there. Folded code will be compiled.

Folding and unfolding is available for syntactic elements of code. Figure 3-8 shows part of `application(_:didFinishLaunchingWithOptions:)` at the top of `AppDelegate.swift` in the example app.

Move the pointer over the code. As you pass over the function, the rest of the code is shown with a gray background so that the function itself is made more prominent. At the top and bottom of the function (lines 17 and 29), small arrows appear in the margin. Click either arrow to fold up the function. When folded up, the function will appear as shown in Figure 3-9. Note the small arrow in the gutter at line 17.

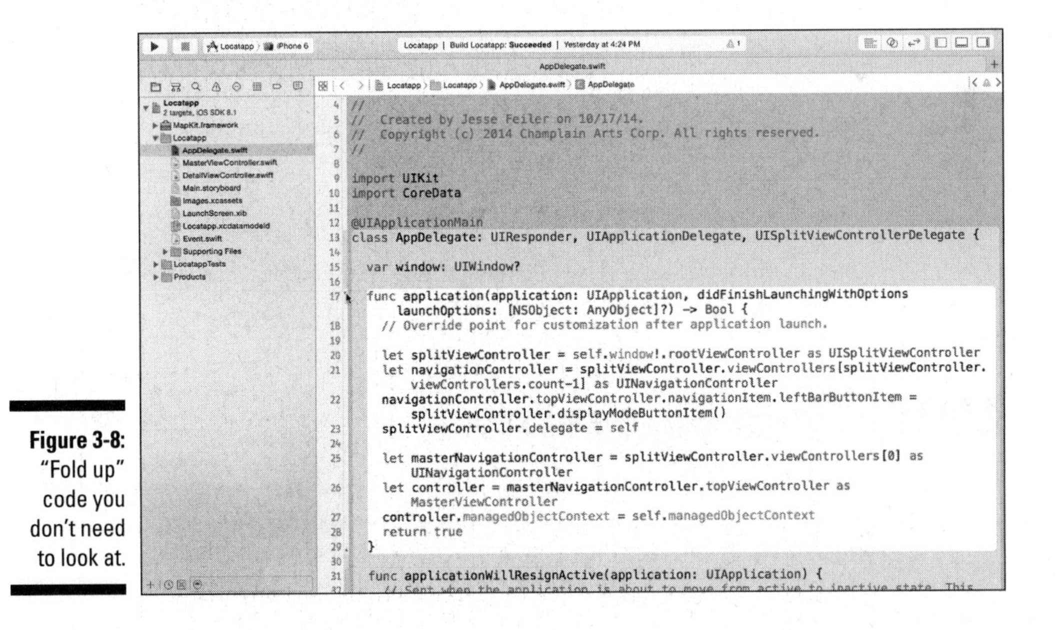

Figure 3-8: "Fold up" code you don't need to look at.

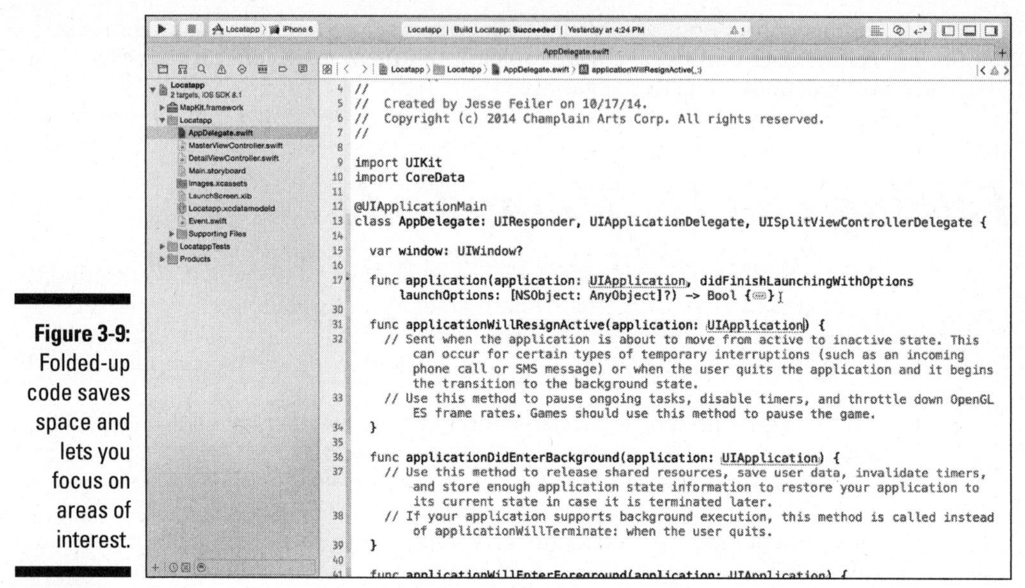

Figure 3-9: Folded-up code saves space and lets you focus on areas of interest.

Folding isn't limited to functions. You can fold up almost any syntactic element: `if`, `switch`, or any of the loop constructs.

There are a number of indications that code is folded up. For example, the yellow *ellipsis* (a series of three dots, as in . . .) that appears in Line 17 of Figure 3-9 is an indicator of folded-up code.

Also, folded-up code produces a discontinuity in line numbers. If you've chosen to show line numbers (an option you can set in the Editing section of the Text Editing tab in Xcode preferences), you can see that the line numbers in this example skip from 17 to 30 because lines 18 to 29 have been folded up.

You can unfold a section by clicking on the arrow in the margin or by double-clicking the ellipsis.

Using Code Snippets

Code completion and Fix-It can both help you speed up your typing and writing of code. Code snippets in the library go even further: They are snippets of code you can just drag into your own code. You can use a snippet as-is, but many have *tokens* — highlighted areas that you can customize with your own variable names or other customizations.

When you drag snippets with tokens into your code, they almost always generate errors because you haven't replaced the tokens yet. This is normal.

In addition to the built-in library, you can create your own snippets. Both methods are discussed in the following sections.

Working with built-in code snippets

Here are the steps to use for working with built-in code snippets.

1. **If necessary, show the utilities area.**

   The utilities, navigator, and debug areas all can be shown or hidden independently, so what is visible depends on what you've been doing. The trio of buttons at the top right of the toolbar (shown in Figure 3-10) let you show or hide each of these areas.

   In order to make the library area as big as possible, you may want to drag the tab bar up, as shown in Figure 3-10.

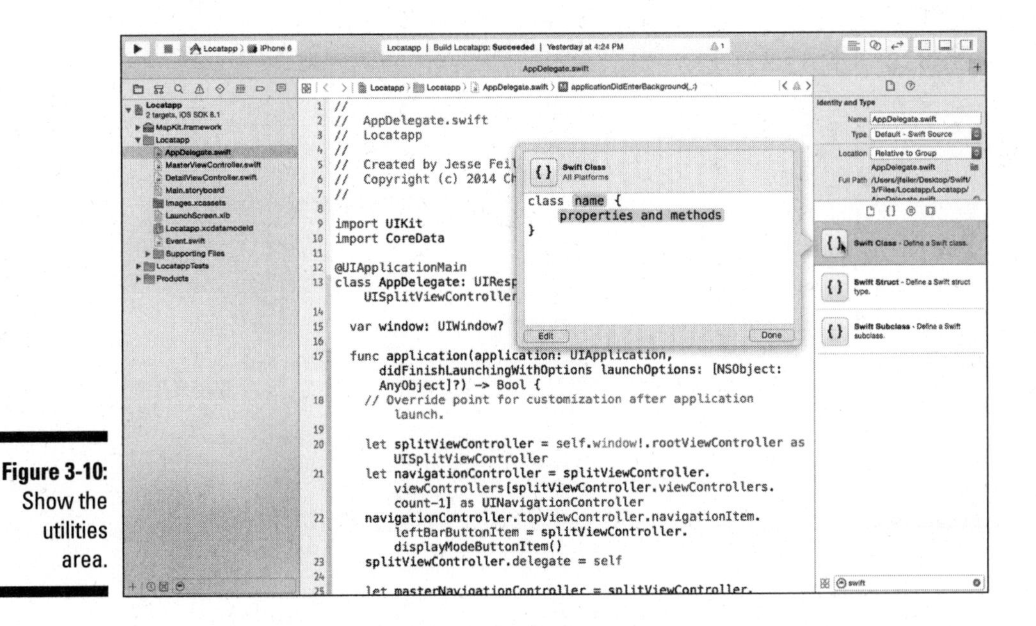

Figure 3-10: Show the utilities area.

2. **Click Snippets in the tab bar — {}.**
3. **Enter *Swift* in the search field at the bottom.**

   The library contains snippets from several languages, so searching for Swift will make certain you're working only with the Swift snippets.
4. **Select the snippet you want to use (as shown in Figure 3-10).**

   Information about the snippet is shown.
5. **Drag the snippet into your source code and place it where you want, as shown in Figure 3-11.**

   If there are tokens in the snippet, you may get error messages until you enter your own data.

   In addition to replacing tokens, feel free to make any other changes you want to the code. When you've dropped a snippet into your code, it becomes part of your code. The fact that it came from a snippet rather than from your own typing doesn't matter.

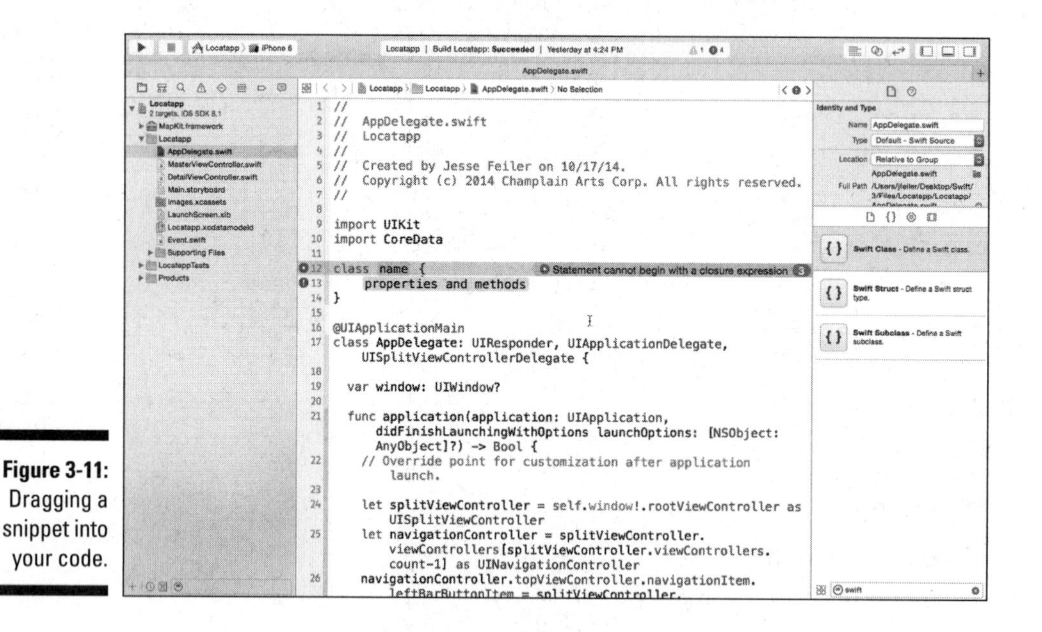

Figure 3-11: Dragging a snippet into your code.

Creating your own code snippets

You can create your own code snippets and add them to the library. You can create these for any code you commonly use, from copyright notices to any other sections particularly relevant to your work.

Here's how to create a snippet of your own:

1. **If necessary, show the utilities area.**

   In order to make the library area as big as possible, you may want to drag the tab bar up. (Refer to Figure 3-10.)

2. **Click Snippets in the tab bar — {}.**

3. **Highlight the code you want to create as a snippet and drag it into the library, as shown in Figure 3-12.**

   Note that Figure 3-12 shows the code of one of the functions in the template being dragged into the library: This is why you can see both the code in the file as well as the code in the process of being dragged.

4. **Select the snippet in the library.**

   Information about the snippet is shown.

5. **Click the Edit button in the lower left, as shown in Figure 3-13.**

6. **Add a good title for the snippet, and, unless the snippet you're creating is language-independent, like a copyright notice, change the language setting to Swift.**

7. **Choose a scope from the Completion Scope pop-up menu, as shown in Figure 3-14.**

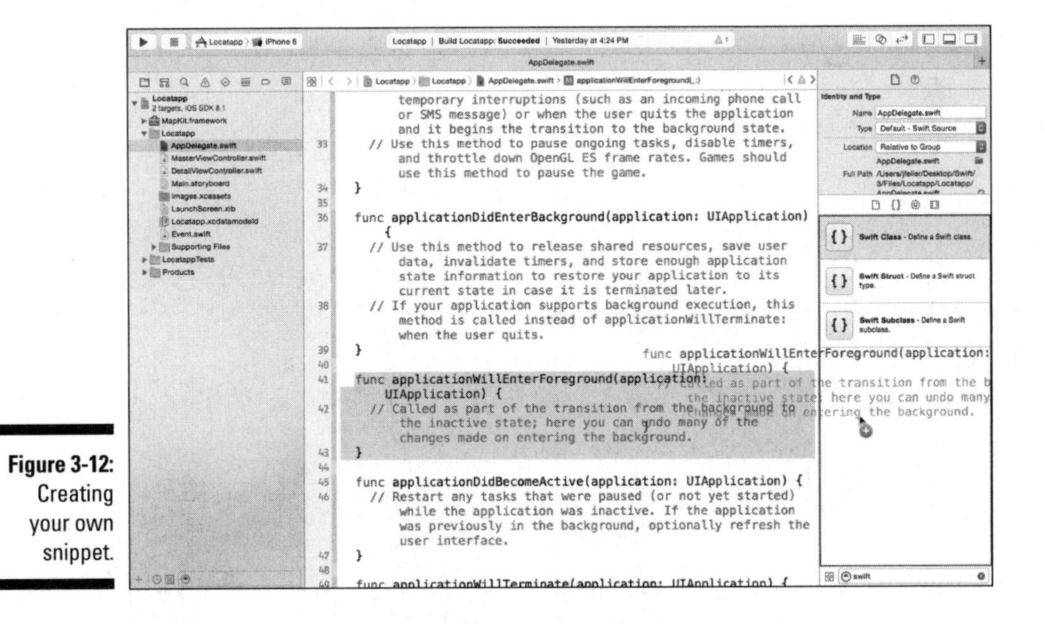

Figure 3-12: Creating your own snippet.

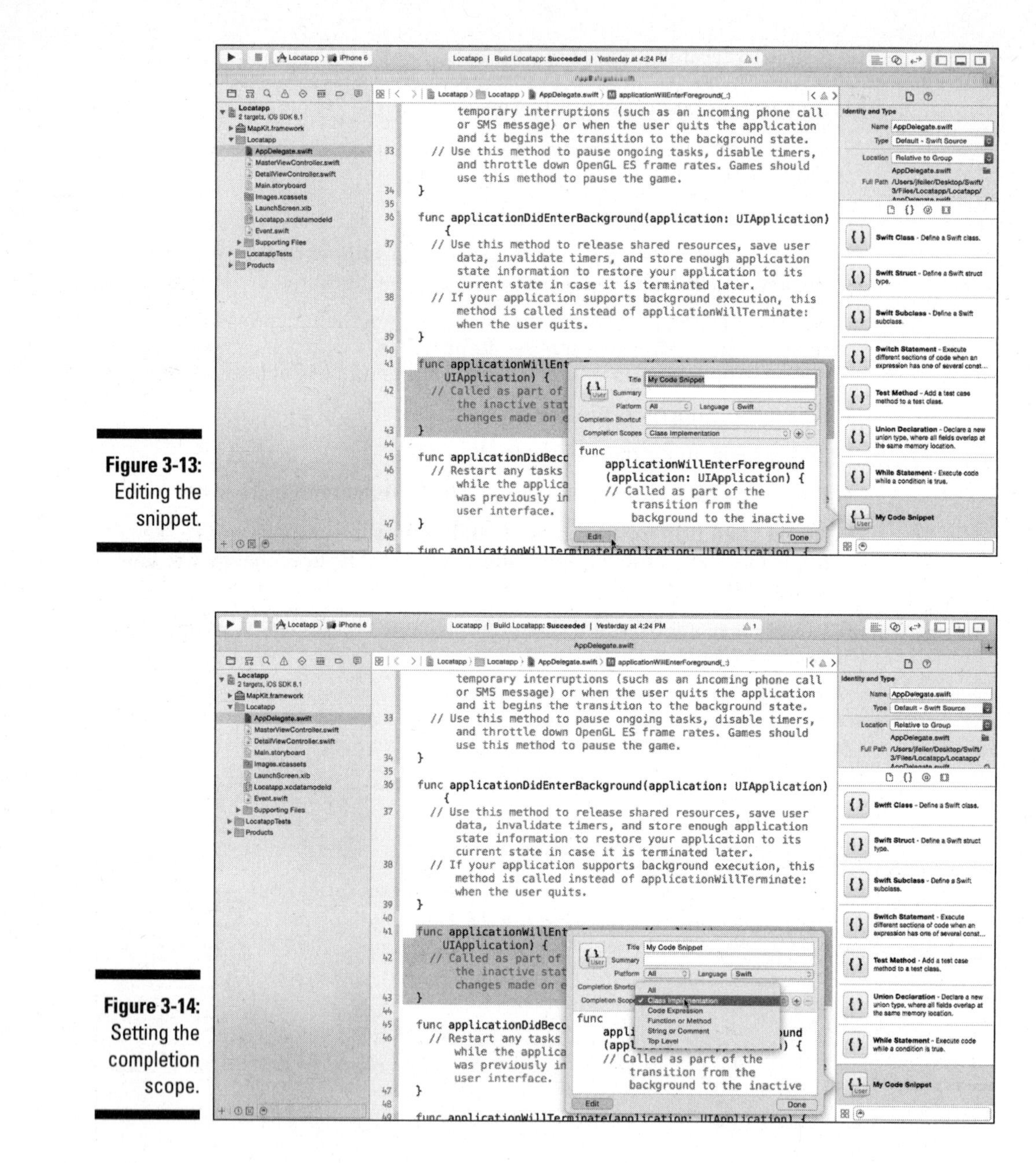

Figure 3-13: Editing the snippet.

Figure 3-14: Setting the completion scope.

Adding a scope makes your snippets even more useful because it prevents you (or your colleagues) from adding the snippet in illogical places.

Set the language setting before choosing the completion scope. The completion scope choices in the pop-up menu change depending on the language selected.

8. **(Optional) Replace the token text, such as the < #myVar# > shown in Figure 3-15.**

   Token text can be more than one word. Until the token is replaced, your snippet will generate an error — again, this is normal.

   Figure 3-16 shows a custom snippet with a token (and the associated errors).

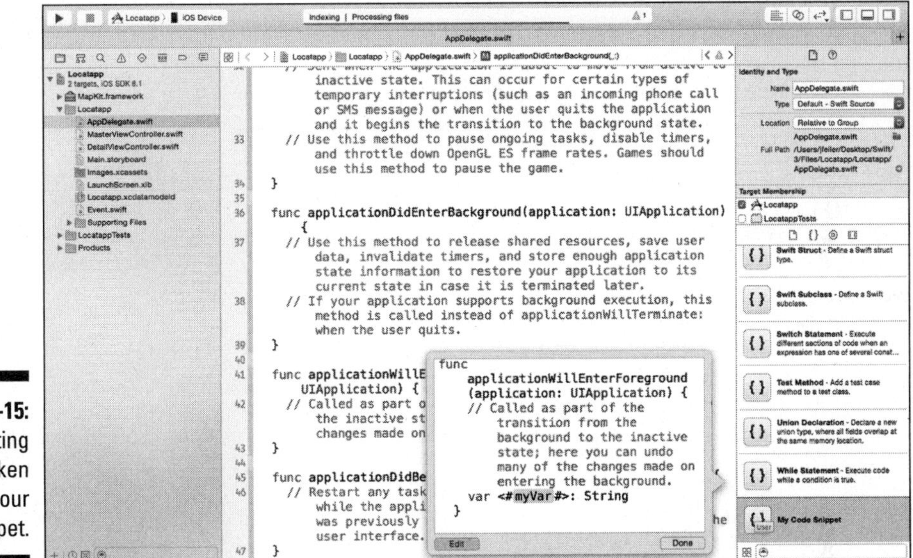

Figure 3-15: Creating a token in your snippet.

Figure 3-16: Using a custom snippet.

Chapter 4

Creating a Swift App

In This Chapter

- Creating and organizing your project's files
- Adding Swift code for your first app
- Testing your app

Chapter 1 shows you how to get started with an Xcode Swift project. As I discuss there, a great deal of your Swift Xcode development involves Xcode's graphical user interface. A lot of the work — particularly at the beginning of a project — is graphical or involves checkboxes.

Chapter 2 shows how to write and test code — particularly small snippets of code — in a playground. This helps you learn Swift syntax, as well as test out code fragments before you add them to your project files.

In this chapter, you take it from the top (as musicians say). I give you a quick review of the steps from Chapter 1 so you can create your version of the example app, Locatapp, you'll be using as you progress through this book. Much like peeling an onion, in this process you must peel back layer after layer. Yes, in some ways this is repetitive, but this only serves to help you become more comfortable with the steps involved in building a Swift app. This approach — a high-level quick overview followed by a demonstration of the basics, which is then followed by in-detail steps is just how engineers at Apple introduce new technologies at the Worldwide Developers Conference (WWDC).

If you've explored the first two chapters of this book, then you've begun to understand Swift's basic tools. This chapter gets down to business. Here you begin to build the example app used in many places in this book. From here on, the exercises I've included consist of steps that you'll use and reuse as you build your Swift apps. If anything in this chapter seems confusing, feel free to browse back to the first two chapters to get the background information. In addition, you can find more information at the author's website at `www.northcountryconsulting.com` and at `www.dummies.com`.

As I pointed out previously, remember to always check the date of information you find on the web. As I write this, OS X Yosemite (10.10) and iOS 8 have just been released. Apple Pay went live yesterday, and the Apple Watch SDK is available to registered developers. By the time you read this, all of these will be in use.

As a preview of what's to come, in the next chapter you explore Xcode's editing tools. There, you'll be writing code in the same way in which you may have written code in a beginning programming class in school. The focus in that chapter is on Xcode's tools that assist you with writing code. The tools and techniques that you find in these first chapters help you to actually create you first Swift app — the Locatapp example app used in this book.

Double-Checking Your Environment

One of the most commonly asked questions new Swift developers ask is, *Can I use an old Mac to develop with Swift (or Objective-C or Cocoa or Cocoa Touch)*? The answer depends on how old your Mac is. In most cases, Macs dating back as much as five years tend to be usable with current development tools.

What does need to be updated when you start developing — at least in many cases — is your operating system. This shouldn't be too much of a challenge: For the last few years, the operating system updates have been free. If you don't have the latest operating system, just download a free copy and get started.

The memory and disk requirements of the operating systems have been relatively stable. Sometimes, you may need to upgrade memory or disk storage — particularly if you've accumulated a lot of files on your disk(s).

Xcode is the development tool we use. It, too, is free, and most of the time you won't need to upgrade your computer to run it. It's true that you may want to upgrade your computer to get added speed for your development efforts, but you often can manage with a slightly slower computer for your development. In fact, many developers find that they need powerful Macs only to help them prepare their app graphics. The code is often not a challenge, even for old computers.

There is one environmental point to attend to. With today's large disks, we all tend to have a lot of files floating around. Developers can easily accumulate version after version of a project's files until it's no longer clear which is which. The solution to this is to create a file organization system and adhere to it. You may think you'll remember which is the latest version of a file, but I assure this isn't always the case. Sometimes you can forget as soon as you've finished your cup of coffee. Organize your files as if they were going to be used by a whole staff of developers, and you'll be in good shape.

Creating the Project

The first step in building an app is to create the project and its basic files. Most of the time, you start from one of the built-in Xcode templates. The templates used in this book are those built into Xcode 6.1, which is the version that supports iOS 8 and OS X Yosemite. Updates will happen over time, but this is the common starting point.

The details of creating a project are described in Chapter 1. Here are some additional points for you to consider.

Choosing the name

You need to choose a name for your project and its targets. Actually, your project can have multiple targets, each with its own name. This section provides a high-level view of the structure of your Xcode project. For now, the simplest way to proceed here is to ignore the complex options. (You can always come back to it later.) Name your project with a simple one-word short name (eight letters or fewer) that doesn't contain non-letter or non-number characters such as spaces, dollar signs, or tildes. For later reference, here are a few of the options that you can consider as you are more comfortable with Xcode and app development.

The *project* is the overall collection of files that you are creating. It is contained within a folder that uses the project name. This name is for your benefit, so you can include abbreviations, department codes, or other shortcuts that you would not reveal to the public.

Be careful of the characters that are not allowed in Finder names such as / , ~, {, (, and spaces. (This list is not exhaustive.) It's safest to stick to upper- and lowercase letters and numbers; limit special characters to dashes. If you're not certain about a character, create a file in the Finder and rename it with the name you're thinking of: If the Finder changes the name automatically, you'll know that you should use either the changed name or a more middle-of-the-road name without special characters.

The project can contain multiple *targets*, each of which can be built with Xcode. One target may be a version of your app for iOS, and another may be a version for Macs. Still another may be designed for testing (the Xcode templates often create a testing target as a companion for your app's target). You can create several targets from the same basic files. (That's a reason for using multiple targets: It's easy to share the common files in the project.)

Another variation on this theme occurs if you'll have several versions of your app — perhaps Your App Lite, Your App, and Your App Pro. A common strategy is to create Your App Lite as a free app, Your App as a priced app, and Your App Pro as a higher priced app. Multiply those three apps by two (for iOS and OS X), and you now are talking about building six apps. If you can write your basic functionality code once for all six apps, you'll be far ahead.

Within a family of devices (iOS or OS X), the differences typically do not require separate apps. For example, you can build an iOS app that runs on both iPhone and iPad; you can build an OS X app that runs on MacBook Pro and iMac.

When you create a new project, you provide the name of the project as well as the name of each target. Review the App Store and Mac App Store guidance for naming conventions so that your names don't confuse anyone. (Browse the App Store Resource Center on `developer.apple.com` for the most current information.)

Also, be aware that there are also restrictions on the ways you can promote Lite and Pro versions. In short, remember that every version of your app should give users a satisfactory experience rather than a sense of frustration when they are suddenly informed that they have to get out their credit card to type even one more keystroke.

In short, naming the user-facing parts of your project — that is, the parts that normally become products — is a more critical and complex matter than naming projects or targets, whose names are visible only to you and other developers. (You have almost total control over the product name if you modify it in the Build Settings section of an Xcode target. Use the Build Settings section under Packaging, where you'll find Product Name — which you can specify separately for debug and release versions.)

Stick with a simple short, one-word product name for your first tests. Get into the complexity of naming products later on.

The name of the project and the targets can be changed later. However, although changing the names is easier than it was in the past, it is often best not to do it if you can avoid it. Renaming can cause problems with bundles, which are described in the following section.

Understanding bundles

A *bundle* identifies your target — that is, the app that you're building. That's the basic definition. The bundle identifier is constructed automatically by Xcode from your organization identifier and your product identifier.

The combination of the two should be unique, and it will be if you use the reverse domain name of your company or organization as the organization name.

Behind the scenes your bundle identifier is further modified by having your developer identifier prepended to it. I said that the bundle identifier is used to identify your app, but this is a bit of a generalization. For iCloud-enabled apps, several apps can share one bundle identifier for their common iCloud storage.

A bundle identifier is key to identifying your app behind the scenes. It is not a user-facing name, although your product name is included as part of the bundle name. Furthermore, although this section describes the default Xcode behavior, be aware that you can modify almost every step of the process to create your own naming conventions.

Reviewing a project's file structure

This section provides some details about how Xcode project files are laid out on disk. In the case of a simple project (such as Locatapp), the structure is very simple: one workspace with one project with one target. This section walks you through that structure. If you want to, you can move onto a workspace with multiple projects, each of which has multiple targets. Alternatively, you can opt for a workspace with a single project with multiple targets. The structures outlined in this section come into play in any of those scenarios, but you only need to understand what you have in the Xcode template you're using: one project called Locatapp that contains two targets, Locatapp (the app you're building) and LocatappTests (a testing app that Xcode automatically creates).

Although right now you're working with a very simple project, having a basic understanding of the structure of more complex projects right from the start can be very helpful. In particular, you can start thinking about future directions for your project, and knowing the options available to you in Xcode can help you think of a complex app or even a suite of apps.

Figure 4-1 shows the structure of the Locatapp project described in Chapter 1. Here are the important points to note about these files and folders (they are discussed from the top down in the figure).

- **`DS_Store`:** This file is normally hidden (this is why it's shown in gray). It's in every folder on OS X, and it contains information about the files in that directory. Developers often use a Terminal command to show hidden files in their folders, but you don't need to worry about that for the moment.

- **Target folders:** The project you create in Chapter 1 has two targets by default. One is the actual app (Locatapp) and the second is code to run automated tests (LocatappTests). A tests target is included by default in many of the Xcode templates.
- **`Locatapp.xcodeproj`:** This file is at the top level of the project folder along with the folders for the two targets (Locatapp and LocatappTests). This is the file you open to start work on your project. In Figure 4-1, it is located between the two target folders (Locatapp and LocatappTests) because the files and folders are shown in alphabetical order.

As noted previously, the structure of files within this project folder is set when you create the project. You can modify locations and relationships using the File inspector in the utilities area, but most of the time, you should leave the locations and relationships alone. If you move things around, Xcode can get confused (as can you). If you must move files around, don't use the Finder. Most developers prefer not to use the Finder to modify, move, or rename files or folders within a project folder. Use the File inspector or the Edit⇨Refactor⇨Rename command to do that.

Working with workspaces

The steps to create a project in Xcode in Chapter 1 represent the most common way to make a project. However, this isn't the only approach: You can create a *workspace* that contains several projects.

The workspace, project folders, and the files within them are managed by Xcode, subject to settings you create in the File inspector in the utilities area.

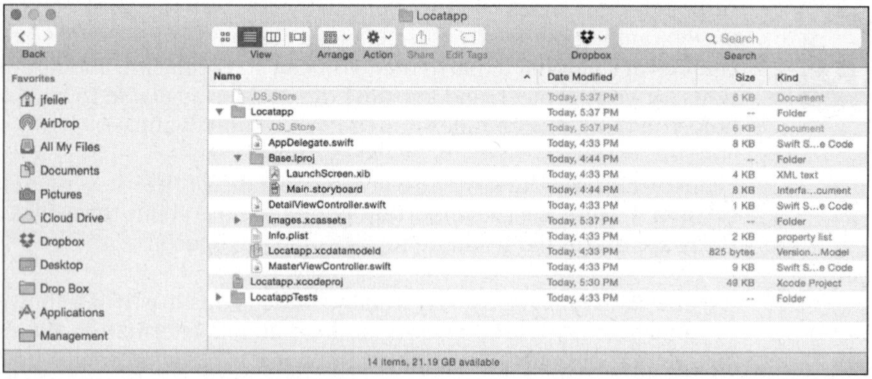

Figure 4-1: Inspecting the project folder.

Within a project folder, you create files and groups of files using Xcode. The groups of files you see in the project navigator may or may not be folders on disk.

You can create a workspace with File⇨New⇨Workspace. A workspace is designed to contain multiple projects. This gives you two hierarchical layers you can use in developing apps:

- A workspace can contain one or more projects.
- A project can contain one or more targets.

One common use of a workspace is for two projects: one designed for iOS and the other for OS X. A shared folder (on disk) or group (in Xcode's project navigator) may contain the shared code.

Multiple targets within a single project tend to have tighter integration and sharing than targets within a project. As you can see in the default templates, the targets within a project may consist of an app with automated tests as well as a user-facing app. You can bring this structure forward so that within a single project, compiler options are used to build Pro and Lite versions.

A workspace is represented by a file with an extension of `xcworkspace`. When you are creating a new project (as described in Chapter 1 and shown in Figure 1-10), an option at the bottom of the sheet lets you place that project into a worksheet, as shown in Figure 4-2. (You also can add it to a project.)

As described in the preceding section, the project is placed in a target folder and is managed by an `xcodeproj` file. If you want to add an existing project to a workspace, drag the `xcodeproj` file into the navigator of the workspace. The file and folder structure of the project remains wherever you have placed it.

Figure 4-2 shows how you add a new project to an existing project or workspace in Xcode: You can add a new project to an existing project or workspace using the pop-up menu at the bottom of the sheet.

When you are adding a file with New⇨File, you can select the target to which to add it with checkboxes in the same location on the sheet as the pop-up menu shown in Figure 4-2. When you add a new target, you select the project to add it to with a pop-up menu on the Options sheet where you specify the project name (shown previously in Figure 1-9). To sum up: Files go in targets; targets go in projects; and projects go in other projects or workspaces.

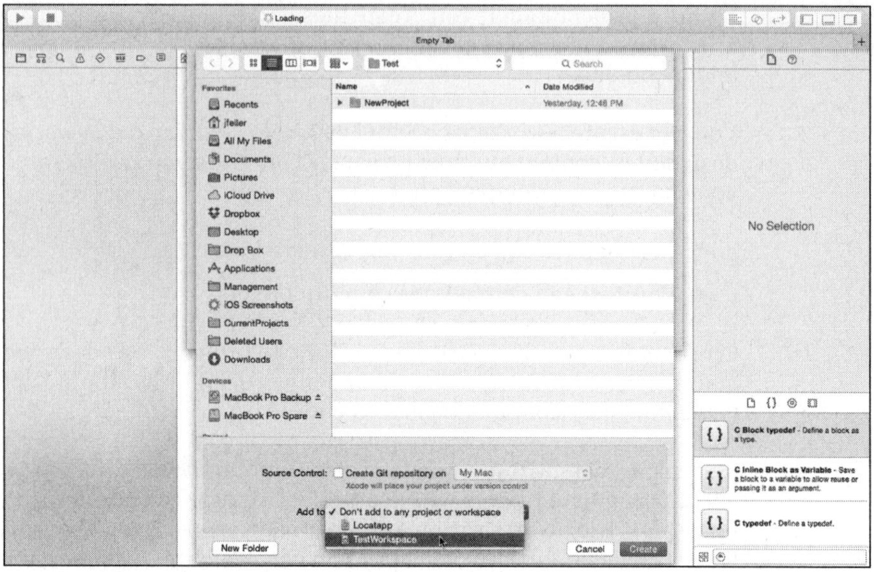

Figure 4-2: Adding a new project to a workspace.

For convenience and simplicity, developers frequently place all of the workspace projects into a single workspace folder, but this is not necessary. In cases with complex workspaces, it's sometimes not even possible.

Testing the Template

At this point — after you have created a new project from a template and are chomping at the bit and ready to get going — run the app. When it runs, you should see a map when iOS Simulator is in landscape mode (use Hardware⇨Rotate Right/Left to get to the landscape view).

If the app doesn't run from the basic template, it won't run for your further additions.

If your app doesn't run, try some of the solutions in the following list, ordered from simple to more complex. Before considering these options, however, take this one very basic step: If you have an error message, read it and see if it describes a problem that you can solve. Failing that, run Console (launch it from Applications⇨Utilities⇨Console) and look for recent messages that may relate to your app's problems. There may not be messages of either type, or you may not understand them. In either case, you can proceed with the solutions listed here:

- **Try again:** For any number of reasons, your second try may succeed. You may have made a mistake the first time in one way or another, or some components of the test (most often iOS Simulator) may need more time to launch. There are two parts to "try again":
  - Try to run the app again using Xcode and iOS Simulator.
  - Create a new project from the Xcode template and try to run that one.
- **Check your components' versions:** Ideally, you are using the latest release versions of OS X and Xcode. (You can download them from `developer.apple.com`). If you are using pre-release beta versions, try again with the release version. (For more, see the sidebar, "A note about switching versions.")
- **Look at Apple Developer Forums:** Most of this area is reserved for registered developers (go to `developer.apple.com` to register or sign in), but even so, it's worth checking to see what you can get to. Use the search tools, because you might find your answer mentioned in passing in a totally unrelated post. Searching on the text of an error message you have found is always a good start.
- **Search the web:** Use a web browser to search on the error message. Remember the reminder mentioned several times in this book: Check the date on postings you find because they may be out of date and cause you to waste time. (That also applies but to a lesser extent with Apple Developer Forums because they are moderated.)
- **Try another template:** Try one of the other built-in Xcode templates to see if you can build and run it. This may narrow down your problem.
- **Use a technical support incident:** If you are a registered Apple developer, you typically get two technical support incidents each registration year. (Note that the year begins and ends on the anniversary of your registration, rather than the calendar year.) You have separate registrations for iOS and OS X, so if you are registered for both programs, you have four technical support incidents that you've already paid for. Many developers hoard their incidents in case they need them, but remember that you've already paid for them (and you can buy more in packages of two for $100). Be aware that you can't use technical support incidents for pre-release software, so make certain you're using the release versions of OS X and Xcode.

- **Contact other developers:** Check `meetup.com` and other sites to find a mutual help group near you. Of course, you'll probably discover that a group met yesterday and will meet for the next time in two months, but even so, it's worth a shot.
- **Social media to the rescue:** As long as you're not dealing with pre-release software from Apple that's covered by non-disclosure, search and then post a message on tools like Facebook or LinkedIn to see if someone else has had the problem. If the problem really isn't your fault (this happens mostly with pre-release software) you may discover other people who have come across this problem (and maybe solved it).
- **Tomorrow is another day:** Create a new Xcode project and test it from the beginning . . . *tomorrow*. In the meantime, get some rest and clear your mind. Do the same for your Mac (that is to say, shut it down and then restart it). Shutting down rather than just restarting may help you get past network issues that may be getting in your way. Particularly if you are using a shared network disk, you may be encountering some kind of network problem that a total restart will either solve or clearly identify.

A note about switching versions

If you decide to try switching to a newer (or older) version of OS X or Xcode, take a moment to consider all the ways this may create problems. If you have a separate Mac that you use for development, you may be able to do a clean install (erasing the hard disk) and then reinstall OS X and Xcode. This gives you a clean environment.

If you don't have a separate Mac, consider creating a new user account in the Finder (using System Preferences➪Users & Groups). This gives you a new user account with its own set of files. You can even reinstall Xcode in the Applications folder of the new account rather than in the Applications folder for all users on the Mac.

If you don't have Time Machine running, do a full backup of your Mac. If Time Machine is running, do a manual backup of the current state of your Mac using System Preferences➪Time Machine.

Although you're focused on getting your app to compile and run, keep a cool head while you make the switch — don't inadvertently break something else!

Setting the Location for iOS Simulator

iOS Simulator is built into Xcode. It lets you run your app as if it were running on a device such as iPhone or iPad. It's a key tool in app development.

I discuss the basics of using iOS Simulator in Chapter 1.

iOS Simulator can't do certain things that an actual device can do. For example, it can manage iCloud synchronization, but in iOS Simulator this is done with a menu command (Debug⇨Trigger iCloud Sync).

Locatapp uses the location manager tools that are built into iOS. When you're running on iOS Simulator, those basic tools are available, but the location that they manage is not the location of the simulated device. In order to test your Locatapp code, you must manually set the location you want to use in iOS Simulator. There are two steps to this: setting your device(s) and setting the location to use.

This process can be a little tricky because the location settings for iOS Simulator may have been set by you or someone else in testing apps on the Mac you're using and you may be mystified by why iOS Simulator thinks it's somewhere strange to you.

When you are testing with iOS Simulator, you don't set your actual location. Rather, you set a specific location — that is, the location returned when you query iOS Simulator. This makes it easier to test your code because you know what the location should be.

Adding devices to iOS Simulator

To set your iOS Simulator location, follow these steps. (Note that these steps also include information about how to check if this setting has already been done.):

1. **To check to see if you have devices that are already configured for iOS Simulator, click the pop-up menu at the left of the toolbar, as shown in Figure 4-3.**

   If the list there contains only the iOS Device command, you don't have any simulators installed. Proceed to the next step.

   If you do have any simulators installed, you can use iOS Simulator for that device, but if you want to simulate a different device, check to see that that device is installed in Xcode. If it isn't, proceed to the next step.

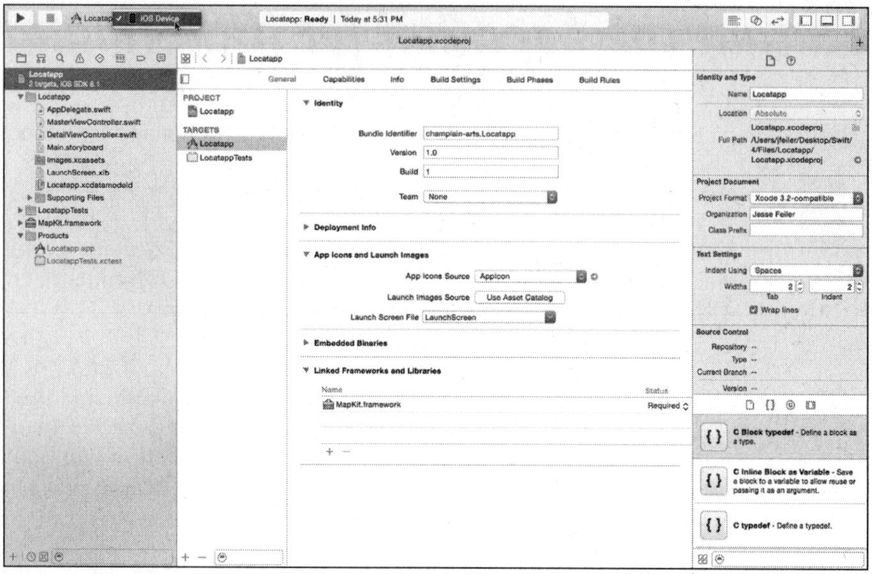

Figure 4-3: Check to see which simulators are installed in Xcode.

2. **In Xcode, choose Window➪Devices or Shift-Command-2, as shown in Figure 4-4.**

   This opens the Devices window.

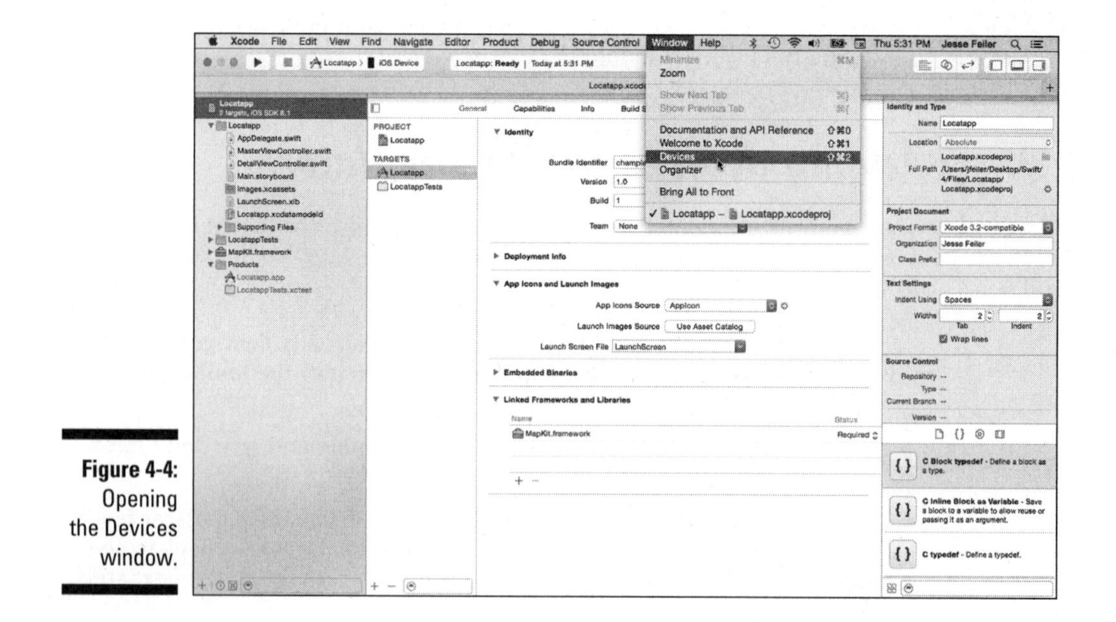

Figure 4-4: Opening the Devices window.

3. **In the Devices window (shown in Figure 4-5), you'll see the devices you are using along with the simulators you have installed.**

   The simulators section will probably be blank; if it has any entries, they may not be for the simulator(s) you want to use. The entries there should match the entries in the pop-up menu shown in Figure 4-3.

4. **To add a new device, click the + at the bottom of the left sidebar of the Devices window.**

   This opens the Create a new simulator sheet shown in Figure 4-6.

5. **Choose your device type from the pop-up menu on the sheet and give it a simulator name of your choosing. Select the appropriate iOS version as well.**

   This allows you to simulate not only a device but also a version of the operating system.

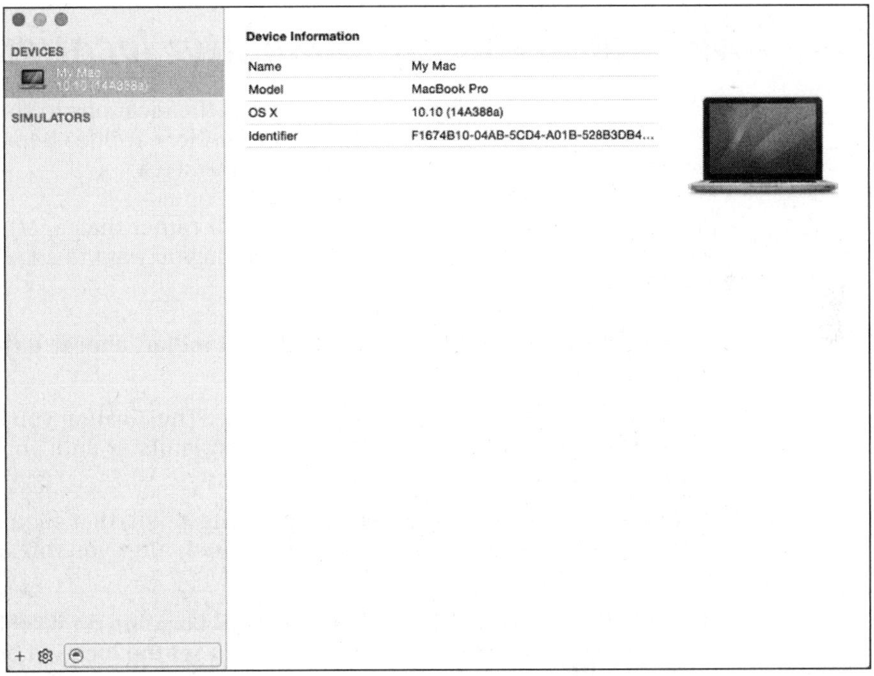

Figure 4-5: Reviewing your devices.

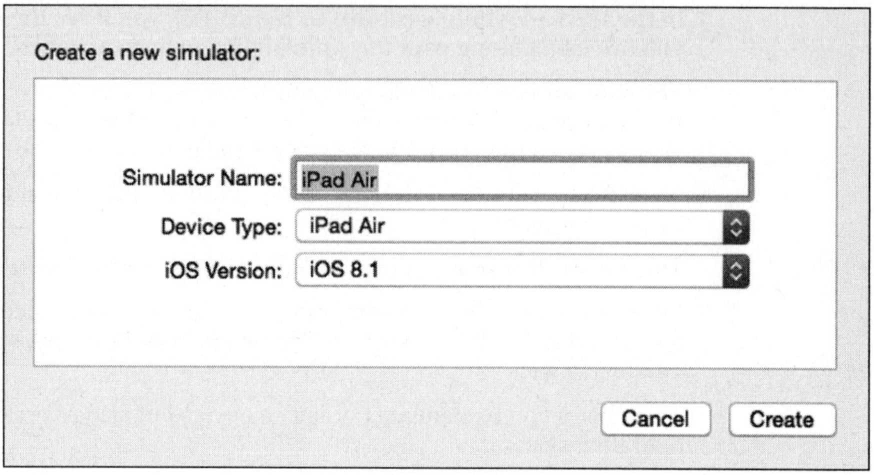

Create a new simulator:

Simulator Name: iPad Air

Device Type: iPad Air

iOS Version: iOS 8.1

Cancel Create

Figure 4-6: Naming and adjusting your new simulator.

Managing the iOS Simulator location

Both Xcode and iOS Simulator allow you to set the locations to simulate. There are two types of simulations you can set. Here are the steps to set them (the details of each are described after the steps).

With your Xcode device(s) set for iOS Simulator rather than a tethered (plugged-in) iPhone or iPad, choose the location you want to simulate by following these steps:

1. **Using the pop-up menu at the left of the toolbar, choose any of the devices listed.**

   It doesn't matter which device you choose: The location you set is for iOS Simulator and all of the devices that it simulates until you change it to another location.

2. **Run an app that uses Core Location.** At this point, that should include the Locatapp template that you have created. After you run an app, iOS Simulator launches automatically.

3. **While the app is running, choose Debug⇨Location on iOS Simulator or Debug⇨Simulate Location on Xcode to set the location on iOS Simulator.**

Your choice of whether to set the debugging location with Xcode or with iOS Simulator reflects the choices and behavior that each one provides, as follows:

- *Setting locations using Xcode:* With a Core Location-using app running, select Debug➪Simulate Location on Xcode to choose a location. As of this writing, your choices include London, England; Johannesburg, South Africa; Moscow, Russia; Mumbai, India; Tokyo, Japan; Sydney, Australia; Hong Kong, China; Honolulu, HI, USA; San Franciscoo, CA, USA; Mexico City, Mexico; New York, NY, USA; and Rio de Janeiro, Brazil.

  In addition, there's a Don't Simulate Location option so you can test out your code to handle the case where a user doesn't have Location Services turned on. Furthermore, there's a menu option to add a GPX file to the project. (A GPX file is an XML schema formally called GPS Exchange Format that can be used for waypoints, tracks, and routes. It lets you add your own location to the Simulate Location menu.)

- *Setting locations using iOS Simulator:* With a Core Location-using app running, select Debug➪Location on iOS Simulator. Your menu choices are different than on Xcode. The location choices include Apple (the Apple campus in Cupertino); City Bicycle Ride; City Run; and Freeway Drive.

  In addition, there is a None option to turn off Location Services, and an option to supply a custom location by entering a latitude and longitude (in digital form rather than degrees-minutes-seconds).

  The ride, run, and drive options in iOS Simulator provide you with a changing location that follows a track on a route and with a speed for a bike, run, or drive. This lets you test code to track a moving current location. That code will be in the Locatapp sample when you're finished, so it will work after you have finished the following section.

With these steps in either Xcode or iOS Simulator, you're ready to test the location code that will be added later in this chapter in the section, "Adding Swift Code to Locatapp."

Adding the Map to the Storyboard and Project

Using the steps described in Chapter 1, you can begin to lay the groundwork for the app you'll build throughout this book. You may want to refer back to Chapter 1 to make sure you've carried out these steps after you have created the project:

1. **Drag a MapKit view from the library in the utilities area into the Detail scene of the storyboard. Place it over the `View` view (which is helpfully named `view`) so that it replaces that view as well as its constraints.**

   If you make certain that it replaces `view`, the constraints will automatically be removed. If you can't see the Detail scene of the storyboard, verify that you have selected `Main.storyboard` in the project navigator, and that you have shown the document outline in the storyboard with Editor⇨Show Document Outline.

2. **Import the MapKit framework with this code at the top of DetailViewController.swift.**

   ```
   import MapKit
   ```

   You need to add the framework to the project as a whole (Step 1) as well as to this file.

3. **Add the code side of the map view you added in Step 1.**

   `IBOutlet` specifies that this variable is an outlet in Interface Builder. (Outlets are interface elements such as views, buttons, and the like.) Xcode makes it simple to do this. Because Xcode will be writing the code for you, you go into Interface Builder inside Xcode and draw a line. Here are the steps:

   a. *Select `Main.storyboard` in the project navigator.*

   b. *Show the Assistant editor with View⇨Assistant Editor⇨Show Assistant Editor.*

   c. *In the jump bar, select Automatic⇨DetailViewController.swift, as shown in Figure 4-7.*

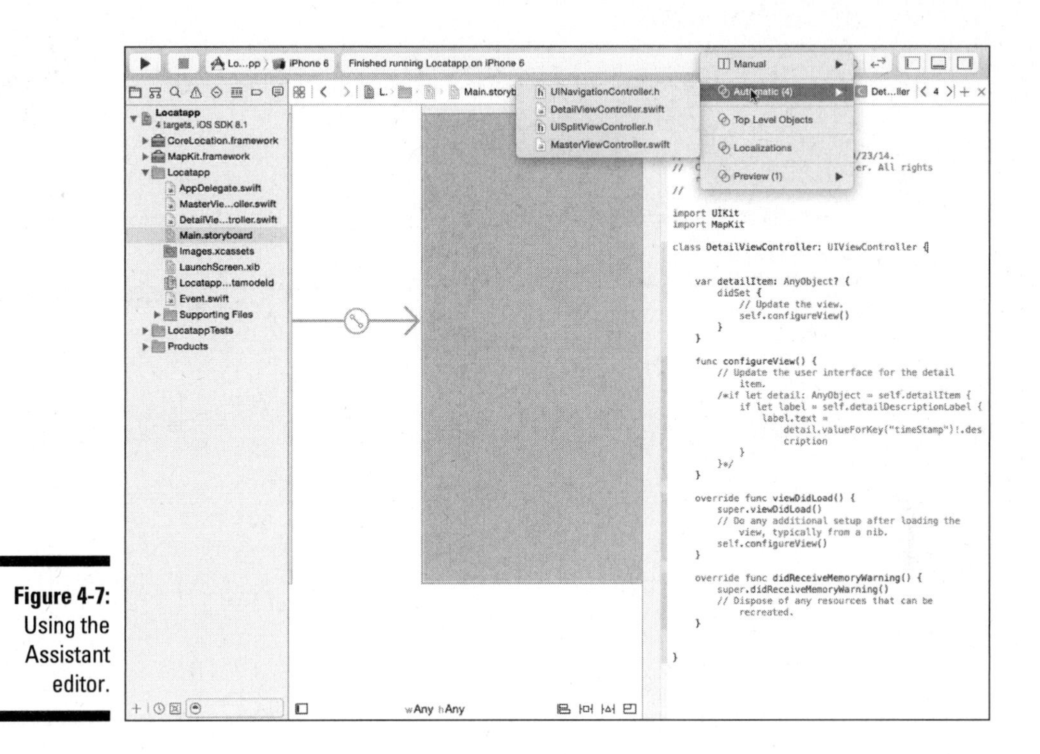

Figure 4-7: Using the Assistant editor.

At this point, you should have `Main.storyboard` on the left and `DetailViewController.swift` on the right. (If your preferences are set otherwise, they may be arranged on the top and bottom.)

d. *If necessary, show the storyboard document outline with Editor⇨Show Document Outline.*

e. *Control-drag from Map View in the document outline to the top of* `DetailViewController.swift`*, as shown in Figure 4-8.*

When you release the mouse button, you'll see a small view.

f. *Enter* ***mapView*** *for the name of the outlet, as shown in Figure 4-9.*

Xcode and Interface Builder will write the following line of code for you and connect it to the user interface you have drawn in Interface Builder:

```
@IBOutlet var mapView: MKMapView!
```

What is that ! for? You'll find out in Chapter 6.

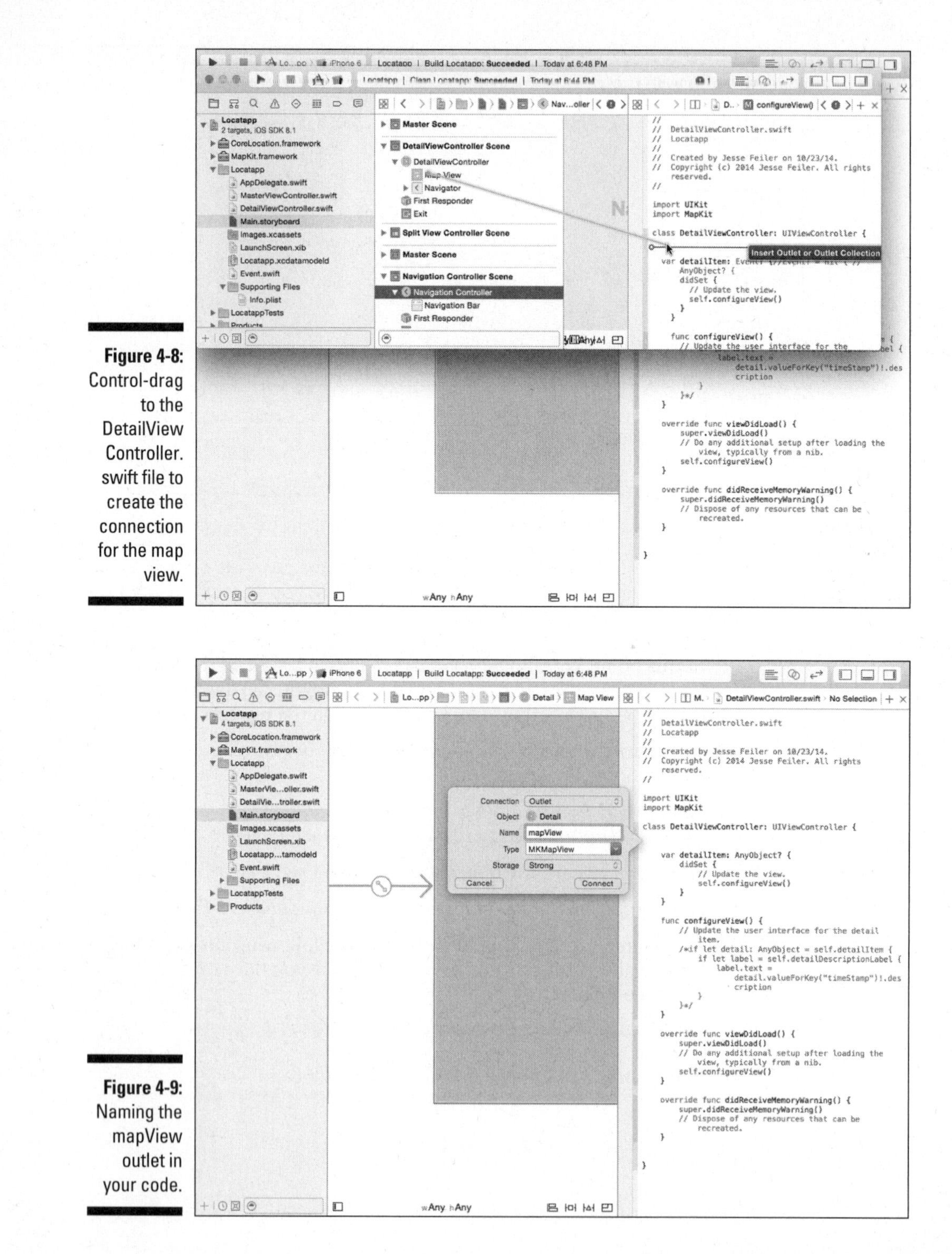

Figure 4-8: Control-drag to the DetailViewController.swift file to create the connection for the map view.

Figure 4-9: Naming the mapView outlet in your code.

4. **Add the MapKit framework to Linked Frameworks and Libraries on the General tab of the project.**

   Use + at the bottom of that section to open a list of available frameworks: Look for `MapKit.framework`, select it, and click Add in the lower-right corner.

Testing the App

When you run the app now, you'll see a map when you're in landscape mode. The user location isn't shown, and if you add a new `Event` object to the database with the + at the top right of the master view controller, it will have a timestamp because that's what the template does.

Figure 4-10 shows the app as it is now. It is running in landscape on iOS Simulator for iPhone 6 Plus. In this configuration, it uses a split screen view with the master view controller at the left and the detail view controller (with the map) at the right.

To complete the first phase of the app, you'll need to enable the map to show the user's location and you'll also need to store the user's location instead of a timestamp. The following sections show you how to do these things.

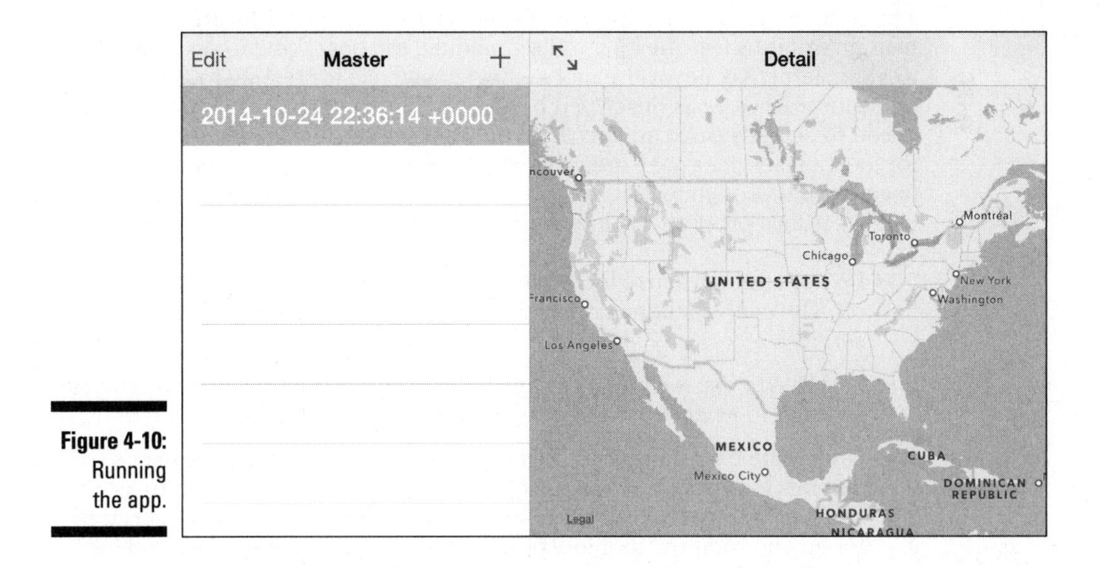

Figure 4-10: Running the app.

In the sections that follow, you see how to add Swift code to the template to make an app that you can use to experiment with throughout this book. The emphasis in this book is on the Swift language, so you'll be using it, but you'll also be using code in the Cocoa or Cocoa Touch frameworks as well as the built-in Xcode templates (primarily the iOS Master-Detail Application template). The frameworks are not described in detail in this book.

Adding Swift Code to Locatapp

In this section, you see how to add the necessary code to display and store the user's location. As noted previously, this requires a good deal of Swift code, and it will give you a basic overview of a number of language features. Later chapters will explore the various features in depth.

Although most of the time you can skip around in this book, it's important to carry out the steps in this chapter in sequence because they rely on one another.

Setting and confirming location settings in iOS Simulator and on devices

The code in the example app checks the user's settings for location awareness. In order to test the app you're building, the best thing to do is to set iOS Simulator, Xcode, or the mobile device you use for testing to allow use of location services as described previously in this chapter. When you move ahead to actually build an app that you want to distribute, the user's settings for location services is an area that you'll need to test. At that time you'll need to do thorough testing so that you know that your app respects the user's settings properly, as follows:

- Do not attempt to use location services if the user has turned them off. The user's action is referred to as *unauthorizing* the use of location services.
- Feel free to use location services if the user has turned them on. This is referred to as *authorizing* the use of location services.
- Even if the user has authorized location services, respect the user's settings for your app. App-specific authorizations are referred to as *enabling* the location services for your app. (Enabling location services for an app requires that location services in general be authorized for the user's device.)

This means that when you're writing a real app, you must check the authorization and enabling of location services and you must monitor changes to both. This is done with the Core Location framework's delegate protocol, which you must adopt in your app. The necessary code is provided in the Swift code in this book; details of its use are in Apple's documentation of location services and MapKit.

For more on protocols, see Chapter 18.

Authorizing location services on a device or simulator

Here are the steps to authorize location services on iOS Simulator; (the steps on an iOS device itself are the same):

1. **Run your app on iOS Simulator as described in the earlier section, "Testing the App," and shown in Figure 4-7.**
2. **Click on iOS Simulator to bring it forward on your Mac, if necessary.**

   Make certain that the menu bar at the top of the Mac's screen is the simulator's menu bar.
3. **"Tap" the Home button by choosing Hardware⇨Home or pressing Shift-Command-H.**

   You should see the iOS Home screen as shown in Figure 4-11 (at the left). The specific installed apps may vary.
4. **Go to Settings⇨Privacy⇨Location and turn on Location Services, as shown in Figure 4-11 (at the right).**

   You may or may not have specific apps listed beneath the main setting. If you have run your app already, you may have a blank space for its name — this will be corrected in the following section.

Writing the code to check authorization and enabling of location services

There are two parts to adding the code to your app to check authorization and the enabled status of location services. The first is to set up the alert for the user to enable location services for your app, and the second is to write the code to respect the user's settings. To do this, follow these steps:

1. **Select the Info tab in the project.**

   Select the project at the top of the project navigator and then click the Info tab.

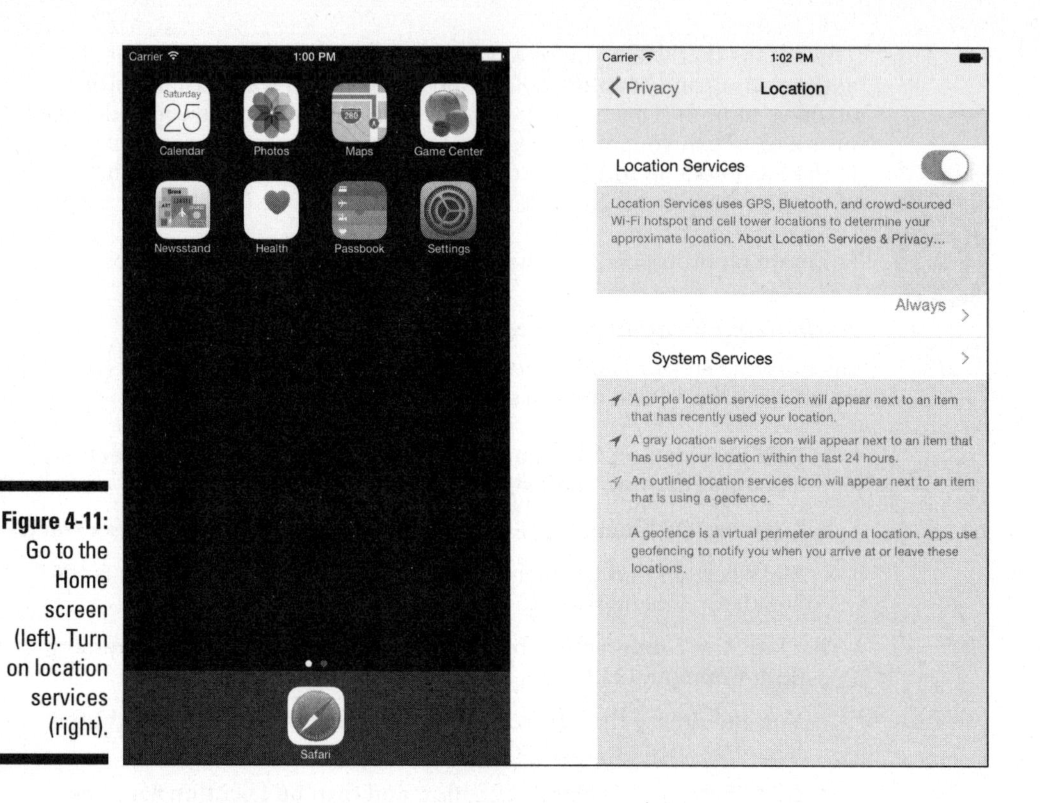

Figure 4-11: Go to the Home screen (left). Turn on location services (right).

2. **Add a new item at the bottom of the list of Custom iOS Target Properties.**

    a. In Figure 4-12, the last item in the list is Required device capabilities. If you hover the pointer over it, you'll see a +. Click that to add a new line to Custom iOS Target Properties.

    b. At the time of this writing, the property you need to use is not in the pop-up list, so type its name into the field at the left. The name is `NSLocationWhenInUseUsageDescription`. (There's a companion setting called `NSLocationAlwaysUsageDescription` but you don't need that for this example.)

    c. The type should be `String` by default, but double-check that it is set correctly.

3. **At the right, enter the text you want to be shown in the alert. This text asks the user to decide whether or not to enable location services for your app.**

    For example, you could use "This will let you see your current location" as shown in Figure 4-13. (Note that this is what it will look like after more code has been added later in the book.)

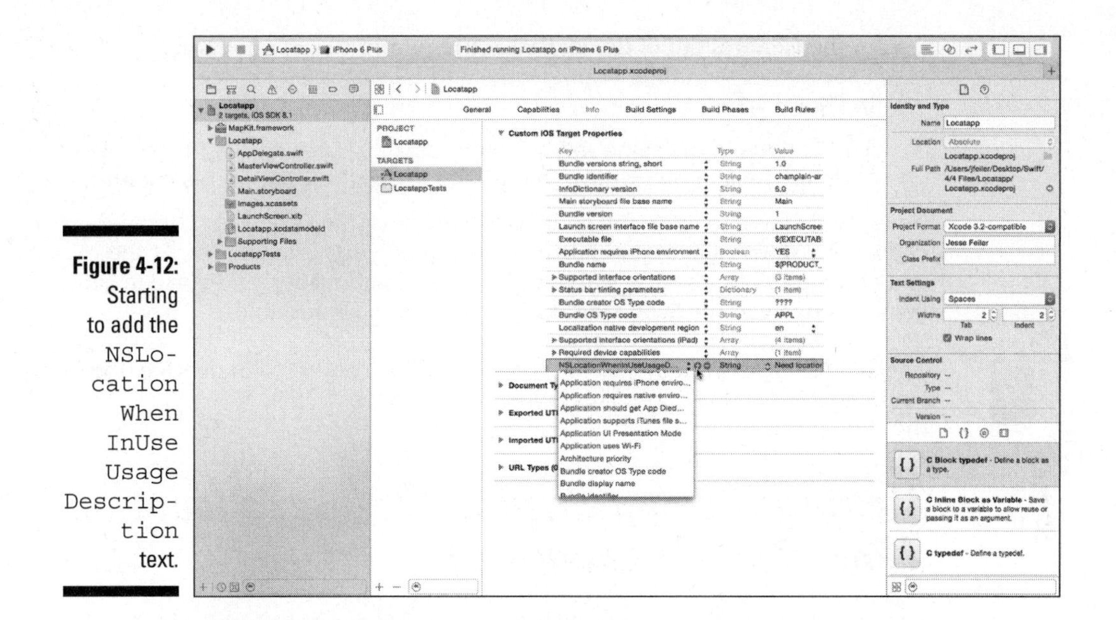

Figure 4-12: Starting to add the `NSLocationWhenInUseUsageDescription` text.

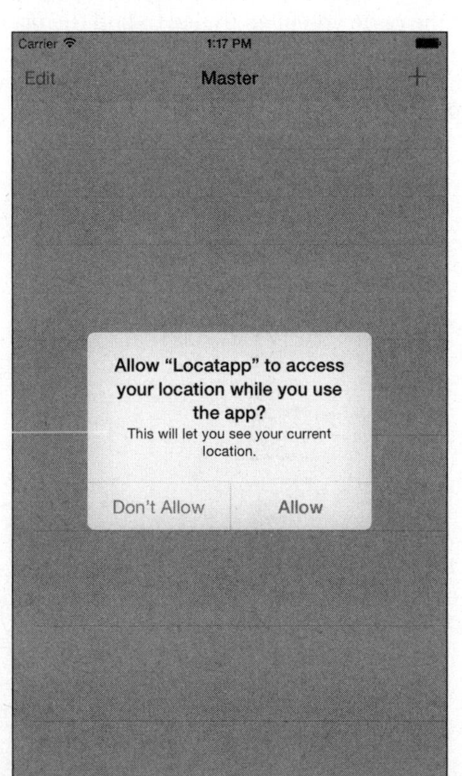

Figure 4-13: Asking permission to use location services.

4. **In the General tab of the project settings, add `CoreLocation.framework` to Linked Frameworks and Libraries as you see in Figure 4-14.**

   This is done in the same way you add `MapKit.framework` there in "Adding the Map to the Storyboard and Project" earlier in this chapter.

Now you do have to write the code to use these settings. There's not much code, but it does require jumping around a bit in your project files. At the end of the process, the app will have its basic functionality, and you can get back to looking at the Swift syntax that makes this all possible.

The details of the Swift syntax shown here will be discussed in depth in the later chapters of this book. This is just an overview.

Making the app display the user's location (Part 1: Core Location)

The Core Location framework (`CoreLocation.framework`) added in Step 4 of the previous section has the code you need to use to find the user's location and to handle other location tasks. Together with the MapKit framework (`MapKit.framework`), the tools you need for managing location and mapping are now part of your app.

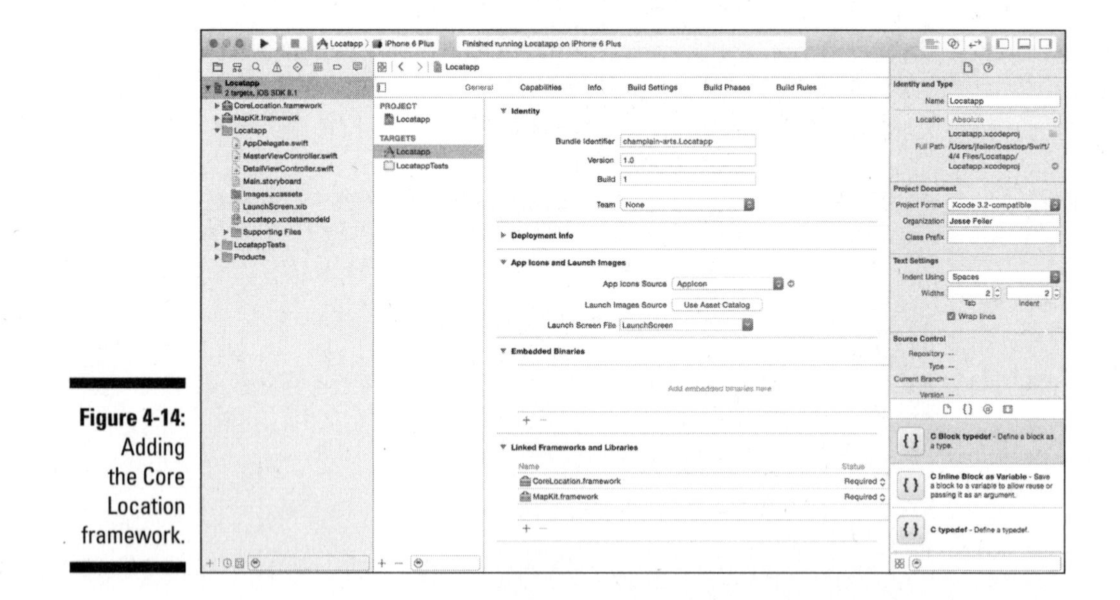

Figure 4-14: Adding the Core Location framework.

All you have to do is use them.

The main object in Core Location is `CLLocationManager`. You create an instance of it to let you find the user's location and track changes as the user moves around.

As is the case with many frameworks, the Core Location framework contains the definition of a *protocol* — code that can be placed in any class to implement parts of the framework. The methods of the protocol are called by the framework itself, and a class that *conforms to* the protocol provides the methods: This is the glue that connects the framework to the app's code. (Chapter 19 provides more details on this common Cocoa and Cocoa Touch design pattern.)

TIP

The methods and properties of the Core Location are prefixed with `CL`. Thus, the protocol you'll need to use is called `CLLocationManagerDelegate`.

In Cocoa and Cocoa Touch, many of the framework objects declare *delegates*. A delegate is a companion object that does some of the work for the framework object itself. A delegate works together with a protocol as you see in the following sections.

REMEMBER

There's much more on protocols and delegates in Chapter 18.

There are four steps to using a protocol, as follows:

1. **Declare the protocol's name, methods, and properties.**
2. **Import the framework or class that declares the protocol into the class you want to use it.**

   Note that the declaration of the protocol could also be done in the file that will adopt it.
3. **In the declaration of an object that will implement the protocol, declare the fact that it *adopts* or *conforms to* the protocol.**
4. **Implement the required methods and properties of the protocol.**
5. **Set a variable of the adopting class to be the delegate.**

The local instance of `CLLocationManager` inside `MasterViewController` will wind up getting the user's location periodically. It will store that current (or last retrieved) location in a variable called `lastLocation` with type `CLLocation`.

Setting up MasterViewController as the Core Location delegate

Here are the steps to make the master view controller the delegate of the Core Location manager. The code for these steps appears afterward in Listing 4-1:

1. **Import CoreLocation to the top of `MasterViewController.swift`.**

   ```
   import CoreLocation
   ```

2. **Add the `CLLocationManagerDelegate` protocol to the declaration of `MasterViewController` at the top of `MasterViewController.swift`.**

   Thus, the declaration at the top of `MasterViewController.swift` will look like this:

   ```
   class MasterViewController: UITableViewController,
           NSFetchedResultsControllerDelegate,
           CLLocationManagerDelegate {
   ```

   `MasterViewController` is a subclass of `UITableViewController`, and it adopts the `NSFetchedResultscontrollerDelegate` protocol as well as (now) the `CLLocationManagerDelegate` protocol.

3. **Create a variable named `locationManager` and set it to an instance of `CLLocationManager`.**

   ```
   let locationManager = CLLocationManager()
   ```

4. **Create a variable named `lastLocation` of type `CLLocation`, which will store the last location obtained from location services.**

   ```
   var lastLocation: CLLocation! = nil
   ```

Listing 4-1 shows the new code along with the code that already exists in the template you used to create Locatapp.

Listing 4-1: Setting Up Core Location

```
import UIKit
import CoreData
import CoreLocation

class MasterViewController: UITableViewController,
  NSFetchedResultsControllerDelegate,
  CLLocationManagerDelegate {

  var detailViewController: DetailViewController? = nil
  var managedObjectContext: NSManagedObjectContext? = nil
  let locationManager = CLLocationManager()
  var lastLocation: CLLocation! = nil
```

Implementing the protocol's delegate methods

Because `MasterViewController` not only adopts the protocol but also serves as its own delegate (that is, as the implementer of the protocol's methods), you need to provide the code for those methods. When you create a delegate, it is generally a good idea to place all of the protocol's delegate methods together so that you can see they are implementing the protocol and are not part of the adopting class's own functionality. The easiest way to do that is to create a separate section using the `MARK` keyword:

```
// MARK: CLLocationManagerDelegateProtocol
```

This comment inserts a title in the list of methods and properties in the jump bar at the top of the editing area, as you see in Figure 4-15.

Listing 4-2 is the Swift code that implements the required protocol methods for the delegate, so enter it now. You can place it at the end of `MasterViewController.swift` before the final } in the file. (It is discussed in the sections that follow, so you'll know what you're doing.)

Even though this syntax is deeply intertwined with Core Location, it's still a good example of Swift code as it's used with the Cocoa and Cocoa Touch frameworks. Not only will you have to learn to write your own Swift code, but you will also have to understand how it's used. A lot of app development consists of making relatively small (and sometimes literally very small) modifications to existing code.

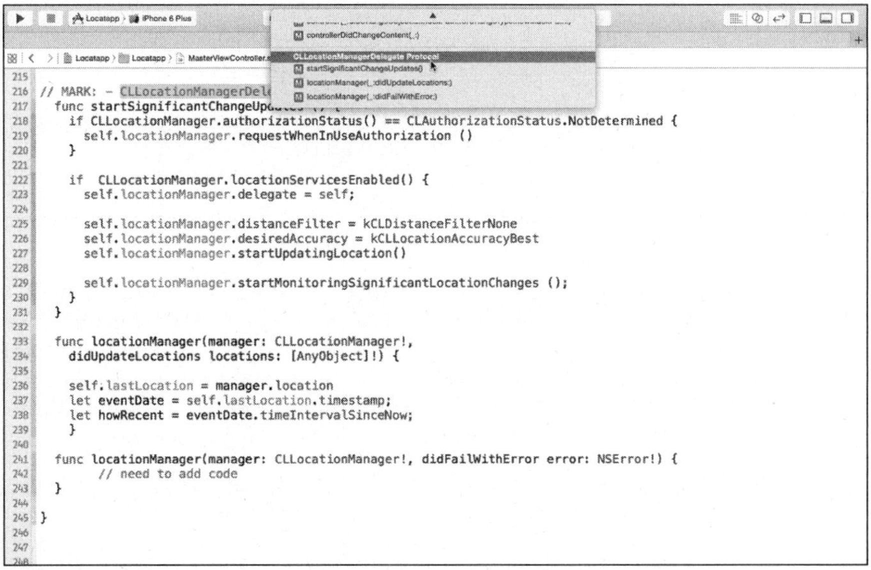

```
216 // MARK: - CLLocationManagerDel
217   func startSignificantChangeUp
218     if CLLocationManager.authorizationStatus() == CLAuthorizationStatus.NotDetermined {
219       self.locationManager.requestWhenInUseAuthorization ()
220     }
221
222     if  CLLocationManager.locationServicesEnabled() {
223       self.locationManager.delegate = self;
224
225       self.locationManager.distanceFilter = kCLDistanceFilterNone
226       self.locationManager.desiredAccuracy = kCLLocationAccuracyBest
227       self.locationManager.startUpdatingLocation()
228
229       self.locationManager.startMonitoringSignificantLocationChanges ();
230     }
231   }
232
233   func locationManager(manager: CLLocationManager!,
234     didUpdateLocations locations: [AnyObject]!) {
235
236     self.lastLocation = manager.location
237     let eventDate = self.lastLocation.timestamp;
238     let howRecent = eventDate.timeIntervalSinceNow;
239     }
240
241   func locationManager(manager: CLLocationManager!, didFailWithError error: NSError!) {
242         // need to add code
243   }
244
245 }
```

Figure 4-15: Putting together all the protocol definitions with a title.

Listing 4-2: Implementing Core Location Delegate Methods and a Local Method

```
// MARK: - CLLocationManagerDelegate Protocol
  func startSignificantChangeUpdates () {

    if CLLocationManager.authorizationStatus() ==
      CLAuthorizationStatus.NotDetermined {

          self.locationManager.requestWhenInUse
           Authorization
        ()
  }

     if CLLocationManager.locationServicesEnabled() {
       self.locationManager.delegate = self

       self.locationManager.distanceFilter =
         kCLDistanceFilterNone
       self.locationManager.desiredAccuracy =
         kCLLocationAccuracyBest
       self.locationManager.startUpdatingLocation()

       self.locationManager.
         startMonitoringSignificantLocationChanges ()
     }
  }

  func locationManager(manager: CLLocationManager!,
    didUpdateLocations locations: [AnyObject]!) {

    self.lastLocation = manager.location
  }

  func locationManager(manager: CLLocationManager!,
    didFailWithError error: NSError!) {
    // need to add code to catch errors
  }
```

There are three functions in Listing 2-2. (Remember that in Swift, class methods are often called functions. The terms are interchangeable.) You've probably never seen the code in Listing 4-2 before, yet it's not hard to pick out these three functions. One of the reasons is that the indentation is consistent. Remember to use the Xcode preferences to choose the indentation settings tab in the Text Editing preference, and remember as you type to not interfere with the indentation you've set.

Double-clicking an opening or closing brace, bracket, or parenthesis in Xcode highlights the text between it and the companion closing or opening symbol. Doing this will frequently catch errors: The highlighted "enclosed" text will immediately appear to be wrong, and you can fix it very quickly in many cases.

These functions are as follows:

- `startSignificantChangeUpdates()`
- `locationManager(_:didUpdateLocations:)`
- `locationManager(_:didFailWithError:)`

The first function is called `startSignificantChangeUpdates()`, and it has no arguments (the parentheses are empty).

The second two functions are part of the protocol the delegate of a location manager must adopt. The declaration of the instance of `CLLocationManager`, which is called `locationManager`, is shown in Listing 4-1. `CLLocationManager` is declared in `CoreLocation.framework`.

The first function, `startSignificantChangeUpdates`, is simply a function of a class (`MasterDetailView`, in this case). It's included in the `MARK` section because it's part of the Core Location implementation. If you wanted to, you could create a separate `MARK` section for it. (This would make sense in a much larger source file with many more functions.)

For much more about classes, see Chapter 15. For more about `locationManager(_:didUpdateLocations:)`, see the section, "Making the app display the user's location (Part 2: MapKit)," later in this chapter.

A class can define a number of delegates. For example, `UITableViewController`, which does exactly what its name suggests, conforms to both a `UITableViewDelegate` and `UITableViewDataSource`. The first manages the user interface, and the second manages the table data. In many cases (including the Master-Detail Template application used here), one class such as `MasterViewController` conforms to both protocols (meaning that it will provide the functionality declared in the protocols) and it declares itself to be the delegate that does this. It could hand off the implementation of the functionality to two other classes. You'll see this structure several more times in this book because it's at the heart of Cocoa and Cocoa Touch. However, don't worry if it takes a few passes through the architecture to be comfortable with this structure.

Implementing a local method

You've seen the structure, and you've seen that the required protocol methods (there are only two of them) have been implemented with the code in Listing 4-2. There's one more thing you have to do.

The method `startSignificantChangeUpdates()` is a local method that's not part of a protocol. (It's commonly used in the examples on `developer.apple.com`.) You've implemented the code in Listing 4-2, but you have to use it. There are certain key locations in classes of Cocoa and Cocoa Touch that serve as choke-points in the sense that they are always invoked at key stages of an object's life. Another one of these choke-points is `viewDidLoad()`, which is a method of `UIView` that's usually overridden to do a custom set-up.

The `self.startSignificantChangeUpdates ()` function is a function of `MasterViewController`, so it's a function of the class you're working on, which is referred to as `self`. Just add a call to this function before the closing bracket of `viewDidLoad`:

```
  self.startSignificantChangeUpdates ()
}
```

If you want to check that the code you've written in this section is working, set a breakpoint on the first line `of locationManager(_:didUpdate Locations:)`. in `MasterViewController.swift`. You should see the app stop there as it checks updates to your location.

If this doesn't happen and you are running in iOS Simulator, check the Debug⇨Location menu to make certain that you haven't accidentally set the location to None. Also check that the Settings for Location in the simulator have Location Services turned on, as described in the section "Setting and confirming location settings in iOS Simulator and on devices," earlier in this chapter.

You can disable checkpoints after you have used them by clicking on them to turn them light blue. You can also just remove them.

Making the app display the user's location (Part 2: MapKit)

This step is very simple. Open `Main.storyboard` and navigate to the Detail scene. Select that map view and use the Attributes inspector to select the option to show the user's location, as shown in Figure 4-16.

The various settings to enable and authorize the use of Core Location services described in this chapter need to be configured for the location to actually be shown. If they are properly configured (and if you set the Debug⇨Location submenu in iOS Simulator to Apple), you'll see your selected location on the map as your current location, when you run your app as in Figure 4-17.

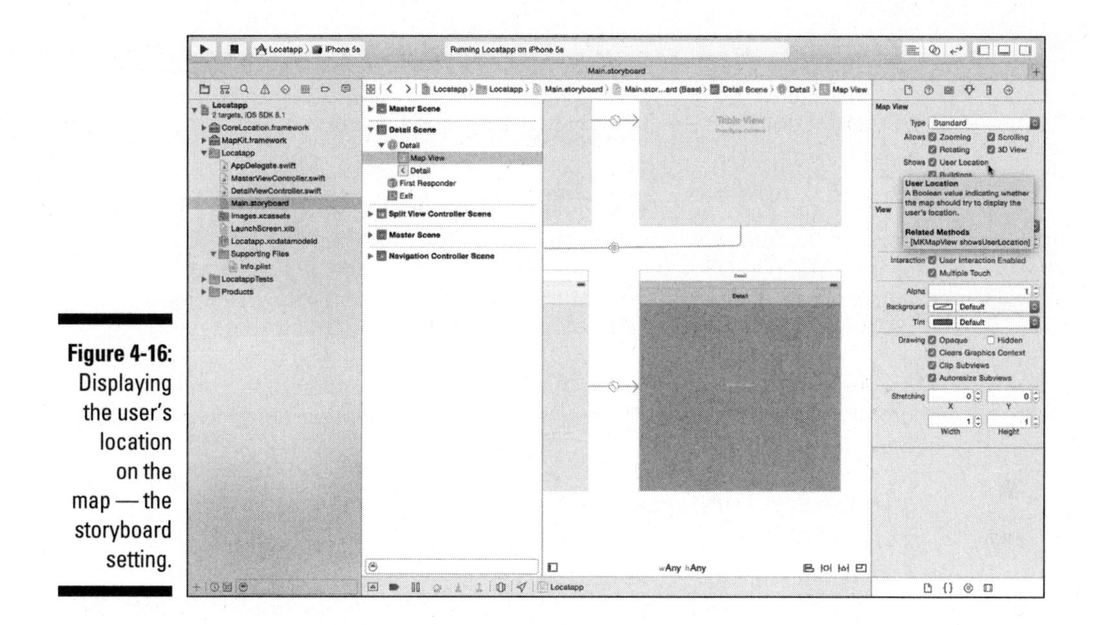

Figure 4-16: Displaying the user's location on the map — the storyboard setting.

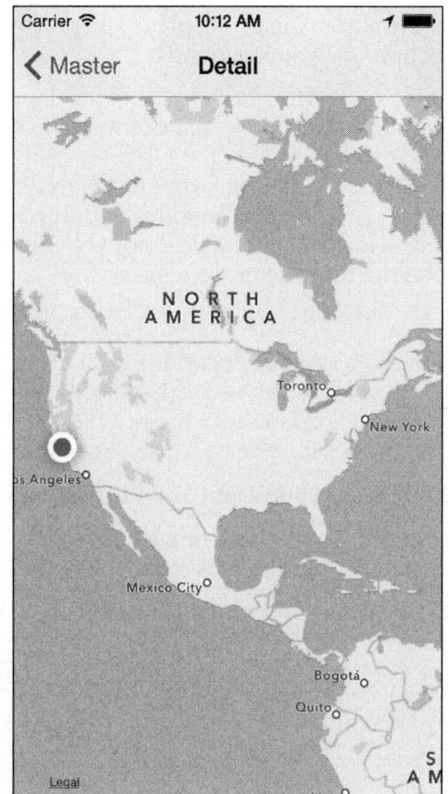

Figure 4-17: Displaying the user's location on the map — the result.

Storing the user's location (Core Data)

In this section, you see how to store the user's location in the Core Data persistent store.

A Core Data data model is frequently used with Cocoa and Cocoa Touch apps. In its default version, it uses the built-in SQLite library for the storage of the data. (On OS X, it can also use XML for storage.) Core Data is a *persistent store* mechanism that has much in common with a relational database, but it *uses* a database or other technology to store its data.

To store the user's location in the Core Data persistent store, you'll have to modify several features In the Master-Detail Application template that is the basis for Locatapp:

- The Core Data persistent store defines an Event entity with a `timeStamp` attribute.
- When you tap the + at the top right of the master view controller, you create a new `Event` entity. Its `timeStamp` is set to the current date and time.
- The master view controller automatically displays all of the `Event` entities — including the new one you've created.
- If you tap the cell for an `Event` in the master view controller, you see a detail view controller with the `timeStamp` data centered in a `UILabel`.

You've already added the `CoreLocation` framework and the code to periodically check the location. (You don't do anything with the location data . . . yet.) In this section, you make a few changes so that you store the user's location rather than the timestamp. To achieve this, you do the following tasks:

- **Store the current location in a `MasterViewController` property:** This process will continue as your app periodically checks the location. You set this up in `self.locationManager.startMonitoringSignificantLocationChanges` in Listing 4-2.
- **Add two `Double` attributes, `latitude` and `longitude`, to `Event`.**
- **When the + is tapped, create a new `Event` object and set its `latitude` and `longitude` to the values from the most recent location.**

These tasks are described in the sections that follow.

As is the case with most of the other tasks you've done to make Locatapp a usable app, many of the tasks in this section are fragmented: They jump from place to place in the Master-Detail Application project. This is typically the case with Swift (and Objective-C). Periodically you get to a section where you do write line after line of code, but, in most cases, such sections aren't very long.

This need to make changes in many places to implement functionality may be one of the reasons why some people believe that coding for Cocoa and Cocoa Touch is difficult. There's something to this belief, but it's also true many modern development environments are like this.

Storing the current location in a MasterViewController property

Because you have set up `MasterViewController` as a delegate for the `CLLocationManager`, `locationManager(_:didUpdateLocations:)`, which is defined as a required function in the `CLLocationManagerDelegate` protocol, is called periodically, and you must implement it. When you have done this, you will always have the most recent location stored in a property of `MasterViewController`, and you can use that value when you need to create a new `Event` object.

Note that this is a very common design pattern in Cocoa and Cocoa Touch: You implement a delegate for some framework or other, which periodically is called from that framework to provide you with an opportunity to update your app's data.

To periodically get and store the current location, follow these steps:

1. **Declare a `lastLocation` property for `MasterViewController`.**

   This will be continually updated as you receive new locations from Core Location so that you will always have the latest value when you need it. Here is the code you should have already added to the top of `MasterViewController.swift`:

   ```
   var lastLocation: CLLocation! = nil
   ```

   If it's not there, `locationManager(_:didUpdateLocations:)` will give you a compile error because it uses this variable. Check to see if that's also missing.

   For details of the `lastLocation` syntax shown here, see Chapter12.

2. **Implement `locationManager(_:didUpdateLocations:)` to store new location values.**

   Note that this was shown in Listing 4-2, so you may already have entered it.

The value of the current location is passed into this function with its first parameter (`manager`) that has a location property as defined in `CLLocationManager` (part of `CoreLocation.framework`).

Adding latitude and longitude attributes to Event

Now you need to add latitude and longitude to `Event`. You do this in the data model. With this, by the way, you have your first brief introduction to Core Data. You also need to convert the data model to a Swift class. This, too is a useful introduction to a common data modeling task.

Don't worry: Each task here is brief and not very complicated.

Follow these steps to add the new attributes:

1. **Select `Locatapp.xcdatamodeld` in the project navigator.**

   It opens in the editing area, as shown in Figure 4-18. If it looks different to you, click the Editor Style button in the lower right section of the main pane to choose the alternate view.

2. **In the Attributes section, click + twice to create two new attributes.**

   They'll be named `attribute` and `attribute1` by default.

3. **Select one of the new attributes. Use the Data Model inspector in the utilities area to set its name (`latitude`) and type (`Double`), as shown in Figure 4-19.**

4. **Do the same for the other attribute: Name it `longitude` and set its type to `Double`.**

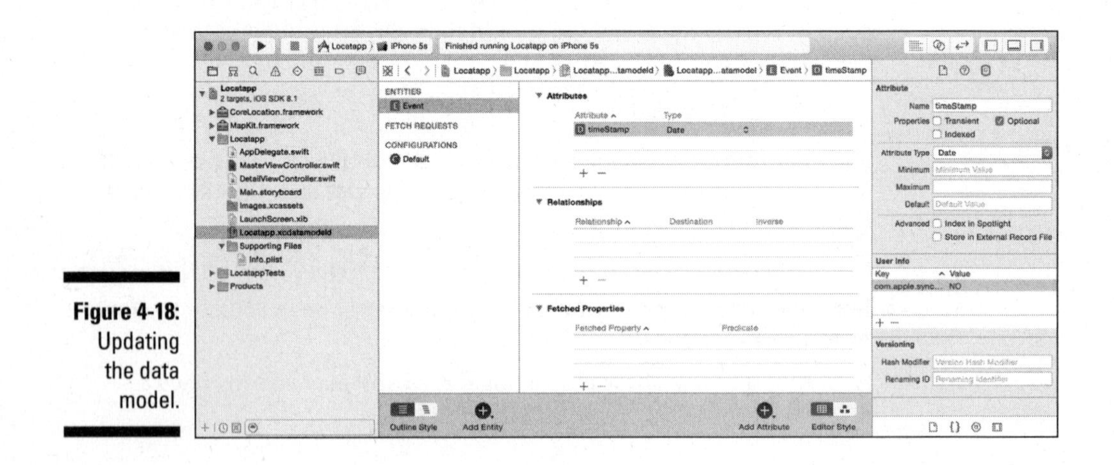

Figure 4-18: Updating the data model.

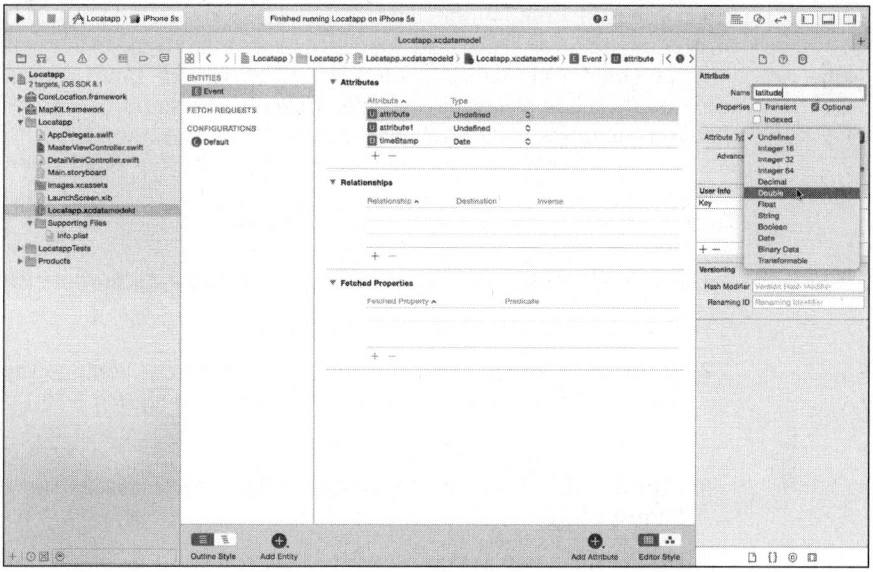

Figure 4-19: Naming attributes and setting their type.

5. **Delete old data stored using the previous data model.**

   If you haven't run your test app at all, this step is unnecessary, but it's a good precaution to take. Use one of these approaches:

   - *If you're using iOS Simulator:* With iOS Simulator running, choose iOS Simulator⇨Reset Content and Settings. This will delete all the data on the simulator.

     Alternatively, go to the Home screen on iOS Simulator with Hardware⇨Home or Shift-Command-H, tap and hold the Locatapp icon, and delete it with the X. This is the same way you delete an app on a device.

   - *If you're using an iOS device:* Tap and hold the Locatapp icon on the Home screen and delete it.

A Core Data model parallels the classes in Objective-C and Swift in some ways. The language of data modeling (not just Core Data) is different from the programming language used in object-oriented programming. In the world of data modeling, an *entity* has *attributes*. In Swift (and Objective-C) a *class* has *properties*. The Xcode Data Model tool built into Xcode can convert a model entity to a programmatic class as well as convert an entity's attributes to the class's properties. (The conversion is one-way: You can't reverse it.)

When you turn a data model entity into a class, the class file is added to your project. If you have previously made this conversion, the existing file(s) for your data model's class is erased. You will be warned, but if you have modified the class files, it is always a good idea to keep a backup that's easy to reach so that you can quickly add the necessary code. This process is not for beginners, but I mention it here so that you may remember it later when you need it.

To convert your data model to a Swift class, follow these steps:

1. **Select the entity you want to convert in the data model editor.**

   In your case, there's only one entity: `Event`.

2. **In the Data Model inspector in the utilities area, change the Class name to `Locatapp.Event` if necessary. (See Figure 4-20.)**

   Note that it may be listed as Event.

3. **Choose Editor⇨Create NSManagedObject Subclass, as shown in Figure 14-21.**

4. **On the next two sheets, confirm that you want to convert the Locatapp data model and the `Event` entity; then click Next.**

5. **On the following sheet, make sure the language is set to Swift (not Objective-C).**

   The other settings are usually correct, but you can save the file wherever you want and place it into whatever project navigator group you want, as shown in Figure 4-22.

You now have the modified data model converted to a class named `Event` that is defined in a new file called `Event.swift`. You can browse it in the project navigator if you want (but don't make changes!).

Figure 4-20: Setting the class name.

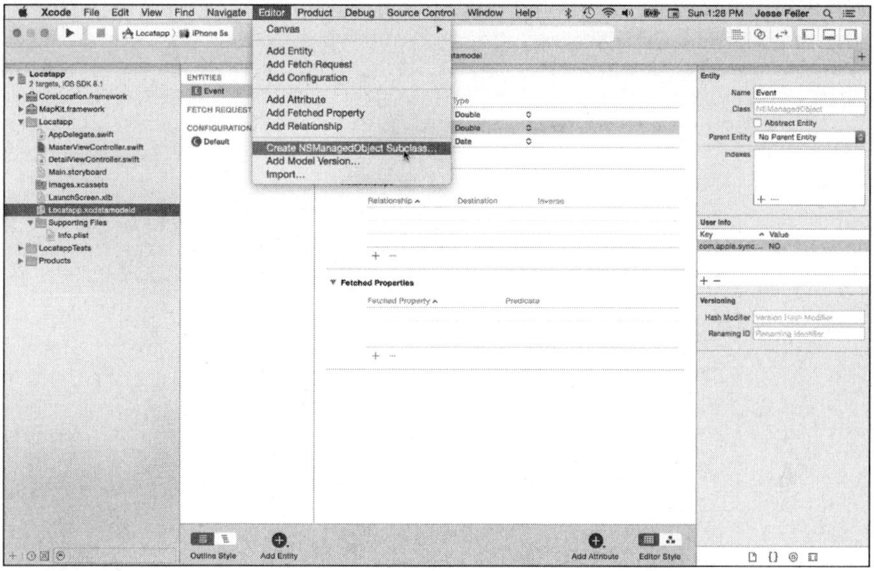

Figure 4-21: Converting the entity to a class.

Creating a new `Event` object and setting its latitude and longitude values

The Master-Detail Application template creates new `Event` objects when you tap the +, so that code is already implemented. All you have to do is to modify it so that instead of setting the new `Event` to the current `timeStamp`, you set it to the current latitude and longitude (which have been stored for you in `lastLocation`, which has been updated by `locationManager(_:didUpdateLocations:)`, as I discussed in the previous section.

To begin with, locate the `insertNewObject` method in `MasterViewController` as it is now (this is the original Master-Detail Application code). Listing 4-3 shows that code for this method.

As you can see, most of the function is devoted to two lengthy comments.

There are two lines of code here you need to worry about:

- The first of these lines, the New Event Entity line, creates a new `Event` entity:

```
let newManagedObject = NSEntityDescription.
  insertNewObjectForEntityForName("Event",
    inManagedObjectContext: context)
    as NSManagedObject
```

Figure 4-22: Confirming the name and language for the conversion.

- The second line stores the `timeStamp` in the attribute. This is done using a technique called key-value coding (KVC), which is common in Cocoa and Cocoa Touch:

```
newManagedObject.setValue(NSDate(), forKey:
 "timeStamp")
```

Don't worry if the details of this aren't clear: I explore this process again in Chapters 6, 12, and 15.

Here's how you make the changes to store the location:

1. **When you create the new object, create it as an instance of the new `Event` type rather than as a `NSManagedObject`.**

Listing 4-3: `insertNewObject` from the Template

```
func insertNewObject(sender: AnyObject) {
  let context =
    self.fetchedResultsController.managedObjectContext
  let entity =
    self.fetchedResultsController.fetchRequest.entity!
  let newManagedObject =
    NSEntityDescription.
      insertNewObjectForEntityForName("Event",
        inManagedObjectContext: context)
        as NSManagedObject

     // If appropriate, configure the new
     // managed object.
     // Normally you should use accessor methods, but
     // using KVC here avoids the need to add a custom
     // class to the template.
  newManagedObject.setValue(NSDate(), forKey: "timeStamp")


  // Save the context.
  var error: NSError? = nil
  if !context.save(&error) {
    // Replace this implementation with code to
    // handle the error appropriately.
    // abort() causes the application to generate
    // a crash log and terminate. You should not
    // use this function in a shipping
    // application, although it may be useful
    // during development.
    println("Unresolved error \(error),\(error.userInfo)")
    abort()
  }
}
```

Change `NSManagedObject` to `Event` in the New Event Entity line in the preceding list so that it reads as follows:

```
let newManagedObject = NSEntityDescription.
  insertNewObjectForEntityForName("Event",
    inManagedObjectContext: context)
      as Event
```

Creating the new object as an instance of `Locatapp.Event` rather than as an instance of `NSManagedObject` is actually optional in this example, but many people (including me) believe that it's a good style to develop, and it is somewhat more efficient than using KVC in high-performance environments.

2. **Set the `Event` class `latitude` property using the value from `self.lastLocation`.**

   You can replace the old `timeStamp` setting code or just leave it there. It's still in the data model, so it doesn't matter at the moment, and it might be useful in debugging if you want to take things one small step at a time.

   ```
   newManagedObject.latitude =
     self.lastLocation.coordinate.latitude
   ```

3. **Set `longitude` in the same way with this code.**

   ```
   newManagedObject.setValue.longitude =
     self.lastLocation.coordinate.longitude
   ```

Displaying the stored location

You've now stored the user's location, but you need to display it. That's a simple task once the previous steps are done. Listing 4-4 shows the `configureCell` code, which displays `timeStamp` in the Master-Detail Application template.

Instead of displaying `object` as an `NSManagedObject`, you display it as an `Event`. If this reminds you of the code in the previous section, you're right: That code worked with the new object as an `Event` in setting its data. This code takes the data out of the `Event` object and displays it. Instead of displaying the `timeStamp`, you display the latitude and longitude along with some string titles.

Listing 4-4: configureCell

```
func configureCell(cell: UITableViewCell,
  atIndexPath indexPath: NSIndexPath) {

  let object =
    self.fetchedResultsController.
      objectAtIndexPath(indexPath) as NSManagedObject

  cell.textLabel.text
    object.valueForKey("timeStamp")!.description

}
```

Here is the code to use to replace the display code in the template:

```
let object =
    self.fetchedResultsController.
      objectAtIndexPath(indexPath) as Event

cell.textLabel.text =
   "latitude: " + object.latitude.description +
   " longitude: " + object.longitude.description
```

Testing the App with Location Data

You should now be able to test the app and get results like those shown in Figure 4-20. You can change the location in iOS Simulator while it is running so that you can get several locations to check. Also, experiment with the master view controller list shown in Figure 4-23: The Edit button works and allows you to delete rows in addition to adding them with the +.

You don't have pins on the map to show individual locations, and you don't have the social media integration, but they will come later in the book.

For now, you've seen enough Swift code that you are ready to dive into the syntax that you've seen here.

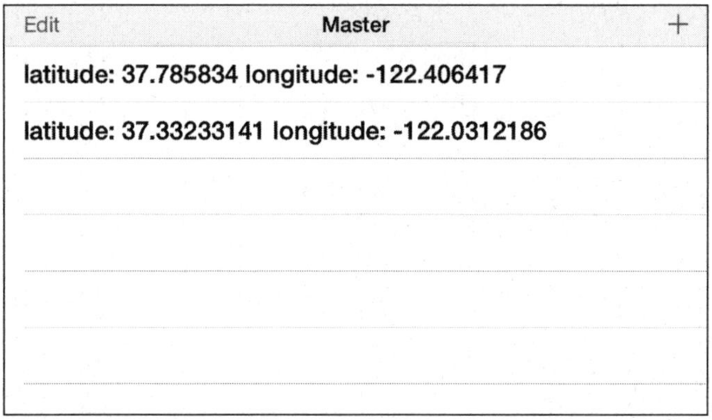

Edit Master +

latitude: 37.785834 longitude: -122.406417

latitude: 37.33233141 longitude: -122.0312186

Figure 4-23: Testing the app.

Part II

Introducing Actions

```
demo — Edited
demo
demo.playground 〉 No Selection

1  import Cocoa
2
3  var h1: NSString = "Hello"                "Hello"
4  var h2: NSString = "Hello"                "Hello"
5
6  var b = h1 == h2                          true
7  b = h1 === h2                             false
```

Find out how to know whether to use a type, collection, flow control, or function to implement an action at `www.dummies.com/extras/swift`.

In this part . . .

- ✔ Manipulate your data with actions.
- ✔ Categorize data with types.
- ✔ Organize data with collections.
- ✔ Manage the sequence of actions.
- ✔ Turn expressions into functions.

Chapter 5

Operating on Data

In This Chapter

- Using a playground to check syntax
- Getting a high-level view of arithmetic operators
- Exploring Swift's Boolean operators

Actions, the subject of this part of the book, are the heart of apps. At the heart of actions, are *operators* — the symbols that act directly on objects or values. Although actions are the heart of apps, you may or may not use them directly. When you're using a framework such as Cocoa or Cocoa Touch, the classes in that framework perform many actions for you — it's the framework's code that invokes the actions that use the operators described in this part of the book.

Some apps live totally in the world of the frameworks with their generic operations to manage data and interface elements whereas others rely directly on their own actions to work with their custom data and interface elements. The specifics of your app — as well as your experience and programming style — determine which of these two approaches you'll use.

Don't worry: It's quite possible to get far in the world of Cocoa and Cocoa Touch apps without touching the topics in this chapter. However, when you need them, they're here. For now, browse over this chapter and the others in Part II so that you have an idea of what's covered. Then, later, when you suddenly need to find out why a simple addition statement seems to have gone awry, for example, check out this chapter's coverage of the addition operator. After all, it's easy to get tripped up by the details of basic points like these.

Note that most operators are special character symbols alone or in pairs such as `+` or `!` or `||`, but some are text, such as AND. In addition, some operators have both symbol and text versions that mean the same thing. And, to keep you on your toes, some symbols are paired with text operators for which the symbol and the text operators are similar but have subtle differences. For instance, as in C, AND is a synonym for `&&` — a logical AND that operates on a Boolean value of true or false; `&` is a bitwise AND that operates on the bits of an entire word.

If you are familiar with other programming languages (and you should be familiar in a general way with at least one), most of these operators won't be totally new to you. However, Swift requires a few tweaks to some of them, so don't skip this chapter, even if you only read it quickly.

Classifying Operators

Whether symbols or text, operators act on *operands,* which are values — either specific values (such as `17.5`) or expressions that yield values (such as `16.5+1`). Combining an operator with the appropriate number of operands yields a value which can then be used itself as an operand in another operation.

Operands are sometimes referred to as the *targets* of operators. Whether you refer to them as *operands*, *targets*, or the more generic *values*, they may be single values such as `17.5` or the result of expressions such as `16.5+1`. See Chapter 10, "Expressing Yourself" for more information on types.

Operators are classified by the number of operands on which they act, as follows:

- **Unary:** Unary operators operate on one target. (The term *target* is often used to describe a unary operand.) In Swift they appear immediately before or after the operand. However, these are not interchangeable — for example, a minus sign must immediately precede a number and cannot follow a number. When a unary operator precedes its target, it's called a *prefix* operator; when it follows its target, it's called a *postfix* operator.
- **Binary:** Binary operators operate on two targets. The basic arithmetic operators (+, –, /, and x) are binary operators. Whereas unary operators can be prefix or postfix operators, binary operators are *infix* operators because the operands (or targets) are placed on either side of the binary operator.
- **Ternary:** Ternary operators operate on three targets. The classic ternary operator in C is also implemented in Swift. It describes a conditional operator using syntax such as the one shown here which evaluates to either the second or third value depending on the test in the condition:

```
(targetValue > 5) ? valueForLessThan5 : otherValue
```

In general, an operator is classified as one of these three. These concepts are present in many computer languages including most of those derived from C.

Answering Syntax Questions with Playgrounds

As with many other languages, the operators in Swift were derived from common operators in other programming languages; Swift's operators include some tweaks and modifications that make them different from the originals, and they include some new operators as well. If you have experience with several languages, it's hard to keep straight all the details of these operators. It's easy to lose track of which tweak belongs to which language. Furthermore, you may not even be aware of these differences: With the as-you-type correction offered in today's powerful editing tools, you may actually type illegal syntax but never see it because Xcode or another tool automatically fixes the error.

Still, it's easy to get stuck over a minor point of syntax. You can look it up (maybe you've bookmarked this page), or you can wait to see if the compiler objects. Playgrounds in Xcode 6 and later are perfect for answering these questions. (Chapter 2, "Playing in the Playground" has more information on playgrounds.)

Consider the simple question of whether a space can be placed between a minus sign and the value it negates. (This is one of the syntax issues that can arise when you decide to standardize indentations to make your code easier to read.) In fact, if you read Apple's documentation carefully, you see that unary operators "appear immediately before or after an operand." That *immediately* means *no space,* but a detail like that is easy to miss or forget.

Using a playground is the easiest way to answer a question like this. To do so, just follow these steps:

1. **Create a playground as described in Chapter 2. Start from a basic playground such as the one shown in Figure 5-1.** Note that this example uses OS X and Swift in setting up the playground. You can tell because `Cocoa` is imported rather than `UIKit`. You can use either OS X or iOS for the examples in this chapter.

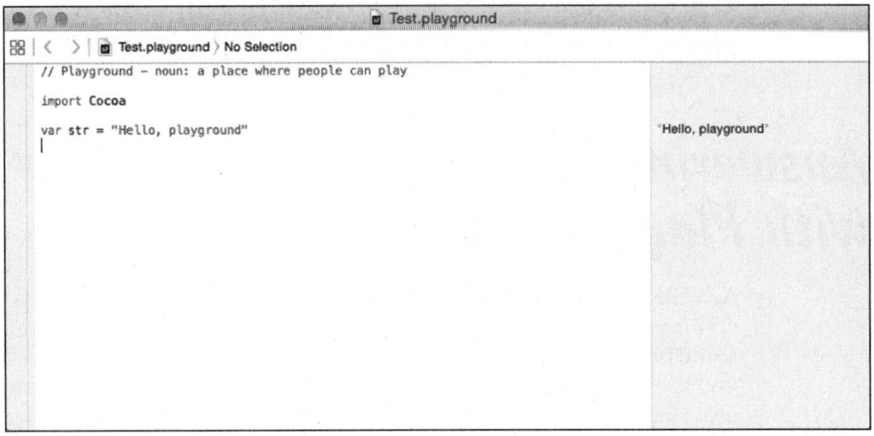

Figure 5-1: Creating a playground.

2. Enter some test code as shown in Figure 5-2. (For this example, make sure your test code includes a negative number.)

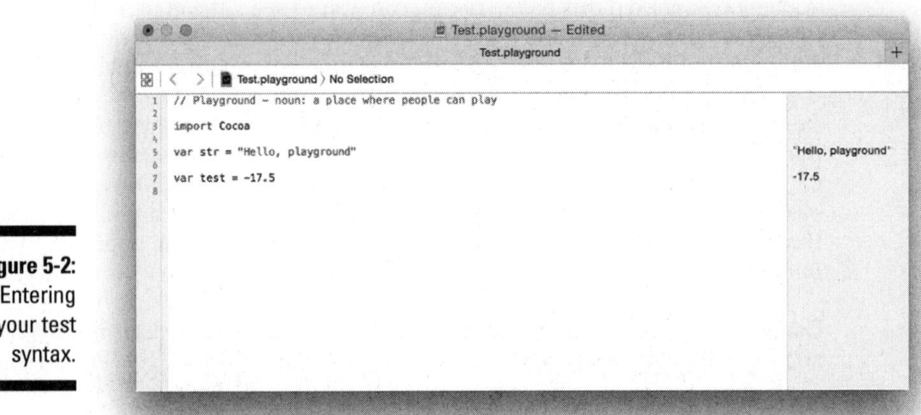

Figure 5-2: Entering your test syntax.

3. Change the syntax for a second test, as shown in Figure 5-3. (For this example, add a space between the negative sign and the number.)

The sequence doesn't matter (you can test with or without the space in either step). The point is to answer the question: "Does the space matter?" It's not hard to imagine a language in which the space is optional (but would you really want to write the language parser for that case?).

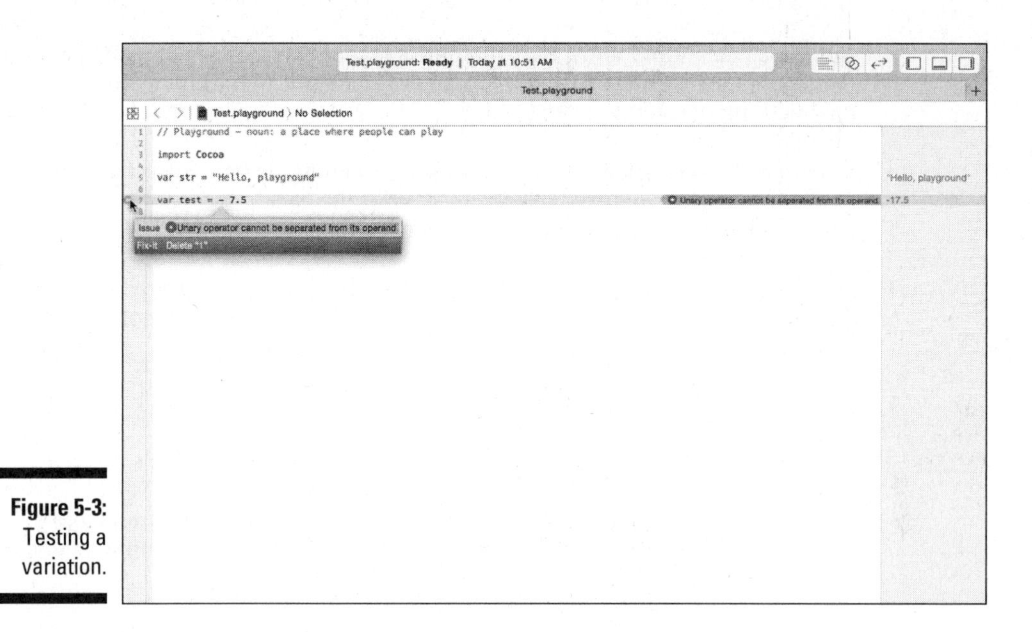

Figure 5-3: Testing a variation.

Leaving a playground window open all the time just for tests like this is a good idea. For many people, typing the test syntax to get an immediate answer to a syntax question is actually faster than looking up the class or language reference.

Clearing the Way for Operators

The operators described in this chapter operate on *operands* — variables, constants, or expressions. Many of the operators are arithmetic, but, as in other languages, logical (Boolean) operators are also implemented in Swift. Bitwise operators operate on the bits of a word just as they do in other languages.

Bitwise operators are used most frequently on integers and particularly on unsigned integers. In the case of unsigned integers, the bits of a word are evaluated as a binary value (such as 0111 being evaluated as 7). As in other languages and operating systems, at the hardware level a Boolean value is true (1) or false (0), and that value is stored in the low-order (0-th) bit of a word. This "wastes" the other bits. Bitwise operations can use all of the bits of a word so that bitwise operations may be significantly faster and take much less memory than operations that use the entire word for storing a Boolean value. The trade-off may come in complexity. This is not a Swift issue, and you can find many discussions of it in textbooks and articles on the web. You should know that the performance advantages of using bitwise operators have been rendered much less important than they were in the past with modern computers.

Whether you're working with numbers, characters, or bits, Swift has one very important design feature that can make your life easier and your code more robust. All variables must be initialized before being used in Swift.

This restriction doesn't apply to many other languages. You can declare a variable and then use it without initialization as in this pseudo-code:

```
integer i;
i = i + 3;
```

What is the value of `i` after these two lines are executed? There's no way of telling because the initial value of `i` is unknown. In some cases, variables are automatically initialized (sometimes to a safe value such as 0 or an empty string in the case of a string). In many other cases, using an uninitialized variable can cause a crash or an undefined result.

In a similar way, pointers can be declared in many languages, but they need not have been pointed to anything in particular before they are used. Preventing the use of uninitialized variables and constants in Swift has been a major objective of the language and its implementation.

Remember this as you read through this section and think about the ways of preventing and recovering from undefined operations. When you don't have to worry about uninitialized variables and constants, you can cross a number of concerns off your to-do list.

Assigning Values with Assignment Operators

Although Swift builds on both C and Objective-C, along with other languages, there are several ways in which it strikes out on a different course. One of these is in the interpretation of the assignment operator (=).

The assignment operator takes two operands: It sets the value of the one on the left to the value of the one on the right, as in

```
a = b
```

or

```
area = width * depth
```

The assignment operator must not be confused with the Boolean comparison operator, which is ==. In some languages, the assignment operator is actually valid in a Boolean comparison, and there are historic reasons for this (possibly related to the limited number of symbols on keypunch machines). For example, the following code is legal in C, Objective-C, and Swift:

```
if (width > depth) {...
```

In C and Objective-C, however, the Boolean > comparison operator can be replaced as follows:

```
if (width = depth) {...
```

The phrase `width>depth` appears to be similar to phrases such as `width<depth` and `width=depth`. All are valid syntax, but tread carefully here.

The comparison operator here (>) has been replaced with an assignment operator (=) rather than a comparison operator that tests for equality. Most of the time, the intent of this code is not assignment or replacement but comparison. To be a comparison, the code should be written as follows:

```
if (width == depth) {...
```

There really is no ambiguity here, but it is the rare developer who has never been caught confusing == and =. Swift addresses this issue by making = illegal in this case. Using == is not optional: It is required in Swift for testing equality in this way.

For the cases in which both assignment and a Boolean test are required, you must use two totally unambiguous statements (one for the assignment and one for the test).

Counting On Arithmetic Operators for Math

The earliest computers in the twentieth century were created to perform arithmetic operations. Indeed, modern computers are often traced to a paper written by Alan Turing in 1936 — *On Computable Numbers*. These days, with music and movies on mobile devices, we've moved far beyond computable numbers, but numbers and arithmetic remain at the core of computers. In Swift, the basic arithmetic operators are supported, although, as with other operators, some have been modified, refined, or enhanced.

Addition

The simple addition operator (+) is available in Swift. It acts on numbers but also can act on strings and characters for concatenation. It also has an additional feature which is shared with the other arithmetic operators that lets you handle over-and underflow conditions (This is discussed in the following section.)

Figure 5-4 shows the addition operator being used for concatenating two strings and a character (the blank space). You'll notice that this string manipulation is different from the techniques in both C and Objective-C. (For one thing, it's simpler than the C `strcat` function and the `stringByAppendingString`: message in Objective-C.)

Handling over- and underflow conditions

Swift provides an extension to basic arithmetic operators to handle the potential over- and underflow conditions that can occur. If you precede an arithmetic operator with `&`, the new operator handles over- and underflow conditions, as well as certain errors. (The new operator — `&+`, `&-`, `&*`, `&/`, or `&%` — is called an *overflow operator*.) If the addition operation, for example, would generate an invalid result (such as a value that cannot fit in the declared type), using `&+` instead of `+` will handle the operation without generating an error.

The most common example of this behavior is demonstrated by setting a variable to the maximum value of an integer and adding 1 to it. Normally, that produces an overflow, but if you use the `&+` operator, the result is 0.

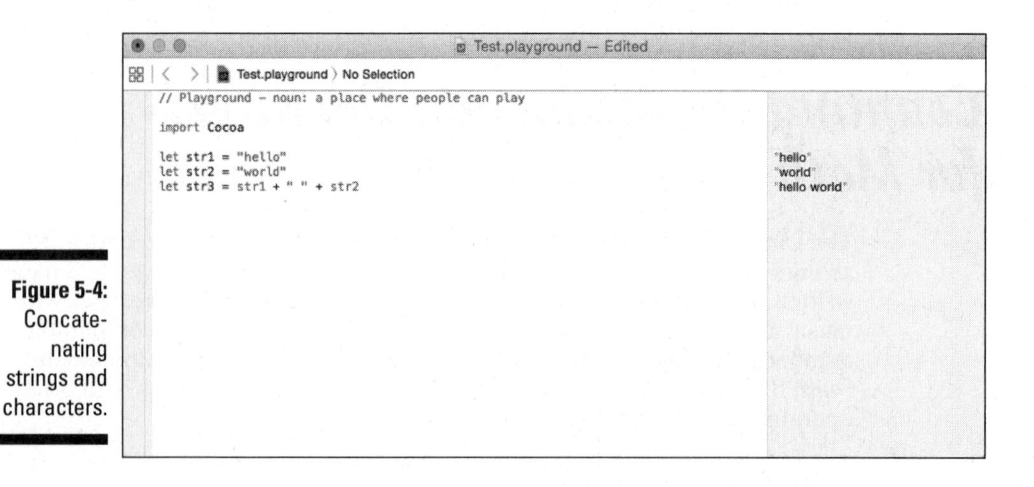

Figure 5-4: Concatenating strings and characters.

Here is the code to ignore the overflow:

```
var testOverflow = UInt16.max
testOverflow = testOverflow &+ 1
```

The first line sets `testOverflow` to the maximum value of an unsigned 16-bit integer. (Working with an unsigned integer is the simplest case because you are dealing only with the binary representation of a number without regard to a sign.) Adding 1 to the maximum value for the type with `&+` results in 0 because the value has overflowed the size of the declared type. (If there were space, the value would be 0 with a leading 1 in the next digit, but there isn't space in the `UInt16` type for that next digit.)

The overflow operator is defined differently for each arithmetic operation. For example, the result of the following line of code is 0 rather than an error. (The syntax error for the code without using the overflow operator may be generated as you type; if it is a result of division attempted with a variable the value of which is unknown until runtime, the error will be flagged at that point.)

```
var testDivision = 5 &/ 0
```

This method of working around a divide-by-zero error is very useful in many cases: You can avoid testing for zero and then forcing the value of zero to the variable that would have been the result of the division operation.

In some cases, the error and accompanying program stop or exception is what you want, but in other cases it's not. The point is, Swift lets you choose. Over- and underflows along with illegal arithmetic operations such as division by zero have been issues from the earliest days of computers. In COBOL, for example, numbers are formatted using a `PICTURE` structure. A `PICTURE` functions much like an odometer in a car: Adding 1 to 99999 rolls the value over to 00000. That is the behavior of `&+`, whereas the behavior of `+` in the same situation is to generate an error.

In the early 1950s this topic was the subject of much debate between the business-oriented programmers working on COBOL and the mathematicians working on FORTRAN. To this day, software that handles numbers that may cause over- or underflows often has code to handle the question of what adding 1 to a number like 99999 should do in the case where the result cannot be stored and/or printed.

Subtraction

The subtraction operator (–), also has a `&` variant. Remember that addition and subtraction turn into the same operation when the values involved are negative numbers.

In cases where you use & with an operator, it must precede the operator directly without an intervening space. The two-character combination is an overflow operator that is handled as a single entity when your code is parsed.

Multiplication

Multiplication, too, can use the overflow operator `&`. Figure 5-5 shows a variable set to the maximum `Int16` value of 32,767 (note the `Int16.max` syntax). Listing 5-1 shows manipulations of that value that are also shown in Figure 5-5.

As the playground shown in Figure 5-5 demonstrates, you can subtract 1,000 from that value without any problem. Multiplying that value using `&* 2`, however, gives the bitwise correct value of –2002, as shown in Figure 5-5, but that type of code is generally considered unadvisable. First of all, it's hardware-dependent. Second of all, it's not clear what you are doing, and anyone modifying the code later on may either misunderstand it or misinterpret your intentions. Perhaps worst of all, someone may "discover" a "bug" in your code and "correct" it to code that doesn't work properly. From a maintenance standpoint, this is a time bomb.

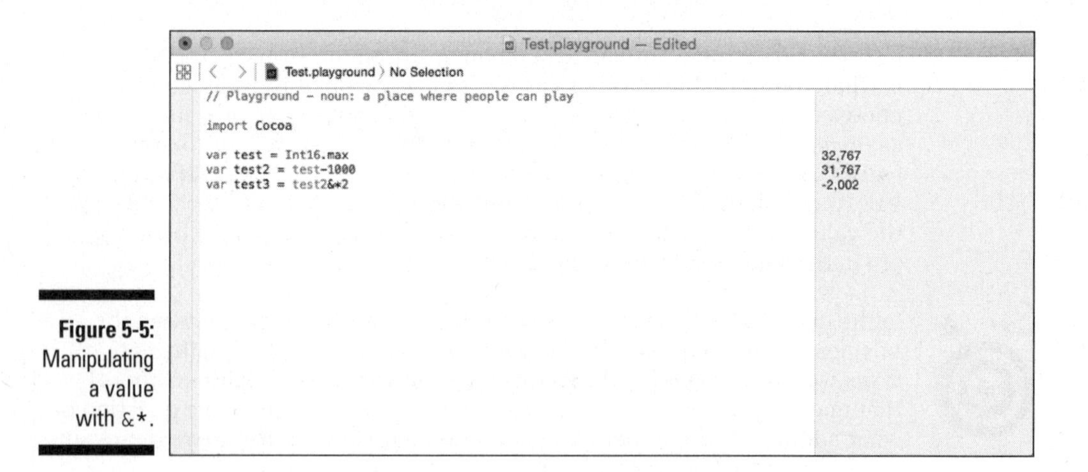

Figure 5-5: Manipulating a value with `&*`.

Listing 5-1: Manipulating a value at the edge of precision

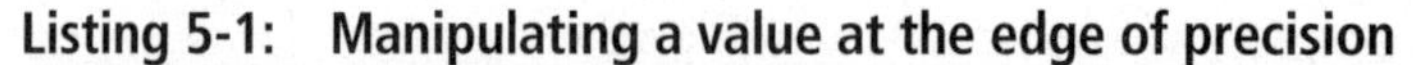

```
var test = Int16.max
var test2 = test-1000
var test3 = test&*2 // result is -2002
```

Do you see how we got to –2002? It's because the result of 31,767 multiplied by 2 overflows the `Int16` type field. If there were space to add digits to the left, the result would be arithmetically correct, but because those high-order bits don't exist, the number is incomplete — and wildly wrong.

Division

Division is an operator that can pose problems in any computer language. The basic operator is `/`, but beyond that a variety of issues arise in any language — including Swift.

Although the topic of handling runtime errors arises here in the context of division, it arises in many other contexts with Swift, so this discussion is generalized. The handling of runtime errors, including handling operations that either cannot be performed or whose results are undefined is something that you need to handle in your apps. You may have dealt with it in other languages (particularly in C or Objective-C, which have the greatest influences on Swift and Cocoa or Cocoa Touch programming). The measures you take to avoid runtime errors generally work in Swift, but you have a wider variety of tools to avoid such errors, and as a result, you can push some of your error-avoidance code into Swift itself using tools such as optionals (see Chapter 6), and overflow operators, as discussed in this chapter.

Handling undefined results and errors

Perhaps the most common issue with division is the divide-by-zero error. The problem arises because dividing a value by zero is undefined. (If you want to investigate some of the history of the topic, look up George Berkeley and his 1734 book, *The Analyst.*) Computers and programming languages don't generally have the ability to deal with uncertainties or, to use a mathematical phrase, *indeterminate forms*. This is not just a piece of history: Problems with undefined results occur frequently in both hardware and software (particularly programming languages and compilers).

This section outlines the major approaches to handling operations that may be undefined. These are general approaches that apply to most programming languages (they're more a matter of system design than of specific languages). At the end of this section, you'll see a very important feature of Swift that can significantly reduce the frequency with which you encounter undefined results. Uninitialized variables are banished from Swift thereby eliminating quite a few common problems in many other languages. (This is discussed in more detail at the end of this section.)

The basic approaches to handling undefined results are as follows:

- **Ignoring undefined results:** One way of handling undefined results is to simply ignore them. Believe it or not, there have been implementations where operators or functions encountering undefined results return a random value (or a random memory location interpreted as a numerical value). The argument for this is that "undefined means undefined," so any value will suit the bill. Fortunately, this way of thinking has pretty much gone out of style.
- **Returning an error:** Another way to deal with undefined operations is to refuse to do them — to cause an error. The error can be anything from a crash of the app (or even the device!) to an error value or message. This technique involves returning two results from the operation — a value result and a status result. Many people believe that this is the most robust coding style because it separates the calculation from the status of the result. Unfortunately, it also adds more code to your app. However, incorporating calculations returning a value and a status into a reusable function or method can minimize any inconvenience.

  This is one of the techniques that Swift uses — in fact, it's the default behavior for the / operator.
- **Returning a defined value:** Logically, you need to return two results from an operation that can fail or be undefined. One classic way of doing this is to perform the operation and test the result (or test the operands before a result is produced). If the test produces an error or undefined result, you can return a known value that indicates an error.

  In some programming languages (and on some computers) a value called a `NAN` (not a number) is returned. Its internal representation can vary, but when printed out, the value can be shown as `NAN`. Typically, a `NAN` cannot be used in further computations. If an error result is returned, it may indicate that the value returned (that is, the `NAN`) is unusable.

  Alternatively, a returned value can be safe to use in further calculations without causing problems even though it is not a valid arithmetic result. In some divide-by-zero situations, returning 1 or the value of the numerator avoids returning an error while making it possible for further calculations to proceed.

  This is another technique that Swift uses. If you divide by zero using the `&/` operator, Swift returns 0, as you can see in line 1 of Figure 5-6. A simple / operator causes a division by zero error.

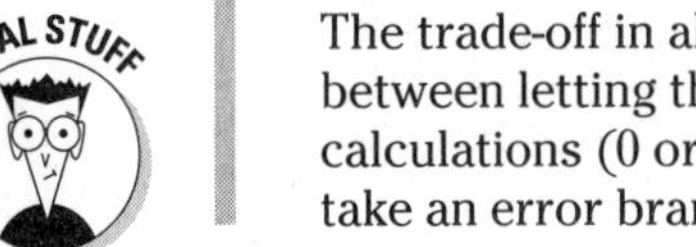

The trade-off in all cases of calculations that are undefined is the balance between letting the program continue even with possibly misleading calculations (0 or 1 to bypass a possible divide-by-zero error) or letting it take an error branch and unambiguously stop its processing.

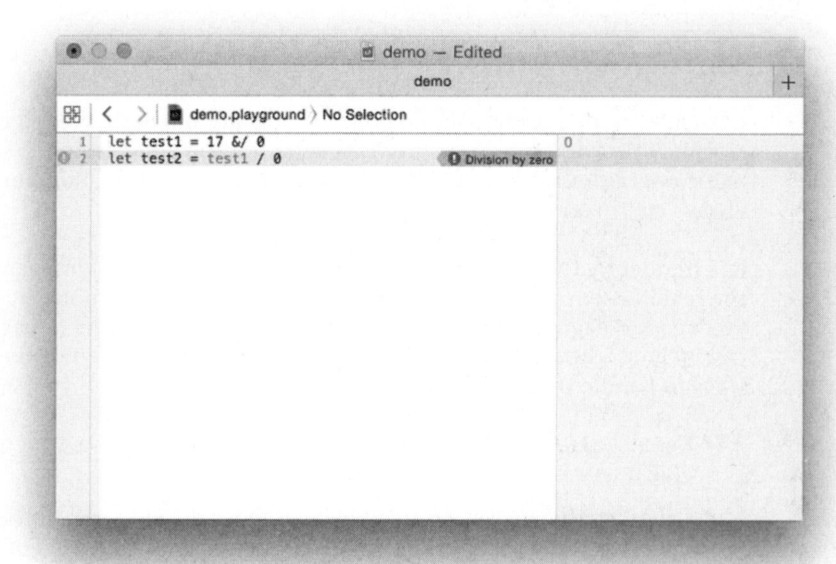

Figure 5-6: Managing division errors with &/.

- **Preventing errors:** The best way to handle an operation that could fail or be undefined is to catch the situation before it happens. Instead of relying on a status result, you avoid even attempting an operation that results in a problem. By moving that evaluation out of the operation itself, you may make your code more maintainable. In most cases, preventing the error means modifying an operand or substituting a "result" that is appropriate as a default for your case.
- **Avoiding errors:** The final strategy is to avoid the possibility of an error. Instead of manipulating the operands or the result, you just don't do anything that could cause the problem. This may be as simple as displaying a message that the area of a polygon can't be calculated in certain circumstances. When a user is, say, selecting a movie to play and encounters a divide-by-zero error, it's usually preferable, particularly in Cocoa Touch apps, to do *something* appropriate rather than to ask the user to help solve the problem.

Remember that Swift goes out of its way to prevent you from having uninitialized variables and constants. There's no guarantee that they will be initialized to correct values, but the fact that you don't have to worry about totally uninitialized variables can make your life as a developer easier than otherwise.

Using remainder division

Even if both the numerator and denominator are integers, the result of division may be a non-integer value. This sets division apart from the other arithmetic operators, whose operations involving integers (any number of them) always return an integer.

It is frequently the case that you need to handle division of integers and use the result as one or more integers. Perhaps the most common case is when you need to paginate some data: Let's say you have 17 items to list and you can include 5 items per page. How many pages will you need? There are two ways to handle this in Cocoa and Cocoa Touch:

- Use `NSTableView` in Cocoa or `UITableView` in Cocoa Touch and don't give it another thought.
- Calculate the answer yourself using integer division and the remainder operator. (There are other ways of doing this, but this section focuses on remainder division so that is the approach that is used here.)

The code in Listing 5-2 defaults the variables to integers, as you can see in Figure 5-7. (You can tell this because in the sidebar they are shown without a decimal point.)

This is basic C code, and it works in Swift. What's important to note is that Swift is inferring the types involved (there's more on this in Chapter 6). The ternary expression in the last line tests to see if `leftOvers` is not equal to 0, and, if so, it adds a single page to the page count to accommodate the leftovers.

In Listing 5-3 (and in Figure 5-8), you can see how things work with the `%` (remainder) operator when the variables are floats (using the `Float` type).

In Figure 5-8 and Listing 5-3, the variables are declared as `Float`, and when they are used in a calculation (see the calculation of `leftOvers`) the result is a floating point number instead of an integer.

Listing 5-2: Using Default Integers for Remainder Operations

```
var itemCount = 17
var itemsPerPage = 5

var pageCount = itemCount/itemsPerPage //3
var leftOvers = itemCount%itemsPerPage //2

var totalPages = pageCount + (leftOvers > 0 ? 1 : 0) // 4
```

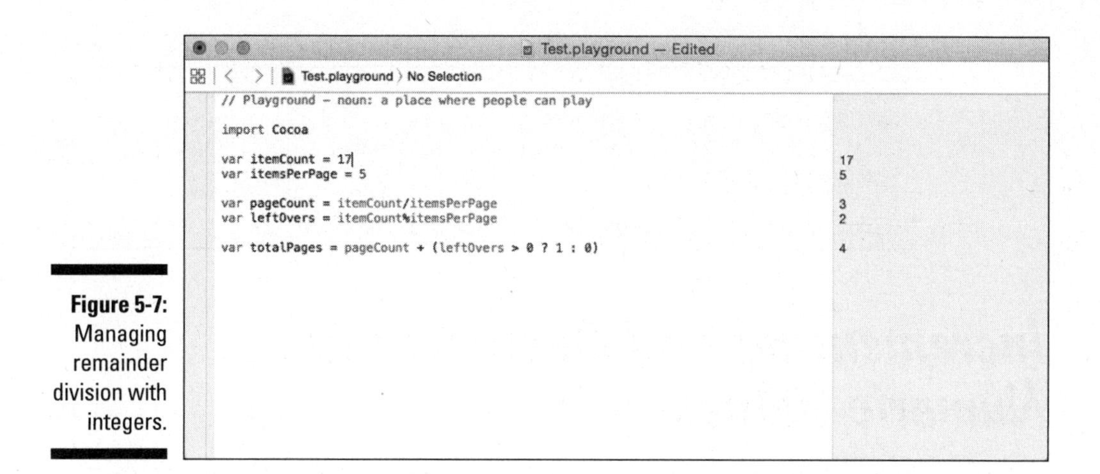

Figure 5-7: Managing remainder division with integers.

Listing 5-3 not only uses floating point numbers, but it also uses the ceiling function (`ceil`) that rounds up the result of a division operation. That is exactly what is needed here. In fact, if the ternanary operation remains as the last line of code, it will produce an incorrect result for `totalPages` because `ceil` has addressed the issue directly.

You don't need to calculate `leftOvers` as shown in Figure 5-3: It is sufficient to use `ceil` to calculate `pageCount`. If you need to know how many items will appear on the final partial page, you do need `leftOvers`, but in many cases you will just use a loop to fill the pages. This reduces the five lines of code in Listing 5-2 to three lines of code. When you reduce the number of lines of code you have to write to accomplish a task, you're almost always on the right track.

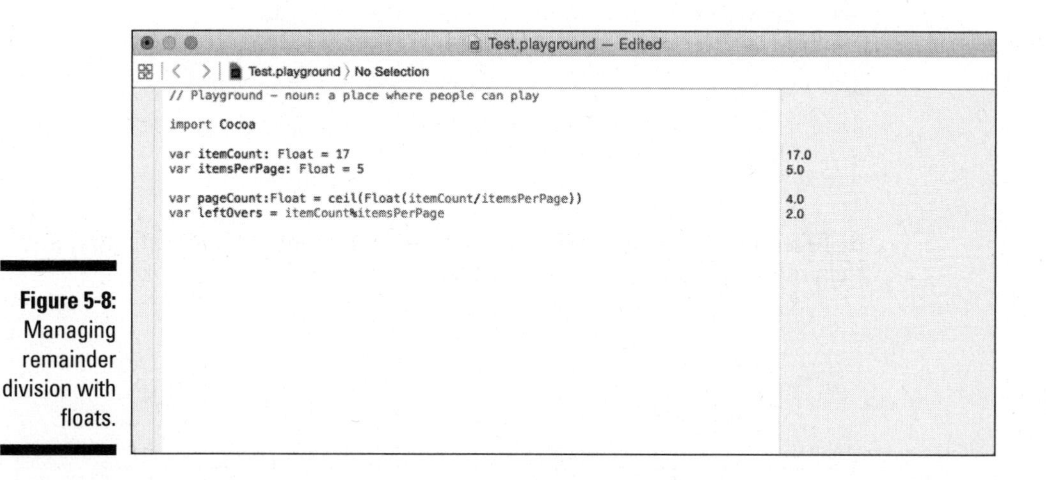

Figure 5-8: Managing remainder division with floats.

Listing 5-3: Using Floats for Remainder Operations

```
var itemCount: Float = 17
var itemsPerPage: Float = 5

var pageCount: Float =
  ceil (Float (itemCount/itemsPerPage))  //4.0
var leftOvers: = itemCount%itemsPerPage  //2.0
```

Incrementing and Decrementing Numeric Values

Although a few features from C and Objective-C aren't implemented in Swift, most of the features from those languages are implemented, the majority of which are implemented without changes. Among the unchanged features are the increment and decrement operators as well as the combined operators.

Increment and decrement operators add or subtract 1 from a value. They are most frequently used in loops, but you can use them anywhere. One form of the syntax is

```
i ++
```

or

```
i --
```

With this syntax, the value of `i` is returned and, after that, is incremented or decremented. You can also reverse the order, like this:

```
++ i
```

or

```
-- i
```

By reversing this order, you increment or decrement the value of `i` first and then return the incremented or decremented value.

Combining Operators

With this pattern in mind, you can combine other operators and operands. The increment/decrement operators function along the lines of combined operators. To use a combined version of an increment operator, for example, you could write:

```
var a = 2
a += 1
```

The value of `a` at the end of this snippet is 3 (1 is added to 2 and `a` is set to the result).

The combined operator `+=` provides more flexibility than the simple `++` operator and its variations (such as the decrement operator and all prefix and postfix positions). You can vary the increment value from 1 and even change the operator so that you get something like this:

```
var a = 2.0
a *= 21.6
```

As I discuss in Chapter 6, Swift's type safety requires you to make certain that you're using appropriate types. Swift can infer types, but it doesn't automatically convert types. Multiplication is not defined for two dissimilar types (an integer and a floating point number, for example). This is why you have to declare `a` with an initial value of a `Float` to prepare for the next line of code. Alternatively, you could rewrite the second line of code as `a *= Int(21.6)` to solve the problem on the other side.

You're not limited to addition or subtraction and you're not limited to a value of 1 as you can see in Figure 5-9.

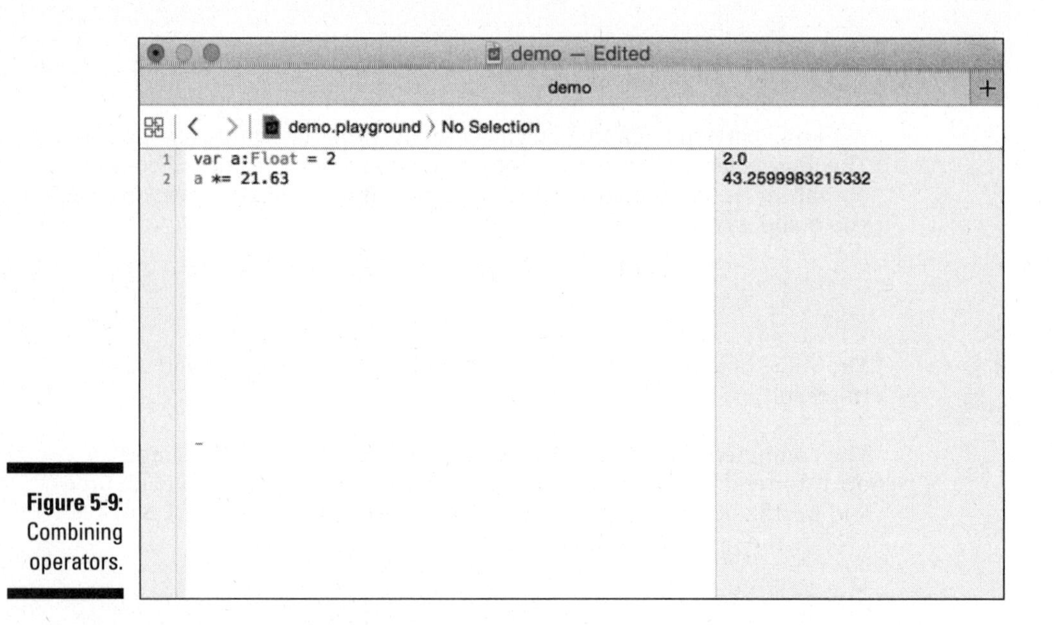

Figure 5-9: Combining operators.

Comparing Values

The standard C comparison operators shown in Table 5-1 are supported in Swift.

Any of the operators can be preceded by a `!` (not) operator.

The *identity* operator may be new to you. It handles a problem, common in object-oriented programming, that occurs when comparing two instances. This issue occurs frequently when you're comparing two `NSString` instances, although it arises in other cases as well.

Table 5-1 Comparison operators

Comparison	*Symbol*
Equal value	==
Identity object	===
Greater than	>
Less than	<
Greater than or equal	>=
Less than or equal	<=

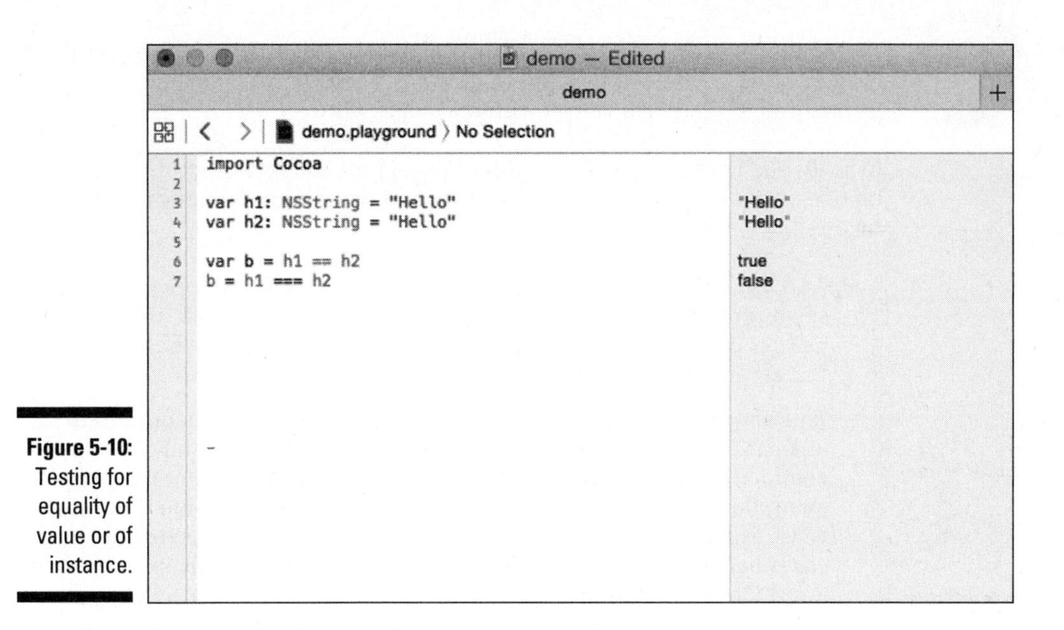

Figure 5-10: Testing for equality of value or of instance.

Here's an example. Assume you have two instances of `NSString`, one containing `Hello` and the other containing `World`. They are not equal and they are not identical. Now change the value of the second string to `Hello`, so that both `NSString` instances contain the same letters. As you can see in Figure 5-10, the values of these two instances are now equal (`Hello`), but their identities are not because they are two separate instances. This is where the identity operator comes in handy. When you want to compare values, use two equal signs (==); when you want to see if two objects are the same instance, use three equal signs (===).

Choosing and Checking Values with Logical Operators

Logical operators operate on Boolean values, which can either be true or false. Depending on your background, this may or may not be a gotcha waiting to strike. A Boolean value is true or false, and it's represented by one bit in a computer word. The remaining bits in that word are irrelevant to the evaluation of the Boolean value.

The actual values representing true and false differ from one language to another: In Swift, the values are `true` and `false`. In Objective-C, the basic values are `YES` and `NO`. In other languages, the implementations of Boolean variables are `0` and `1`, with the underlying type being an integer.

Rather than wasting the remaining bits in a word, there are bitwise operators that compare the bits in two words, thereby potentially using many (perhaps as many as 64) Boolean values within a single word.

In Swift, each of the logical operators has a graphical representation based on one or two characters. The operators and those representations are as follows:

- **And `&&`:** This operator evaluates to a `true` value if both operands themselves are `true`. Put another way, if any operand is `false`, the result is `false`. Because of this, as soon as the operating system encounters a `false` operand, the result of the operation is set to `false`.

  This shortcut that triggers as soon as a `false` value is encountered in an `AND` (or, conversely a `true` value is encountered in an `OR`) is a common optimization in many programming languages and their implementations, but it means that if an operand is an expression that sets a value as part of its operation, that expression will not be executed in all cases because it may be unnecessary when a shortcut has been encountered. This means that the order of these expressions matters in your code. If there's a byproduct of a Boolean expression that sets a value and a shortcut is taken before that expression is evaluated, you may have created a bug that's difficult to find.

- **Or `||`:** With this operator, if any operand is true, the expression will evaluate to true. The same rule about sequence applies.
- **Not `!`:** This is a unary operator that inverts the Boolean value of a variable or expression.

You can combine Boolean operations into a complex expression. As is the case with arithmetic expressions, you can use parentheses to control the order of execution of the various parts of the full expression. Parentheses, together with indentation and line spacing in your source code can make your intention clear. Furthermore, consider the people who will maintain your code in the future and think about splitting overly complex expressions into several parts that may be easier to read and maintain.

Chapter 6

Using Swift Types

In This Chapter

- Exploring Swift types
- Refining type declarations and references
- Using types to improve readability of code
- Working with tuples and optionals

In most programming languages, variables and constants not only have values, they also have *types*. C (the progenitor of many of today's languages) provided four basic arithmetic types (`char`, `int`, `float`, and `double`) that can then be enhanced with optional specifiers, such as `signed`, `unsigned`, `short`, and `long` to form more complex and sophisticated types.

Adding types for variables and constants means that the compiler at run-time can perform more efficiently and can more easily check for errors. For example, in most languages, assigning "Hello" to an `int` type is a mistake likely to raise an error or exception at compile- or run-time. In a properly written app, every error or exception raised is a crash that's been averted (provided that you've done your part by adding the necessary error- and exception-checking code to catch those errors).

Together with assertions (which are discussed at the end of this chapter), Swift types let you know what a variable or constant is in terms of its type as well as its content (that's where assertions come into play). This makes code more maintainable over time.

This chapter shows you the what, why, and how of Swift types. You see what the types are, why they're present in the language, and how you can use them most productively.

Types are intimately related to declarations, which are discussed in chapter 11, and to initializers, which are discussed in chapter 12.

Understanding Types and Type Safety

If you want a thorough discussion of types in computer languages, read *Types and Programming Languages* by Benjamin C. Pierce (The MIT Press; ISBN 0-262-16209-1). A sentence from that book sums up the concept of types nicely: "A type system is a syntactic method for enforcing levels of abstraction in programs." You can make a good case that everything done in the digital world of programming is an act of abstraction — a move from the real world of concrete objects and ideas to the digital world of ones and zeroes — but this interesting conversation is beyond the scope of this book.

Pierce's book tells you everything you need to know about types in a mere 648 pages. In *Swift For Dummies,* on the other hand, I examine Swift types in a much less-detailed manner, so you understand only what you need to know to use types efficiently in Swift.

The discussion of types and variables in this chapter applies to constants as well.

Considering type safety

Swift implements *type safety,* which basically means that you can't use a variable inappropriately for the terms of its type. In other words, according to the rules of type safety, you can divide by zero — that's not a type error — but you can't perform an arithmetic operation with a string unless you do some conversions first.

Type safety can be described in a language specification and is enforced in a development environment like Xcode; it can also be enforced with careful programming. That's part of the problem: Without enforced type safety, it's very easy to slip up and create unsafe code. In many environments, unsafe code may fail the first time you run it — this is the best-case scenario. Unfortunately, the most common scenario is that the code fails at various times. Often its failure has to do with the memory your app has to work with, so the unsafe code may fail depending on what other apps or functions are running at the time. Letting the development environment enforce type safety is the safest way of handling these problems. (Relying on the good intentions of people is, alas, not always the wisest choice.)

The Swift language specification describes its type safety as part of the language; the entire language specification is enforced by the compiler as well as by the Xcode development environment. In common usage, however, people often say things like "Swift enforces type safety." In fact, Swift only provides the specification; it's Xcode and the LLVM compiler that do the enforcement. Nevertheless, unless there is a reason to make a distinction between the Swift specification and its implementation in Xcode and the compiler, this book refers in a general way to Swift.

Swift takes two approaches to enforcing type safety: tightening up coding standards and inferring types. It uses other approaches as well — you'll see examples throughout this book — but these are the major ones.

Tightening coding standards

There has long been a trade-off (some people would call it a *battle*) between the coding practices of strict and loose typing of variables. Strict typing is more trouble, and it can cause compile errors as the compiler objects to vaguely-typed variables. Loose typing is simpler to write and incurs fewer compiler errors, but it can cause more runtime errors and crashes.

Swift tightens coding standards. To a large extent, these standards consist of language limitations that prevent unsafe code. Here are some of the type safety measures that Swift puts in place and enforces:

- **Pointers:** Pointers let you access memory directly, which can lead to all sorts of problems. The basic Objective-C syntax for accessing an instance of a class involves a pointer: This is not the case with Swift.

  TECHNICAL STUFF

  When you declare an instance of a class such as `UIView` in Objective-C, you do so with code such as `UIView *myView`. That asterisk indicates that you're working with a pointer (this is plain old C syntax). If you are used to Objective-C, most of those asterisks are history for you. The exception is if you are mixing Objective-C and Swift. See the PDF document called *Using Swift with Cocoa and Objective-C* on `developer.apple.com` for details.

Using type aliases to clarify code

Like all other names in your app, type names should be descriptive. Sometimes finding an appropriate descriptive name can be difficult, however, particularly when you're working with code from several sources. In these cases, you can declare a type alias to improve your code's readability. You can do this using syntax such as the following:

```
typealias myAlias = myStrangeTypeName
```

This is purely a cosmetic issue: The type name is not changed.

- **Initialization:** Variables must be initialized in Swift before use. There is no way to use uninitialized variables in Swift. (See the following section, "Inferring types.")
- **No `nil`:** In other languages, `nil` is often used to provide a value that can be tested to see if an object exists. In Swift this is handled with optional types (discussed later in this chapter in the section, "Using optional types for values that may or may not exist").
- **Memory management and overflow checking:** Swift has inherited Objective-C's features implemented with advanced compiler behaviors, such as Automatic Reference Counting (ARC).

Inferring types

Because Swift requires variables (and constants) to be initialized before being used, the compiler and runtime library always have a value for each variable. (Note the exceptions with optionals, however, that are discussed later in this chapter.) From this value, Swift can infer a type without your having to specify it. In other words, you can specify the type for any variable, but you don't have to do so if that variable is initialized with a value from which Swift can infer the type.

Arrays and dictionaries in Swift must contain instances of the same type. Thus, when you create an array or dictionary, you must either explicitly specify its type or provide initial values so that Swift can infer the type of the array or dictionary. In either case, Swift can determine the type of the values in the array or dictionary.

When you are dealing with classes and subclasses, you may want to use an explicit type. If your array or dictionary is eventually going to contain instances of subclasses of a given class, you may initialize it with several of those subclasses. For example, an array that will contain various instances of `UIView` subclasses can be initialized with one or more `UILabel` instances. However, there is no way Swift could infer `UIView` from instances that do not include all possible `UIView` subclasses. So if you're aware that you'll want to add (say) `UIButton` instances later on, you may prefer to explicitly type the array as `UIView` so all of the `UIView` subclass instances are welcome.

Exploring Swift types

Swift's handling of types is similar to other languages, but each language has different emphases and rules. In general, these rules have to do with the ways typing must be implemented in cases where there is ambiguity. How much does the language (or its compiler or runtime library) do to ensure type compatibility? Swift's approach to these issues, as you'll see, is different from other languages. Don't skip this section.

Broadly speaking, Swift has two categories of types. In the first category, four types are built into the Swift standard library, and these are available to you without further ado. They're described in the following section, "Swift Standard Library Types."

In the second category are the types you can create. These fall into three groups:

- structures (`struct`)
- enumerations (`enum`)
- classes

Structures and enumerations are basic C types, whereas classes are at the heart of object-oriented programming. All of these let you group data together into an element that can be assigned to variables (or constants) and passed around with a simple assignment statement.

If you're not used to using structures, enumerations, and even classes, it's worthwhile to take the time to learn about them. This book provides a good basic introduction for Swift developers, but if you want more details, you can find them in books about basic programming techniques. Although it may take a little while for you to get used to using these complex types, it's worth it. The point is, by using a complex data structure, you can reduce the amount of code you have to write because much of the complexity is in the data structure rather than in your code.

Swift Standard Library Types

As with other languages, Swift provides developers a common library of utility code that's frequently used in development. A library like this is separate from the language itself, although it uses the language's syntax and features. Although you can replace this library with another, non-standard one, most people prefer the standard library, and, in fact, replacements are very rare.

The contents of a standard library reflect the language and its intended uses. For example, the C standard library (sometimes called the ISO C Library; it's available online at `www.open-std.org/jtc1/sc22/wg14/www/docs/n1570.pdf`) contains routines for string handling, mathematical functions, input/output, and character manipulation. The library represents nearly 300 pages of the entire 650-page C language specification.

By contrast, the Swift standard library is 50 pages long at this time; it contains:

- types (discussed in this section), which include:
  - strings
  - arrays
  - dictionaries
  - numeric types
- protocols (discussed in Chapter 18)
- free functions (discussed in Chapter 9)

If you want to delve deeply into the C library as well as Swift, you'll find that some of the functionality described in the C library is implemented directly in Swift as well as in the Cocoa and Cocoa Touch frameworks. What matters at this point is that the standard library is the ultimate reference for Swift types.

Strings

A Swift string is an ordered set of characters. When you use a string literal, you enclose the characters in quotes like this.

```
"ABCDE"
```

The Objective-C syntax is not used so you can forget the @:

```
@"ABCDE"
```

Swift begins from the premise that its users will be international, so any Unicode character is acceptable as a string value or for the name of a constant or string.

Arrays

Arrays are discussed in Chapter 7, "Collecting Objects." Swift arrays are similar to arrays in other languages except that all elements of an array must be of the same type, and the array is then said to be of that type. In the case of classes, as opposed to values (enumerations and structures), the common type for elements of an array may be a superclass. Thus, an array of `UIView` instances can still be a `UIView` array if it contains `UILabel` and `UIButton` instances, which are both subclasses of `UIView`.

Unlike arrays in Objective-C, Swift arrays are not classes; they are actually implemented as structures.

Dictionaries

Dictionaries are also discussed in Chapter 7. Like arrays, dictionaries have a common type for their elements. In other languages, dictionaries are called *associative arrays*. Each element has a key value rather than a number index. The key values are converted to index values that can locate a dictionary value.

Numeric types

The Swift standard library provides support for common numeric types. The basic types are:

- **Boolean:** The `Bool` type has values `true` and `false`. (Note that this differs from Objective-C, which supports `YES` and `NO` as well as `TRUE` and `FALSE`.)
- **Integer:** The `Int` type is a full word interpreted as a single binary integer. The size of words changes from time to time (at the moment, both 32- and 64-bit words are common, depending on the device). Because of this variation and the likely changes in the future, make no assumptions about word size. Also additional types exist for signed and unsigned integers, as shown in Table 6-1.
- **Floating point:** `Double` is the most commonly used floating-point type. It uses 64 bits — but a 32-bit `Float` is also available.

Protocols

Protocols are implemented in a number of object-oriented languages. Sometimes, as in Java, they're called *interfaces.* To a certain extent, pure virtual functions in C++ abstract classes are also very much like protocols in Objective-C and Swift.

In the simplest sense, protocols are the methods and properties of a class but without the class. In Swift, they can be implemented by any class, structure, or

Table 6-1 Swift Integer Types

Length (bits)	*Signed*	*Unsigned*
8	`Int8`	`UInt8`
16	`Int16`	`UInt16`
32	`Int32`	`Uint32`
64	`Int64`	`Uint64`

enumeration that *adopts* the protocol, and each class that adopts the protocol may implement it in a different way, using its own data and rules for that data.

For more details on protocols and their syntax, see Chapter 13, "Expanding Objects with Extensions."

The Swift standard library has three protocols:

- `Equatable`
- `Comparable`
- `Printable`

These protocols have default definitions, but you can write classes, structures, and enumerations that conform to the protocols and implement the protocol properly in the context of your class, structure, or enumeration and its data. However, don't think that you have to implement these protocols: You only need to implement the protocols if you want to change the default behavior.

The first two of these Swift standard library protocols involve overloading binary comparison operators (==, for the first, and <, >, <=, and >= for the second). If you want to play with the un-overloaded built-in operators as you read this chapter, create a playground with the code in Listing 6-1. You can then change the values and operators as you go along. (See Figure 6-1.) Note that `b3` on the left of Figure 6-1 is set to 3; on the right, it's set to 4. This changes the result of `bTest`.

Equatable

This protocol returns a Boolean value that indicates whether two compared arguments are equal. It overloads the == operator. As I discuss in Chapter 13, this function takes two arguments (`lhs` and `rhs`) of the type `Self` (which means the type that adopts the protocol). Here is the definition of the overloaded operator in the protocol:

```
func == (lhs: Self, rhs: Self) -> Bool
```

Protocols defining overloaded binary operators often use `lhs` and `rhs` to refer to the two arguments — left side and right side.

What does *equality* mean? The definition differs depending on the factors being compared. A class that works with various representations of integers,

Listing 6-1: Experiment with Built-in Operators

```
var b3 = 3
var b4 = 4
var bTest = b3 == b4
```

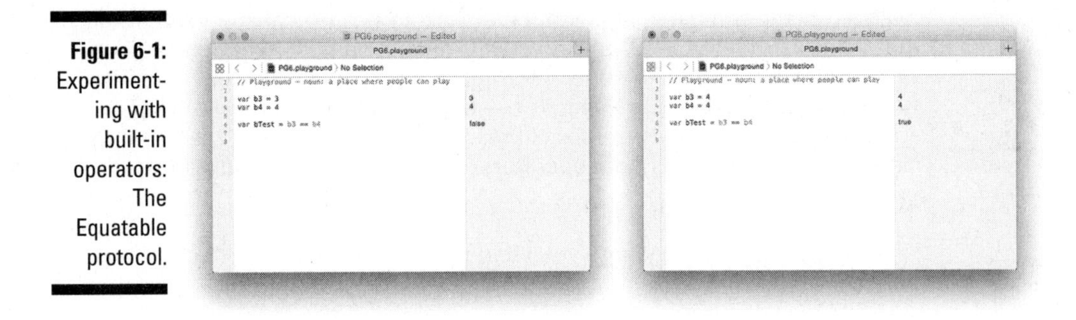

Figure 6-1: Experimenting with built-in operators: The Equatable protocol.

for instance, might make `VIII` equal to `8` and to `eight`. This is the point of writing a protocol for your class to adopt or of assigning your class to conform to a protocol written by someone else: The protocol defines the action, but you implement it for your own environment.

Experiment in your playground with the code shown in Listing 6-1 and Figure 6-1. Try changing the value of `b3` to `4` and watch the result as shown in Figure 6-2. Remember that it may take a few moments for the playground to catch up to your typing if you type quickly.

Comparable

The `Comparable` protocol returns a Boolean value that says whether or not an argument to the `<` operator is less than another. It requires you to overload the `<` operator. The definition of the overloaded operator is:

```
func < (lhs: Self, rhs: Self ) -> Bool
```

Figure 6-2: Experimenting with built-in operators: The Comparable protocol.

Swift treats the comparison operators as a group — a logical approach, when you think about it. After all, you already have either a built-in or overloaded test for equality with the == operator. And an overload for the < operator also implies an overload for the > operator — because you can turn $y>x$ into $x<y$ simply by reversing the two sides of the expression and flipping the operator. The <, then, can serve as both operators, depending on how you set up the expression.

Thus, merely by overloading < you wind up with overloads for ==, <, >, <=, and >=.

Experiment with the code in Listing 6-1 by changing == to < and changing values of `b3` and/or `b4` to make the expression true or false. Without supplying your overloading code, replace the operator in Figure 6-1 and Listing 6-1 with <, as shown in Figure 6-2.

Printable

The `Printable` protocol returns a text representation of an instance of a type. This is done through the `description` property.

Here is the declaration of the property (note that the `get` makes it a read-only computed property):

```
var description: String { get }
```

Test this protocol by adding a `println` function call to your code, as shown in Figure 6-3. Compare the results shown at the right of the window. When `b3` and `b4` are set to values of `3` and `4` respectively, the results are shown at the right. These are numeric values generated by the playground.

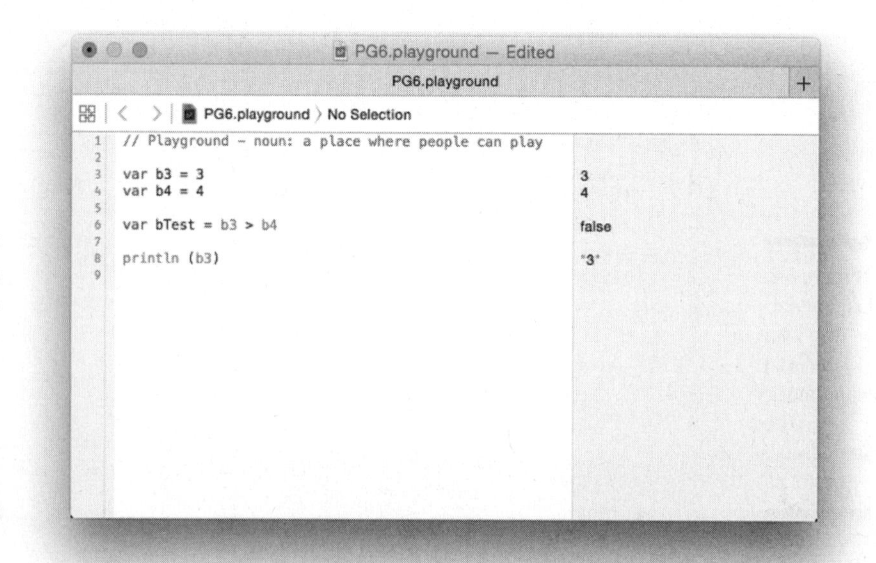

Figure 6-3: Experimenting with built-in operators: The Printable protocol.

When you print out the variables with `println`, Swift invokes the `Printable` protocol and returns the `description` property of the variable, which is a string (note the quotation marks).

You can access the `description` property of the protocol directly. To demonstrate this, add the following line of code to your example (as shown in Figure 6-4):

```
var s = b3.description
```

Note the quotation marks again in the sidebar: You have asked `b3`, which is an `Int`, to provide its `description`, which is a `String`.

How do you know `b3` is an `Int`? See the section, “Specifying Variable or Expression Types with Type Annotations,” later in this chapter.

Free functions

In object-oriented programming, most methods and functions (interchangeable in this discussion) as well as properties are declared inside classes. That goes along with the notion that globals in general are not a good programming practice.

However, in some cases, *free functions* — functions that aren’t part of any class — are useful. The two most commonly used free functions in the Swift standard library are `print` and `println`.

PG6.playground — Edited

PG6.playground

PG6.playground 〉 No Selection

```
1  // Playground - noun: a place where people can play
2
3  var b3 = 3                                        3
4  var b4 = 4                                        4
5
6  var bTest = b3 > b4                               false
7
8  println (b3)                                      "3"
9
10 var s = b3.description                            "3"
11
12
```

Figure 6-4: Accessing the Printable protocol’s description property.

In Objective-C, there is a common base class (`NSObject`) with an accompanying `NSObject` protocol. Almost every object in Objective-C descends from `NSObject` and therefore conforms to the `NSObject` protocol. General-purpose functions such as description wound up in the `NSObject` protocol for Objective-C but in the `Printable` protocol for Swift. Perhaps this is because there is not a common base class like `NSObject` in Swift. Almost every object-oriented language has come to grips with the issue of where to put general-purpose utility functions of this sort.

Printing

The heart of printing is preparing a printable version of an instance. That is done in the `description` method of the `Printable` protocol, and it is implemented for the standard types. If you create new types that are not subclasses of standard types, you can decide whether or not to conform to the `Printable` protocol and implement `description`. You can print out a value or a summary or anything you want.

In Swift, the printing code itself goes into the pair of free functions — functions that are part of no class but that are globally available to any class instance. `println` is used as it is used in C. If you pass an instance to `println`, its `description` is printed out.

As is true in many languages, `println` adds a new-line (return) character to the printed string. `print` does not; if you want a new line, use `\n` inside the `print` function string.

Algorithms

The Swift standard library provides some algorithms for common tasks such as sorting and finding. You can implement them to make your classes and structures sortable and findable. This is an area of Swift that is still in progress as this is written.

Specifying Variable or Expression Types with Type Annotations

This section provides some examples of the use (and misuse) of type syntax in Swift. It sets the stage for the further discussions of type syntax that follow in this chapter.

Some languages help you out by automatically converting one type to another when the conversion is obvious. The problem with automatic conversions, however, is that they work their magic behind the scenes. This is very convenient, but in some cases it can be dangerous. For example, a simple typo can send the conversion off in the wrong direction; there are cases where such a typo and misleading conversion generate an error or crash months or years later. Such data-dependent bugs are notoriously difficult to track down.

Long battles have been waged about whether the convenience of self-correcting compilers is a good or bad thing. Swift comes down emphatically on the side of demanding that you keep your types strictly defined and synchronized. Although conversions don't happen behind the scenes, Swift does infer types from values that you provide. Thus, the value 2 is inferred to be an integer type, whereas 2.0 is inferred to be a floating point type. These inferences can be overridden, and so with Swift the process of typing variables (and constants) is more in your control than it may be in other languages. Furthermore, you have playgrounds to use as a tool to test type inference. As you can see in Figure 6-5, playgrounds allow you to test code and get immediate feedback. You can't multiply an integer by a string, and that's the end of the story.

Figure 6-5 should raise a question for you: Why does Swift assume `i` to be an integer? In some very early programming languages, such as FORTRAN, the first letter of the variable determined its type. Variables beginning with I, J, K, L, M, and N were understood to be integers, and that was the end of the discussion. This coincided with common algebraic usage, so it seemed obvious. (In fact, algebra is where the variable-naming rule came from.) But typing variables based on the first letter of their name is a long-discarded technique.

Swift knew `i` was an integer because it is initialized to an integer — 17. In Swift, variables and constants must be initialized, and from that initial value, their type often can be inferred. (However, you can add a specific type *annotation* to remove any ambiguity.) An annotation follows a colon after a variable name as in

```
var i: Int
```

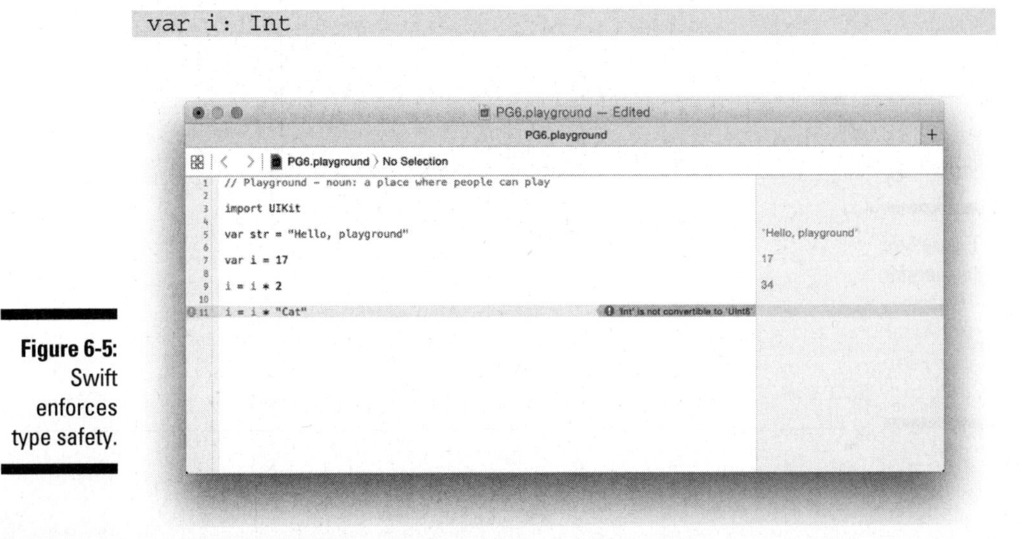

Figure 6-5: Swift enforces type safety.

An annotation is not required because if a variable is initialized, Swift can often infer the type from the value and format of the initializer (for example, 25 as opposed to 25.0).

Figure 6-6 shows another example of Swift's insistence on type safety. You can follow these steps to duplicate the example.

1. **Create a new playground for iOS and Swift.**

   If you want, delete the `import UIKit` and `var` statements.

2. **Declare a variable i and initialize it to 17.**

   Swift infers that it is an integer (`Int`).

   ```
   var i = 17
   ```

3. **Set `i` to 25.0 (or attempt to).**

   You get the error shown in Figure 6-6. This is because you cannot assign a `Double` (or `Float`) to an `Int`.

   ```
   i - 25.0
   ```

You may disagree with Swift in this matter, but 25.0 is not an integer, and so it must be converted from a floating point number to an integer before you can assign it to an `Int`. Although 25.0 and 25 are mathematically equal, they are different types, with different representations in memory (because floating point numbers have an exponent and mantissa).

Although modern computers do not have the inconsistencies in converting integer and floating point representations of the same number from one to the other that older computers had, some inconsistencies persist. These inconsistencies arise most often in borderline

Figure 6-6: You cannot assign a `Float` or `Double` to an `Int`.

cases (such as when using very large numbers, very small numbers, or specific numbers that are notorious for causing trouble in the binary-to-digital conversion of floating point numbers).

4. **Convert 25.0 to an `Int` and assign it to an `Int` variable as shown in Figure 6-7.**

```
i = Int(25.0)
```

5. **You can change the declaration of `i` to explicitly be a `Float` even though it's initialized as an apparent `Int` value.**

```
var i: Float = 17
```

6. **Now Swift will allow you to set `i` to 25.0 (a `Float`). (See Figure 6-8.)**

   It also allows you to set it to 25 (because this conversion is safe).

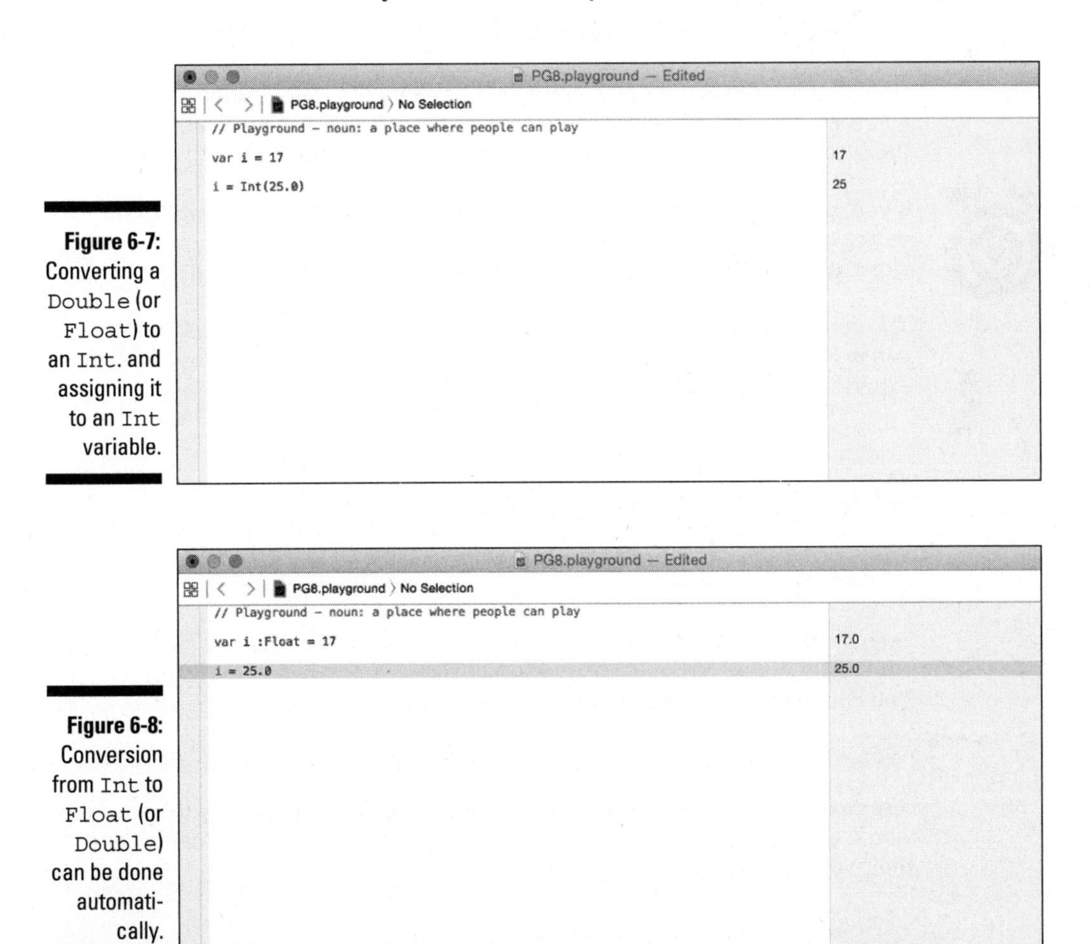

Figure 6-7: Converting a `Double` (or `Float`) to an `Int`. and assigning it to an `Int` variable.

Figure 6-8: Conversion from `Int` to `Float` (or `Double`) can be done automatically.

Dealing with Tuples

As I discuss in Chapter 7, in Swift, both arrays and dictionaries let you combine values into groups, much as they do in other programming languages. No matter how many elements you have in an array or dictionary, all are included in the collection that you can reference by its name (such as `myArray`). Unlike arrays and dictionaries, a tuple can consist of a variety of types, but those types are part of the tuple definition as you will see in the following paragraph.

Tuples provide another way of combining many values into one named group. With tuples, the values can be the results of expressions, constants, variables, or literals. For instance, this is a single tuple consisting of three values (in this case, literals):

```
var myTuple = (5, 103, true)
```

Note that a tuple is not just a collection of elements. The number of elements and their types must be the same in each use. (You'll see more about this in the section, "Type safety with tuples," later in this chapter.)

If you glance at samples of Swift code, including the various examples on `developer.apple.com`, you'll find that tuples are used extensively. Pay close attention to this section, then. It's important to understand.

The code snippets discussed in the following sections are shown in Listing 6-2 and in Figure 6-9. (Use either of the first two lines to declare `myTuple`; then experiment with the other line.)

Decomposing a tuple

You can *decompose* a tuple into separate variables. Consider our original tuple:

```
var myTuple = (5, 103, true)
```

You can decompose it with the following code:

```
let (myDecompose1, myDecompose2, myDecompose3) = myTuple
```

After a tuple's elements have been decomposed, you can access them as you would any variable or constant. In a playground, just type their names and their values will appear at the right.

```
myDecompose1
myDecompose2
myDecompose3
```

Listing 6-2: Experimenting with Tuples

```
var myTuple = (5, 103, true)
//or
var myTuple = (anInt: 5, aFloat: 103, aBool: true)

myTuple.anInt
myTuple.aFloat
myTuple.aBool

myTuple.0
myTuple.1
myTuple.2

let (myDecompose1, myDecompose2, myDecompose3) = myTuple

myDecompose1
myDecompose2
myDecompose3

let (_, myDecompose, _) = myTuple

myDecompose //to show value
var myTuple2 =
  (anInt: Int(), aFloat: Float(), aBool: Bool() )
println (myTuple2)

myTuple = (99, 99, false)
myTuple = (99, 99.5, false)
myTuple = (99, 99, 99)
```

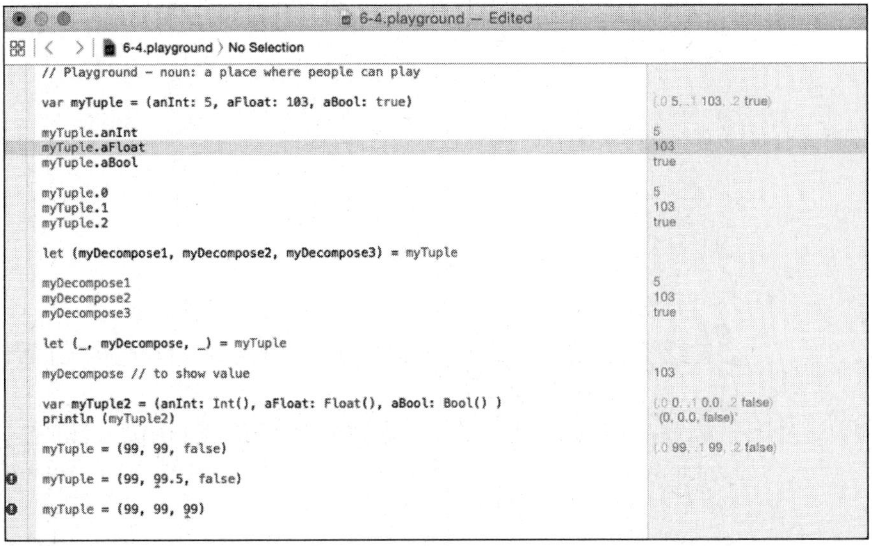

Figure 6-9: Experimenting with tuples.

This is the declaration of `myDecompose1`, `myDecompose2`, and `myDecompose3`: Note that you don't have to create a separate variable before decomposing the tuple.

Accessing tuple values with names

You can name the elements of a tuple when you create it. For example, you can create the same tuple shown previously with names. (This is the difference between the two alternate first lines in Listing 6-2.)

```
var myTuple = (anInt: 5, aFloat: 103, aBool: true)
```

Accordingly, you can decompose it using these names as in the following code:

```
myTuple.anInt
myTuple.aFloat
myTuple.aBool
```

Accessing tuple values with index numbers

The tuple notation in the previous example demonstrates the use of names. However, you can also decompose a tuple using index numbers to refer to its elements. In fact, you can always use index numbers, for any tuple, but you can use names only if you provided them when creating the tuple. Here's an example of using index numbers to decompose a tuple (note that the index numbers start at 0):

```
var myTuple = (5, 103, true)
//or
var myTuple = (anInt: 5, aFloat: 103, aBool: true)

myTuple.0
myTuple.1
myTuple.2
```

Skipping tuple values with underscores

If there are any tuple values you don't care about, you can skip them by including underscore characters when you decompose the tuple. Using the tuples shown previously (either named or unnamed), you can write the following code, which creates a single `myDecompose` variable and ignores the other tuple data:

```
let (_, myDecompose, _) = myTuple
myDecompose //to show value
```

Creating a tuple with types

When you are creating a tuple, it can be useful to get into the habit of naming the elements and explicitly setting their types. You can do that with code such as the following.

```
var myTuple2 =
  (anInt: Int(), aFloat: Float(), aBool: Bool())
```

This sets the elements and their names to instances of `Int`, `Float`, and `Bool`. You can then set their values. The names and types are now unambiguous.

Type safety with tuples

As noted previously, when you create a tuple, you specify the number of values as well as their types. When those values are literals, constants, variables, or expressions, however, you can implicitly specify the types, and allow Swift to infer the type of each element.

The list below demonstrates how to create tuples, using constants, variables, or literals whose types are inferred from their initial values. If you created the tuples in earlier sections, you can use these steps in this list to experiment with type safety.

In the following list, I deliberately ask you to create errors to demonstrate type safety (specifically in steps 4 and 5). After creating errors like these (intentionally or accidentally), you must fix the error or delete the test code to reset the playground; otherwise, the playground may not evaluate the rest of the code.

1. **Declare a tuple.**

   You can name the elements or not — it doesn't matter for this exercise. To make things simple, use only one of the following lines of code:

   ```
   var myTuple = (5, 103, true)
   var myTuple = (anInt: 5, aFloat: 103, aBool: true)
   ```

2. **Set the tuple to new values with the following code.**

   Use this code exactly as shown here:

   ```
   myTuple = (99, 99, false)
   ```

3. Now set your tuple to the following values:

```
myTuple = (99, 99.5, false)
```

You should get an error. (Type 'Int' does not conform to protocol 'FloatLiteralConvertible.')

4. Try setting it to these values:

```
myTuple = (99, 99, 99)
```

You should also get an error. (Type 'Bool' does not conform to protocol 'IntegerLiteralConvertible')

From the initial tuple creation in Step 1, Swift infers that your tuple consists of three elements (you can see that) and that they are an `Int`, another `Int`, and a `Bool`. This is inferred from the initial values: Names have nothing to do with it. Thus, an element created as an `Int`, such as `aFloat`, cannot be set to the floating-point value 99.5. Similarly, an element whose initial value was of Boolean type, such as `aBool`, cannot be set to an integer value like 99.

Working with Optional Types

Type safety and strict typing are all well and good, but sometimes the real world intervenes. The most common problem with strict typing in computer languages is handling non-existent values (that is to say, empty variables). This has been a problem since the dawn of computer programming. You may have probably seen some of the workarounds for this problem.

Workarounds for missing data

A common workaround to handle non-existent values is to designate a type-conforming value (often 0, –1, and 99 — or its companions 999 and 999999999) to have a special meaning.

This allows you easily to identify real data and to distinguish it from non-data values. There are many examples of multiple special values. (See the nearby table for some possibilities.)

Value	*Meaning*
99	Missing data
0	Data being entered
–1	Invalid data (present but not usable)
–2	Data not verified

Is this a good workaround? How would you like to work on an app that uses these special values? Take a moment and think about how you would compute the average of data values. (If you know anyone who worked on the Year 2000 problem, ask them how much time they spent turning 1999 from a special value to an actual date.)

As the nearby sidebar, "Workarounds for missing data," shows, designating special values is a poor solution, but the need to flag missing data still exists. Objective-C uses a value of `nil` to represent an instance of a class that has no value yet. That works well, as far as it goes, but what do you do for structures, enumerations, and even basic C types that don't exist?

To address this issue, Swift uses *optional types*. An optional type is created by including the modifier `optional` before a type name, as in `optional Double`, or, more commonly, by writing `Double?`.

In practical terms, a variable (or constant) can be an optional type only when that variable has either the specified type or the special value of `nil`. Any type can be optional. Thus, optional types allow you to have a `nil` value for an `Int?`, a `UIView?`, or anything at all.

Don't read too much into the word *optional*. The term means only that the variable can be either the specified type or it can be `nil`. It can't be another type.

Optional types are often referred to as *optionals,* as in "That property is optional," or "That property is an optional." The fact that a type is optional can be more important in some contexts than the type of which it is optional. All optionals can have a value of `nil`, and that is their commonality. Putting it in reverse, if you need to be able to specify a value of `nil` for a variable, it must be an optional. In Swift, `nil` is the only non-data value that can be stored in a variable. It is conceivable that someone will add a new wrinkle to Swift in which other special non-data values (perhaps "estimated") would exist, but that's not planned as far as we know. If you need to manage non-data values for a variable or constant, you have to implement your own mechanism.

Using optional types for values that may or may not exist

Optional declarations look like this.

```
var testOptionalInt: Int?
var testOptionalView: UIView?
```

If you inspect an optional variable immediately after you declare it, you'll see that it has been automatically set to `nil`. This goes along with Swift's insistence that all variables be initialized. In the case of an optional, the initial value must be `nil` unless you specify something else.

The most common reason for creating an optional when you do know the initial value is to reserve the ability to set that variable to `nil` sometime later. As you can see in Figure 6-10, playgrounds display the values of optional variables with the keyword Some.

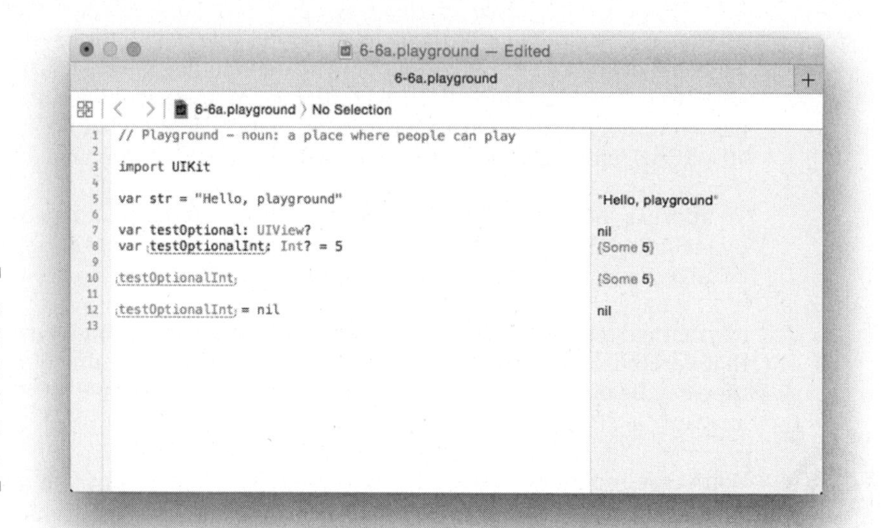

Figure 6-10: Declaring and using optionals in a playground.

Using forced unwrapping with exclamation marks

You can test whether or not an optional has data simply by testing its value for `nil`. If it's not `nil`, it must be the specified type, and you can access its underlying value. This is called *unwrapping*. You can unwrap an optional by following the variable name with an exclamation mark. (See Figure 6-11.) However, you must make certain there is something there before you unwrap it (in other words, is must not be `nil`).

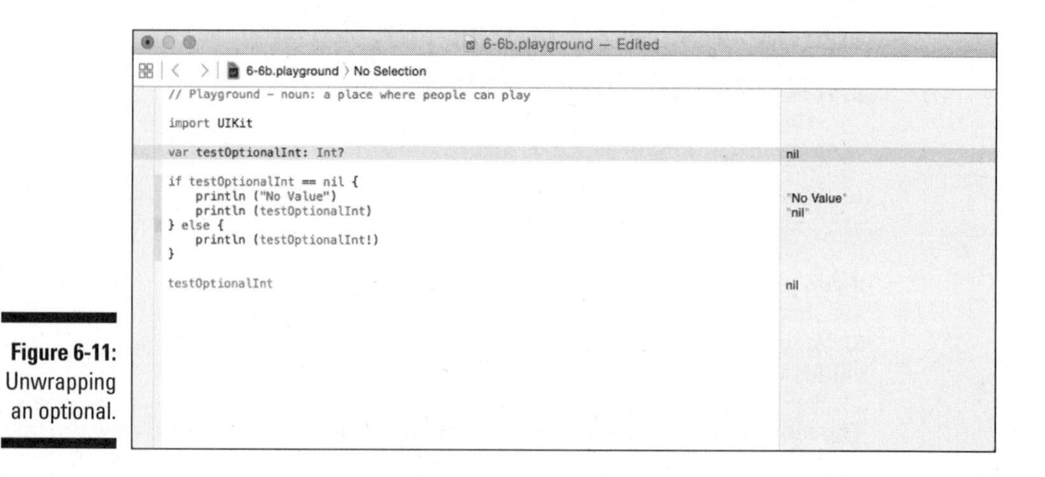

Figure 6-11: Unwrapping an optional.

The steps below help you experiment with optionals. When you work with optionals, you'll frequently follow these steps. (The result is shown in Listing 6-3.)

1. **Declare an optional of the type you want.**

   You can do this by typing in the following code:

   ```
   var testOptionalInt: Int?
   ```

   At the right of the playground window, you'll see that Swift has set your optional to `nil`.

2. **Test whether it is `nil`.**

   Type in the following line:

   ```
   if testOptionalInt == nil
   ```

3. **If it is, print out a message.**

   ```
   println ("No Value")
   ```

4. **If it is not `nil`, it has a value. Unwrap that value and print it out.**

   ```
   println (testOptionalInt!)
   ```

5. **Print out the unwrapped value before you get to the `if` statement.** This will cause an error because there is nothing to unwrap. That's why you always need to test an optional for `nil` before unwrapping it.

   ```
   var testOptionalInt: Int?

   println (testOptionalInt!) // this will cause an error
   if testOptionalInt == nil{
   ```

Listing 6-3: Unwrapping an Optional

```
var testOptionalInt: Int?
if testOptionalInt == nil{
  println ("No Value")
} else {
  println (testOptionalInt!)
}
```

Using optional binding to access an optional value

Optional binding is a special case involving optional types that lets you combine the assignment and the test in a single line of code. It lets you quickly test to see if a variable that's optional (that is, that may have a nil value) exists, and, if it does, to access the value. The following line of code comes from the completed Locatapp example (in DetailViewController.swift):

```
if let activityURL =
  NSURL (string:"http://champlainarts.com") {...
```

As is often the case with complex code, it's easiest to parse it from the inside out. Here's what goes on here:

- A NSURL instance is created and initialized with a string (string:"http://champlainarts.com").
- The NSURL instance is assigned to a local variable (activityURL).
- The if statement tests to see if activityURL exists (that is, if it's not nil).

Using Generic Types

Swift provides the ability to use generic types to simplify your code. Generic types are specified with a type *placeholder* — often called T. Two common uses of generic types are: generic functions and generic types.

Using a generic function

When declaring a generic function, the placeholder is placed just after a function name, as in:

```
func myFuncWithPlaceholder <T>
```

You can then use T as a type name in the function. Many times, T is used as a parameter; to use it this way, declare a function like this:

```
func myFuncWithPlaceholder<T> (a: T, b:T)
```

This common style lets you declare a function that takes two parameters (a and b) that may be of any type, although both a and b must be of the same type.

Using a generic type

In the case of a generic type, you can use a generic anywhere in a function — as the type of a variable or parameter, as the type of an array, or as the return value of a function.

You declare the generic type in the same way as you do a function — by placing it in brackets after the name of the entity, as in:

```
struct myStructWithPlaceholder<T>
```

You have to let Swift know what the generic type will be when you use the object. (In the case of generic functions, Swift only enforces that both uses of the generic type are of the same type.)

Here's how you would use a generic type:

```
var myUseOfGeneric = myStructWithPlaceholder<Int> ()
```

Then, each occurrence of `T` within your structure (or class or enumeration) is assumed to be an `Int`.

When used within a class, enumeration, or structure, your placeholder type is not placed in brackets. In other words, don't write `<T>`; just use `T`.

Chapter 7

Collecting Objects

In This Chapter

- Working with mutable and immutable collections
- Starting with arrays
- Storing data in dictionaries

It's often convenient to be able to group objects into collections so that you can handle them together. Whether you're talking about students in a class, items in a desk drawer, or values in an array, collecting items together makes your code easier to read (and write!).

Swift has two types of collections: arrays and dictionaries. Arrays are the standard indexed collections of values that can be accessed by their index. Dictionaries are associative arrays in which the values are accessed by a key value and a hash routine.

As is true in most languages that support arrays and dictionaries (or associative arrays), the syntax for manipulating these collections and their data values is different for the two forms of collections. Associative arrays are usually thought to be a specific type of array rather than a separate concept altogether. For most programming languages, including Swift, the indexes for arrays are integers. Associative arrays, on the other hand, can use other types of objects as indexes. Access to integer-based arrays usually involves use of the arithmetic index, and for associative arrays, a hash routine, which is used to convert the index value to a number. In languages other than Swift and Objective-C (as well as Python, REALbasic, and .NET), associative arrays can be called *hashes*, *hash tables*, or *maps*.

Playing by Swift Collection Rules

If you have experience with other programming languages (and you should have experience with at least one), you must have already encountered arrays and possibly associative arrays (or *dictionaries,* in Swift-speak). However, don't just assume that arrays in Swift are same as the arrays you know from a language like C: There are some important differences.

Arrays are basic building blocks in many languages for many programs. If you have taken formal programming courses, you may already be familiar with arrays and iterators (`for` or `while` loops).

Although Swift, Cocoa, and Cocoa Touch use arrays and iterators, they use them in an object-oriented way, so you may need to adjust your thinking a bit for the object-oriented world of Swift and Cocoa/Cocoa Touch.

In Locatapp, the Swift location app you built in Chapter 4, the iPhone version provides a master list of objects as shown in Figure 7-1.

As you add or delete items from the master list, this display changes. Surely, you may be thinking, this is an array. After all, it's a classic example of array manipulation. You have a list (collection) of objects, and you want to do the same thing to each one (display it). From the user's point of view, if one of the items is tapped, you want to carry out the same process no matter which item has been tapped (albeit with different data, depending on which item has been tapped).

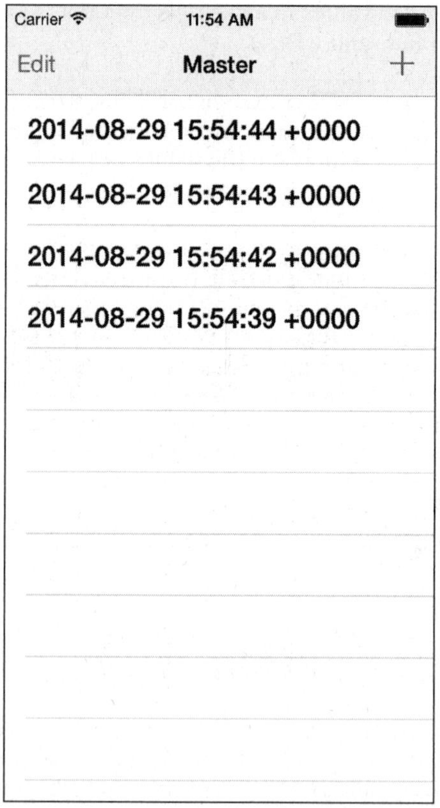

Figure 7-1: Viewing the master list in Locatapp.

But in Swift or in most object-oriented languages, this sort of thing isn't done with just an array. Yes, you *could* use an array, but that wouldn't be the most effective way of handling it. The sections that follow present an overview of how it's done in the Master-Detail Application template (the basis for the app you build in this book). This is the basic design pattern for handling lists like the master list in object-oriented programming.

As you will see, there *is* an array at the heart of things, but that array is inside an object that is an instance of `NSFetchedResultsController`. The array (`fetchedObjects`) is created and accessed by functions in `NSFetchedResultsController` that add functionality and sophistication to the simple indexed array of results.

As noted in Chapter 4, the Social Media Location App (Locatapp) built on the Master-Detail Application template in Xcode 6 (or later) is used throughout this book. You may want to review Chapter 4 at this point to remind yourself what the built-in template does before you modify it.

Managing a collection of objects

Listing 7-1 shows you how the Master-Detail Application template configures the cells in the master view controller without directly using an array or any other collection object. I guide you through this code in various other chapters in this book, but for now I'll give you a high-level overview. This overview pinpoints the way collections are managed in Swift, and it shows you how Swift functions are written.

This code configures a cell in the master view controller list (as its name suggests). The `UITableViewCell` named `cell` is the cell in the list that needs to be configured with data. It is passed into `configureCell` by reference and the appropriate data is placed in it (specifically, in its `textLabel.text` property). Because it's passed in by reference, it doesn't need to be returned: The updated data is placed into the `cell` instance, which is then available to the calling code after the completion of this function.

Listing 7-1: Configuring a Cell in the Master-Detail Application Template

```
func configureCell(cell: UITableViewCell, atIndexPath
  indexPath: NSIndexPath) {

  let object =
    self.fetchedResultsController.objectAtIndexPath
      (indexPath) as NSManagedObject

    cell.textLabel.text =
      object.valueForKey("timeStamp").description
}
```

This code needs to deal with two objects — the cell in the list and the data to be placed into the cell. The cell in the list is passed into the function, so it's available with the name `cell`.

The data to be placed in the cell has been retrieved from the persistent store that uses Core Data. Core Data has been designed for tasks like this. It's a framework that has built-in functionality for retrieving and managing collections of objects. In the built-in template, Core Data is retrieving a collection of data objects containing timestamps that will be shown in the master detail list, as in Figure 7-1.

Core Data itself manages lists of data, and it can handle the multi-dimensional lists that frequently occur in data of this sort. The multi-dimensionality is actually implemented by building a tree of nested arrays in which each array implements a dimension. The resulting object is an `NSIndexPath`. An `NSIndexPath` instance contains the various indexes of the nested arrays that combine to create a multi-dimensional index.

Each data element in these lists is identified by a `NSIndexPath` instance, and each element can be found using that index path. Thus, the function shown in Listing 7-1. retrieves a single object of the fetched results from Core Data. The appropriate index path is passed into the function as the named parameter `atIndexPath` and the parameter `indexPath`. (`atIndexPath` is the name that makes the function more easily read by humans, and `indexPath` is the name that you use in your code).

The ability to use internal and external names for parameters of functions is inherited by Swift from Objective-C. The external names can help a function and its named parameters form a complete phrase or sentence — (`configureCell: atIndexPath`) for the function shown in Listing 7-1. Inside the function, a less precise name (`indexPath`) may be used because the inside of the function has a different audience from the outside declaration. You can easily imagine a series of related functions, all of which use an internal name of `indexPath` to support externally visible function names such as `configureCell: atIndexPath`, `removeCell: fromIndexPath`, `addCell: afterIndexPath`, and so forth. (Note that these function names are provided as examples of the concept rather than of specific functions.)

```
let object =
    self.fetchedResultsController.objectAtIndexPath
      (indexPath) as NSManagedObject
```

If you're used to working with arrays, this line of code may seem a bit too complex. Why can't you just write

```
let object = retrievedObjects [i]
```

where `i` is an index number passed into the function, and `retrieved Objects` is a simple array of retrieved objects?

The answer is that the object-oriented pattern gives you a function that's a much more extensible function than an array and a one-dimensional index. The code in the `configureCell:atIndexPath:` function can handle multi-dimensional index paths without modification (although at the present time on iOS, you only have to worry about single-dimensional paths).

The lessons to take away from this are:

- Collections are implemented in Swift, but very often they are used inside objects that manage them in more sophisticated ways than either an array or dictionary can.
- If you are used to using arrays, remember that they are available in Swift along with dictionaries, but you may be better off using classes that are "smarter" than arrays and dictionaries. (And you may be working with such classes rather than arrays and dictionaries in the frameworks and templates you use in Xcode.) Of course, if you're writing your own collection classes, you may decide to use arrays and dictionaries within them while exposing your own UI to clients of the collection you develop.

If you really want to get deeper into the concepts of collections in object-oriented programming and functional programming, native Swift collections are actually built on `struct` objects.

Looking inside a Swift collection object

Whether you're working with an array or a dictionary, a collection object contains collected items (that's just simple English). In Objective-C, the collected items are objects — subclasses of `NSObject`. A collection can contain an `NSWindow` alongside an `NSManagedObjectContext`. These are all subclasses of `NSObject`, and they can all be placed in the same Objective-C collection.

In Swift, there is no base or root class like `NSObject` from which all other classes descend. (For all practical purposes, base and root classes are the same thing.) If a Swift class is a subclass of another class, you or the framework you're using must establish that hierarchy rather than relying on a standard base class of `NSObject`. The root class may be any class whatsoever — its chief distinguishing feature is that you cannot make calls to `super` in a root class that you define. Otherwise, your base class in any circumstance can be any class.

There is no intrinsic commonality among Swift classes provided by a root class such as `NSObject`. Each class can have its own superclass root with its own functionality. What *is* common across Swift classes is the functionality and syntax of the language itself.

In part because of this deliberate lack of a common root class, heterogeneous collections (that is, collections with objects of various types) are problematic and are not allowed. (There are other reasons why collections are restricted to instances of a single class; this is just one of them.)

Of course, nothing prevents you from creating a root class of your own for whatever purpose you want and then using instances of its subclasses in a collection.

Looking deeper into a collection in Swift, you'll see that the items in the collection need not even be objects. They can be instances of a class, but they can also be typed values such as `Int` or `Double`. This means that you can use Swift collections for all of your collecting needs. In Objective-C, the collection of objects is done in `NSArray` and its subclasses whereas the collection of non-object values is done in standard C arrays. In Swift, you just use arrays and dictionaries.

Mutability of collections

Whether you are dealing with arrays or dictionaries, Swift (like Objective-C), provides a pair of classes. Both arrays and dictionaries can be either *mutable* or *immutable*. Mutability refers to whether or not the collection can be modified.

As I discuss in Chapter 6, you can create constants with `let` and variables with `var`. With collections, as well as with other types, a constant created with `let` is immutable — it can't be changed. A variable created with `var`, however, can be changed. Among the advantages of this arrangement is that the compiler and the operating system know when they're dealing with immutable objects, which can make a number of processes (especially regarding memory management) quicker and more efficient.

This use of `var` and `let` to distinguish between mutable and immutable collections has two important benefits:

- It is consistent with the treatment of other types in Swift. Mutable collections thus use the same syntax as other mutable types such as

  ```
  var aFloat: Float
  var aBool: Bool
  ```

- It is simpler than creating pairs of classes as is the case in Objective-C, which has `NSArray` and `NSMutableArray`, along with `NSDictionary` and `NSMutableDictionary`.

There are some significant differences between Objective-C and early versions of Swift compared to the current version of Swift. Mutability refers to changes to the collection or its contents. In Objective-C and in early versions of Swift, you could change the values of elements in immutable arrays, but this is no longer true. Replacing the value of the element at index N in an immutable collection is not allowed. Because this has changed during Swift's development, and because it's different from the behavior of the corresponding classes in Objective-C, watch out for mutability issues in Swift code, and make certain you know what you're dealing with.

Switching mutability

Because of the efficiencies of memory management when dealing with immutable arrays, a great deal of code in Objective-C exists for the purpose of converting an immutable array to and from a mutable one so that it can be modified as a mutable array. Although this is extra work for the processors, the work required is often outweighed by limiting the use of a mutable array to only a brief period of time.

The basic benefit of using an immutable array is that if it needs to be moved from memory temporarily, it can be restored from the known version — intermediate modifications will not have been made to an immutable array.

Creating classes and objects to use in collections

In Chapter 15, I show you how to create classes; in Chapter 10, I show you how to create instances of those classes. I don't want to delve into the details of classes and instances here; however, sometimes a little knowledge on one concept (such as classes and instances) is necessary to understand another (such as collections). Here is a quick reference for creating classes and instances. This code is used in examples in this chapter. See Chapters 10 and 15 for the details:

- Declaring a class containing a string property:

```
class MyClass {
  var instanceName = "New
    Instance"
}
```

- Creating an instance of the class:

```
var instance = MyClass ()
```

Organizing Data Sequentially with Arrays

The basics of working with arrays consist of creating arrays, adding and removing elements, finding elements, and modifying them. As noted previously, arrays (like dictionaries, and, as noted, any constant or variable) can be either mutable or immutable; however, they can't be changed from one to the other. It is possible, however, to copy one to the other as I show in the following sections. The typical use copies the elements of an immutable collection into a mutable collection where they can be modified; the modified collection elements are used to initialize a newly-created immutable collection.

Comparing full and shorthand array syntax forms

There are two forms of syntax you can use to create arrays: a full type and a shorthand type. The Swift documentation uses the shorthand type, and so does this book. As an example, here is the full version of an array type annotation:

```
Array<MyClass>
```

By comparison, the shorthand version is provided without a label:

```
[MyClass]
```

This is a shorthand version of an array declaration for an array consisting of elements of `MyClass`. Note the square brackets.

There's another use for square brackets, a specific shorthand style that you encounter frequently. It's called an *array literal*, and it's a way of writing an array together with its contents. It consists of zero or more array elements enclosed in square brackets. These elements can be literal values, such as strings or integers, or they can be class instances. Here are some examples of array literals:

```
["String 1", "String 2", "String 3"]
[1, 2, 3, 4, 5]
[classInstance1, classInstance2, classInstance3]
```

Thus, within the brackets that delimit an array literal you can provide literal values, class instances, or a type that specifies the type of the array elements that will be provided. When literal values are provided, Swift infers the common type that they represent.

Remember that a class, structure, or enumeration can be treated as a type in cases like this.

If you have declared `myClass1` and `myClass2`, where `myClass2` is a subclass of `myClass1`, creating an array that mixes instances of the two classes would be interpreted by Swift as an array of `myClass1` instances because `myClass1` is the common class of `myClass1` and `myClass2`. (If you think there will be any ambiguity in interpreting the array's type, you can always declare it with the class notation to prevent confusion.)

Creating arrays

You can create empty arrays and populate them as needed or you can create arrays that have one or more elements in them. In either case, the array is assigned to a constant or a variable. Arrays assigned to variables (with `var`) are mutable and can be modified. Arrays assigned to a constant (with `let`) are immutable and cannot be modified. Creating an empty array and assigning it to a constant is legal but improbable.

One case in which you may want to assign an empty array to a constant is during development. You could write the code that checks for elements in the array and, if found, acts on those elements. You can write that code without fully implementing it and run your app against an empty immutable array until you are ready to go back and recreate the array as a mutable array (with `var`). Doing something like this can eliminate the possibility of accidentally modifying array elements as you are building your code. If you do something like this, make sure to comment it carefully so that you don't tear your hair out when you get around to finishing the implementation and don't understand why you can't update the array.

Whether you create an empty array or a populated array, you must set its type (that is, the type of its elements) either explicitly or by letting Swift infer it from the elements in an array literal.

Here are the ways to create an array with elements of type `MyClass` (remember that the elements can be types such as `Int` as well as classes):

- Create an empty immutable array:

```
let myArray = [MyClass]
```

- Create an empty mutable array:

```
var myArray = [MyClass]
```

- Create a populated immutable array from an array literal:

```
let myArray: [MyClass] = [instance]
```

- Create a populated mutable array from an array literal:

```
var myArray: [MyClass] = [instance]
```

Working with arrays and their elements

Swift uses Swift language features to let you access array elements not just by their index but also by their ranges. In most programming languages, you can access an array element with a specific index or with a variable that contains an integer, as in the following code.

```
myArray [4]

var myIndex = 4
myArray [myIndex]
```

Adding and removing elements by index and range

If you have created a mutable array with `var`, you can modify its elements. You can add them, remove them, or change their values. Here are the basic tools you'll need. Remember that, like dictionaries, arrays are functional (not object-oriented) features of Swift, and are frequently used inside classes that provide object-oriented logic above and beyond basic array manipulation.

The examples here build on an array that consists of instances of a class that you create, as noted in the sidebar "Creating classes and objects to use in collections." Follow these steps to explore array behaviors. (Note that the full code for this experiment is shown later in this chapter in Listing 7-2.)

1. **Create a class in a playground.**

   You can delete the comment and import statement, if you want. You won't need them for this experiment, but they do no harm.

   ```
   // Playground - noun: a place where people can play
   import UIKit
   ```

2. **Create a class with a single string instance variable called `instanceName`.**

   ```
   class MyClass {
     var instanceName = "New Instance"
   }
   ```

3. **Create four instances of that class.**

   ```
   var instance = MyClass ()
   var instance2 = MyClass ()
   var instance3 = MyClass ()
   var instance4 = MyClass ()
   ```

4. **For each instance, set `instanceName` equal to a unique string so you can tell them apart.**

   Remember that the class initializer already sets this property to a common value, which you are changing.

   ```
   instance2.instanceName = "Instance 2"
   instance3.instanceName = "Instance 3"
   instance4.instanceName = "Instance 4"
   ```

5. **Create an immutable array using this class and a single element.**

   Remember that with `let`, you can't modify the array. You'll see the array and its single element at the right in the playground window, as shown in Figure 7-2.

   Note that in the sidebar at the right of the playground shown in Figure 7-2, each element of the array is shown inside brackets and quotes. The quotes delimit the string that is now the value of the instance variable, and the brackets denote each instance. After the `let` statement, you see an array (delimited by square brackets) containing one instance (delimited by curly braces) and containing a string (delimited by quotes).

   ```
   let myArray = [instance]
   ```

6. **Create a mutable array of `MyClass` instances named `myArray10`, and set it to an array literal consisting of the first instance you created in Step 3.**

   ```
   var myArray10:[MyClass] = [instance]
   ```

Figure 7-2: Creating an immutable array.

7. **Create `myArray11` using full syntax instead of shorthand. Set this array to include `instance2`.**

   I specify full syntax here only to familiarize you with both methods. It doesn't matter whether you create `myArray11` with full or shorthand syntax. (For that matter, you can create `myArray10` with either syntax.) You'll need both later on, but using the two syntax forms is just to demonstrate them.

```
var myArray11: Array<MyClass> = [instance2]
```

8. **To add elements to an array, use an array literal and the += operator, as follows:**

```
myArray10 += [instance3]
myArray11 += [instance4]
```

   Note the square brackets around the array literals.

9. **Use the `count` function on the three arrays to count them.**

   Figure 7-3 shows the result. `myArray` has one element, and each of the other two has two elements — the `New Instance` element created in the initializer, and the one you added in Step 8 to each array.

```
myArray.count
myArray10.count
myArray11.count
```

10. **You can access an individual array element by index number. In a mutable array, you can set it to another value. Set the 0-th element of `myArray11` to `instance3`. Check the count to confirm that you still have the same number of elements.**

```
myArray11 [0] = instance3
myArray11.count
```

11. **Create a new array from the range [0...1] in `myArray11`. Count that array and you'll see that there are two elements. (Refer to Figure 7-3.)**

    Note that this is the syntax you could use to copy some or all of the elements of an immutable array to a mutable array.

```
var subArray = myArray11 [0...1]
subArray.count
```

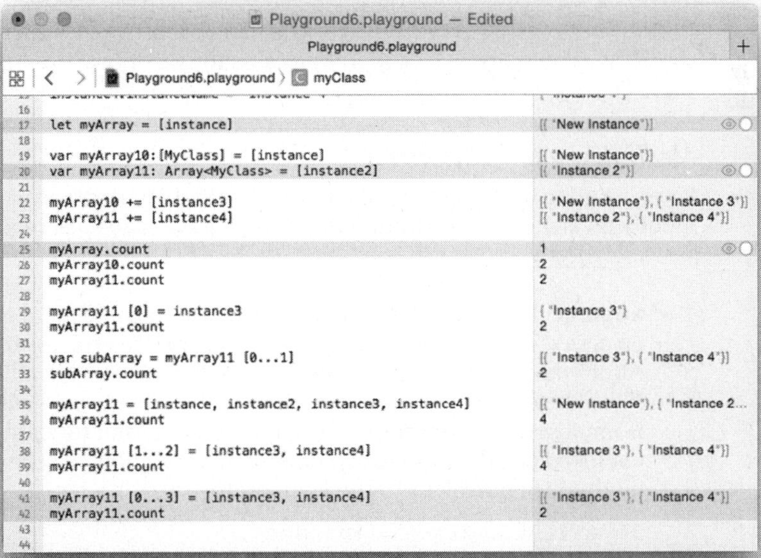

Playground6.playground — Edited
Playground6.playground
Playground6.playground > myClass

```
16
17  let myArray = [instance]                                   [{"New Instance"}]
18
19  var myArray10:[MyClass] = [instance]                       [{"New Instance"}]
20  var myArray11: Array<MyClass> = [instance2]                [{"Instance 2"}]
21
22  myArray10 += [instance3]                                   [{"New Instance"}, {"Instance 3"}]
23  myArray11 += [instance4]                                   [{"Instance 2"}, {"Instance 4"}]
24
25  myArray.count                                              1
26  myArray10.count                                            2
27  myArray11.count                                            2
28
29  myArray11 [0] = instance3                                  {"Instance 3"}
30  myArray11.count                                            2
31
32  var subArray = myArray11 [0...1]                           [{"Instance 3"}, {"Instance 4"}]
33  subArray.count                                             2
34
35  myArray11 = [instance, instance2, instance3, instance4]    [{"New Instance"}, {"Instance 2...
36  myArray11.count                                            4
37
38  myArray11 [1...2] = [instance3, instance4]                 [{"Instance 3"}, {"Instance 4"}]
39  myArray11.count                                            4
40
41  myArray11 [0...3] = [instance3, instance4]                 [{"Instance 3"}, {"Instance 4"}]
42  myArray11.count                                            2
43
44
```

Figure 7-3: Creating mutable arrays.

12. **Set `myArray11` to all four instances and count the array: Confirm you have four elements. (Refer to Figure 7-3.)**

```
myArray11 = [instance, instance2, instance3,
        instance4]
myArray11.count
```

13. **Set the range [1...2] of `myArray11` to `instance3` and `instance4`. Confirm that you still have four elements in the array.**

```
myArray11 [1...2] = [instance3, instance4]
myArray11.count
```

14. **Set the range [0...3] to `instance3` and `instance4`. Confirm that the element count is two.**

    This is correct because although the range [0...3] can hold four values, you have only provided two, and Swift has adjusted the array and indexes appropriately.

```
myArray11 [0...3] = [instance3, instance4]
myArray11.count
```

    Listing 7-2 provides the full code from this experiment. It's also downloadable from this book's companion website, as described in the Introduction.

Working with specific array elements

In addition to using array indexes, you can access specific elements of the array. There are two built-in functions for this purpose: `first()` and `last()`.

Modifying a mutable array

If you've gone to the bother of creating a mutable array with `var`, you can modify its structure in addition to modifying its values. Here are the methods you use:

- **append:** The `append` method is used to add an element to the end of an array. The element must be the appropriate type for the array. After you use this method, the array will be one element longer than it was before. Note that the method takes a single parameter, which is enclosed in parentheses (as all method parameters are), and not enclosed in brackets (which delimit an array literal). The append method is equivalent to the `+=` operator.

```
myArray11.append (instance)
```

Listing 7-2: Experimenting with Arrays

```
// Playground - noun: a place where people can play

import UIKit

class MyClass {
  var instanceName = "New Instance"
}
var instance = MyClass ()
var instance2 = MyClass ()
var instance3 = MyClass ()
var instance4 = MyClass ()
instance2.instanceName = "Instance 2"
instance3.instanceName = "Instance 3"
instance4.instanceName = "Instance 4"

let myArray = [instance]
var myArray10:[MyClass] = [instance]
var myArray11: Array<MyClass> = [instance2]

myArray10 += [instance3]
myArray11 += [instance4]

myArray.count
myArray10.count
myArray11.count
myArray11 [0] = instance3
myArray11.count

var subArray = myArray11 [0...1]
subArray.count

myArray11 = [instance, instance2, instance3, instance4]
myArray11.count

myArray11 [1...2] = [instance3, instance4]
myArray11.count

myArray11 [0...3] = [instance3, instance4]
myArray11.count
```

- **`insert`:** You can insert an element at a specific location in an array by using the following line:

  ```
  myArray11.insert (instance1, atIndex: 3)
  ```

- **`remove`:** You can remove an element from a specific location in an array by using the following line:

  ```
  myArray11.removeAtIndex (3)
  ```

The `remove` methods that work on single elements (`removeAtIndex` and `removeLast`) return the element that has been removed so that you can do something with it if you want.

In each of these methods, the array itself and indexes are adjusted for the new index numbering after the element(s) are added or removed.

Iterating or enumerating over an array

You can access array elements by index or by iterating through the array. Swift's iteration methods are highly optimized and quite efficient. You can iterate (or enumerate) a collection using standard C for loops, but you can also use the highly-optimized fast enumeration method introduced in recent versions of Objective-C. Fast enumeration is object-oriented and imperative rather than procedural (or functional, if you prefer that term).

There are two versions of the Swift collection fast enumerations, as follows:

- **Fast enumeration over array elements:** The syntax for this is simple:

  ```
  for anElement in myArray {
    // do something with anElement
  ]
  ```

  Each element in turn is presented to you in `anElement`, and you can do whatever you want with it — create a list, query each element's value, or anything else you like.

- **Fast enumeration over array elements and indexes:** You frequently need to know the index for the elements that you are iterating. For these situations, Swift has a different method for you:

  ```
  for (index, anElement) in enumerate (myArray) {
    // do something with index and anElement
  }
  ```

  Note that `enumerate` is a built-in function, but the other names are up to you. Although `index` is frequently used as the name for the index value of each element, you can use any name you like.

There are other array functions available in Swift, but these are the major functions and features that are used most often.

Organizing Data Logically with Dictionaries

Arrays are sequentially ordered sets of data; their order is maintained by array indexes, which are not stored in the array. The fifth element of an array is known because it comes immediately after the fourth element and immediately before the sixth element. If it is deleted, the former sixth element becomes the new fifth element, and so on. Again, the array itself contains only the element values — not the indexes.

On the other hand, dictionaries work a little differently. Dictionaries don't use array indexes to maintain order. Instead, they have key values that identify the elements stored within. Unlike arrays, dictionaries store the key values along with the data. Because the keys are stored with the values, deleting one element from a dictionary has no effect on the key values of other elements.

Because a dictionary's keys need not be sequential numbers, there is no such thing as a "next" or "previous" value in a dictionary. Each data value just has its own key, and that's the end of the story.

Dictionaries and arrays suit different purposes. Neither is better than the other: They're just different.

Dictionaries have been around for a while, but they came into use after arrays. In that long-ago era of mainframes and early personal computers, dictionaries were thought to be inefficient. Some people believed that the cost of accessing data values from a dictionary required more computational firepower than it cost to access them in an array. In those days, the cost of performing a hash (which usually involved at least one division operation, and possibly some follow-up disambiguation operations) was a serious concern for programmers. Today, although these concerns still exist, the reality is that the "inefficiency" of accessing data in a dictionary doesn't matter very much.

If you haven't used dictionaries or associative arrays extensively, the word *dictionary* may suggest a thick volume with thousands of entries. Don't be fooled. The reality is that in Swift (as in Objective-C), dictionaries are very frequently used to store small numbers of data values — two or three entries, for example.

Because keys are located by using a hash routine, keys in Swift must be *hashable,* meaning that they must be of type `String`, `Int`, `Double`, and `Bool`, or of any type that conforms to the `Hashable` protocol.

Comparing full and shorthand dictionary syntax forms

As with arrays, dictionaries have full and shorthand syntax forms. For each, as with arrays, dictionaries must contain elements of the same type — which may be the same class, same superclass, or a combination of classes and superclasses that all have (or are) the same superclass.

The full syntax form: `Dictionary<KeyType, ValueType>`

The shorthand form: `[KeyType: ValueType]`

Note that in full syntax, `KeyType` and `ValueType` are separated by a comma; in shorthand syntax, on the other hand, they're separated by a colon.

Creating dictionaries

The simplest way to create a dictionary is to use a dictionary literal like this:

```
var myDictionary: Dictionary = ["MyKey": "MyValue]
```

Note that either the key or the value (or both) can be an expression.

Working with dictionaries and their elements

Dictionaries use the same syntax as do arrays; the difference is that instead of an index, you use a key. To access an element in an array, you might write

```
let myIndex = 5
myArray [myIndex] = "someValue"
```

Whereas, to access an element in a dictionary, you could write:

```
let myKey = "someKey"
myDictionary [myKey] = valueForSomeKey
```

Or you could also write:

```
myDictionary.updateValue (valueForSomeKey forKey: myKey)
```

You can remove the value for a key by using code such as this:

```
myDictionary.removeValueForKey (myKey)
```

To query a dictionary, use the `count` and `isEmpty` methods, which return integer and Boolean values, respectively.

Fast enumeration over a dictionary

You can enumerate dictionaries in a manner similar to enumerating arrays. Here's a sample of the code:

```
for (key, value) in myDictionary {
  println ("\(key), \(value)")
}
```

Remember that you can use your own names for `key` and `value`; however, these are the most commonly used names. In a quoted string inside a `println` statement, a backslash (\) preceding parentheses around a variable prints out the value of the variable.

Reporting errors with a dictionary

Locatapp uses the Master-Detail Application template, and within that template is a common use of a dictionary. it's used in the process of creating a persistent store coordinator which is used in managing the Core Data store for the app.

As is frequently the case with database accesses, this process can fail in several ways. It contains some error-catching code that relies on a dictionary. Here is a summary of the key dictionary calls that are used to construct an error object that is passed back to the app to report the error.

In the Objective-C version of the Master-Detail Application template, the accessor (specifically the getter) for `persistentStoreCoordinator` checks to see if the object exists. If it does, it is returned. If it doesn't, it is created and then it is returned.

In Swift, this is handled more easily (and with less code). The `var persistentStoreCoordinator` is declared with the following initialization code. The keyword `lazy` at the beginning of the declaration indicates that this code should be used for *lazy loading* — don't execute it until you actually need to reference the variable. If for some reason the app never needs to reference `persistentStoreCoordinator` (that would probably only occur if it encountered an error during startup), this code would never execute.

The full code is shown in Listing 7-3, but don't let its length bother you. Immediately after Listing 7-3, the code is broken apart into manageable chunks — one of which shows you the details of using an error dictionary.

As noted previously, this code is the declaration and initialization of a variable (persistentStoreCoordinator). It is loaded lazily (that is, as needed). It is an optional of type NSPersistentStoreCoordinator (see Chapter 6 for more about optionals). An initializer can have parameters, although this one doesn't. It does, however, have the parentheses that would be needed for parameters. Thus, the basic structure is:

```
lazy var persistentStoreCoordinator:
  NSPersistentStoreCoordinator? =
{
  //create coordinator
  return coordinator
} () //no initialization parameters
```

After some setup processing, addPersistentStoreWithType is called on coordinator, which was created in the setup processing. For the moment, there's only one line of setup code that matters:

```
  var error: NSError? = nil
```

A variable named error of type NSError is an optional (that's the significance of the question mark), and it's set to nil.

If the function fails to return a persistent store, that means there's an error. Here's the call to the function and the test for the result:

```
    if
      coordinator!.addPersistentStoreWithType(NSSQLiteStoreType,
        configuration: nil,
                  URL: url,
              options: nil,
                error: &error) == nil
      {
```

This pattern is used frequently, so it's worth taking the time to understand it. At the highest level the test is whether or not the result of addPersistentStoreWithType is nil. If it is, that means that the persistent store couldn't be created and the app can't really continue — although failing gracefully is a desired outcome.

In order to fail gracefully, addPersistentStoreWithType uses an inout parameter for the error parameter. The & indicates that the parameter is returned with a value (other parameters are not passed back by a function).

Listing 7-3: Using an Error Dictionary

```
lazy var persistentStoreCoordinator: NSPersistentStoreCoordinator? = {
  // The persistent store coordinator for the application. This
  // implementation creates and return a coordinator, having added
  // the store for the application to it. This property is optional
  // since there are legitimate error conditions that could cause
  // the creation of the store to fail.

  // Create the coordinator and store
  var coordinator: NSPersistentStoreCoordinator? =
    NSPersistentStoreCoordinator(
      managedObjectModel: self.managedObjectModel)
  let url =
    self.applicationDocumentsDirectory.URLByAppendingPathComponent
      ("Locatapp.sqlite")
  var error: NSError? = nil
  var failureReason =
    "There was an error creating or loading the application's
     saved data."
  if
    coordinator!.addPersistentStoreWithType(NSSQLiteStoreType,
      configuration: nil,
               URL: url,
            options: nil,
              error: &error) == nil
    {
      coordinator = nil
      // Report any error we got.
      let dict = NSMutableDictionary()
      dict[NSLocalizedDescriptionKey] =
        "Failed to initialize the application's saved data"
      dict[NSLocalizedFailureReasonErrorKey] = failureReason
      dict[NSUnderlyingErrorKey] = error

      error = NSError(
        domain: "YOUR_ERROR_DOMAIN",
          code: 9999,
      userInfo: dict)

      // Comment deleted
      NSLog("Unresolved error \(error), \(error!.userInfo)")
      abort()
    }

  return coordinator
  }()
```

Thus, there are two results of this function call:

- The result of the function call can be `nil` (failure) or a value of the persistent store coordinator.
- If there has been a failure, the `inout` parameter `error` has a value that it passes back. The startup processing sets `error` to `nil`, and it's only set to another value in the function if there's been an error.

If the result of `addPersistentStoreWithType` is `nil` (that is, there was an error), the coordinator that got an error on `addPersistentStoreWithType: configuration: URL: options: error:` is set to `nil`, and the error is reported. Here's the code:

```
coordinator = nil

// Report any error we got.

let dict = NSMutableDictionary()
dict[NSLocalizedDescriptionKey] =
  "Failed to initialize the application's saved data"
dict[NSLocalizedFailureReasonErrorKey] = failureReason
dict[NSUnderlyingErrorKey] = error

error = NSError(
  domain: "YOUR_ERROR_DOMAIN",
    code: 9999,
userInfo: dict)

// Comment deleted
NSLog("Unresolved error \(error), \(error!.userInfo)")
abort()
```

A mutable dictionary (`dict`) is created. The keys `NSLocalizedDescriptionKey`, `NSLocalizedFailureReasonErrorKey`, and `NSUnderlyingErrorKey` are set to appropriate values. Note that the value of the `&error` parameter that was returned from the function is used to set `NSUnderlyingErrorKey`.

A new `NSError` is used to reset the error variable. `NSError` is initialized with constants for domain and code, but notice that the `userInfo` parameter is initialized with the entire contents of the `dict` dictionary. This means that all of the information can be displayed in this log statement:

```
NSLog("Unresolved error \(error), \(error!.userInfo)")
```

You'll encounter this code many times, so it's worthwhile to look at it. It's a bit complex because it mingles Swift and Objective-C code, but after you understand the basics of dictionaries and variables, you'll see that it's all just a matter of combining keys and values in a dictionary — and that a dictionary itself can contain another dictionary as one of its elements.

Chapter 8

Controlling the Flow

In This Chapter

- Redirecting the flow of Swift's code with flow controls
- Using `for` and `while` loops
- Working with conditions

Code is executed sequentially — line after line of code. That sequential flow is interrupted in two ways:

- **Through the use of *flow controls* — code structures that modify the sequential flow of code.** Usually the term *flow controls* refers to conditional statements and various types of loops. Occasionally they explicitly change the flow by forcing the app to jump out of the current function either to a specific command or, more frequently, to whatever it was that called the function. All of these force the "next" line of code to be something other than the next line of code in the source file.
- **By *functions and closures* — sections of code implemented in response to certain conditions.** Those conditions can be events, such as the completion of an asynchronous process, or they can be references within the code that fire off synchronous or asynchronous processes. All of these disrupt the next-line structure to start processing in response to an event.

These concepts are implemented in different ways in different languages. This chapter gives you the basics of flow controls in Swift.

Looping through Code

No matter which programming languages you know (and you do know at least one, don't you?) you'll have encountered loops. Swift also supports loops, and, as you'll see, Swift's loops include variations and simplifications not found in other languages.

There are two basic types of loops: *for loops,* which include some kind of counter, and *while loops,* which rely on specified conditions for their continued operation.

There's another form of loop that you may have used: a *polling loop*. This loop repeatedly checks (or *polls*) a condition, such as whether the user's mouse button is still down or whether a communications link is still active. You can implement a polling loop in Swift with a `while` loop — but *don't.* Polling loops are very expensive: In order to repeatedly check their condition, they tie up the computer's resources. With a message-based operating system such as Cocoa or Cocoa Touch, you can observe the event or condition and be notified only when its state changes. In this way, the operating system and the framework do the polling for you. You'll find more on this topic in Chapter 18, "Using Protocols to Provide Templates for Functionality."

Using for loops

`For` loops are one of the most basic programming structures: They let you execute a section of code repeatedly based on some type of control (which is the *for* in a `for` loop).

Swift supports two types of `for` loops:

- `for-in` loops
- `for-condition-increment` loops

These are discussed in the next few sections.

These loops aren't new: `for-condition-increment` loops have been around since the dawn of computer languages, whereas `for-in` loops (sometimes called *iterators*) are closely intertwined with object-oriented programming and were first seen in the 1970s. Even if you've been programming for a while, `for-in` loops may be new to you. In the sections that follow, I discuss for-in loops at more length than other loops — partly because they're somewhat rare, and partly because some Swift developers find that they use them more than the other types of loops.

Working with for-in loops

Although they may be new to you, `for-in` loops are not unique to Swift. They're used in other object-oriented programming languages (such as Python, Scala, and C++), and are particularly useful in working with collections of items — as opposed to indexed values in arrays.

Objects indexed in an array have a clear, unambiguous sequence. (Two elements can't have the exact same index). If you want to construct a loop that processes each array element, then using a `for` loop to work with indexes is a great approach, as I discuss in the next section, "Working with `for-condition-increment` loops."

In collections of objects or other data elements, however, the contained elements may be unindexed and in no obvious order. In these cases, the elements are members of some collection or other, and are identified individually through means other than index numbers. In fact, in some collections, identifying individual items is not necessary or even impossible. For these collections, all you may know is it's a collection, and that it has elements.

For more information about collections, see Chapter 7, "Collecting Objects."

Scanning through an array in undefined order can be a nuisance, but in a large number of cases, the sequence of presentation is irrelevant: You simply want to deal with each bank account, each appointment, each bill, each friend, and so forth. As long as you access each element, and omit none, everything is fine.

The object behind the Swift syntax for a `for-in` loop relies on two protocols: `Sequence` and `Generator`. `Generator` contains a `next` function, which is the heart of the matter. If you have a class or structure that adopts the `Sequence` protocol (and through that, adopts `Generator`), you can access the `next` function that can be used by an iterator. Whether `next` is interpreted to be random or ordered depends on the class or structure that contains it. The interpretation of `next`, in other words, is dependent on the class or structure: It may be a random `next` element or it may be an ordered `next` element. From the high-level Swift perspective, `next` is undefined except that it provides an element according to the rules of the structure or class that is considered to be "next." In life, we usually pair "next" with some context such as "next student in line," "next meeting," or "next week." In writing your code, it is usually safest to assume that there is no predetermined order unless you are certain that there is one.

The Swift syntax for `for-in` loops is

```
for <item> in <collection> {
  <statements>
}
```

Note that all italicized terms (and the < and > characters) are general descriptions of missing syntax elements. They aren't intended to be seen as part of the syntax itself, or to be typed verbatim. In the syntax above, these terms are:

- **`<item>`**: This refers to an element of a collection. It contains a different element each time the loop is evaluated.
- **`<collection>`**: This can be any structure or class that conforms to the `Sequence` protocol. Don't bother looking it up in the Swift documentation, however: Most of the time you'll just use a `collection` object, as I discuss in Chapter 7.

  You can also use a range or an array here. For more on ranges, see Chapter 5.
- **`<statements>`**: These refer to Swift code statements, and can include more or less anything you want (and as many statements as you want).

Why are there so few `for` loops in frameworks and templates?

A great way to learn Swift (or Objective-C, for that matter) is to create new projects from the built-in Xcode templates. Just create a project, build it, and run it in iOS Simulator (or directly on your Mac). Explore the code and watch how it functions. If you do this and then use the Search navigator to find instances of the word *for* in the source code, you may be surprised by the results. You'll find *for* in comments — as in, say, part of the word *before* — and you'll find it in named parameters such as `forKey`, but you won't often find it in actual `for-in` loops (or in other loops) in the templates.

The absence of `for` loops here reflects the role of the frameworks and, to a lesser extent, the templates. Frameworks provide your app's overall structure. They typically take care of the user interface and the basics of user interaction, and it's here, among these processes, that loops often occur. Generally, you'll only be concerned with overriding classes for specific data elements or functions. This sort of management happens in the framework, often by looping, and in most cases you provide these loops' internal functionality. In other words, the loop and other UI code control the flow, but your implementation of a specific class provides the detailed functionality.

This means that a large part of your app's flow control is already implemented for you in Cocoa and Cocoa Touch. Although you need a basic understanding of loops and the ways control works in an app, most of the time you should be focused on other matters — namely, the details of your implementations of functionality that take place underneath the top-level flow control. If you're tempted to write loops to work through every window or every button or every, well, *anything* — give it a second thought. This is typically the framework's job, and your effort is probably better spent elsewhere.

The following steps build code on which you experiment with a `for-in` loop. It will be shown later in Figure 8-1 and Listing 8-1 with some additions that will be added later. As you have seen in other chapters, start by creating a playground using Swift for either iOS or OS X.

1. **Declare a collection for the `for-in` loop to use.**

   Make this declaration by using a statement such as the following:

   ```
   var elements = [1, 3, 5, 17, -1]
   ```

   In this case, the declared collection is a variable, but it could be a constant or any other type of collection.

2. **Create the `for-in` loop.**

   Here's an example:

   ```
   for myElement in elements {
     // do something with myElement
   }
   ```

   Note that this is the loop's declaration. You don't need to add a separate declaration for `myElement`. In fact, doing so declares a separate variable.

   The loop uses the collection you declared or referenced in Step 1. Here `myElement` is filled with each value of the loop; you can use it inside the loop.

   You can do whatever you want with the iterated element inside a loop.

Here are some variations on `for-in` loops.

- **Performing a test on the item:** Often you perform a test on item, but you may also use it as part of an operation. Sometimes you do both. As an example, the following code, placed within the loop, tests whether the value of the iterated element is a negative number; if it is, it prints out that value.

  ```
  if myElement < 0 {
    println (  " \(myElement.description) is a negative
      number")
  }
  ```

- **Breaking out of the loop:** If you're searching a collection for the highest or lowest numeric value, such as the highest game score, you'll have to search all the values in the collection, so this variation won't help you. On the other hand, if you're trying to find a specific value, or a value that fulfills certain conditions, this one's for you. When doing such a search, you'll want to stop searching the moment you've found the value you're looking for. To terminate the loop at that point, just add a `break` statement. This statement drops you out of the loop and executes the next statement beyond it, as shown here:

```
if myElement < 0 {
  println (  " \(myElement.description)is a negative
    number")
  break;
}
```

- **Identifying the `item` in each iteration:** As you may recall, the `item` in a `for-in` loop contains the element from the collection. This element may be a value, as shown in the code here, but it can just as easily be an object. In the case of an ordered collection, such as an array, you may want to know the element's index number. Because this information isn't part of the `for-in` loop, you'll need to calculate it.

  See the section, "Working with for-condition-increment loops," later in this chapter, to see another way of getting this information.

  To perform this calculation, you must first create a counter. This counter creates a unique value for each element within the loop. To create one, follow these steps (refer to Figure 8-1 or Listing 8-1):

  a. *Create a counter variable outside the loop.*

     Make certain this is a variable declared with `var`, not a constant declared with `let`. Use a statement such as the following:

     ```
     var index = 0
     ```

  b. *Inside the loop, increment the counter.*

     ```
     index++
     ```

  Now the body of your loop may look like this:

  ```
  var index = 0
  if myElement < 0 {
    println (  " \(myElement.description)at \(index) is
          a negative number")
   }
  index++
  ```

  Before adding your counter, decide how you want to number the elements in the `for-in` loop. The index values in an array begin at 0, but depending on your needs, you may want to set your counter value to start at 1 or any other number. In the first step above, set your initial counter/index number. If you want the first element that passes through the loop to be 0, place your increment statement at the end of the loop. This ensures that your counter will remain 0 the first time through. However, at the end of the first iteration, the counter's value will be 1, which will be the value used during the second iteration (that is, for the second value).

If you want to start at 1 right away, however, set your counter variable to 1 when you create it. (Or, alternatively, set it to 0 and increment it at the beginning of the loop.)

- **Ignoring the `item`:** Sometimes, you don't need to do anything to the `item` returned from each iteration. In that case, you can replace it with an underscore character, as in the following:

  ```
  for _ in elements {
  ```

  In this case, if you find you need to reference the `item` later, use the technique described in the previous bullet to identify it.

- **Iterating over a dictionary:** You can iterate over a dictionary in exactly the same way that you iterate over any other collection. The only difference is that the `item` in the syntax (that is, each item that's passed to the loop as it processes) is a tuple consisting of the key and value for a dictionary element. Thus, a `for-in` loop for a dictionary will look like this:

  ```
  for (myKey, myValue) in myDictionary {
    //do something with myKey and myValue
  }
  ```

Figure 8-1 and Listing 8-1 show the code as it may be at this point (not all of the options discussed are shown in the code).

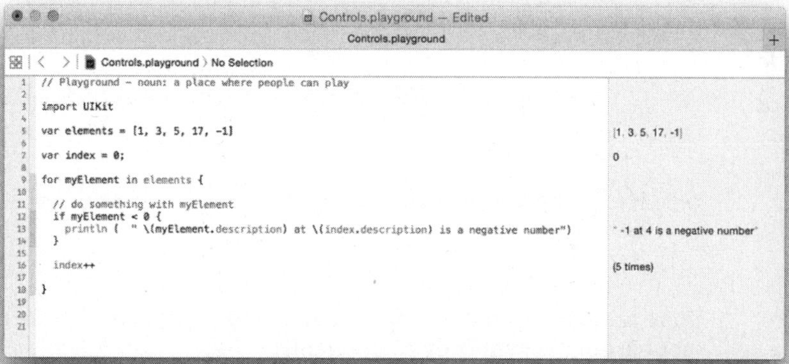

Figure 8-1: Using a `for-in` loop.

Listing 8-1: Using a for-in Loop to Manage a Collection

```
// Playground - noun: a place where people can play

var elements = [1, 3, 5, 17, -1]

var index = 0;

for myElement in elements {

  // do something with myElement
  if myElement < 0 {
    println (  " \(myElement.description) at
      \(index.description) is a negative number")
  }

  index++
}
```

Working with for-condition-increment loops

Now we can turn our attention to `for-condition-increment` loops, which are the classic `for` statements you may have seen in C and other legacy programming languages. Swift's way of handling these loops is more or less what you might expect — with one possible exception: The loop control does not need to be enclosed in parentheses. It *can* be, that is, but it need not be.

The Swift syntax for `for-condition-increment` loops is:

```
for <initialization>; <condition>; <increment>{
  <statements>
}

for <initialization>; <condition>; <increment>{
  <statements>
}
```

Here are the non-syntax components of the syntax (remember the < and > are not part of the syntax or component):

- **`<initialization>`:** Initializes the index counter. The index counter must be declared before it is used.
- **`<condition>`:** Specifies the condition according to which the counter continues to be incremented. This condition is checked during every pass through the loop, and the counter is incremented (by *`increment`*, discussed next) until *`condition`* fails. When *`condition`* fails, the *`for-condition-increment`* loop terminates.

- **<*increment*>**: Specifies the expression to use to increment the index counter. A common increment is `myCounter ++`, which increments the counter by 1, but you can use any increment you want — including fractions, negative numbers, and even expressions.
- **<*statements*>**: These refer to Swift code statements, and can include more or less anything you want (and as many statements as you want).

Listing 8-2 recasts the loop from Listing 8-1 using a `for-condition-increment` loop. Note the fourth line of code: You might expect this line to appear with parentheses, as follows:

```
for (myElementCounter=0; myElementCounter <5;
  myElementCounter ++) {
```

You can use the parentheses, but you don't have to. Do whatever is easiest for you and the people you work with. (Remember that you're usually writing for other people on your team — either today or in the future.) Whatever you do, try to be consistent.

Here are the steps to create a `for-condition-increment` loop like the one in Listing 8-2. Begin with a new playground set up for iOS or OS X.

1. **Declare a collection for the `for-condition-increment` loop to use.**

   You can either create a new collection or use the collection (`elements`) defined in the previous section:

   ```
   var elements = [1, 3, 5, 17, -1]
   ```

Listing 8-2: Using a for-increment Loop

```
// Playground - noun: a place where people can play

var elements = [1, 3, 5, 17, -1]

var myElementCounter = 0;

for myElementCounter =0; myElementCounter <5;
  myElementCounter ++ {

  // do something with myElement
  if elements[myElementCounter] > 15 {
    println (  " \(elements[myElementCounter].description)
      at \( myElementCounter.description) is greater than
      15")
  }
}
```

2. **Create and initialize a variable to use as a counter, such as `myElementCounter`.**

   As you may recall, this step is unnecessary with basic `for-in` loops, whose "counter" is implicitly declared in the `for` statement. (Incremented counters aren't used in `for-in` loops; instead, each element in the collection is returned one-by-one.) If you need to be able to identify the n-th element of the collection, you will need to calculate your own index with a `for-in` loop just as you are doing here.

3. **Set up the loop control.**

   Here's where you write the `for` statement. Make sure to initialize your counter variable correctly and to set the *`condition`* and *`increment`* according to your needs. An example:

```
for myElementCounter =0; myElementCounter <5;
  myElementCounter++ {
```

4. **Inside the loop, process each element.**

   Instead of simply getting the element as part of the `for` statement, as in `for-in` loops, with `for-condition-increment` loops, you must subscript the array using the counter (see Figure 8-2):

```
  // do something with myElement
  if elements[myElementCounter] > 15 {
    println (  "
      \(elements[myElementCounter].description)
      at \( myElementCounter.description) is a
   negative
      number")
  }
```

   If you think this makes `for-in` loops simpler than `for-condition-increment` loops, well, you're right.

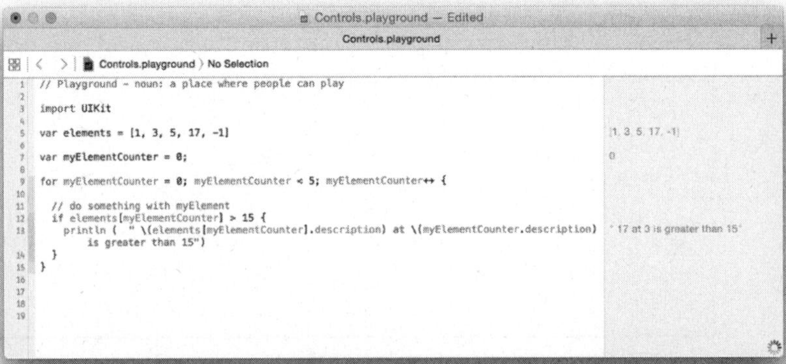

```
Controls.playground — Edited
Controls.playground
Controls.playground > No Selection
1  // Playground - noun: a place where people can play
2
3  import UIKit
4
5  var elements = [1, 3, 5, 17, -1]                         [1, 3, 5, 17, -1]
6
7  var myElementCounter = 0;                                0
8
9  for myElementCounter = 0; myElementCounter < 5; myElementCounter++ {
10
11   // do something with myElement
12   if elements[myElementCounter] > 15 {
13     println (  " \(elements[myElementCounter].description) at \(myElementCounter.description)
         is greater than 15")                                " 17 at 3 is greater than 15"
14   }
15 }
16
17
18
19
```

Figure 8-2: Using a for-condition-increment loop.

Using while loops

As is the case in other languages, Swift supports `while` loops. In `for-condition-increment` loops, the syntax requires both a condition and an increment, as you may recall. However, in `while` loops, the basic syntax requires only a condition. Here's a simple `while` loop:

```
while myValue < 10 {
  // do something
]
```

In this loop, `myValue` is the condition. Keep in mind, however, that you must eventually change the value of `myValue`. If `myValue` remains unchanged while the loop is executing, the loop is either an infinite loop or one that doesn't execute at all.

Note, though, that the condition in a `while` loop also can be an expression, so at times a `while` loop can closely resemble a `for-condition-increment` loop, as in the following (see Figure 8-3):

```
var myValue = 5
while myValue++ < 10 {
  // do something
]
```

The three components of a `for-condition-increment` loop are present here — the declaration of `myValue` and its initial value (remember, Swift requires initialization); the condition (`< 10`); and the increment (`myValue ++`).

`While` loops have two formats:

- **`do <action>-while <condition>`:** With this format, the *`action`* is always performed at least once. The *`condition`* is evaluated only after the *`action`* is performed, and if found true, the *`action`* is performed again (possibly even more times).
- **`while-<condition>-do <action>`:** Here the *`condition`* is evaluated first. If it's true, the *`action`* is performed. The loop repeats by performing the *`action`* and then re-evaluating the *`condition`*.

Both forms of `while` loops are similar to those in other languages. The one slight difference is that the condition in other languages may need to be placed in parentheses.

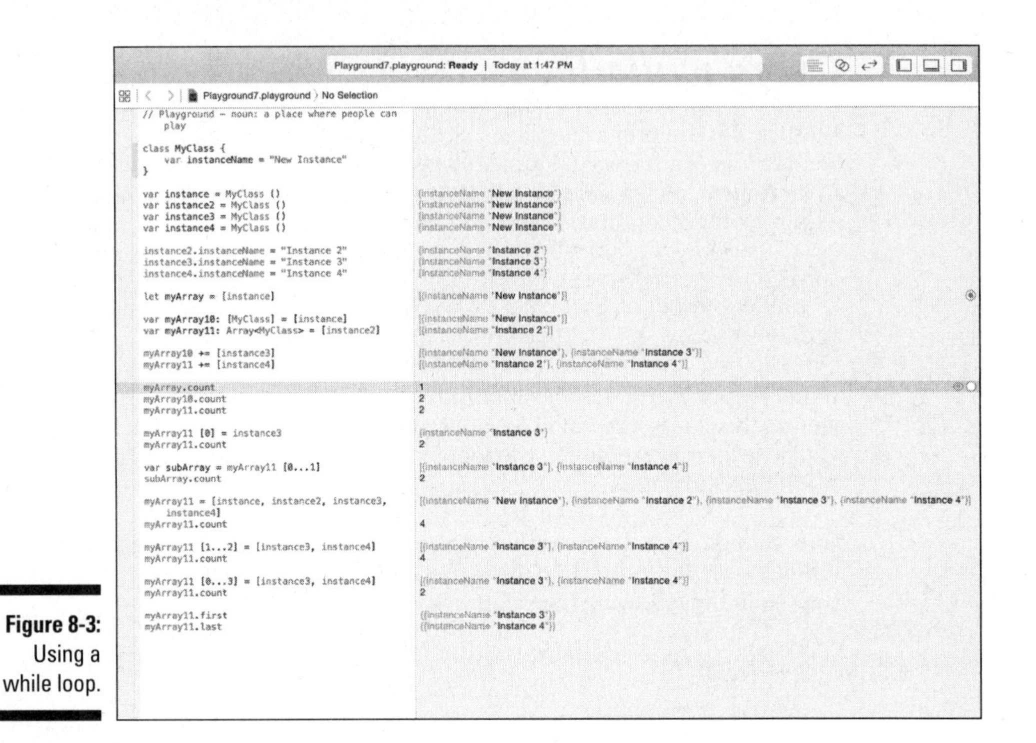

Figure 8-3: Using a while loop.

Using Conditions

The one-thing-after-another structure of most code is interrupted in a number of ways. The most basic way is to use *conditions* — in Swift, as in most other programming languages, this means using `if` or `switch` statements.

`if` statements in Swift are very similar to those in other languages, whereas switches have significant variations.

Cocoa and Cocoa Touch, together with the Darwin core on which OS X and iOS rest, support sophisticated messaging. Messaging allows non-linear processing — a critical component of iOS and OS X. With messaging, you set up your app or sections of it to receive notifications rather than periodically (or constantly!) checking to see the status of something. This tends to reduce the use of conditional statements.

Working with `if` statements

In Swift, `if` statements are easy to discuss because they're used in a way that's similar to the way other languages use them. Here's the Swift syntax for a simple `if` statement:

```
if <condition> {
  <statements>
}
```

Similarly, a *compound `if` statement* (sometimes called an *`if-else` statement*) has two branches:

```
if <condition> {
  <statements for true>
} else {
  <statements for false>
}
```

The biggest difference between the way Swift and most other languages use `if` statements is that, in Swift, the condition doesn't have to be placed in parentheses. It *can* be, but it's not required.

Another difference: in Swift, *`condition`* can be a Boolean expression, or an expression or variable of any type that conforms to the *`BooleanType`* protocol. This difference isn't obvious from the syntax examples, but it's a very important aspect of Swift. It's an example of how a protocol can allow a type to be of one type (or a subclass of one type) and also conform to a protocol which in some ways has the appearance of a class. Thus, a class can combine features of itself or its superclass(es) with the methods of a protocol. (See Chapter 18 for an in-depth discussion of protocols.)

Working with switches

Here's the formal syntax of `switch` statements in Swift:

```
switch <control expression> {
  case <pattern 1>:
     <statements>
  case <pattern 2> where <condition>:
    <statements>
  case <pattern 3> where <condition,
     <pattern 4> where condition>:
    <statements>
  default:
    <statements>
}
```

Figure 8-4 shows a `switch` statement in a playground. Note that the spacing in Figure 8-4 is different from the spacing shown in this chapter. This doesn't matter from the standpoint of syntax, but it does matter in making your code readable. Choose whatever style you like (and set your Xcode preferences to match in the Text Edit tab of Preferences).

Swift `switch` statements have some significant differences from `switch` statements in other languages. A list of the differences suggests the problems that people have had over the years with C-style `switch` statements. These include the problems that are solved with the following Swift features:

- **Exhaustivity:** A `switch` statement in Swift must cover every possible value for the control expression. Before you tear your hair out, remember that you can accomplish that goal by always including a `default` case.
- **Falling through:** Just about every programmer has experienced the "joy" of falling through from one `case` statement to the next. In many other languages, a `break` statement must be included at the end of a `case` statement; if it isn't, control passes to the next `case` statement. With Swift, after you move into a `case` statement and it executes, control passes to the first statement after the `switch` statement.
- **Guard clause:** As in other languages, a `switch` statement contains one or more `case` statements. In Swift, you can add a *guard clause,* which begins with `where`. This allows you to have several `case` statements that match a single control expression value and to further refine their structure with the guard clause. A guard clause is similar to an `AND` statement in a query in that it refines the basic `case` statement with additional considerations.

```
8a.playground — Edited
8a.playground 〉 No Selection
// Playground - noun: a place where people can play

var elements = [1, 3, 5, 17, -1]                                   [1, 3, 5, 17, -1]

var myElementCounter = 0                                           0

for myElementCounter = 0; myElementCounter < 5; myElementCounter++ {
    if elements [myElementCounter] > 15 {
        println ( " \(elements[myElementCounter].description) at \(myElementCounter.description) is greater than 15")   " 17 at 3 is greater than 15"
    }
}
```

Figure 8-4: Using a Swift `switch`.

In Figure 8-4, you see an example of a guard clause:

```
case "sample text" where guardExpression == "guard":
```

This `case` statement is executed on in the case where the control expression at the top of the `switch` statement is equal to "sample text" *and* another variable called `guardExpression` is equal to "guard." You could also have additional `case` statements, such as the following:

```
case "sample text" where guardExpression == "guard 1":
case "sample text" where guardExpression == "guard 2":
case "sample text" where guardExpression == "guard 3":
```

A guard clause often eliminates the need to place an inner `switch` statement inside a `case` statement.

Transferring Control

A few other control transfer statements exist in Swift, such as those in the following list. Note that the first two are similar to statements in other languages:

- **`continue`:** You can use the `continue` statement in any of the loop statements discussed in this chapter. It ends that particular iteration of the loop and proceeds to the next one. Any further statements within that iteration are not performed.
- **`break`:** A `break` statement terminates a loop iteration or the current case of a `switch` statement. Control transfers to the first statement after the `switch` statement or loop.
- **`fallthrough`:** This statement explicitly duplicates the behavior of `case` statements inside `switch` statements in other languages. When placed within a `case` statement, it transfers control to the next `case` statement in the `switch` statement.

Many people believe that relying on this type of structure is dangerous, and they avoid using this technique.

Using Assertions

Assertions aren't new in software development. The first known reference to them is from a talk given by Alan Turing in 1949. Turing's point, which is still valid today, is that it is not practical to thoroughly check every single decision point in a program. The combinations of choices in conditional statements (much less the variations in data and hardware conditions) quickly make the number of combinations and permutations enormous. Although we do attempt to check every decision point and design assumption, assertions are a powerful tool for keeping an app running properly.

An assertion simply presents a condition in the form of a Boolean expression that must be true. Regardless of the programming path that has been taken (which may contain design or implementation errors), without regard to the data (which may contain user errors), and without considering hardware and network connections that may act in erratic and sometimes non-repeatable ways, a certain condition must be true (or false) if the app is to continue.

In the development and debugging phases of app development, assertions can help you work back to find logical flaws. These assertions may be removed (or, more commonly, commented out) in the production versions of the app. Other assertions may remain in a shipping app to catch serious problems.

Assertions may or may not display an error message to the log (they typically do), and they cause the app to terminate. This is a pretty dramatic step, but it is invaluable during debugging, and may be needed in a shipping app because in the case of an erratic error, the message may be able to guide you (and users) to the true source of the problem.

The global function `assert` is used to implement an assertion. It takes two parameters: a Boolean expression and an optional string, as in:

```
assert (idNumber == 0, "missing ID number")
```

Note that this is an error condition that probably could be managed in validation routines for data entry. However, if you are far from data entry in your app and must assume that all of those validation routines have already been passed, this assertion would catch a deliberate deletion of the value by a line of code that is wrong.

Wherever possible, use standard error-checking routines and other techniques instead of assertions.

Chapter 9

Functioning Successfully

In This Chapter

- Looking at functions
- Adding functions for location support
- Creating an action function

In Swift, functions and types play a larger role than they do in some other object-oriented languages. The whole idea of objects containing both data and functionality (or, in Swift terms, properties and methods) is central.

It makes for a neat package.

Named types share important characteristics with objects. One of the most important shared characteristics is that all named types can contain functions: Yes, you can place functions in structures and enumerations as well as in classes. (In classes, however, functions are generally referred to as *methods*.)

That last point is very important. This chapter is about functions wherever they reside — in classes, enumerations, structures, or even inside other functions or at a global level of your app. When in classes, functions are referred to as methods, but they're still functions underneath. Keep this in mind as you read this chapter.

In 'Chapter 4, you set up Locatapp to use as a running example in this book. In this chapter (and in many that follow), you build on Locatapp. If you haven't created it, you have three choices:

- Download it from the Chapter 4 files at this book's companion website, as described in the Introduction.
- Work through Chapter 4 to create it.
- Use the summary that follows to create it. This is a shorter version of the steps in Chapter 4. It can serve as a review as well as a guideline for creating new apps once you've read the in-depth instructions in Chapter 4.

Setting the Stage for the Social Media Location App

This book focuses on Swift, but other components are important for app development in iOS and OS X, including Xcode (the integrated development environment — IDE) and Objective-C, as well as the Cocoa and Cocoa Touch frameworks.

Although Swift is the future of development for Cocoa and Cocoa Touch, many frameworks are still written in Objective-C. The interface between Objective-C and Swift works both ways, so you can easily interact with Objective-C frameworks. In fact, the interaction is so simple, you can do this without even knowing much about Objective-C.

In this section, you work with the project that is the main example in this book. These steps guide you through the creation of the project itself. Accordingly, not all of these steps are Swift-related, strictly speaking, but they help you create a project so you can write and rewrite your Swift code. Just follow these steps, and you'll be on your way.

Introducing Locatapp

In Part I, "Getting Started with Swift," I provided an overview of Xcode and showed you how to put a project together. In Chapter 4, I described the app that serves as an example in this book — a social media location app. It uses Cocoa Touch and its frameworks to let you display a user's location and store it in a Core Data store. Part of the beauty of this app is that it does a lot without much work on your part. It has an interface to social media, such as Facebook and Twitter, as well as other communication tools like messages and email. It also has a fully-functioning database, although the example app uses only the basics.

How can a database be part of "only the basics"?

Some people wonder how a database can find a place in an app that uses "only the basics." The fact of the matter is that data management is emphatically one of the basics of modern app development. There are a number of ways of managing app data: You can store it using tools such as key-value coding (KVC), which is built into the Cocoa and Cocoa Touch frameworks. You can store the app's data for each user on the local device, or in iCloud (or both). In addition to structuring data using KVC, you can use Core Data, the persistent store that's built into

Cocoa and Cocoa Touch. It uses the SQLite library for its actual storage (optionally XML as well on Macs), and it's an object-oriented relational database system that provides more complex data storage than does KVC.

Other apps use data stored in places such as Amazon Web Services (AWS) and other cloud services. This is a good solution for data that needs to be shared between iOS or OS X apps and other apps and systems.

The amount and type of data storage that's needed depends on the app. For some games and lifestyle apps (such as HealthKit apps), it's sufficient to store game scores for each game and environmental or personal readings of items such as blood pressure and precipitation. Often, KVC is a good tool for this type and amount of data, and it's easy to share it with other Cocoa and Cocoa Touch apps. On the other hand, data such as the details of each move in a multi-person game may need more flexible and larger storage features that a persistent store like Core Data can provide or that a relational database accessible to other apps and systems can provide.

Finally, you can write out some data in your own format in a scratchpad that you create in your app's sandbox. That type of idiosyncratic data storage is probably the most widely used across the range of apps today, but the problems this type of storage creates are legion. They range from security to reliability to maintainability and back to security again.

With an understanding of this app — a mobile location-aware app that is integrated with social media — you're well on your way to building a wide variety of apps. In this chapter, you explore functions (called "*methods*" when they're in classes). In previous chapters, you learn the basics of Swift actions with the data (and collections of data) and flow control that you can use to build an app. Starting with this chapter, you put those basics together into an app.

There are a few points to bring up before we launch into the code. The first is the pretty obvious fact that the name "*Social Media Location App*" is a bit of a mouthful. From here on, I'll call it *Locatapp*.

Creating the Locatapp project

The Locatapp project is created from the built-in Master-Detail Application template in Xcode. The steps to do this are the same as they always are with building an Xcode project from a template: In summary, you create a new project from the Master-Detail Application template, save it to disk, and — this part is *very important* — run it as a test. If the unchanged template doesn't work properly, resolve the problems. Remember: Waiting for magic to happen is not a viable strategy.

If you have problems, use the resources you have as a registered developer, including access to the developer discussions on `developer.apple.com`. Searching on the web also works, but be sure that the results you find are for Swift and for the current version of Xcode that you're using. Outdated analyses and recommendations can cost you a lot of wasted time. Also, if you are a member of one of Apple's paid developer programs, remember that you are permitted two technical support incidents each year for each program. (This makes a total of four if you're both an iOS and OS X developer.) Using a tech-support incident to get yourself up and running can be a good investment. Another useful resource is Meetup — use it to find a local group.

The following steps create the Locatapp project from the Master-Detail Application in Xcode:

1. **Choose File➪New➪Project to open the dialog box shown in Figure 9-1.**
2. **Select Application from the iOS group at the top left of the dialog.**
3. **Select Master-Detail Application in the main section of the dialog.**
4. **Click Next.**
5. **Provide the product name and the other data, as shown in Figure 9-2.**

   Depending on your preferences and your past use of Xcode, some of the data such as the organization name and identifier may be filled in for you already. You can change the filled-in data if you want (and the changed organization name and identifier will be used automatically for your next project as well). The bundle identifier is created for you automatically as you enter the product name.
6. **Verify that the language is set to Swift.**

   The Universal devices option (both iPhone and iPad rather than only one or the other) is used in this book, along with Core Data if it's available (Core Data is not available for all of the project templates). If you

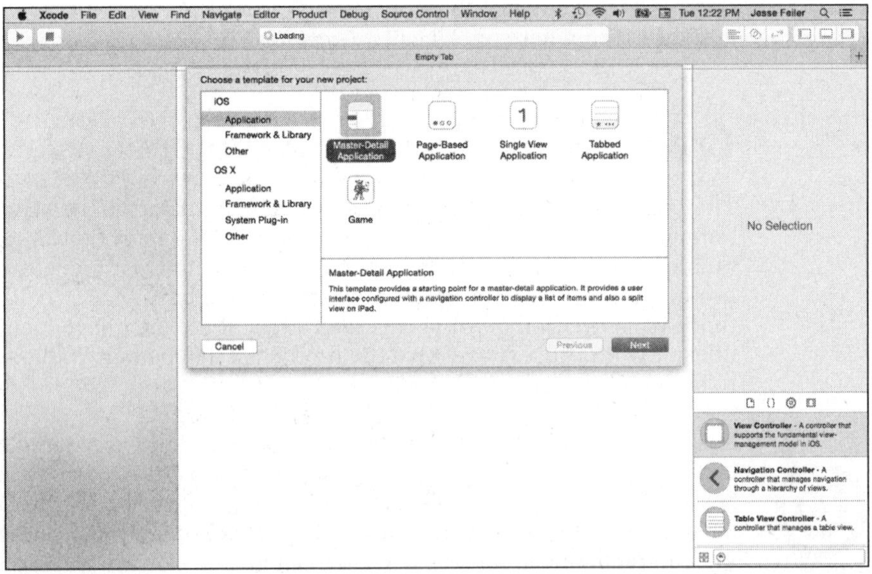

Figure 9-1: Choosing the Master-Detail Application template.

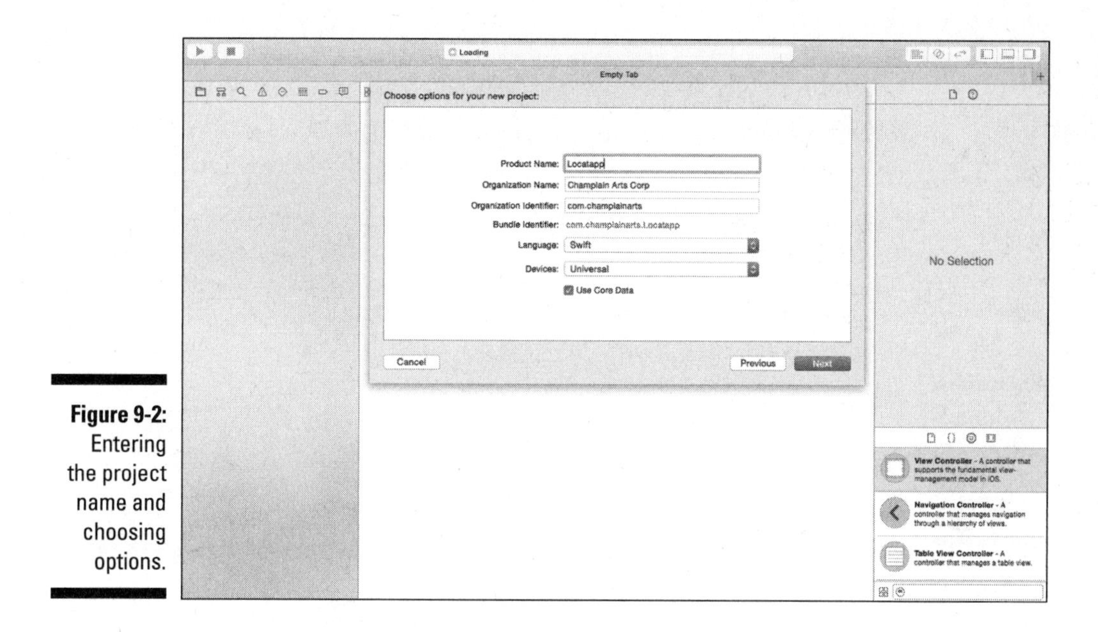

Figure 9-2: Entering the project name and choosing options.

have experience with Xcode and prefer other options, however, feel free to use them.

7. **Click Next.**
8. **Choose a location for your new project and click Create.**

   Whether to use the Source Control checkbox to create a Git repository is something you can decide for yourself. The simplest rule of thumb is: If you don't know what Git is, don't use it. (Even so, at some point you should learn about source control because it makes your life as a developer easier.)

9. **Review your project summary as shown in Figure 9-3.**

   Remember that the layout of the Xcode workspace window may change depending on your preferences. Using that project navigator at the left, choose the project itself and check out the files (shown in Figure 9-3) and the settings in the editor. At this point, having Team set to None (the default) is OK. An error because of the missing team may be shown, but that error can be ignored for now.

10. **Build and run the project.**

    You see the iOS Simulator with your app running in it. The simulator uses whatever device you have chosen at the top-left of the workspace window. You see the launch image (the leftmost screen in Figure 9-4) and then an empty list of objects (the second screen in Figure 9-4).

11. **Click + in the upper-right to add an entry (the third screen in Figure 9-4).**
12. **Select the entry. You now see it on the detail view (the last screen in Figure 9-4).**

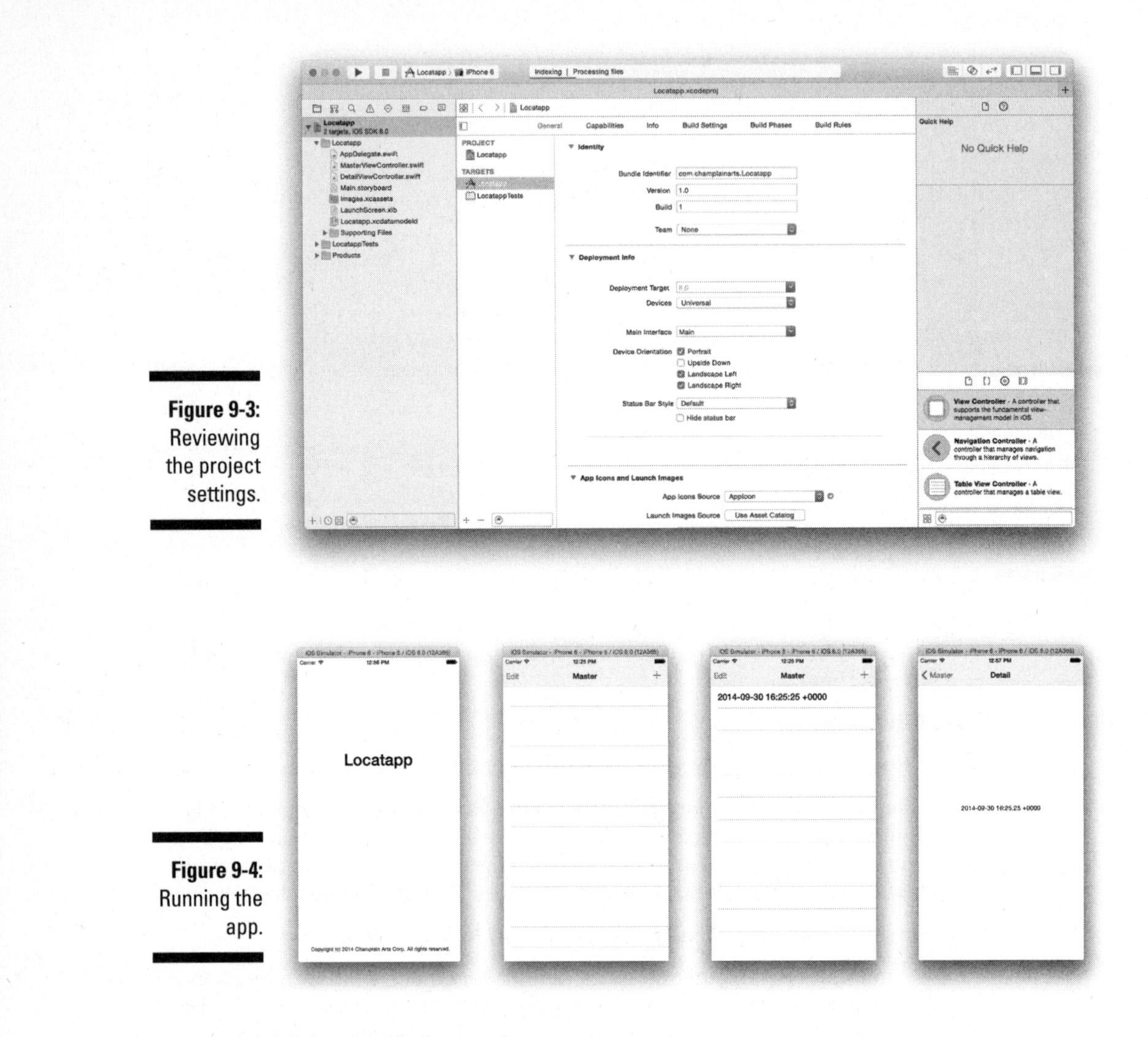

Figure 9-3: Reviewing the project settings.

Figure 9-4: Running the app.

Modifying the template

The default template lets you add events with the +; each one is annotated with a timestamp. For Locatapp, you use the same basic structure, but instead of creating entries with a timestamp, you will create entries that automatically pick up your location. The master view that lets you add entries and that displays the list of entries will now show the locations. When you click on a single item in that list, instead of showing the timestamp in a a full-screen view (as in the last screen in Figure 9-4 in Step 12 above), you'll see it on a map.

This app lets you work with MapKit and Core Location. Together with the table view controller built into the template, you're well on your way to building a customized and useful app.

As the name of the template suggests, this architecture relies on a master view and a detail view. It's a very common structure. Here's a bit more information about these views:

- **Master view:** This is the view shown in the middle two screens in Figure 9-4. It's a list of the items that have been created in the app. This list is implemented with a custom class called `MasterViewController` that is located in `MasterViewController.swift` in the template. `MasterViewController` is a subclass of `UITableViewController`.
- **Detail view:** When you select an item from the master view list, you see its details in the detail view (shown in the last screen in Figure 9-4). This is done with a custom class in the template called `DetailViewController`; it is a subclass of `UIViewController`, and is implemented in `DetailViewController.swift`.

The concept of master and detail views and their controllers is very common. They can be named anything you want, but frequently the naming conventions used here (master and detail) are used.

In the template, the detail view controller manages a view (an instance of class `UIView`) that contains a `UILabel` object (shown with the timestamp in the last screen in Figure 9-4). This view hierarchy is implemented in `Main.storyboard`.

A *storyboard* or *xib file* is the standard way of designing view hierarchies. Storyboards are the more modern way of doing so. `Main.storyboard` is built into the template. You draw your interface on a *canvas* in the storyboard. Although a few examples of storyboards appear in this book, storyboarding itself (as are all details of the Cocoa and Cocoa Touch frameworks) is beyond the scope of this book.

The following list gives you a high-level overview of the modifications to the Master-Detail Application template that you make at this point. Don't worry: The following sections provide the step-by-step details for you:

1. **Change the detail view controller so that it manages an instance of `MKMapView` rather than an instance of `UIView` with an instance of `UILabel` within it.**
2. **Remove references to the `UILabel` instance to avoid an error (referencing an object that's not there).**
3. **Adjust the map to show the user's location.**

4. **Make necessary changes to the data model so that instead of a timestamp, a location with latitude and longitude is stored.**
5. **Modify the master view controller so that the + creates a new entity with the user's current location rather than the current timestamp.**

Adding a `MKMapView` *view and removing the* `UIView` *and* `UILabel` *views*

Here are the steps to replace the `UIView` with a `MKMapView` in the detail view controller:

1. **Select Main.storyboard from the project navigator, as shown in Figure 9-5.**
2. **If necessary, choose Editor ⇨ Show Document Outline to reveal the document outline at the left. (That is, at the left of the editor; the project navigator is shown at the far left of the workspace window with the utilities area at the right.)**

   The editor's main section is the *canvas* with the graphical representation of the user interface and the optional document outline at the left.
3. **Open Detail Scene, and Detail view controller within it.**
4. **Select View within Detail as shown in Figure 9-5.**

   You may need to do some rearranging of the window. Figure 9-5 shows the utilities area at the right.
5. **With View selected, delete it with the Delete key.**

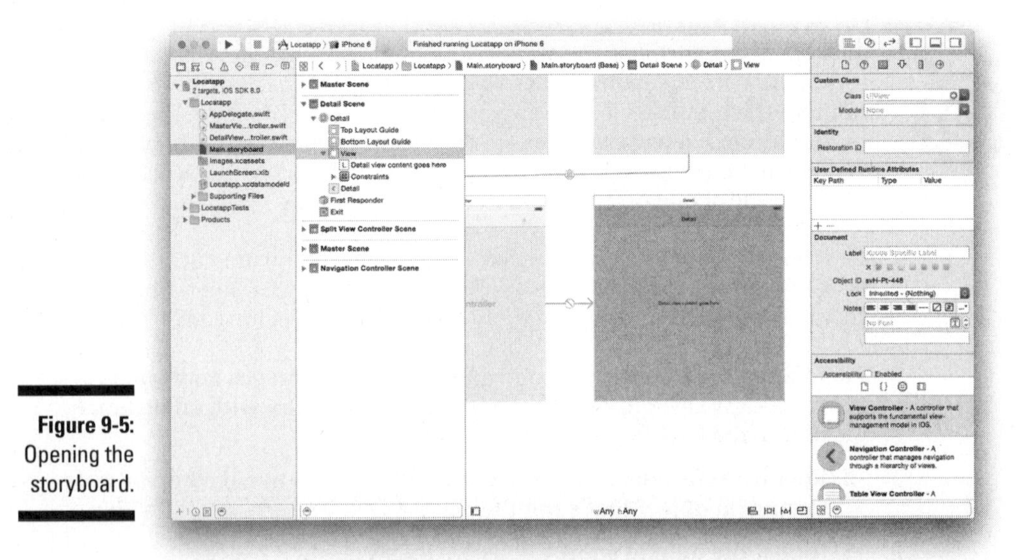

Figure 9-5: Opening the storyboard.

If it was opened, its subviews, layout guides, and constraints (shown in Figure 9-5) will also be deleted.

6. **Check that the document outline looks like the one in Figure 9-6.**
7. **Find `MapKit` View in the lower-right of Library, as shown in Figure 9-7.**

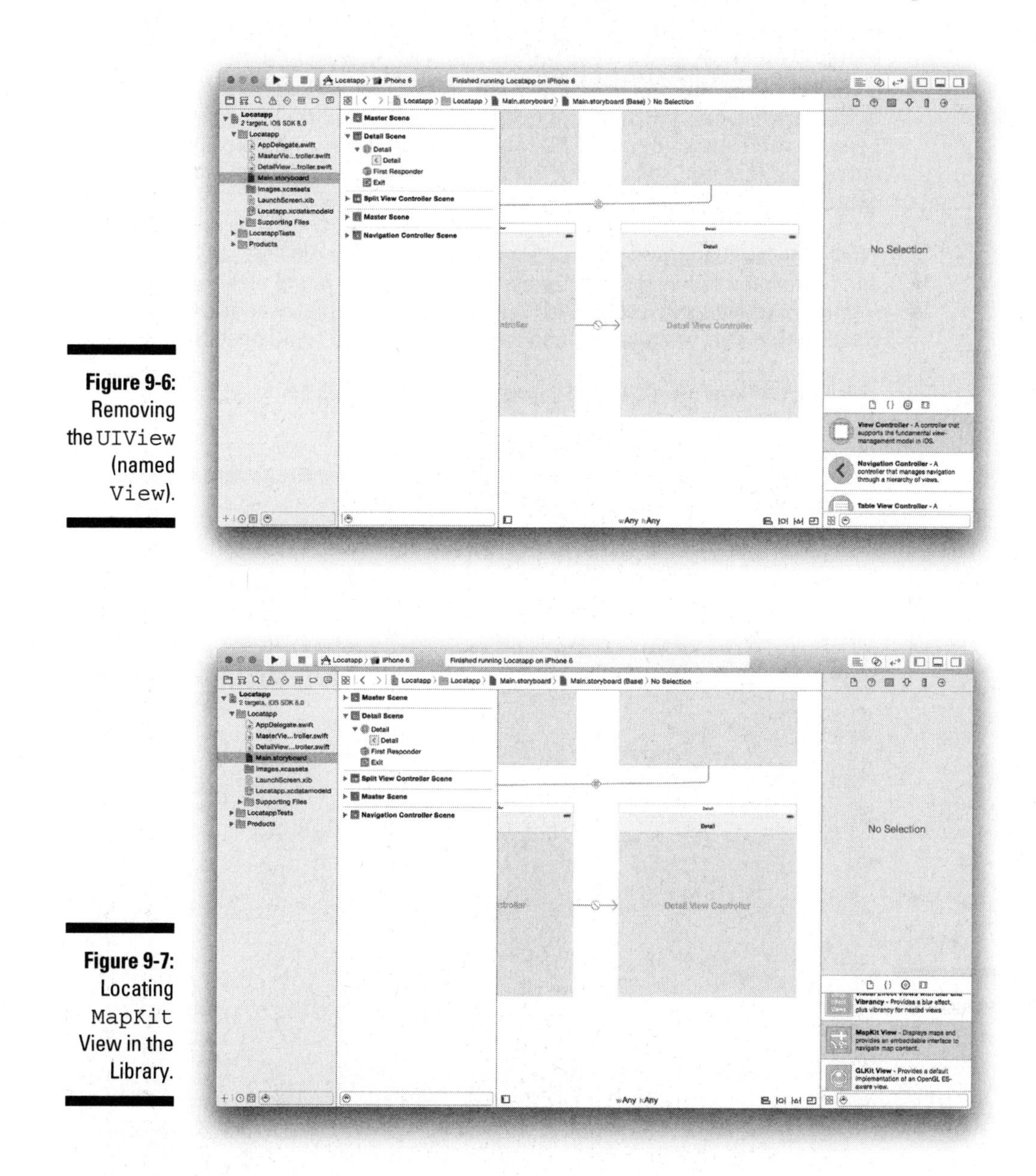

Figure 9-6: Removing the `UIView` (named `View`).

Figure 9-7: Locating `MapKit` View in the Library.

8. **Drag a `MapKit` view into the document outline. Place it inside View and above Detail, as shown in Figure 9-8.**

   You can also drag it directly onto the canvas. Just make certain it winds up in the proper place in the document outline.

Removing reference to the `UILabel` view and adding a reference to the `UIMapView` view

If you try to run the app now, it will fail. In fact, depending on the sequence in which you work, you may not even be able to build the app. That's because there are still remnants of the template there. Specifically, there's a detail item that you select from the list in the table view in the master view controller. It no longer exists, but the code is still there.

The following list shows you the steps to remove the old `UILabel` view code and to do a few other miscellaneous cleanups. Performing cleanups like these is good practice for working with this and other templates — it's the kind of cleanup that you often have to do as you modify and repurpose them:

1. **Start by opening `DetailViewController.swift`.**

   That's where most of the changes will be made.

2. **Change the `import` statements at the top of the file to add the `MapKit` framework.**

```
import UIKit
import MapKit //add this line
```

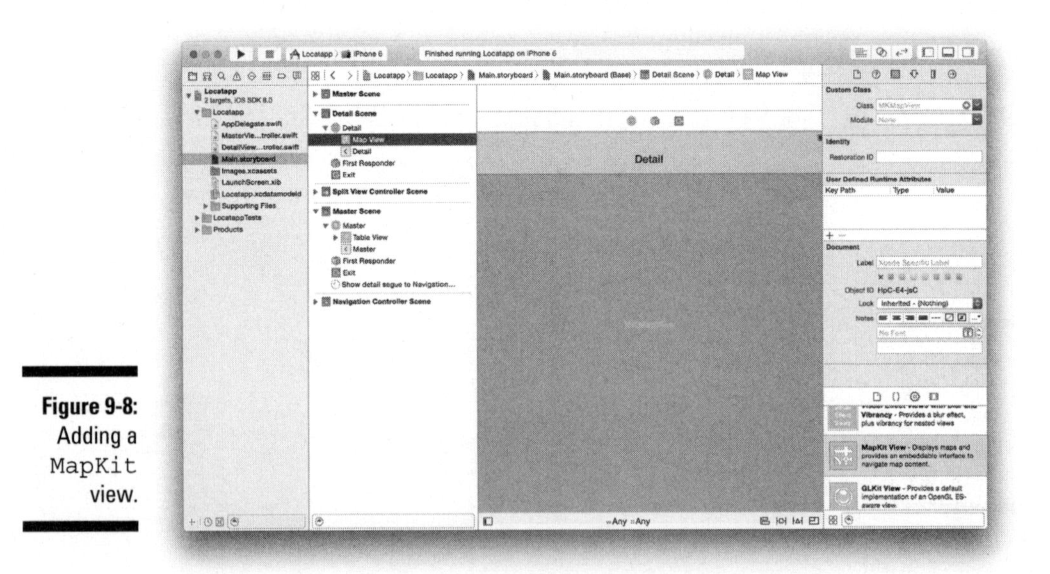

Figure 9-8: Adding a `MapKit` view.

3. **Open the storyboard and `DetailViewController.swift` in the Assistant editor.**
4. **Control-drag from the map view to the property at the top of `DetailViewController.swift` as shown at the right in Figure 9-9.**
5. **Name the new connection `mapView`.**

   Names of properties start with lowercase letters and use "camelCase" (internal caps for each word). This is a convention, not a syntax requirement.

   Double-check the other settings, as shown in Figure 9-9.
6. **Click Connect to create the connection and the property declaration, as shown in Figure 9-10.**
7. **Delete a line.**

   The line should be somewhere around line number 14 or 15, if you have line numbers turned on in Text Editing tab in Xcode Preferences. This is the line to delete:

   ```
   @IBOutlet var detailDescriptionLabel: UILabel!
   ```
8. **Delete the body of the `configureView` function.**

   It's a few lines below the area where you worked in Step 7. This is the code you will delete.

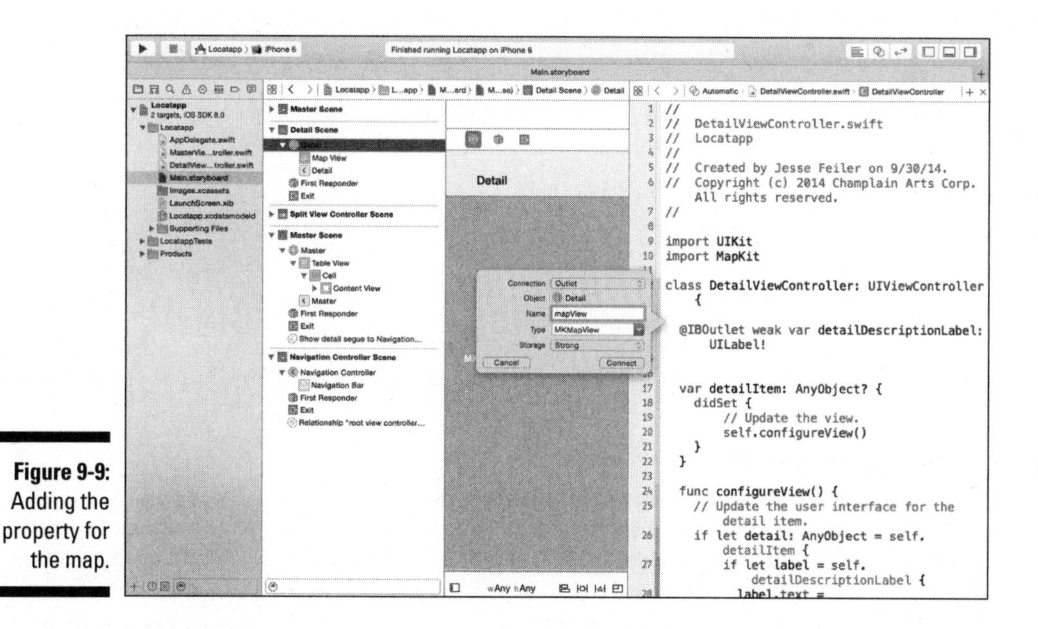

Figure 9-9: Adding the property for the map.

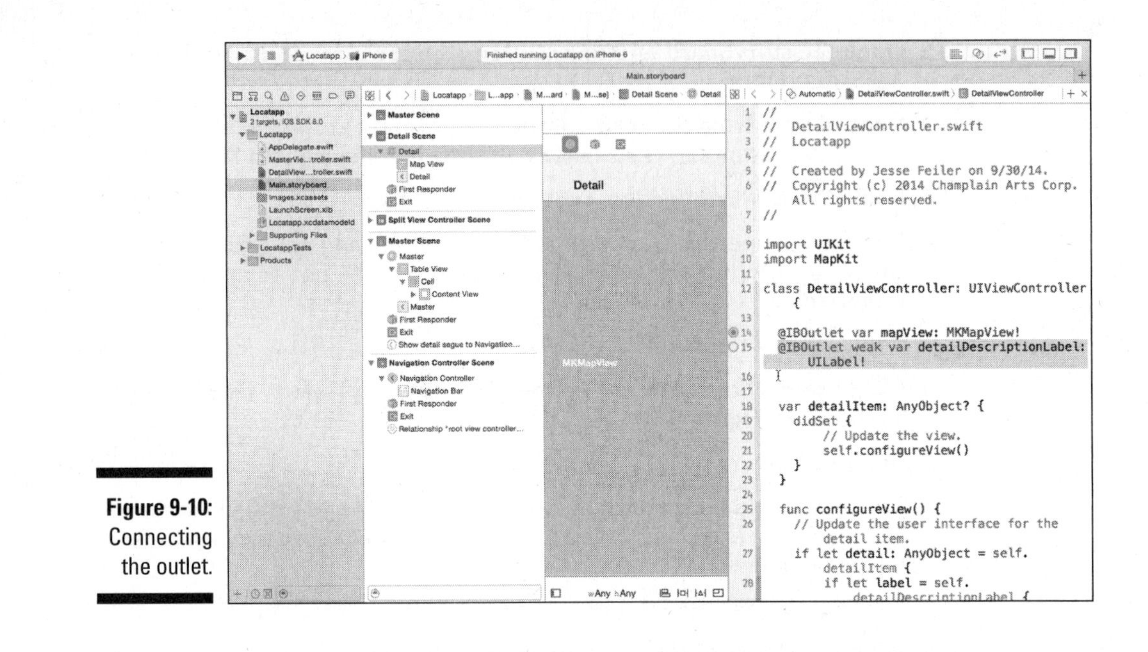

Figure 9-10: Connecting the outlet.

```
if let detail: AnyObject = self.detailItem {
  if let label =
    self.detailDescriptionLabel {
      label.text
        detail.valueForKey("timeStamp")!.description
    }
  }
```

The function should now look like this:

```
func configureView() {
  // Update the user interface for the detail item
}
```

9. **Run the app.**

   You should be able to add a timestamp on the master view controller with +. Click the timestamp you just added and you should see a map, as shown in Figure 9-11.

Showing the user's location

To move ahead, you need to show the user's current location on the map. That requires getting into the MapKit framework, but, as is the case with the use of many frameworks, you can use the framework without getting deep into it (at least to start).

If you reuse code that you've found to use a specific framework, remember to check its date. Frameworks (and now the languages) have evolved over time.

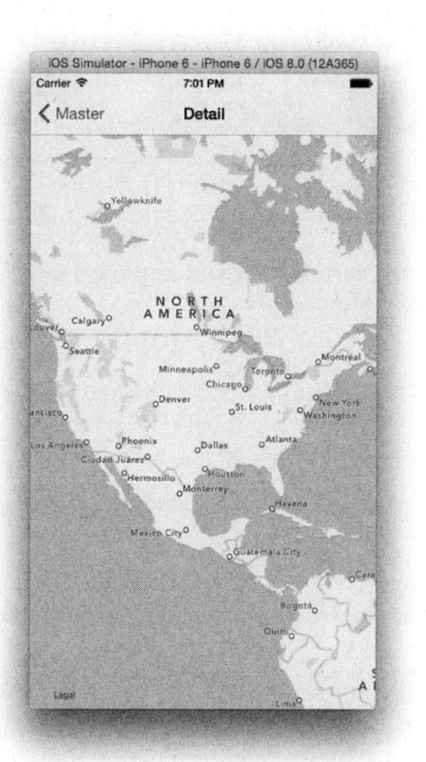

Figure 9-11: Running the app.

Conceptually, there are six steps to complete in order to get the user's location. Although getting deeply into the MapKit framework isn't necessary, knowing these basic steps is necessary if you'll be using locations in your app. You'll do this work in `DetailViewController.swift` because the detail view controller now contains the map view rather than the label view.

Here's an overview of the steps:

1. **Adopt protocols for Core Location and MapKit.**
2. **Add `DetailView` as delegates for Core Location and `MKMapView` so that you can use the frameworks and view.**
3. **Add a location manager so that you can interact with Core Location.**
4. **Add Core Location UI.**

   This includes arranging to ask the user's permission to use the current location.
5. **Use an option to show the user location on the map.**
6. **Set the location in the iOS Simulator. This is only for testing.**

Adopting protocols and adding your class as a delegate to use them is a common Cocoa and Cocoa Touch scenario.

What follows are the steps to get this done. Note that although they are numbered, you don't have to do them in sequence. Just know that as soon as you start on the steps, you will get syntax and compile errors. Don't worry about them until you get to the end of the sequence when they should all be resolved.

1. **In DetailView.swift, make certain that you import MapKit at the top of the file with this line of code:**

```
import MapKit
```

2. **Add `MKMapViewDelegate` and `CLLocationManagerDelegate` to your class declaration of `DetailViewController`.**

   The declaration should now read as follows:

```
class DetailViewController: UIViewController,
  MKMapViewDelegate,
  CLLocationManagerDelegate {
```

3. **Verify that you have the map view connected to a property with this line of code:**

```
  @IBOutlet var mapView: MKMapView!
```

   I showed how to do this previously in the section, "Removing reference to the `UILabel` view and adding a reference to the `UIMapView` view," earlier in this chapter. You should see a small circle with a dot in the middle in the gutter to the left of this line. If you click on it, you will see what the connection is, as shown in Figure 9-12.

Figure 9-12: Checking the map connection.

4. **Add a `locationManager` property to `MasterViewController.swift` and set it up.**

   Create an instance of `CLLocationManager` and set the property to that instance. There is more on classes, instances, and initialization like this in Chapters 12 and 15. While you're here, also add a variable `lastLocation`, which you will update periodically with the user's location so that you always have a recent location to use in storing the current location.

   The property and its initialization can go with the existing properties shown at the top of the file so that section looks like this with the `locationManager` property added.

```
class MasterViewController: UITableViewController,
  NSFetchedResultsControllerDelegate,
  CLLocationManagerDelegate {

  var detailViewController: DetailViewController? =
        nil
  var managedObjectContext: NSManagedObjectContext? =
        nil

  let locationManager = CLLocationManager()
  var lastLocation: CLLocation! = nil
```

5. **Start checking the user's location.**

   Add code to the end of `viewDidLoad` in `MasterViewController.swift` to start finding the user's location. Note that this line of code will fail because it calls a function you haven't written yet, but you will write it shortly.

```
self.startSignificantChangeUpdates ()
```

6. **Set up the UI for asking the user's permission.**

   Select the Info tab in the project, as shown in Figure 9-13.

7. **At the bottom of the properties list, select the last item and then click + to add a new property.**

   It will be named Application Category (the first from the pop-up menu).

8. **Change the name of the new property to `NSLocationWhenInUseUsageDescription`, as shown in Figure 9-14.**

   Make certain that it is a string and add text such as "This will let you see your current location." This will be shown to the user when permission is asked.

9. **Run the app. As soon as it launches, adjust the iOS Simulator's location as shown in Figure 9-15.**

   In the iOS Simulator, use Debug ⇨ Location to choose a location for the simulator to use. You only have to do this once: the iOS Simulator will remember the location until you wipe out its local data with IOS Simulator ⇨ Reset Content and Settings.

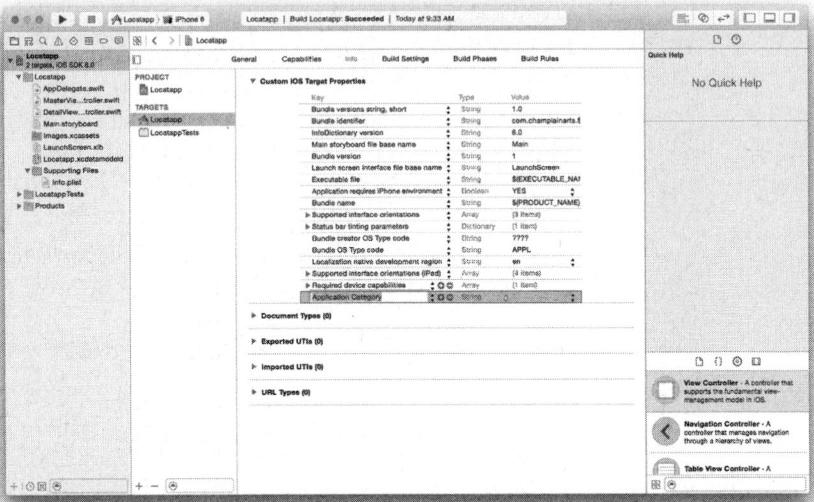

Locatapp | Build Locatapp: Succeeded | Today at 9:33 AM

No Quick Help

General Capabilities Info Build Settings Build Phases Build Rules

Custom iOS Target Properties

Key	Type	Value
Bundle versions string, short	String	1.0
Bundle identifier	String	com.champlainarts.$
InfoDictionary version	String	6.0
Main storyboard file base name	String	Main
Bundle version	String	1
Launch screen interface file base name	String	LaunchScreen
Executable file	String	$(EXECUTABLE_NA
Application requires iPhone environment	Boolean	YES
Bundle name	String	$(PRODUCT_NAME)
Supported interface orientations	Array	(3 items)
Status bar tinting parameters	Dictionary	(1 item)
Bundle creator OS Type code	String	????
Bundle OS Type code	String	APPL
Localization native development region	String	en
Supported interface orientations (iPad)	Array	(4 items)
Required device capabilities	Array	(1 item)
Application Category	String	

Document Types (0)

Exported UTIs (0)

Imported UTIs (0)

URL Types (0)

Figure 9-13: Selecting the project's Info tab.

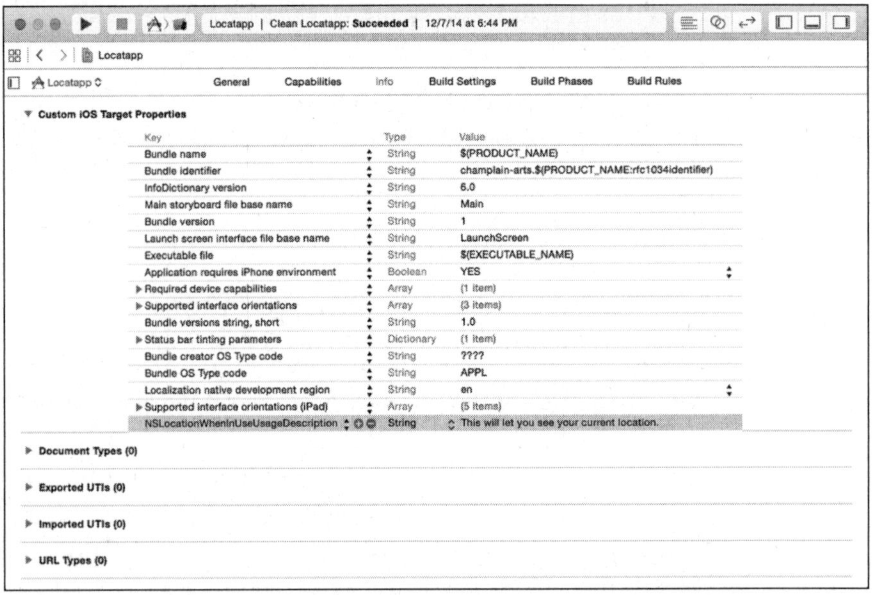

Locatapp | Clean Locatapp: Succeeded | 12/7/14 at 6:44 PM

Locatapp

General Capabilities Info Build Settings Build Phases Build Rules

Custom iOS Target Properties

Key	Type	Value
Bundle name	String	$(PRODUCT_NAME)
Bundle identifier	String	champlain-arts.$(PRODUCT_NAME:rfc1034identifier)
InfoDictionary version	String	6.0
Main storyboard file base name	String	Main
Bundle version	String	1
Launch screen interface file base name	String	LaunchScreen
Executable file	String	$(EXECUTABLE_NAME)
Application requires iPhone environment	Boolean	YES
Required device capabilities	Array	(1 item)
Supported interface orientations	Array	(3 items)
Bundle versions string, short	String	1.0
Status bar tinting parameters	Dictionary	(1 item)
Bundle creator OS Type code	String	????
Bundle OS Type code	String	APPL
Localization native development region	String	en
Supported interface orientations (iPad)	Array	(5 items)
NSLocationWhenInUseUsageDescription	String	This will let you see your current location.

Document Types (0)

Exported UTIs (0)

Imported UTIs (0)

URL Types (0)

Figure 9-14: Adding the new property.

10. **Quit the app and rerun it. If necessary, add a new timestamp and select it. If you already have one, select it. You should see the alert shown in Figure 9-16. Click Allow.**

11. **Check that your location is marked as shown in Figure 9-17.**

    Even on the iOS Simulator, it may take a few moments to obtain the location. (On a mobile device, it will take longer — just be patient.)

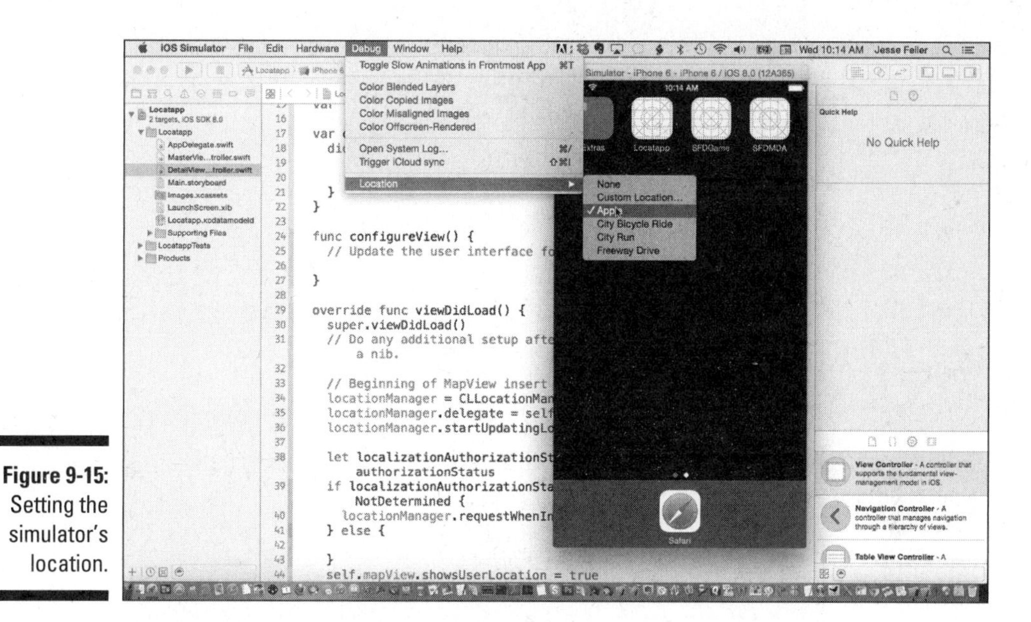

Figure 9-15: Setting the simulator's location.

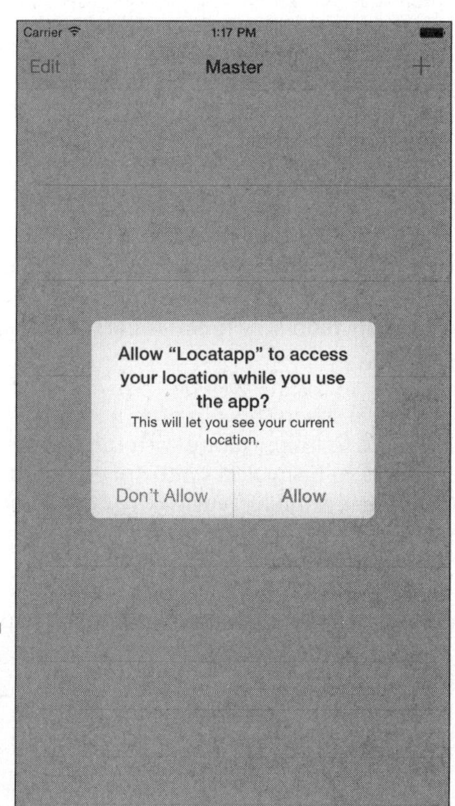

Figure 9-16: Allowing access to location data.

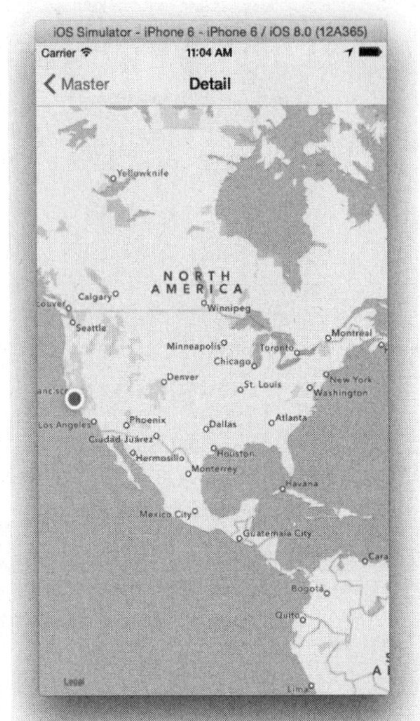

Figure 9-17: Adding the new property.

Exploring the Functions in Locatapp

Now that you have an app that's running, it's time to explore it in some detail. Each of the chapters in the remainder of this book will focus on a different area so that you can explore and develop new functionality in this app and the apps that you'll develop.

If you haven't worked through the steps in this chapter, now is a good time to do so: You'll need that source code to follow along with the rest of the book. Working through those steps helps to bring you up to speed not only with Swift but also with Xcode and a basic familiarity with the Cocoa and Cocoa Touch frameworks (although Cocoa Touch is the primary framework used in this book, it includes many Cocoa frameworks).

If you haven't worked through the steps outlined so far in this chapter, you can download Locatapp as described in the Introduction. Make certain that you download the version from Chapter 9.

Understanding the Locatapp Architecture

There are three Swift files in the Master-Detail Application template (and, thus, in your Locatapp project so far). That makes it easy to look at the app architecture (and, as noted previously, most apps share a fairly similar architecture). The three files are:

- **AppDelegate.swift:** This contains the overall app code (refer to Chapter 4, "Looking at a Swift App" for more details.
- **MasterDetailViewController.swift:** This is the controller for the list of items in the app. Other app templates do not have this file, but they have different files at the second level (that is, below the app delegate).
- **DetailViewController.swift:** This is the detail view controller for a select item from the master detail view's list. In this chapter, you have replaced the default `UILabel` view with a `MKMapView` view.

If you want to drill down into those three files, Xcode has a tool for you. In the jump bar above the editor area, you have a list of the functions for the current file, as shown in Figure 9-18. Exploring those functions provides an overview of the architecture.

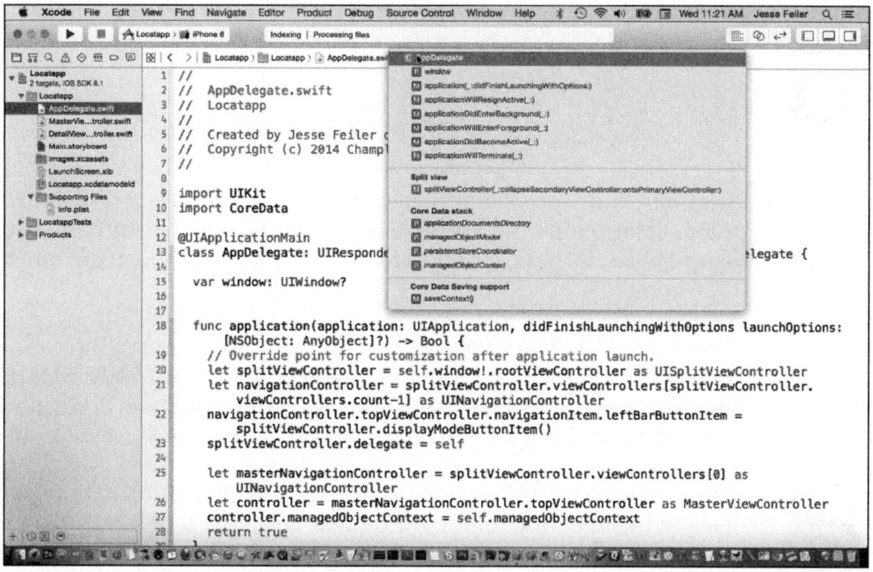

Figure 9-18: Viewing the functions in an Xcode file.

Uncovering the Function Features

Armed with the high-level view represented in the three points shown previously in this section, you can look at the functions in each file. Doing so will let you explore the features of functions. In the sections that follow, you will find references to the file in which each function is declared.

In most of this book, you find text and step lists to help you create code. In this section, the process is inverted so that you have the code (primarily from the template) and you take a look at how it works. This combination of top-down and bottom-up views can help you to become more familiar with Swift.

Not every function is discussed. This section provides an overview of the structure and uses it to point out features of functions. You'll find those features used repeatedly throughout the frameworks, the templates, and this book.

Basic function syntax — configureView()

File: `DetailViewController.swift`

The `configureView` function is as basic as you can get. Here's what it looks like.

```
func configureView() {
  // Update the user interface for the detail item
}
```

Swift functions (or *methods* when they're in classes) start with the keyword `func`, followed by the function name. Parameters (if any) are placed inside parentheses. If there are no parameters, the parentheses are empty as is the case here.

The body of the function is placed within brackets. As is the case here, the body can be empty. This would happen either if you have a placeholder function that will be filled in later or, as is the case here, if you have deleted the body code from a template function that you may use later on.

The comment in the function body is technically optional, but when you come back to this function tomorrow or next year, you'll be glad you used it. And if you are submitting samples of your work for a job, those comments may well make the difference between a paycheck and a career in some other field.

Overriding a function — viewDidLoad()

File: `DetailViewController.swift`

Like other object-oriented languages, you can override functions (methods) in Swift. Unlike some other object-oriented languages, you must specify an override. Omitting the modifier `override` is a compile error. This rule prevents accidental overrides due to typos.

Here is an example from `DetailViewController.swift`:

```
override func viewDidLoad () {
```

In addition to `override`, you can also designate a method as `final`. That means that the method cannot be overridden by a subclass. The syntax for a final method is:

```
final func myFinalMethod () {
```

This rule applies to methods, properties, and subscripts of a class, as follows:

- **No modifier:** The method, property, or subscript can be overridden.
- **`override`:** This is the override of a declaration in a superclass.
- **`final`:** You cannot override this in a subclass.

This rule prevents a number of problems that can occur when several people work together on code, or where there are several levels of inheritance so that it's easy to create a new method that accidentally overrides a higher-level method.

Calling the super function — viewDidLoad()

File: `DetailViewController.swift`

When a function overrides a function you can call the overridden function from within your override using syntax like this:

```
override func viewDidLoad () {
  super.viewDidLoad ()
```

Often, calls to the super function are the first or last line of the override function.

Adding a parameter to a function — controllerWillChangeContent (_:)

File: `MasterViewController.swift`

If a function takes a parameter, it is provided along with its type inside the parentheses as shown in the following code segment. The parameter's name is `controller`. In good programming style, the function's name describes what it will do — a controller will change content. The controller in question is passed in as a parameter. The controller's type is `NSFetchedResultsController`.

```
func controllerWillChangeContent (
  controller: NSFetchedResultsController) {
  self.tableView.beginUpdates()
}
```

The controller that is passed in is not used in the basic function. That's not an error. Parameters need not be used. A function like this one is often provided for the specific purpose of being overridden. It gives you an entry point into a process so that if you want to change the behavior, you have a function ready to override for that purpose.

Using multiple parameters in a function — controller (_:didChangeSection:atIndex:for ChangeType:)

File: `MasterViewController.swift`

If you need multiple parameters to be passed into a function, separate them with commas, as in the following:

```
func controller(
  controller: NSFetchedResultsController,
  didChangeSection sectionInfo:
    NSFetchedResultsSectionInfo,
  atIndex sectionIndex: Int,
  forChangeType type: NSFetchedResultsChangeType) {
    switch type {
      case .Insert:
        self.tableView.insertSections(NSIndexSet(index:
          sectionIndex), withRowAnimation: .Fade)
```

```
        case .Delete:
          self.tableView.deleteSections(NSIndexSet(index:
             sectionIndex),
          withRowAnimation: .Fade)

        default:
          return
        }
    }
```

Now that you have multiple parameters in a function, there are some additional points to notice. The first parameter is named `controller`, and it is of type `NSFetchedResultsController`. Because this is a protocol function that is implemented by a delegate, the first parameter is the object that has sent the message. (See more in Chapter 18.) For non-delegate functions, this sender parameter is missing. Next comes the name of the function (`didChangeSection`), and then three parameters (`sectionInfo`, `sectionIndex`, and `type`). The combination of sender (if present), function name, and parameters (if present) uniquely identifies a function with a class.

Using external names for parameters — controller(_:didChangeSection:atIndex:forChangeType:)

File: `MasterViewController.swift`

The code shown in the previous section also demonstrates the use of external names.

The second parameter has both an internal and external name `sectionInfo` and `didChangeSection` respectively). Inside the function, either can be used, but the external name is used when referenced from outside the function. The internal name is required in all cases in the declaration; if the external name is not provided, use an underscore (_) as a placeholder; the internal one is assumed. Thus, in the previous example, the first parameter's internal and external names are both `controller`.

This internal/external naming syntax is used to improve readability for two audiences — the engineers originally writing the function who may prefer the internal name and the developer/users who use the function. It also improves interaction with the Objective-C code in the frameworks that use this style.

Returning a value from a function — numberOfSectionsInTableView(_:)

File: MasterViewController.swift

If a function returns a value, it's placed after the main part of the declaration with ->:

```
override func tableView
  ( tableView: UITableView,
    canEditRowAtIndexPath indexPath: NSIndexPath) -> Bool
         {
    // Return false if you do not want the specified item
         to be editable.
    return true
  }
```

If you want to explore other elements of these functions, a good place to start is Chapter 10, which deals with expressions.

Adding Location Support

At this point, you have the code to show the user's location on the map using the iOS Simulator. What you don't have is the ability to access that location from your code. You'll need to do that if you want to store the user's location with the +. You'll also need to add `startSignificantChangeUpdates ()`, which you referenced from `viewDidLoad` in `MasterViewController.swift` earlier in this chapter (in the section "Showing the user's location").

You can place that function together with two protocol methods at the end of the file with the code described in this section. First, it's good practice to use the `MARK` directive to set off sections of code. These three functions support the `CLLocationManagerDelegate` protocol (it's discussed further in Chapter 18).

Listing 9-1 shows the setup code you need to use to get the location manager up and running. This code was described in Chapter 4. As a review, this is the critical code that's added to `MasterViewController.swift` there. (Remember to follow the steps to have the MapKit view show the user's location.)

The functions in Listings 9-2 and 9-3 fulfill the promise you made to conform to the `CLLocationManagerDelegate` protocol (see Chapter 18 for more on protocols). Note that `locationManager (_: didUpdateLocations:)` in Listing 9-2 is where you take the location from the `locationManager` and

Listing 9-1: startSignificantChangeUpdates

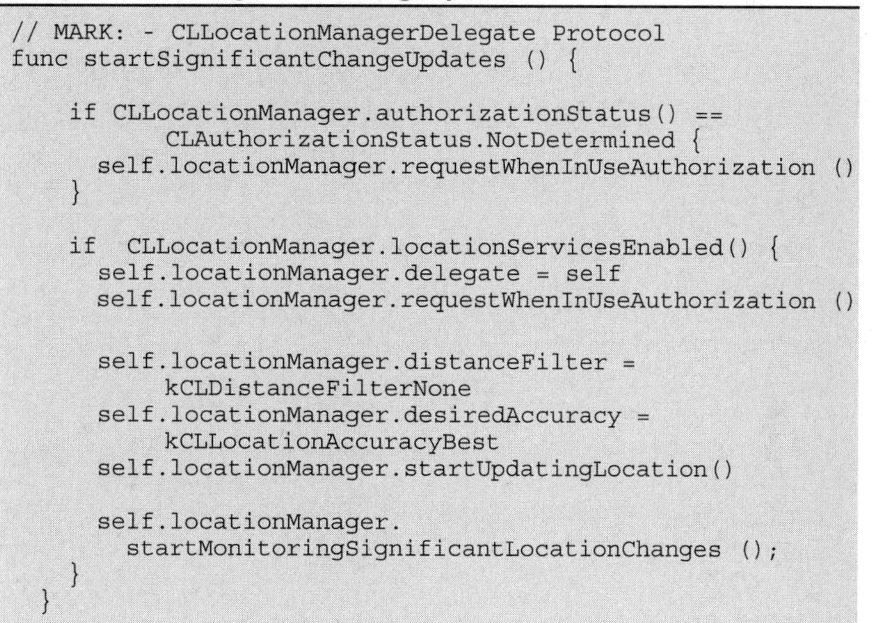

```
// MARK: - CLLocationManagerDelegate Protocol
func startSignificantChangeUpdates () {

    if CLLocationManager.authorizationStatus() ==
         CLAuthorizationStatus.NotDetermined {
      self.locationManager.requestWhenInUseAuthorization ()
    }

    if  CLLocationManager.locationServicesEnabled() {
      self.locationManager.delegate = self
      self.locationManager.requestWhenInUseAuthorization ()

      self.locationManager.distanceFilter =
           kCLDistanceFilterNone
      self.locationManager.desiredAccuracy =
           kCLLocationAccuracyBest
      self.locationManager.startUpdatingLocation()

      self.locationManager.
        startMonitoringSignificantLocationChanges ();
    }
  }
```

Listing 9-2: locationManager (_: didUpdateLocations:)

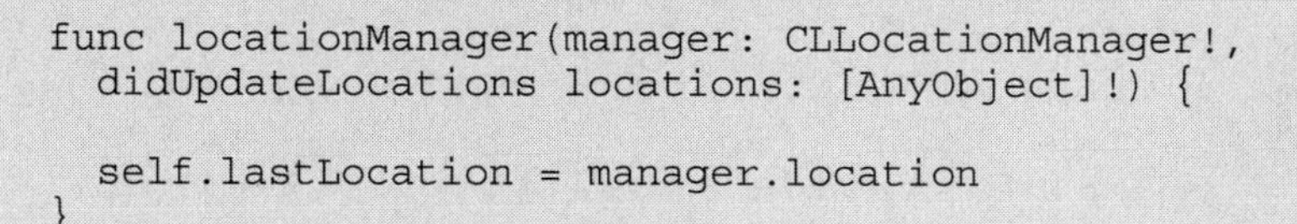

```
func locationManager(manager: CLLocationManager!,
  didUpdateLocations locations: [AnyObject]!) {

  self.lastLocation = manager.location
}
```

Listing 9-3: locationManager (_: didFailWithError:)

```
func locationManager(manager: CLLocationManager!,
        didFailWithError error: NSError!) {
      // need to add code to handle errors
}
```

store it in `self.lastLocation`, which you declared earlier in this chapter at the very top of `MasterViewController.swift`. It's there waiting for you to use it when you add a new location with +.

You also need to update the data model to store the location that you've picked up in Listing 9-2. This is described in Chapter 4.

Part III

Putting Expressions Together

```
//
//  AppDelegate.swift
//  Locatapp
//
//  Created by Jesse Feiler on 10/23/14.
//  Copyright (c) 2014 Jesse Feiler. All rights reserved.
//

import UIKit
import CoreData

@UIApplicationMain
class AppDelegate: UIResponder, UIApplicationDelegate, UISplitViewControllerDelegate {

    var window: UIWindow?


    func application(application: UIApplication, didFinishLaunchingWithOptions
        launchOptions: [NSObject: AnyObject]?) -> Bool {
        // Override point for customization after application launch.
        let splitViewController = self.window!.rootViewController as
            UISplitViewController
        let navigationController = splitViewController.viewControllers
            [splitViewController.viewControllers.count-1] as UINavigationController
        navigationController.topViewController.navigationItem.leftBarButtonItem =
            splitViewController.displayModeButtonItem()
        splitViewController.delegate = self

        let masterNavigationController = splitViewController.viewControllers[0] as
            UINavigationController
        let controller = masterNavigationController.topViewController as
            MasterViewController
        controller.managedObjectContext = self.managedObjectContext
        return true
```

Find out how to initialize stored properties in a class or structure at `www.dummies.com/extras/swift`.

In this part . . .

- Use basic expressions, blocks, and closures.
- Explore symbols, patterns, and ranges.
- Initialize and deinitialize objects and structures.

Chapter 10

Expressing Yourself

In This Chapter

- Understanding optional types
- Choosing types of expressions
- Using lazy loading for properties with closures

Expressions in Swift are very similar to expressions in other programming languages, but there are some differences (of course). Some of these differences arise from Swift-specific features, whereas some simply reflect the requirements of a 21st-century language designed to be developed on extraordinarily powerful computers.

Swift is designed to be easily modified by Apple as circumstances change. In addition, you can define new operators for your own apps. A great deal of flexibility is built in, but in the future there may be added expression syntax both from Apple and from other Swift developers.

Expressions involve not just operators and variables but also the Cocoa and Cocoa Touch frameworks. The best reference for all of these is `developer.apple.com`. Even without registering, you can search the site for information about the developer tools and languages, making this the first place to turn if you have questions.

Surveying the Types of Swift Expressions

Expressions involve targets (which themselves can be expressions, variables or values) as well as operators. Typically, a single expression contains one operator as well as one, two, or more targets. To get started, remember that there are four kinds of expressions in Swift. They are distinguished by the placement of an operator in relation to its target, as follows:

- **Prefix** expressions include an operator that affects the target that follows it.
- **Postfix** expressions include an operator that affects the target preceding it.
- **Binary** expressions include an operator that applies to the targets that surround it on both sides.
- **Primary** expressions don't contain an operator at all (except when the expression includes a parenthetical expression that happens to contain an operator).

With the exception of primary expressions, then, Swift expressions include an operator. Because of this, it's worth taking a moment to explore some issues with optional type operators in Swift. These show up frequently in expressions.

Exploring optional type operators

First of all, don't misread the heading. *Optional type operators* is a term used frequently in Swift documentation, but it may require a bit of parsing. In Swift, there is a concept of optional types, and the term *optional type operators* refers to operators that operate on optional types (and not to type operators that are optional — no such thing exists in Swift).

Optional types can either be a known type (either built-in or user-defined) or they can contain `nil`. If you are used to languages such as Objective-C, you may wonder what the fuss is about — in such languages, which rely on pointers to objects, instances of *any* type can be `nil`. As an example, in Objective-C, the following declaration and initialization code is no problem:

```
UIWindow *window = nil;
```

In this line, `window` is the variable, the asterisk is a pointer to an object, and `UIWindow` is the type; here `window` is set to `nil`, and this is perfectly legal.

You can't use this line in Swift. For one thing, in Swift the order of the variable name and type would be reversed:

```
var window: UIWindow
```

However, even if you correct the order of terms, the Objective-C line would be illegal. The following line, a direct paraphrase of the Objective-C code, would still be illegal in Swift:

```
var window: UIWindow = nil
```

`?` is a postfix operator for a type or an expression. As a postfix operator for a type, it is used in syntax such as this property declaration from the beginning of `AppDelegate.swift` in Locatapp:

```
var window: UIWindow?
```

This common style declares a variable called `window`; it is of optional type `UIWindow`. That means that it can either be a `UIWindow` value or it can be `nil`. `UIWindow?` and `UIWindow` are not the same type, so comparing them in type comparisons will generate an error.

The other postfix operator for optionals is `!`. It provides *forced unwrapping* of the optional to its underlying type. (There is an example of this in Chapter 6.)

Here are some examples, which you can try for yourself in a playground.

```
import UIKit
var window: UIWindow
window
```

This creates a variable called `window` that is of type `UIWindow`. The last line references that variable, but it will fail because it is used before the variable has been initialized.

Let's borrow the Objective-C style to see if that lets you initialize it:

```
import UIKit
var window: UIWindow = nil
window
```

Here the second line fails because you cannot set an instance of `UIWindow` to `nil`.

Here's another way of writing the code:

```
import UIKit
var window: UIWindow? = nil
window
```

This approach succeeds because Swift allows you to set the optional `UIWindow?` to `nil`. When you reference the variable in the third line, the playground reveals its value at the right of the window: `nil`.

You can unwrap the variable `window` in the last line by adding `!` to the end. Thus, given the code immediately above, `window!` will generate an error because unwrapping a `nil` value is an error.

Changing the last line of the code above to `window?`, however, successfully yields `nil` because this is a legal value for an optional.

As shown in Chapter 6 (and in the final version of Locatapp, as well as a number of Xcode templates), *optional binding* is another way to deal with optionals. Here's the code from Chapter 6:

```
if let activityURL =
  NSURL (string:"http://champlainarts.com") {...
```

TECHNICAL STUFF

The heart of the `if` statement is the assignment of a possibly `nil` value to `activityURL`. If `activityURL` is not `nil`, the body of the `If` statement proceeds. If it is `nil`, the body is not executed. (A common reason for this syntax is when an operation, such as the `NSURL` initializer in this case can fail, leaving the result as `nil` rather than as a value.)

TIP

Sometimes people refer to optionals as *nullable* or, less frequently, as *nillable*.

For more details of operators, see Chapter 5.

Prefix expressions

Prefix expressions consist of an operator that acts on an expression that follows the prefix. Swift supports these standard C (and other languages) prefix operators as prefix expressions:

- ++ (adds 1 to the expression that follows)
- -- (subtracts 1 from the expression that follows)
- ! (negates the expression that follows — `logical NOT`)
- ~ (negates the bits of the expression that follows — `bitwise NOT`)
- + (*unary plus* normally provides no action but may clarify an expression as being positive)
- – (*unary minus* negates the value of the expression that follows)

Postfix expressions

Postfix expressions are also found in many other C-derived languages. These include:

- ++ (adds 1 to the expression that precedes it)
- -- (subtracts 1 from the expression that precedes it)

Wait, you may think, *are ++ and -- prefix or postfix operators?* The answer is simple: The operators are defined, but their placement determines whether they are prefixes or postfixes. This means that the operation (adding or subtracting one from the target expression) is done before or after the expression is evaluated.

Binary expressions

A binary expression consists of two expressions (hence "binary") joined by one of the binary operators. Binary operators can be simple arithmetic operators performing addition, subtraction, division, or multiplication; bitwise logical operators such as AND and OR; as well as comparative operators such as less than or equal to.

Perhaps the most commonly used binary operators are the various assignment binary operators that range from simple assignment with = to the compound assignment operators such as ≤, +=, *=, and the like.

Although most Swift operators are similar to those in other languages, several are uncommon and I describe these here in this chapter. Remember that these are lists of some of the operators that may be new to you: They are not intended to be exhaustive lists of the operators in each category.

See the discussions of range operators and patterns in Chapter 11.

Cast operators

Cast operators take an expression of one type and use it as another type. You can't just jump around from one type to another: The casting has to follow the rules of the object hierarchy. A common type of casting is to cast a general type (for example, `UIView`) to a subclass (such as `UILabel`). Cast operators are designed to fail gracefully so that you can attempt to cast an expression in order to find out whether it's possible. Cast operators use `is` or `as`, depending on the situation, as follows:

- **`is`:** You can check an expression using the `is` operator. For example, in the following snippet, the value is `true` if `myExpression` can be down-cast from `myType` — in this case, down-casting means testing for a subclass of `myExpression`.

  ```
  myExpression is aSubClassOfMyType
  ```

- **`as`:** The `as` operator is used to cast an expression to a specific type, as in

  ```
  myExpression as myType
  ```

  or

  ```
  myExpression as? myType
  ```

  If the cast cannot be performed, `as` returns a runtime error. In the same circumstance, `as?` would return `nil` in the optional `myType?`.

Ternary conditional and nil coalescing operators

The *ternary conditional operator* is comparable to the traditional `C ?` syntax, which is referred to variously as a *conditional operator,* an *inline `if`* (`iif`), or a *ternary `if`*. This syntax is "ternary" in the sense that it uses three target values. With this operator, an expression that evaluates to a Bool (that is, as true or false) is used to choose which of the two expressions is used — often in an assignment statement. Here is a typical use in Swift:

```
a > b ? <some expression for true> :
        <some expression for false>
```

The *`nil` coalescing operator* (`??`) provides a somewhat similar functionality, but it tests whether or not the first expression is `nil`. You can use this code to choose between two values, the first of which can be `nil`.

```
a ?? b
```

If `a` is `nil`, this expression returns `b`; if `a` can be unwrapped to a non-`nil` value (as would be the case if you wrote `a!`), the expression returns `a` rather than `b`.

You can always rewrite a `nil` coalescing expression as a ternary conditional expression, but using the `nil` coalescing operator (`??`) saves a few keystrokes and can make your code clearer.

Primary expressions

Primary expressions are among the most commonly used Swift syntax elements (some people would say they're *the* most commonly used element). You can divide them into two major groups: Swift expressions and common expressions.

The Swift expressions include expressions that are both unique to Swift and common to other modern languages. These are the major Swift expressions:

- **Literal expressions:** These let you write an array or dictionary with its data using a single line of code.
- **Type and class expressions (explicit and implicit):** These let you refer to an object (a property or function in most cases) that is part of a class, structure, or extension. They use dot syntax (as in `myClass.myProperty`).
- **Self and super expressions:** These let you reference an object itself or its superclass.
- **Closures:** These are blocks of code that can be passed around in your code; they are often executed at another time and place (as in a completion handler that is executed asynchronously when an operation such as a read or write completes).

The next few sections of this chapter describe these Swift expressions in greater detail.

The common expressions include those that you may have learned in an introductory programming class at any time from the mid-1950s to the present day. These are among the common expressions that are supported in Swift and that are part of the basic programming language repertoire in almost every language today:

- **Parenthesized expressions:** Parenthesized expressions establish an order of operations. As in other languages, the innermost parenthesized expressions are evaluated before the next-innermost expressions.
- **Function call expressions:** These behave as they do in other languages. Some Swift extensions are discussed in Chapter 9.

Literal expressions

Array and dictionary literal expressions (often just called *literals*) let you write an array or dictionary in a single line of code, so you don't have to construct the object.

For arrays, for instance, you use `[` and `]` to enclose the elements of the array as in

```
[element1, element2]
```

You can also write an empty array by typing

```
[]
```

This is commonly used to initialize a `var` array which will be filled later on as the data becomes available.

Dictionaries use keys to identify their elements, so they consist of pairs of keys and values. To write a dictionary literal, use brackets, just as you would with an array literal. Within the brackets, you type each element as a key-value pair — the colon is part of the data. Thus, a simple dictionary literal might look like

```
[key: value, anotherKey: anotherValue]
```

An empty dictionary is written as

```
[:]
```

Some literals are used frequently in debugging statements, such as these:

- **`__FILE__`:** A literal representing the name of the file.
- **`__LINE__`:** A literal representing the line number.
- **`__COLUMN__`:** This is a remnant of the long-gone days when punched cards were used to write programs: It is a literal representing the position in the line of source code where the code in `__LINE__` and `__FILE__` begins.
- **`__FUNCTION__`:** A literal representing the name of the function being executed at the time of evaluation.

Note that each of these literals is preceded and followed by *two* underscores (not one).

Type and class expressions (explicit and implicit)

Swift uses what is commonly referred to as *dot syntax* — syntax that allows you to specify an identifier, the name of a method or function, or some other object in the context of its owning object. (Remember that the owning object in Swift can be a class, a structure, or an enumeration.) Expressions using dot syntax are called *explicit member expressions*.

This isn't as complicated as it may sound. Here's an example:

```
someType.someMemberOfThatType
```

You can use dot syntax by specifying the class or object that contains the property or method you're looking for, but you can also use either of these reserved words:

- **`self`** as in `self.someProperty` or `self.someFunction()` means that the property or function is a member of the class in which you are writing the code.
- **`super`** as in `super.someProperty` or `super.someFunction()` means that the property or function is a member of the superclass of the class in which you are writing. The reserved word `super` is frequently used in initializers and deinitializers. (For more, see Chapter 12.)

You can also use *implicit member expressions.* These are expressions that frequently follow explicit member expressions. You can omit the name of the owner if it is clear from the context what it would be.

Many people prefer not to use implicit member expressions because if you move them or place additional lines of code before them, the context for them may change or be unclear.

Message formats versus dot syntax

This is one of the most significant differences between Swift and Objective-C. In Objective-C you might write

```
[someClass someObjectIn
  ThatClass]
```

Because Objective-C is a message-based language, what that syntax means is that you send the `someObjectInThatClass` message to `someClass`; by convention, the `someObjectInThatClass` would be an accessor method that returns `someObject InThatClass`.

Just to make things more interesting, it has been possible for some time to use dot syntax in Objective-C, so although you may not be used to the message syntax, it is used in many of the Cocoa and Cocoa Touch frameworks.

Dot-syntax is consistent with many other modern languages, so it shouldn't be too much of a challenge to get used to it.

`self` and `super` expressions

These use the keywords `self` and `super` to let you refer to an object itself or its superclass. The most common usage is to refer to an identifier or expression as in the following examples

```
self.myName // property
self.myMethod () // expression
```

You also can refer to an object itself using `self`.

Closures

In Swift, *closures* allow you to declare blocks of functionality that you can refer to elsewhere in your code. You can assign names to them and pass them around as parameters. If this sounds somewhat like functions, you're on the right track. In fact, in Swift, functions are a special case of closures.

As in almost any language, Swift's functions let you declare blocks of functionality. Inside a function, you can use variables, properties, and methods that are local to the function (that is, they are declared within the function). You can also refer to variables, properties, and methods that are declared in the same context as the function but not within it.

Closures go one step further: They can reference variables, properties, and methods that are declared in the same context as the closure, but because the closure can be passed around just as any other variable or function and can be assigned to a variable or property, they carry all these references with them. The closures are said to be *bound* to the variables and properties of the context in they are declared. Thus, the closure consists of the block of code together with the bindings to variables and properties.

Closures can be assigned to multiple variables or properties. Closures are treated as first-class reference types, which means that if you assign the same closure to two variables or properties, both variables or properties refer to the same closure.

In Java, closures are known as *lambdas*, and, closer to home, they're called *blocks* in Objective-C.

In Objective-C and similar languages, they are often used as *completion routines* — code called upon the completion of an operation (often an asynchronous operation). This structure allows you to fire off an asynchronous task to load data or otherwise. When the process is complete, the completion handler fires and that code executes. When the completion handler is implemented as a block (Objective-C) or a closure (Swift), all the variables and properties bound to it when it was referenced in the code you used to start the operation are available to the closure whenever it executes.

Blocks in Objective-C and closures in Swift are basically the same thing. Although some subtle differences exist, the biggest difference is just the name.

The use of blocks as completion handlers has increased since they were first introduced in OS X Snow Leopard (OS X 10.6) in 2009 and iOS 4.0. By now, they are used for many of the completion handlers in the Cocoa and Cocoa Touch frameworks. (Before 2009, functions were passed as completion handlers.)

With Swift, closures easily take on another role — they allow *lazy loading* (or *lazy initialization*) of properties and variables. (This is discussed in the next section.) An example from the Master-Detail Application template shows how they can be used in this way. This is a good programming style to adopt.

Understanding Lazy Loading

Lazy loading is a *design pattern* (a solution paradigm that addresses similar problems in various contexts). Like many modern software environments, Cocoa and Cocoa Touch use lazy loading extensively. In this context, *lazy loading* most frequently means that when a large amount of data is called for by the user, it is displayed one screen or page at a time. The lazy loading part of the pattern is that the initial data retrieval operation does only enough work to be able to present the bare minimum of data: The data for each screen or page is retrieved only when that page is retrieved.

On OS X, you can spot lazy loading when you power on your Mac. The first screen you see after you've logged in may be the image of the last screen you saw before your Mac shut down. As the seconds pass, if you look closely, you'll see that some of the app icons and other images change as the stored shut-down image is replaced by the new live data.

On iOS, you can spot this on individual apps. As part of the app, you can create a *launch image,* which is the basic app screen without any data. The launch image may consist only of a background, or it might be a background and a toolbar. This image is shown immediately when you launch the app. As the app continues its startup, the actual data is displayed. To the user, it can appear that the data is being overlaid on a background, but in fact the launch image is being replaced by a live user interface.

With less powerful computers than those in use today (including smartphones), lazy loading was sometimes discouraged because the total amount of processing power needed to retrieve the summary data and then each page of data in turn is greater than doing all the work at once. From a user's point of view, however, the process is faster. Mainframe systems tended not to use lazy loading, because the computing resources of the mainframe are relatively scarce and need to be shared. On personal computers, there is spare computing power while a user does other things (such as taking a sip of coffee).

The following sections compare lazy loading with Objective-C and lazy loading with Swift so that you can see the differences and get used to using Swift closures in cases such as these.

Lazy loading with Objective-C

Lazy loading is frequently used for asynchronous processes. Setting up the Core Data stack in Cocoa or Cocoa Touch is a great example of this design pattern. Setting up the Core Data environment (called the *Core Data stack*) can require that the app goes out to a data store such as an SQLite database, which may be located on a network device. Initializing the Core Data stack is something that must be done before any access to the persistent store data is carried out.

If you're not precise, you might think that this initialization is something that has to be done when the app starts up. This is generally true, but more specifically it must be done before the first data access occurs — and usually this happens as part of the start-up process. But with lazy loading, things can be structured for efficiency.

Objective-C has an accessor method for the `managedObjectModel` property (`managedObjectModel` is basically the database schema). Following the Objective-C style of being a function (that is, a *method* in Objective-C talk) with the same name as the property (`_managedObjectModel`), this method returns an instance of `NSManagedObjectModel`, which is the managed object model in question. It is shown in Listing 10-1.

In Objective-C, properties are usually backed by variables that share the property name and are prefixed with an underscore. Thus, `managedObjectModel` (the property) is backed by `_managedObjectModel`. (Don't worry about these details: I steer us back back to Swift shortly.)

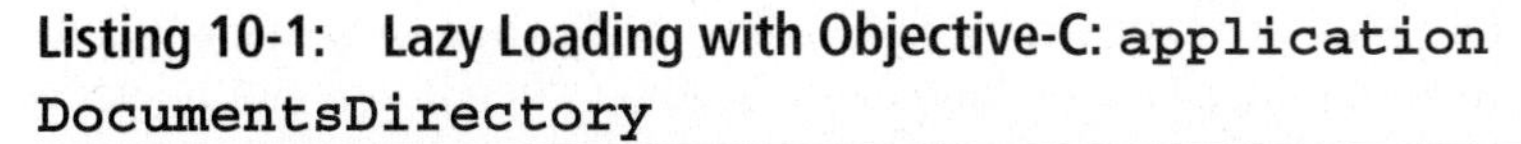

Listing 10-1: Lazy Loading with Objective-C: `applicationDocumentsDirectory`

```
- (NSManagedObjectModel *)managedObjectModel {
  // The managed object model for the application. It is
  // a fatal error for the application not to be able to
  // find and load its model.

  if (_managedObjectModel != nil) {
    return _managedObjectModel;
  }

  NSURL *modelURL =
    [[NSBundle mainBundle] URLForResource:@”LocatappObjC”
      withExtension:@”momd”];

  _managedObjectModel = [[NSManagedObjectModel alloc]
    initWithContentsOfURL:modelURL];

  return _managedObjectModel;
}
```

What is important is that the first thing in this accessor method is a test to see if `_managedObjectModel` exists. If it does, then it is returned as the result of the method. This is the code that does that:

```
if (_managedObjectModel != nil) {
  return _managedObjectModel;
}
```

Thus, after the managed object model has been created, all that the accessor does is test for it; if the test passes, it is returned. This is a very efficient process.

For the first-time access (the lazy part of the process), the managed object model is created and initialized with this code:

```
NSURL *modelURL =
   [[NSBundle mainBundle] URLForResource:@"Locatapp"
     withExtension:@"momd"];

_managedObjectModel = [[NSManagedObjectModel alloc]
  initWithContentsOfURL:modelURL];
```

This can be a lengthy process, but it is done only on an as-needed basis when the managed object model doesn't exist.

This is an efficient way of doing the initialization only when it is necessary and not doing it at the launch of the app (when it may not be needed).

Technically, this is "lazy initializing" rather than "lazy loading." Still, *lazy loading* is the more common term.

Lazy loading the easy way with Swift

Swift includes some features that replace commonly used code in Objective-C. Over the years, it's become obvious that certain code segments are written over and over, which is tedious and an invitation to typographical errors.

Listing 10-2 in Locatapp (actually in the Swift version of Master-Detail Application) shows Swift's version of lazy loading of the managed object model. As with Listing 10-1, this can be used as a model for other lazy loading properties.

The most important difference to notice here is that in the Swift code, the `if` statement at the beginning of Listing 10-1 is missing.

Listing 10-2 shows the declaration of the `managedObjectModel` property in `AppDelegate.swift`. Listing 10-1 relies on a separate declaration in the header file for `AppDelegate.h`. Swift gets rid of header files and separate declarations.

Listing 10-2: Lazy Loading with Swift

```
lazy var managedObjectModel: NSManagedObjectModel = {
  // The managed object model for the application. This
  // property is not optional. It is a fatal error for the
  // application not to be able to find and load its
  // model.

  let modelURL =
    NSBundle.mainBundle().URLForResource("Locatapp",
      withExtension: "momd")!

  return NSManagedObjectModel(contentsOfURL: modelURL)!
}()
```

The declaration in Listing 10-2 declares `managedObjectModel` as a `lazy var` property. As I discuss in Chapter 6, a `var` property is a variable — as opposed to a constant, which is introduced by `let`.

In Swift, `lazy` pushes the `if` statement from Listing 10-1 into the language itself. If the `managedObjectModel` property exists, it is returned when you access it, but if it has not been created, the code in the function shown in Listing 10-2 is executed to create it.

The code in Listing 10-2 is a *closure*, and this is a common use of closures in Swift. Closures are also commonly used as completion handlers, but, as noted previously, that usage is comparable to their usage in Objective-C. The `lazy` keyword and its use, as illustrated in Listing 10-2, is a Swift-only feature.

Summarizing lazy loading

Because lazy loading is so efficient and is used so frequently (and should be used in your Swift apps), I've recapitulated the process in Figure 10-1 and in this section.

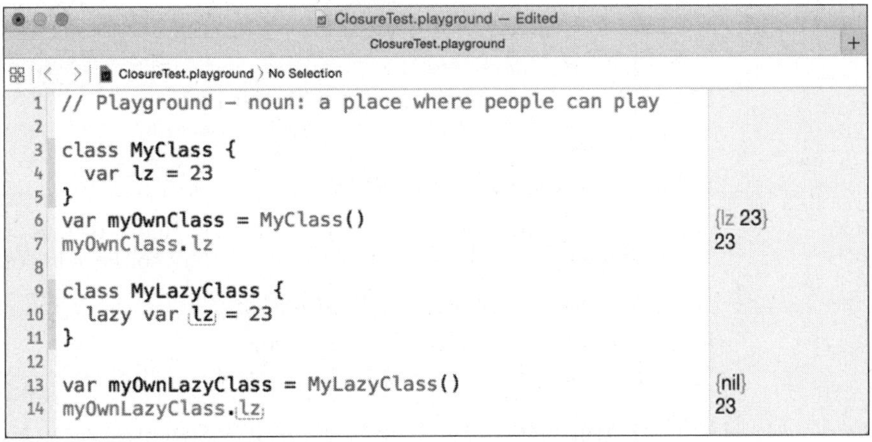

ClosureTest.playground — Edited

ClosureTest.playground > No Selection

```
1  // Playground - noun: a place where people can play
2
3  class MyClass {
4    var lz = 23
5  }
6  var myOwnClass = MyClass()                          {lz 23}
7  myOwnClass.lz                                       23
8
9  class MyLazyClass {
10   lazy var lz = 23
11 }
12
13 var myOwnLazyClass = MyLazyClass()                  {nil}
14 myOwnLazyClass.lz                                   23
```

Figure 10-1: Experimenting with closures in a playground.

To the experiment with closures and lazy loading in a playground, follow these steps:

1. **Declare a class called `MyClass`.**

   ```
   class MyClass {
   }
   ```

2. **Add a variable called `lz`.**

   If you don't initialize it, you will get an error, so you must set it with a line like this.

   ```
   var lz = 23
   ```

3. **Create an instance of the class.**

   In the right-hand sidebar of the playground, you'll see that the property `lz` has been initialized to 23 (this is shown in Figure 10-1).

   ```
   var myOwnClass = MyClass()
   ```

4. **Access the `lz` property with this code.**

   ```
   myOwnClass.lz
   ```

   You'll see that it is 23.

5. **Create a new class called `MyLazyClass` with this code.**

   ```
   class MyLazyClass {
   }
   ```

6. **Add a `lazy` variable called `lz` with this code.**

   ```
   lazy var lz = 23
   ```

7. **Create an instance of the class.**

   In the right-hand sidebar of the playground in Figure 10-1, you'll see that the property `lz` has been initialized to `nil` (not to the value of 23).

   ```
   var myOwnLazyClass = MyLazyClass()
   ```

8. **Access the `lz` property with this code:**

   ```
   myOwnLazyClass.lz
   ```

   The playground shows that it now has the value you set in Step 6.

The point to remember is that until you try to access the lazy property, its value isn't set, and that is done for you automatically as part of the Swift language as long as you provide the closure code.

Chapter 11

Declaring the Symbols

In This Chapter

- Using the symbol navigator
- Improving error-checking with assertions
- Exploring subscript expressions
- Recognizing and using patterns

For many developers, the project navigator in the navigator area is their preferred tool for navigating through a project (with the search navigator a close second). Of course, how you use Xcode is totally up to you.

Another navigator, however, is often useful: the symbol navigator, which lets you explore the symbols in your project both alphabetically and hierarchically. Basically, the project navigator lets you navigate by file and group, the search navigator helps you locate something when you know its name, and the symbol navigator looks at your project's code structure. Yes, it's possible to sit at your Mac and ask yourself, "Where in the world did I place that code sequence?" but the navigators can help eliminate those painful moments.

In addition to looking at the symbol navigator, this chapter provides information on a few other technologies that don't fit easily into other chapters, such as Swift assertions, ranges, and patterns.

Navigating through Symbols with the Symbol Navigator

The project navigator gives you a view of your project using files and groups. The symbol navigator, on the other hand, looks at the logical structure. The most common symbols are classes; they typically contain properties (including variables) and methods (which in many contexts are known as functions). Here is the full list of symbols shown in the symbol navigator:

- **Classes:** The member properties and classes are shown. For more on classes, see Chapter 15.
- **Properties:** For more on properties, see Chapter 16.
- **Protocols:** For more on protocols, see Chapter 18.
- **Functions:** For more on functions, see Chapter 9.
- **Structures:** For a brief discussion of structures, see Chapter 9.
- **Unions:** For a brief discussion of unions, see Chapter 9.
- **Enumerations:** For more on enumerations, see Chapter 17.
- **Types:** For more on types, see Chapter 6.
- **Globals:** In common practice, globals are rarely used these days.

Choosing types of displays

In the figures that follow, you can see the project in a hierarchical order (Figures 11-1 and 11-2) or in an alphabetical one (Figure 11-3) using the buttons at the top of the navigator. Clicking on any symbol opens the relevant file in the editing area so that you can see its declaration.

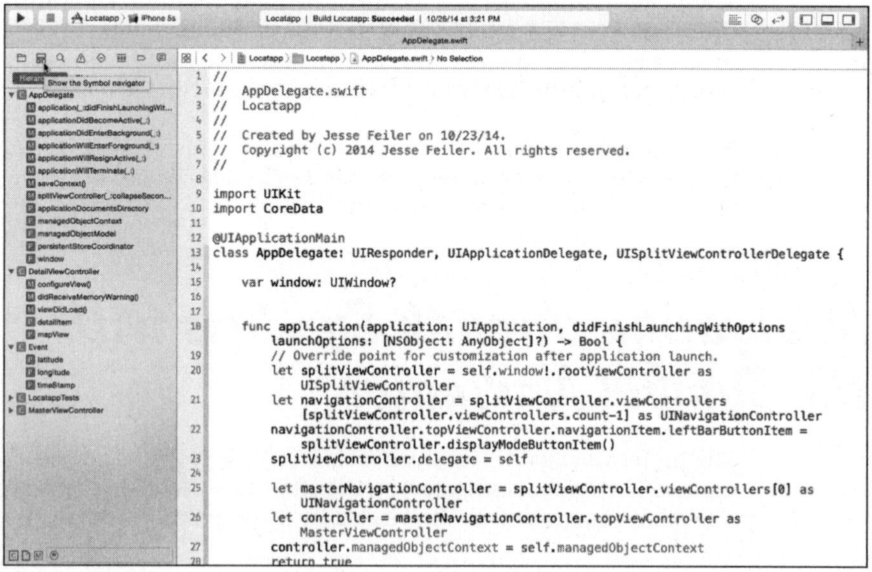

Figure 11-1: You can use the symbol navigator.

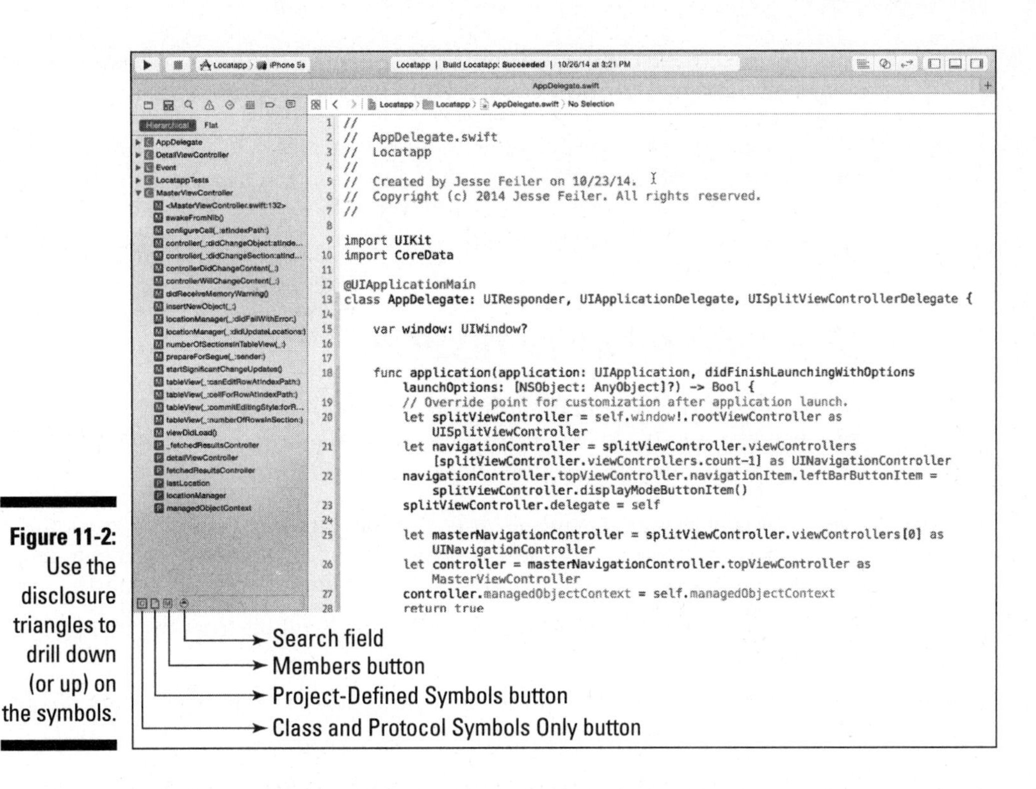

Figure 11-2: Use the disclosure triangles to drill down (or up) on the symbols.

Figure 11-3: You can see the symbol navigator and a file side-by-side in the Assistant editor.

Note that this is the completed Locatapp project, so if you are following along and building your own copy, it has a few more symbols than you will have at this point.

The flat display (shown in Figure 11-3) is similar to the hierarchical display for many projects because, in the hierarchical display, at any level of the hierarchy the symbols are listed alphabetically.

Choosing what to display

The buttons at the bottom of the symbol navigator let you choose what to display. Each is a toggle to control if its data is displayed. From left to right, the buttons turn on (and off) the following displays:

- **Class and protocol symbols only (button C):** Global symbols are not displayed (these are the other symbols in the list shown at the beginning of this section — functions, structures, enumerations, and so forth).
- **Project-defined symbols (document icon):** Symbols from the frameworks aren't shown.
- **Members (button M):** For the most part, these are the member properties and methods of classes or protocols.

In addition to the three buttons, a filter (search) field lets you further limit the symbols that are displayed.

I leave the middle button (project-defined symbols — the document icon) on and the other two off. I also leave the Classes and Protocols symbols expanded. That gives me the information I most frequently look at, but your choices and your projects may be different.

Preventing Disasters with Assertions

Everyone can agree that apps shouldn't crash. But, as a wise manager once said, "Remember that people shouldn't lie, cheat, or steal." Yes, none of those things (including software crashes of all kinds) should happen — but they do.

Our job is to prevent such problems as much as possible.

One way to do this is to check in the code to see if a potentially problematic situation has arisen — perhaps a database is offline or a needed resource is `nil`. If the problem is found, you can gracefully end your app and write a message to the log, as well as inform the user.

This is the gold standard, but it's also the most expensive approach, in terms of resources. It's what should be done for the most extreme cases.

In Swift and other languages, assertions provide a less extensive (if less user-friendly) approach. An assertion (using the built-in global `assert` function), tests whether a condition is true or not. If it is true, processing continues, but if it is false, a message is provided to the user, and the app terminates then and there. (If you are running on a device or the iOS Simulator in debug mode, you can see exactly where the assertion failed.)

Assertions are often provided to catch issues during debugging when the terseness of the message is enough to let developers and testers know an area needs further attention. During the development process, it's not uncommon to see a number of `assert` calls in a particularly problematic section of code.

An example of an `assert` statement is

```
assert (someValue<0, "someValue is out of range (<0)")
```

Patterns

In `switch` statements and other tests, you can match patterns instead of values. You may be used to `switch` statements that match on values, as in the following snippet (adapted for Swift syntax):

```
let val = 15
switch val {
case 15:
    println (15)

case 20:
    println (20)

default:
    println ("Other result")
}
```

The value of `val` is set in the first line. The `switch` statement then tests for values of 15 and 20. Because Swift switches must be exhaustive, a `default` case is included so that the `switch` statement will execute some case no matter what value you set `val` to. Try it with several numeric values.

If you try changing the first line to a non-numeric value, however, you'll get an error because the two `case` statements both expect a number. (That is a form of pattern matching.)

Now try another `switch` statement, such as the following:

```
let val = 20

switch val {
case let x:

    println ("The value is \(x)")

default:
    println ("Some other value")
}
```

Here, `val` is set to 20 as a value. However, note that you could also take the position that `val` is set to a single value. (In fact, both of these statements are correct — it's set to an integer with the value of 20.)

The selection of the case to use doesn't match the value of 20; rather, it matches the *pattern* of an integer. The `case` statement doesn't consist of a value (as in the first example — 15 or 20). Instead, the case statement matches an *expression,* which, in this case, is

```
let x
```

By itself, `x` would be a value for the `case` statement; `let x`, on the other hand, is an expression. Because the `case` statement provides an expression, it assumes to match on the pattern of that expression rather than a value. The pattern of a single value matches `let val = 20`, so the `case` statement executes. The `case` also succeeds for `let x = "test"` (still one value).

Now consider a more elaborate pattern by using a collection of values, as in this example:

```
let val = (1, 2, 3)

switch val {
case let (a, b, c):
    println ("The values are: (\(a), \(b), \(c)).")

default:
    println ("Some other value")
}
```

The pattern matches. Try changing the first line to this:

```
let val = (4, 5, 6)
```

It still matches. The pattern is three elements, so the following will also work:

```
let val = (1, "two", 3)
```

Add or remove one of the values, however, and you'll get an error. The magic number is three. For example, neither of these will work:

```
let val = (1, 3)
let val = (1, 3, 4, 6)
```

It is the `let` expression rather than the value that makes this a pattern-matching `switch` statement.

Ranges

Ranges are useful when you are working with `for-in` statements. They come in two variations: closed and half-open.

A closed range used in a `for-in` statement looks like this:

```
for index in 1...5 {
  //do something
}
```

Note the three dots in the range. This statement executes 5 times (experiment with it in a playground and you'll see.)

A half-open range looks like this

```
for index in 1..<5 {
  //do something
}
```

Instead of three dots, there are two dots and a <. If you experiment in a playground, you'll see that it executes 4 times. Half-open ranges are useful for arrays that start at 0 because you want to step through them starting from 0 to one less than the count of elements in the array. (An array with 5 elements in it can start at 0 and go to 4 — not 5.)

You can combine ranges with `switch` statements as in the previous section. The following code works for a range of values:

```
let val = 4

switch val {
case 1..<5:
  println ("in range")
default:
  println ("not in range")
}
```

Experiment with changing the value of `val` as well as the value of the `case` statement. For example, with the code shown here, if you set `val` to 14 in the first line, it is not in range. Try experimenting with a range like `"abc"..."def"` and see what you get.

The half-open range only works with `..<`. Any character other than < at the end is an error. If you want a different comparison, reverse the sign on the expression or otherwise make it comport with `..<`.

Chapter 12

Initializing and Deinitializing Data

In This Chapter

- Understanding the reasons for initialization
- Initializing properties and variables
- Creating initializers and adding parameters
- Observing changes to properties
- Deinitializing properties and variables

In Swift, every instance of a class, structure, or enumeration must be initialized before being used. Accordingly, Swift gives you several ways to create various types of initializers to handle the process. You can also perform the initialization yourself by setting an initial or default value, which initializes the instance. In addition, many parts of the Cocoa and Cocoa Touch frameworks handle initialization for you.

For example, if you use Interface Builder to design your interface in Xcode, you can draw views and other interface elements on the Xcode canvas. At runtime, the framework instantiates the views and other interface elements that you have drawn, and in the process, it initializes them.

As another example, consider the Master-Detail Application template that is the basis of Locatapp, the example used throughout this book. Do a search for *init* in Locatapp and you'll only get an error message ("Failed to initialize the application's saved data") from the Build Settings pane. The many initializers that you use through that template (and your app) are all hidden deep inside the Cocoa Touch framework.

It's nice that Cocoa and Cocoa Touch can help out with initialization, but for classes that you create, you'll have to think about creating and using initializers yourself. You also may have to think about *deinitializers* — functions called when an instance is about to be deallocated. This chapter introduces you to both of these parts of the initialization process.

This chapter shows you how to manage initialization in the classes that you create. Perhaps more important, it shows you how to use the initializers in classes that you use from the frameworks. There are a number of other initialization techniques that you can use in your own classes, but often you are confronted with initialization code that you must use when you use the Xcode templates or the sample code on `developer.apple.com`. This chapter helps you with initialization tasks you'll need to do even if you're not creating your own classes.

Understanding Initialization

Enforcing Swift's initialization rule means that you cannot have uninitialized instances lying around, and this, in turn, means that you cannot accidentally attempt to access an incomplete instance object. Try this in a playground:

```
var w: UIWindow
println (w)
```

You'll get an error right away (or at least as soon as the playground finishes parsing your code). You can see the result in Figure 12-1.

What if you don't know what you want to set `w` to? You can get around this problem by making `w` an optional, as in this example (shown in Figure 12-2):

```
var w: UIWindow?
println  (w)
```

In this code, the variable has been automatically set to `nil`, and, therefore, it is initialized with that value, so you can use it without creating an error.

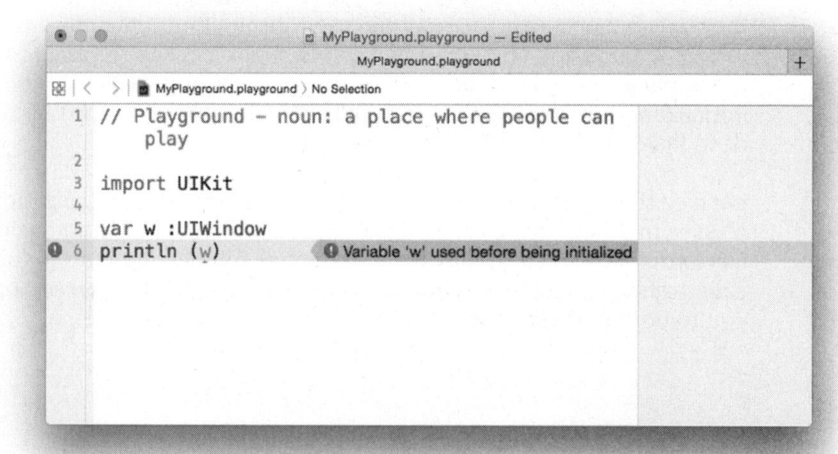

Figure 12-1: If you use an uninitialized variable, you'll get an error.

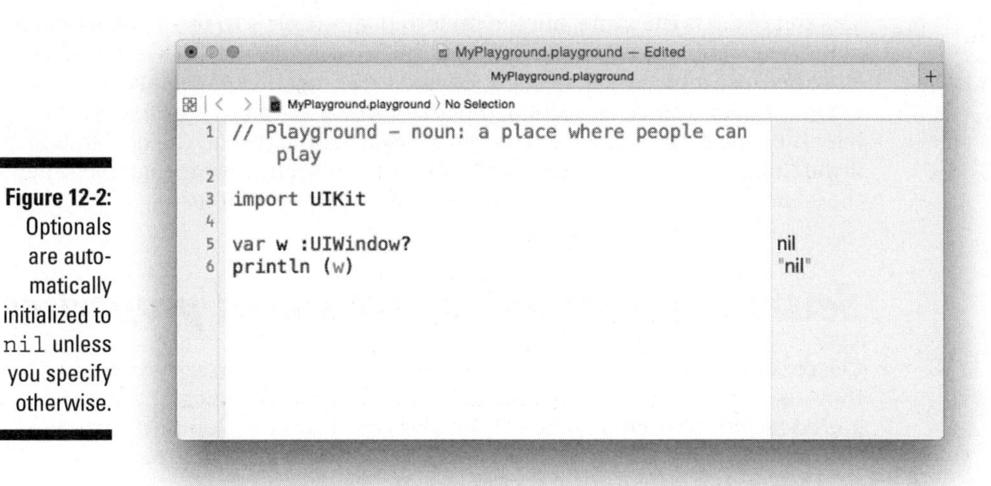

Figure 12-2: Optionals are automatically initialized to `nil` unless you specify otherwise.

You may think that you can get around all of this initialization stuff just by declaring everything as an optional. It's true that this approach keeps you from having to initialize everything — because everything is automatically set to `nil` — but does this really save time or effort? You can still access these initialized properties or variables, but before you do so, you'll have to check to see whether each property or variable is `nil`. This means that your code is going to be littered throughout with phrases like this:

```
if  w != nil {do something with w}
```

You're going to have to include a line like that every time you use `w`. In the end, it's better to initialize properties without using optionals. Initialization takes a little more typing, but it also takes serious consideration of the way you'll be using the property or variable, which can be invaluable as you build your app (and also as you become more and more familiar with Cocoa or Cocoa Touch).

Performing Initialization

There are a number of ways to initialize stored properties. The major ones fall into two categories:

- ***Default values*** are set in a declaration, as in:

  ```
  var x = 17
  ```

- ***Initial values*** are set in an initializer, as in:

  ```
  x = 17
  ```

The end result is the same, but the preferred approach is to use a default value in the declaration when possible. There are two reasons why this is preferred: First, because it places the declaration and value together, it can make maintenance easier over time. Second, the use of a default value can allow Swift to infer the type of the property. You can always add the type to the declaration if you think that the type might not be inferred correctly (as for example, when the inferred type is a subclass of the class you really want to use).

Setting default values for stored properties

Classes and structures in Swift both can contain *stored properties* because they are stored as part of the object they belong to. Technically, they are stored as part of each instance of the class or structure. Computed properties are calculated as needed and are not stored; they are not initialized because nothing is stored. (See Chapter 16 for more.)

As with variables that aren't part of a structure or class, stored properties can be constants (declared with `let`) or variables (declared with `var`). Their type is either declared or inferred from the initial value. If you do not provide an initial value, you must provide a declared type. Classes in most object-oriented programming languages can contain some kind of properties or other declarations. Structures can contain fields or components (or other terms) in C and its derivatives. The ability to place functions or other code in objects is common in object-oriented programming languages but placing them in structures is less so.

A stored property is declared in a class or structure as I describe in Chapter 6. Except for optional properties, every property in a class or structure must have a value when initialization is completed. Figure 12-3 shows how you can set default values using a playground and demonstrates the use of stored properties (`myInstance.myProperty`), as well as the use of global variables (`myProperty`), and the initialization of both.

There is more on properties in Chapter 16.

The following steps show you how to produce the code in Figure 12-3:

1. **Declare a global variable called `myProperty` (line 5) and set its default value to 6.**

```
var myProperty :Int = 6
```

2. **Declare a class called `MyClass` (line 7).**

```
class MyClass {
}
```

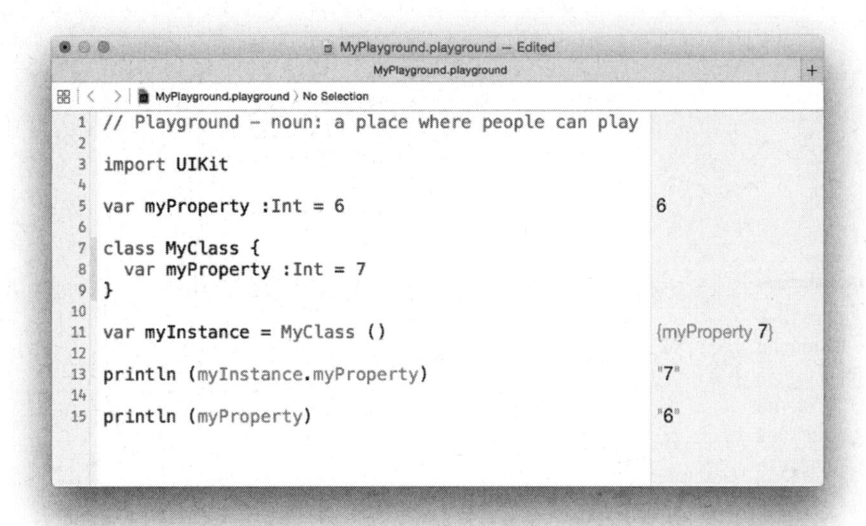

Figure 12-3: Initializing a global variable and a stored property.

3. **In the body of the class, declare a property called `myProperty` (line 8) and set its default value**

   ```
   myProperty :Int = 7
   ```

4. **Create a global variable called `myInstance` and set it to an instance of `MyClass` (line 11).**

   ```
   var myInstance = MyClass ()
   ```

5. **Print the instance `myProperty` (line 12).**

   Note that the value is 7.

6. **Print the global `myProperty` (line 14).**

   Note that the value is 6.

You can use instances of classes as values for stored properties as you see in Figure 12-4. In this case, there are two classes (`MyClass` and `MyClass2`). `MyClass` is the same as the one shown in Figure 12-3, but it has an additional stored property — `myProperty2`. It is set to an instance of `MyClass2`, which is created inside `MyClass`. Figure 12-4 shows the values of the global property (`myProperty`), the stored property (`myInstance.myProperty`), and the new stored property containing an instance of `MyClass2`.

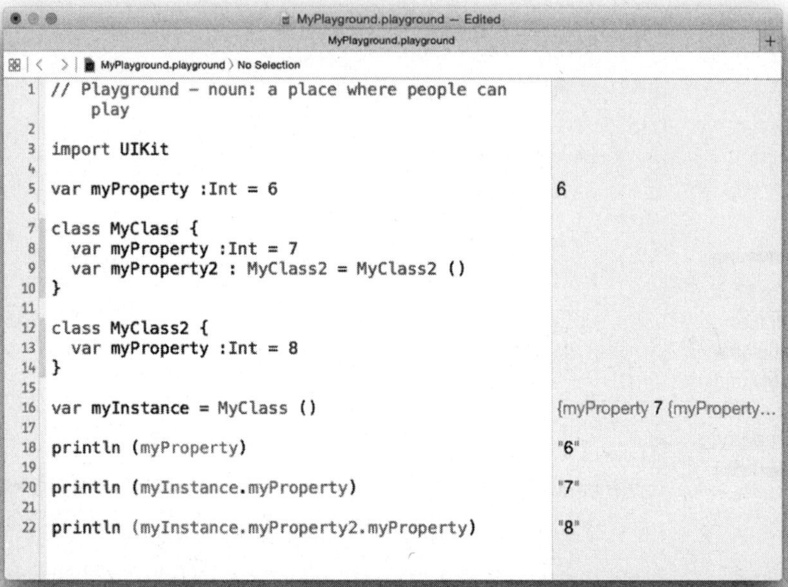

MyPlayground.playground — Edited
MyPlayground.playground
MyPlayground.playground 〉 No Selection

```
1  // Playground - noun: a place where people can
     play
2
3  import UIKit
4
5  var myProperty :Int = 6                              6
6
7  class MyClass {
8    var myProperty :Int = 7
9    var myProperty2 : MyClass2 = MyClass2 ()
10 }
11
12 class MyClass2 {
13   var myProperty :Int = 8
14 }
15
16 var myInstance = MyClass ()                          {myProperty 7 {myProperty...
17
18 println (myProperty)                                 "6"
19
20 println (myInstance.myProperty)                      "7"
21
22 println (myInstance.myProperty2.myProperty)          "8"
```

Figure 12-4: Creating initial values for stored properties that use instances of other classes.

Creating initializers for stored properties

You can declare an initializer function (or method — choose whichever name you prefer) rather than setting a default value. The initializer will be called automatically when a class or structure is instantiated as an instance. For this to happen, the initializer must be placed inside the structure or class, and it must have the name `init`.

The following steps show you how to do this. (The code needed for these steps is shown in Listing 12-1.) They start from the use of a default value, as described previously, and show how you can replace that code with an initializer — or with several initializers. The example uses a class that contains a location stored as latitude and longitude values, along with an optional name for the location:

1. **Create the class or structure.**
2. **Create stored properties and set them to the latitude and longitude of a place, as well as its optional name.**
3. **Create instances of the class and structure and store them in global variables `myLocationClass` and `myLocationStructure`.**

   Figure 12-5 shows what your playground should look like now.

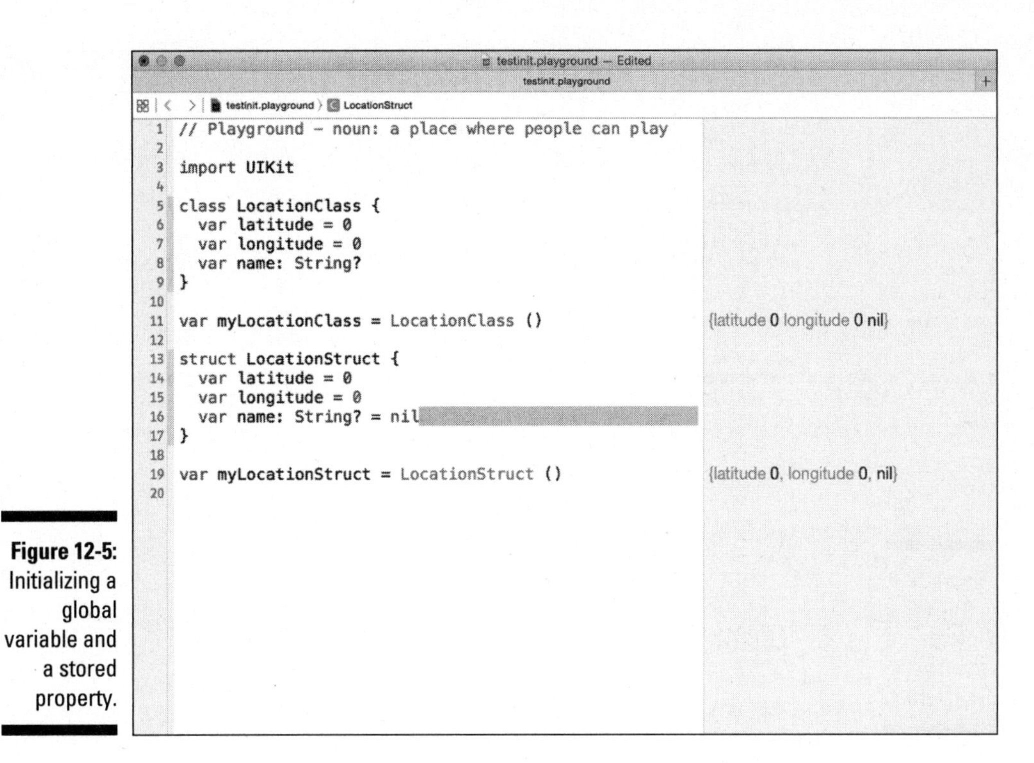

Figure 12-5: Initializing a global variable and a stored property.

4. **If you remove the initial values of the stored properties, you will get a variety of errors, as shown in Figure 12-6.**

   Note that there is no error with `name` in either the class or the structure. That is because it is an optional and is set to `nil` if you don't provide another value.

5. **Create initializers for both the class and structure. Each must have the name `init`, and it must add values to the stored properties `latitude` and `longitude`.**

   The values need not be constants: They could be the results of calculations or they could be expressions that include results of class methods. Figure 12-7 shows the use of constants. This is the initializer code for the class:

```
init () {
  latitude = 10
  longitude = 20
}
```

Note that the initializers are *within* the class and structure objects.

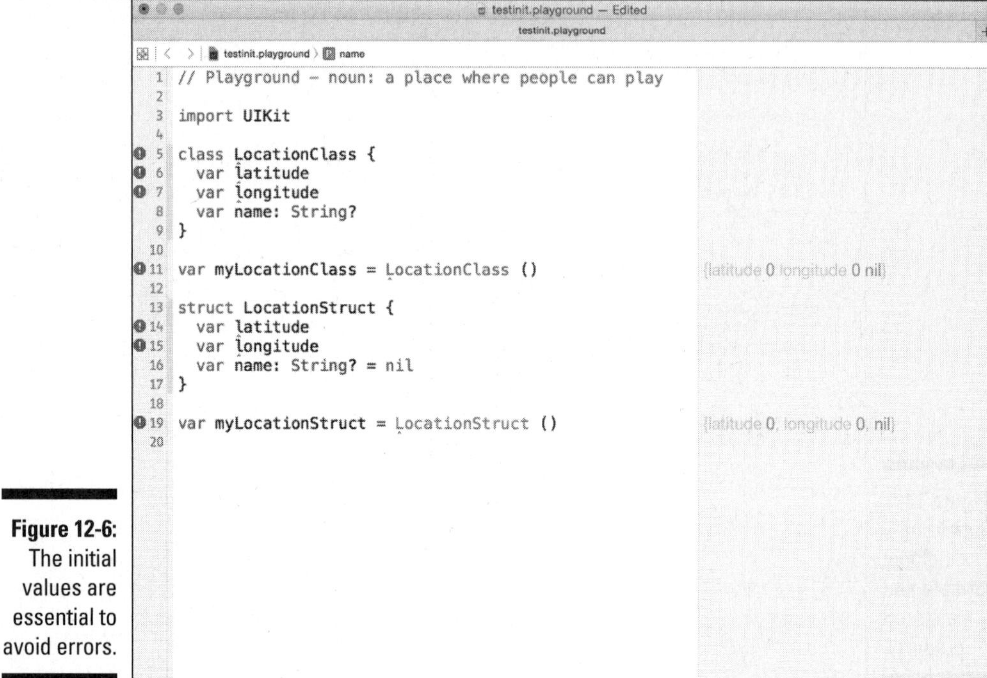

Figure 12-6: The initial values are essential to avoid errors.

Adding parameters to initializers

Listing 12-1 and Figure 12-7 show the simplest initializer syntax. You can make more complex initializers by adding parameters. When you add parameters to an initializer, you create a specific initializer that uses those parameters — even though its name is `init`.

Setting initial values in an initializer

For example, instead of using constants like 10, 20, 30, 40, and so forth, you could actually pass in the values for `latitude` and `longitude`. This means that the code to create and initialize `LocationClass` would look like this:

```
var myLocation = LocationClass
  (latitude: 10, longitude: 20)
```

The initializer inside the class declaration would look like this:

```
    init (latitude: Double, longitude: Double) {
      self.latitude = latitude
      self.longitude = longitude
    }
```

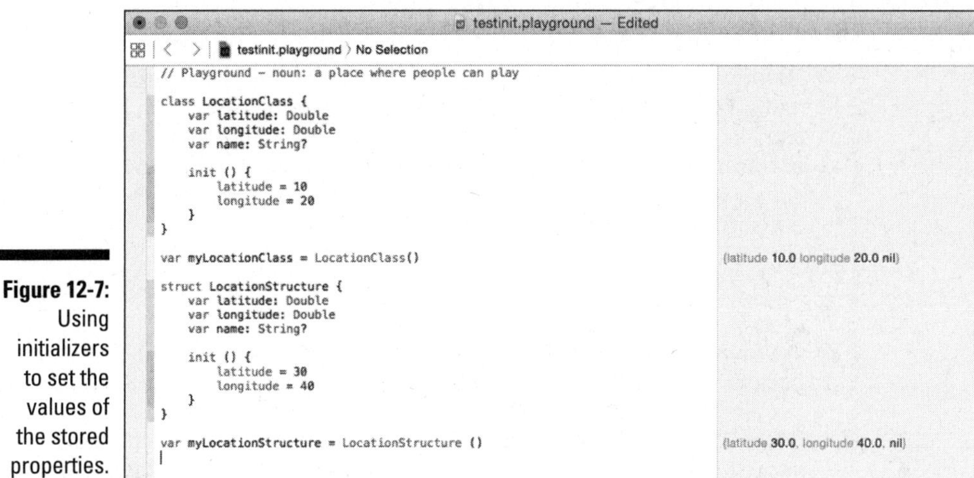

Figure 12-7: Using initializers to set the values of the stored properties.

Listing 12-1: Using Initializers for a Class and a Structure

```
// Playground - noun: a place where people can play

import UIKit

class LocationClass {
  var latitude: Double
  var longitude: Double
  var name: String?

  init () {
    latitude = 10
    longitude = 20
  }
}

var myLocationClass = LocationClass ()

struct LocationStruct {
  var latitude: Double
  var longitude: Double
  var name: String? = nil

  init () {
    latitude = 30
    longitude = 40
  }
}
var myLocationStruct = LocationStruct ()
```

Here are two points to notice:

- **Handle ambiguous names:** Because you have parameters to `init` named `latitude` and `longitude`, there is ambiguity if you leave the names of the properties in the function as `latitude` and `longitude`. In this case, make it clear that you are setting the class properties to the values of the `init` parameters. Change the code to reference `self` (the class itself), as in the following:

```
self.latitude = latitude
self.longitude = longitude
```

- **Optionals don't need to be set:** You can always come back and set name because it is an optional (notice the question mark in `String?`). Some people prefer to initialize every stored property including those that don't necessarily need it (the optionals). Other people prefer to initialize every *necessary* stored property including those that could be automatically set to `nil` but that you want to set to a value that you consider more usable.

Using external names in an initializer

Each of the arguments to `init` can have an external name that may or may not be the name of the property. Using the previous example with external names, the code could look like this:

```
var myLocationClass = LocationClass (
  digitalLatitude longitude: 15,
  digtitalLongitude longitude: 25,
  name: "The Place")
```

The initializer that uses external names would now look like this:

```
  init (digitalLatitude latitude: Double,
        digitalLongitude longitude: Double,
        name: String?) {

   self.latitude = latitude
   self.longitude = longitude
   self.name= name
}
```

For the declaration of `init`, you provide the external name, the internal name, and the type for each parameter. When you call the initializer, you provide the external name and the value for each parameter. Note that in this case, the external names are longer and provide more information (the fact that these are digital and not degree-minute-second values). Internally, the simpler name is used.

If no external name is provided, you can just use the internal name when you call the function.

This is an area of Swift that has changed over time.

Using an expression in an initializer

You don't have to pass values for properties into the `init`. Instead, you can pass in a separate value that is used to calculate one or more properties. Here is an example of an `init` that accepts an address string and geocodes (through the magic of a comment) it into latitude and longitude values:

```
init (address: NSString) {
  // do geocoding to set self.latitude and
  // self.longitude
}
```

Using multiple initializers

All initializers are named `init`, but they may vary based on their parameters. Figure 12-8 and Listing 12-2 show two initializers in the example code that

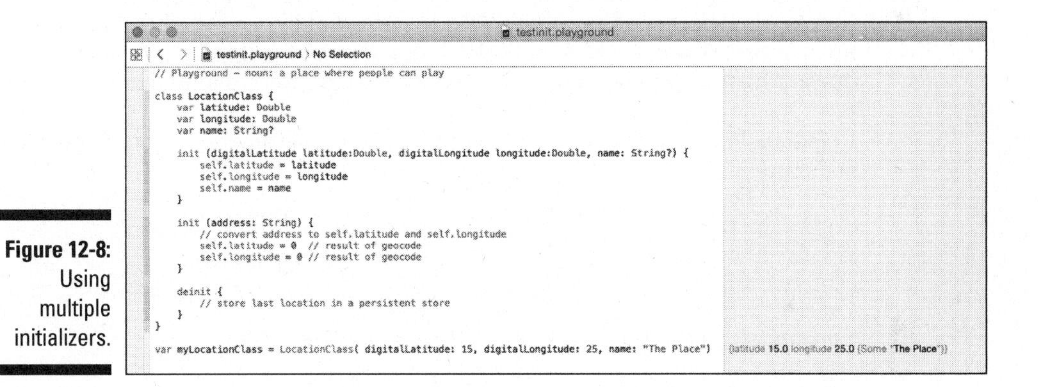

Figure 12-8: Using multiple initializers.

Listing 12-2: Using Multiple Initializers

```
class LocationClass {
  var latitude: Double
  var longitude: Double
  var name: String?

  init (digitalLatitude latitude: Double,
        digitalLongitude longitude: Double,
        name: String?) {
    latitude = latitude
    longitude = longitude
    self.name = name
  }

  init (address: NSString) {
    // convert address to self.latitude and self.
          longitude
  }
}
```

has been used in this chapter. One sets the stored properties based on values passed in, and the other uses the expression shown in the previous section. You can write both initializers (or even more) and then use which one you want.

Understanding Deinitialization

A deinitializer is named `deinit`. It has no parameters. You can use it to clean up a class when it is deallocated. (Although intializers are available to classes and structures, deinitializers are available only to classes.)

Deinitialization may mean moving values from properties that are about to disappear to other properties that will remain (such as in a Core Data persistent store). You don't have to worry about releasing memory: Swift uses Automatic Reference Counting (ARC) to get rid of unneeded objects and free up memory. However, although ARC handles the object memory issues, it doesn't handle data persistence, which is one use for a deinitializer.

Deinitializers are all called `deinit`; they take no parameters. Here's the basic structure:

```
deinit {
  // store last location in a persistent store
}
```

You could use this to keep track of the last location used.

Part IV

Using Components and Subcomponents

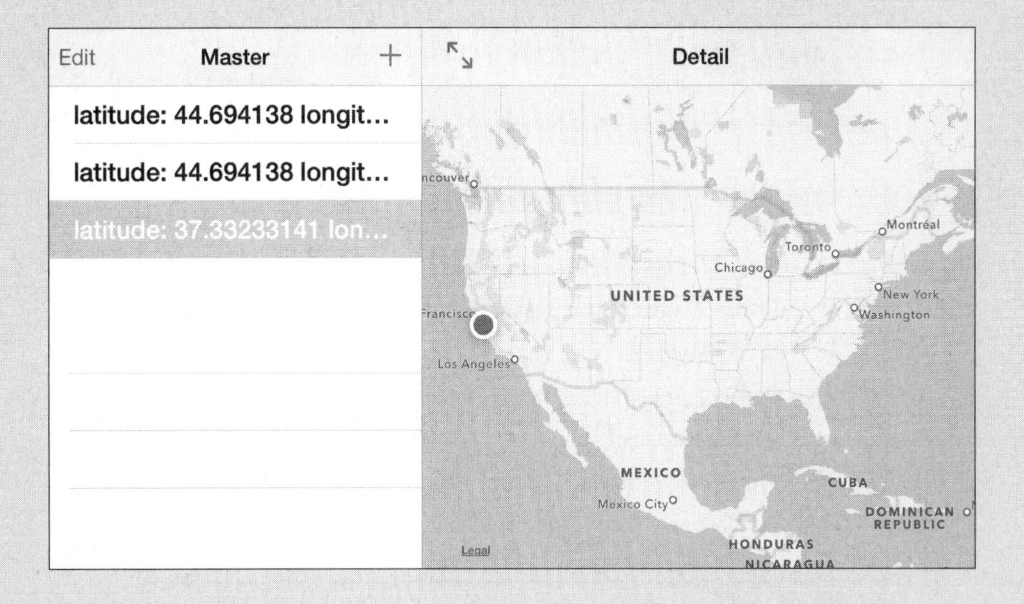

Find out how to let Xcode create actions and outlets for you at `www.dummies.com/extras/swift`.

In this part . . .

- Extend framework classes.
- Control access to your classes.
- Create Swift classes.
- Connect properties, variables, outlets, and actions.
- Enumerate values.
- Work with protocols.
- Put Objective-C and Swift together.

Chapter 13

Expanding Objects with Extensions

In This Chapter

- Looking into a Swift extension
- Extending a built-in type with a Swift extension
- Using a complex extension

In many object-oriented languages, adding subclasses (or *subclassing*) is the most common way of expanding or reusing a class. Over the years, however, additional techniques to expand classes have become common as more and more people use object-oriented programming techniques.

When it comes to reusing code and expanding classes, subclassing is now seen as a pretty blunt instrument. With subclassing, a common approach is to start from a basic class (sometimes called a *root* or *base* class), and to subclass it to add new functionality or customize existing functionality. The root class is often an abstract class that is not designed to be implemented. In an oft-used example, the root class might be *building,* and its first-level subclasses might be *residential building* and *commercial building.* You could then subclass residential building to *single-family* and *multi-family*. On and on you go, subclassing and subclassing until you have the specific class you need — perhaps a multi-family residential building consisting of condominiums (as opposed to co-ops or rental units), and with residency restrictions limiting it to a certain income range and age range.

Swift (like Objective-C and some other modern object-oriented languages) allows you to add methods and properties to classes without necessarily subclassing them. This chapter provides an overview of these Swift *extensions* (sometimes called *class extensions*).

Swift extensions are similar in many ways to Objective-C categories. Objective-C class extensions add methods as well as properties and instance variables to classes at compile time; you need access to the source code for the class. Objective-C categories add methods to classes, but you don't need access to the source code (you also don't need access to the source code to use Swift extensions). Just to make things perhaps a little murkier, Objective-C class extensions are sometimes referred to as anonymous categories: The two concepts are distinctly different but related in that they both can add methods (and in the case of class extensions properties and instance variables) to classes.

Working with a Swift Extension

If you've used Objective-C in the past, you may have heard or read about extensions. Yes, they can extend classes without the subclassing architecture, but they're a little confusing to many people. It's not unreasonable that the topic of Objective-C extensions is often discussed in the "Advanced" section of documentation and training materials.

You can create a new project from the Xcode template for an iOS Game; it contains an extension that you can use to investigate Swift extensions. Here's how to do that:

1. **Create a new project.**
2. **Use the iOS Game template.**
3. **In the Options sheet, give it a name (like testSpriteKitGame).**
4. **Fill in the organization name and identifier as you have done in Chapter 9 and as you see in Figure 13-1.**
5. **Set the language to Swift and devices to Universal.**
6. **For Game Technology, choose SpriteKit.** This is the only setting that's different for a game template project than from other templates.

Now, take a look at the top of `GameViewController.swift` shown in Listing 13-1. At the top of the file, you'll find an *extension* on `SKNode`.

The purpose of the extension in Listing 13-1 is to add a new method to a class (`GameViewController`). In order to do that, the extension is actually added to `SKNode`, which is part of SpriteKit. Figure 13-2 shows the documentation for `SKNode`. You can find it in Quick Help by typing in the name.

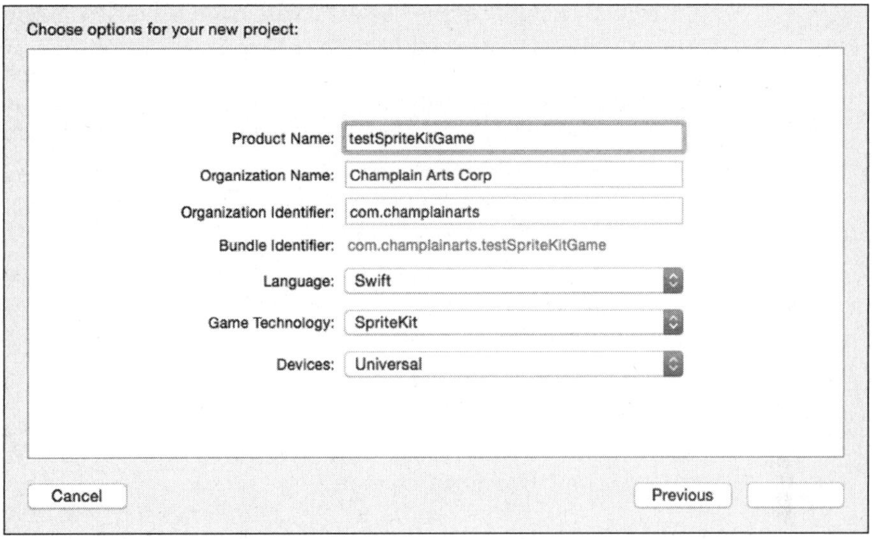

Figure 13-1: Create a new project based on the Game template and using SpriteKit.

Listing 13-1: Swift Extension

```
import UIKit
import SpriteKit

extension SKNode {
  class func unarchiveFromFile (file : NSString) ->
    SKNode? {
      if let path =
        NSBundle.mainBundle().pathForResource(file,
          ofType: "sks") {
          var sceneData = NSData(
             contentsOfFile: path,
             options: .DataReadingMappedIfSafe,
             error: nil)!
          var archiver = NSKeyedUnarchiver(
              forReadingWithData: sceneData)
          archiver.setClass(self.classForKeyedUnarchiver
            (), forClassName: "SKScene")
          let scene = archiver.decodeObjectForKey
            (NSKeyedArchiveRootObjectKey) as GameScene
          archiver.finishDecoding()
          return scene
        } else {
          return nil
        }
    }
}
```

This is a good example of the use of an extension because the new method (`unarchiveFromFile`) is added to:

- **`SKNode`:** A class of SpriteKit to which you don't have the source code. After it's added, it is also available to descendants of `SKNode` such as . . .
- **`SKScene`:** A subclass of `SKNode` for which you also don't have the source code. After it's added, it is also available to descendants of `SKScene` such as . . .
- **`GameScene`:** A descendant of SpriteKit, which is a part of the template.

Thus, by adding an extension to SKNode, you can use it as shown in the boldface type in Listing 13-2.

This section shows you what you'll end up with. How do you decide where to place the extension? You can work backwards from the code you want to write. Here's how you might do that:

1. **Write the code in Listing 13-2 (or a similar function).**
2. **Use a yet-unwritten function where you need it.**

   In Listing 13-2, this is `GameScene.unarchiveFromFile`. You'll get a compile error because it doesn't exist. Don't worry, keep going.

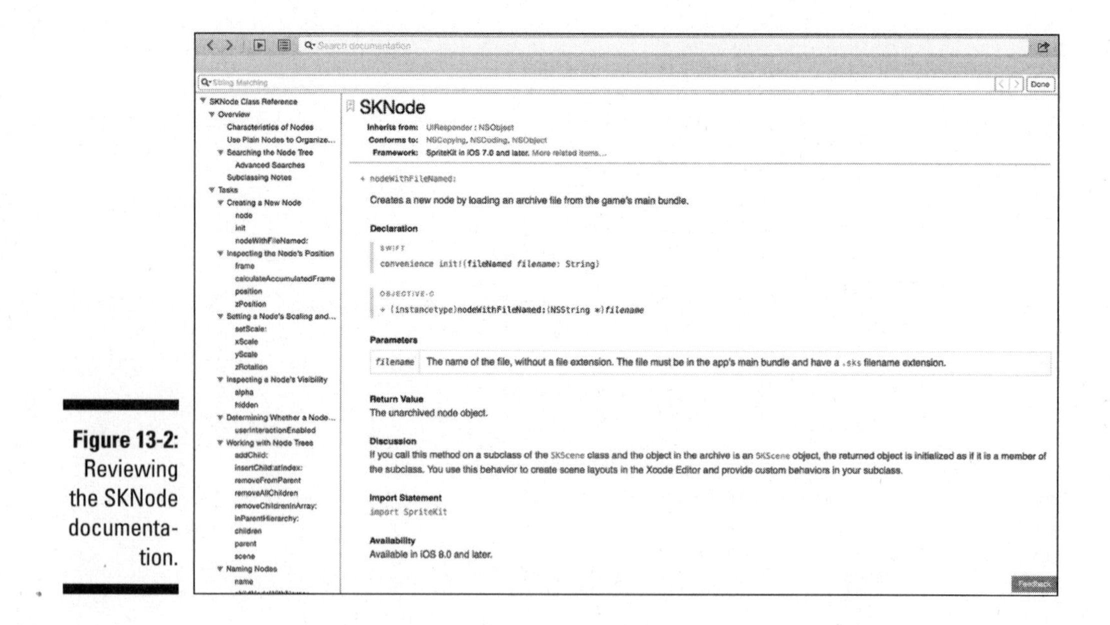

Figure 13-2: Reviewing the SKNode documentation.

Listing 13-2: Using an Extension in a Local Class

```
class GameViewController: UIViewController {

  override func viewDidLoad() {
    super.viewDidLoad()

    if let scene = GameScene.unarchiveFromFile
                ("GameScene") as? GameScene {

      // Configure the view.
      let skView = self.view as SKView
        skView.showsFPS = true
        skView.showsNodeCount = true

      /* Sprite Kit applies additional optimizations
         to improve rendering performance */
      skView.ignoresSiblingOrder = true

      /* Set the scale mode to scale to fit the window */
      scene.scaleMode = .AspectFill

      skView.presentScene(scene)
    }
  }
```

3. **Highlight `GameScene` and look at it in Quick Help.**

   You see its inheritance chain. Alternatively, you can search on it in your project. In either case, you'll find that it is a class defined in the template; its superclass is `SKScene`.

4. **Click on the superclass (`SKScene`) to see it in Quick Help.**

   You see its description and inheritance chain.

5. **Repeat Step 4 to move up the inheritance chain.**

   Alternatively, you can skip a link in the chain and move up two steps. At each step, review the description. You're looking for the place to add your extension.

6. **Decide where to place the class extension based on how broadly you want to make it available.**

   The higher up the inheritance chain you place it, the more instances of subclasses have access to it.

7. **Move up to `SKNode`, as shown in Figure 13-2.**

   This is where the template has placed the extension.

Because it's not difficult to change the class on which you place the extension, you can experiment. Some people like to place the extension on the immediate class where it's needed or on that class's superclass. If you need it to be more widely available, just change the code at the top of Listing 13-1 to choose another class for the extension. This is the line of code you would change:

```
extension SKNode {
```

Using Swift Extensions with a Built-In Class

Classes, enumerations, and structures in Swift share many features; among them is the fact that any of them can be extended with a Swift extension. Swift extensions can be very lightweight elements, and this section shows you how to build basic Swift extensions onto the `Int` class. If you're used to thinking of Objective-C extensions and categories as advanced topics (or even very advanced topics), this section is for you.

You extend a class, enumeration, or structure by creating an extension *on* it.

The following list offers a series of experiments you can make in a playground to learn about extensions. You start by creating an extension on `Int` that automatically calculates half of the value of the `Int`.

1. **Create a new playground for Swift.**

   You can use OS X or iOS for this example.

2. **Create and initialize an `Int` variable called `i`.**

   ```
   var i: Int = 20
   ```

3. **Create an extension on the `Int` class.**

   By convention, the extension should precede the use of the class. All import statements, extensions, and similar constructs are generally placed at the top of a Swift file, so place this *above* the line you wrote in Step 2. (Remember, this is a convention, not a requirement.)

   ```
   extension Int {
   }
   ```

4. **Create a function in the extension.**

   You can call it `halfValue`.

   ```
   func halfValue () -> Int {
   }
   ```

5. **Divide the value of the `Int` by 2.**

   Store the result in a variable. Note that self is the value of the `Int`.

   ```
   let halfValue = self/2
   ```

6. **Return halfValue.**

   ```
   return halfValue
   ```

7. **You can now access the `halfValue` function you have added with the `Int` extension.**

   ```
   i.halfValue()
   ```

Your example code should look like Listing 13-3.

Figure 13-3 shows the result in the playground.

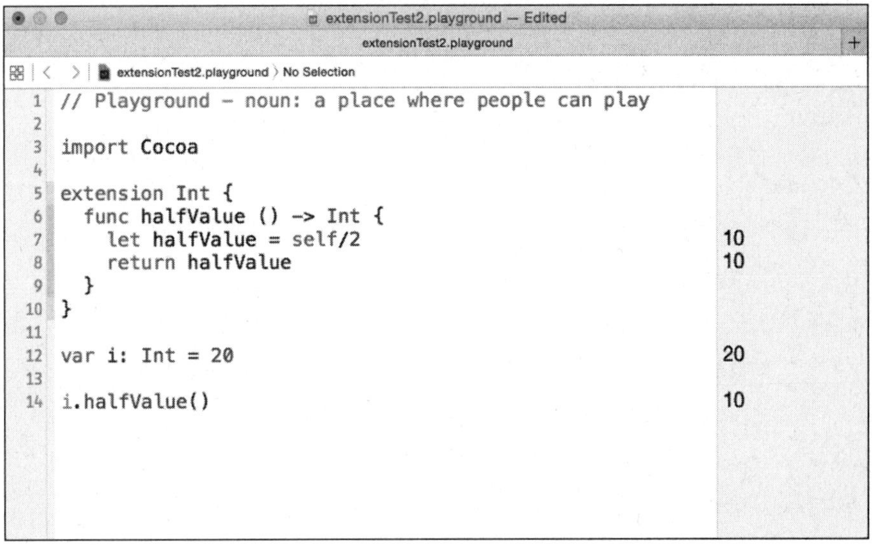

```
extensionTest2.playground — Edited
extensionTest2.playground
extensionTest2.playground > No Selection
1  // Playground - noun: a place where people can play
2
3  import Cocoa
4
5  extension Int {
6    func halfValue () -> Int {
7      let halfValue = self/2                    10
8      return halfValue                          10
9    }
10 }
11
12 var i: Int = 20                               20
13
14 i.halfValue()                                 10
```

Figure 13-3: Using a playground to test an extension.

Listing 13-3: Creating a Simple Extension on Int

```
extension Int {
  func halfValue () -> Int {
    let halfValue = self/2
     return halfValue
  }
}
var i: Int = 20
i.halfValue
```

Experiment with your playground to see how it behaves as you change the value of `i`.

This is a very small step, but you can build on it to become more comfortable with extensions. The operation that this extension performs (dividing the value by 2) is very simple and basic. You can make it somewhat more complex by making it operate on another value rather than `self`. To do that, you modify Steps 4 and 5 in the previous list so that instead of looking like this

```
func halfValue () -> Int {
    let halfValue = self/2
```

they look like this

```
func halfValue (intIn: Int) -> Int {
    let halfValue = intIn/2
```

Listing 13-4 shows what the new extension looks like.

Figure 13-4 shows the result.

Listing 13-4: Modifying the Simple Extension on Int

```
extension Int {
  func halfValue (intIn: Int) -> Int {
    let halfValue = self/2
    return intIn
  }
}
var i: Int = 0
i.halfValue (i)
```

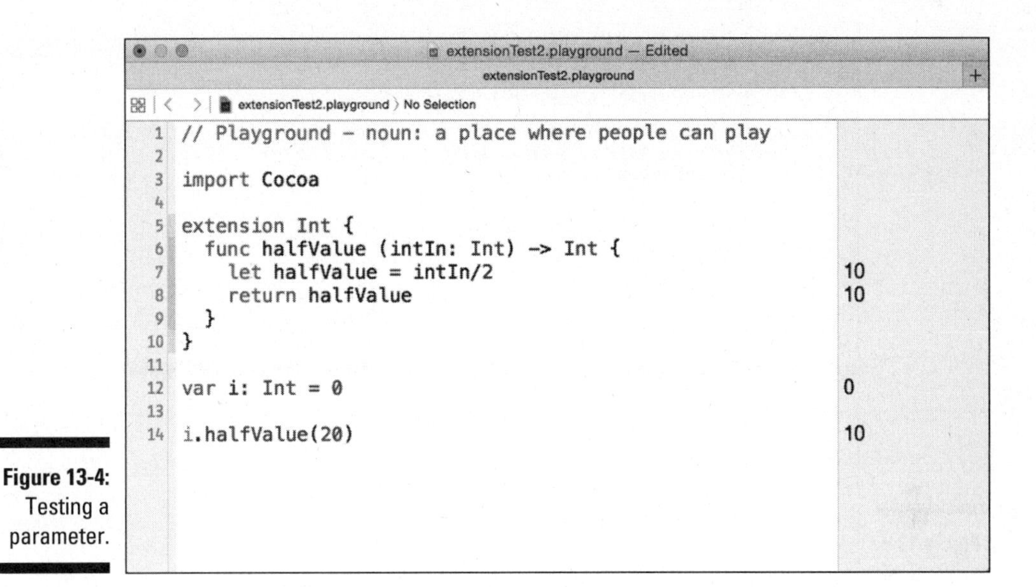

Figure 13-4: Testing a parameter.

You can also test other values, such as

```
i.halfValue (1234)
```

Because Swift is strict about typing, you can't use a `Float` or `Double`. As you see in Figure 13-5, you will get an error if you try the following line of code:

```
i.halfValue (1234.75)
```

The function in the extension expects an `Int` rather than a `Float` or `Double`.

With language constructs such as these lightweight extensions, you may be thinking that you can use Swift structures and enumerations together with extensions in many of the ways that you are used to working with large-scale and heavyweight classes — and you'd be right.

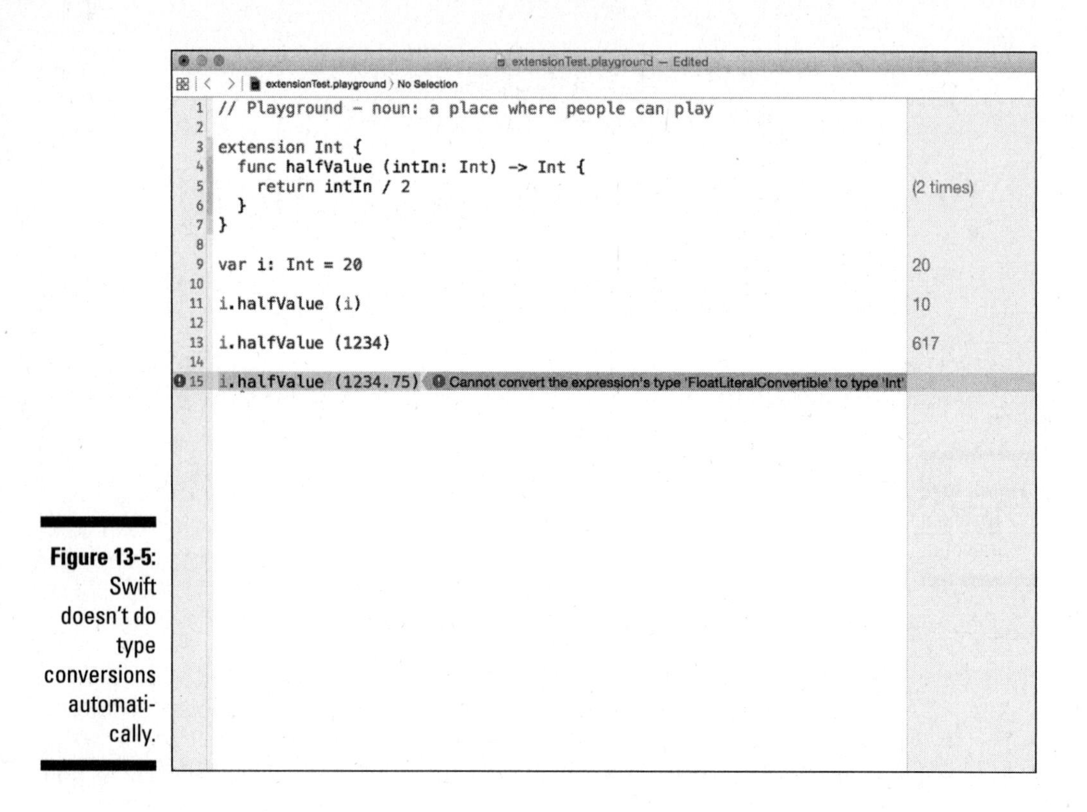

Figure 13-5: Swift doesn't do type conversions automatically.

Chapter 14

Managing Access Control for Your Objects

In This Chapter

- Understanding access control levels
- Defining access control terminology
- Working with access control modules, files, and entities

Access control isn't new with Swift: It's found in many languages. The idea has been around for a long time — for as long as developers have confronted the need to reuse code in a variety of environments. If you're writing code that's meant to be shared among a number of projects (whether the code is a framework or a library), you need to think about the access you'll grant to users of your code. (Users, in this sense, are developers who use your code rather than the end users who run the apps.) Often you can handle this issue by making everything open and public. This works if you're within a firewall and in a secure environment, but it also works if you are working on a project that's public and open.

For environments that aren't totally open (either globally or within a secure organizational environment), remember to consider setting access controls when you develop your code.

Even if none of these circumstances apply to you, you still may not be off the hook for access control issues. If you *use* shared code, you have to respect the access controls that are in place. Because it's hard to conceive of any iOS or OS X apps that don't use the Cocoa or Cocoa Touch frameworks, you're probably a client of access controlled code.

This chapter shows you both sides of the picture and helps you create and use access controlled code.

Introducing Access Control Levels

Access control can be implemented in a very crude way by managing permissions on files: You set permissions so that people can either read the files, write them, or execute them. This approach is often sufficient for files, but when it comes to code, these permissions are unwieldy.

Creating well-structured code often involves dividing the code into separate files. This facilitates reuse and modularity; it also makes multi-person projects more manageable and productive. In a multi-file project, relying simply on operating system permissions for files just won't do the job. That's where access control comes in as part of the development environment. It is designed to work with code and code files. It has the flexibility that you need for code development, and, at least with Xcode and OS X, it works well along with the built-in file permission structures of the operating system.

Access control with Swift has three levels: public, private, and internal. Their meaning is simple, but there are some implementation issues about which you need to be concerned:

- **Public:** Entities whose access level is public can be used within any file in that Xcode project. The Cocoa and Cocoa Touch frameworks are typically imported into your code, and their entities are declared as public. If you build your own frameworks, you usually set them to public.
- **Internal:** This level is used for entities that can be used within any file inside the Xcode project you're working in. This is the default access level, so, whether you know it or not, it's the level you're probably using for the code that you write.
- **Private:** This level is used for entities that can only be used within the source file in which they are defined.

Because you're a developer, and therefore a consumer of shared code such as frameworks, you typically use code specified as `public` by the framework developer (Apple, in most cases). And because you develop the code for your own projects, your own code is given `internal` access control by default.

On the other hand, if you are a developer who is a provider of shared frameworks for yourself and others, you usually set the interfaces of the frameworks to `public` and the implementation details (functions, properties, types, and so forth) to `private`.

This means that you can safely ignore most access control issues in the code that you're writing for your own apps, particularly if you're developing apps the way you and others developed them for Objective-C (that is to say, accepting the default access levels that make interface files — .h Objective-C files — `public` and implementation files — .m Objective-C files — internal.

With Swift, more and more developers are creating frameworks for shared code, so you may become a framework provider — even if it's only to yourself for other projects. In that case, you need to worry about access control both as the provider and consumer of your own frameworks. This takes a little more effort, but it makes your life as a developer easier.

Using Swift Access Control Terminology

Swift documentation discusses the three levels of access control using the three modifiers you use (`public`, `private`, and `internal`), but it also covers three other access-control–related terms you should be aware of. These terms may be new to you, or you may know them from other contexts, but either way, they refer to concepts that you already have dealt with. They are described in the following sections.

Modules

In the context of access control, a *module* is a product of an Xcode build target. Mostly, it is an app or a framework. If you allow other people (or other projects of your own) to use a module by using an `import` statement, you must set access control for the module to allow that use (`public` is the least restrictive and may be a good place to start). A module can consist of a number of files.

Files

Files in the context of access control are just plain everyday files — there's nothing special about them. You manage them with the Finder just as you manage spreadsheets, PDF files, and other documents. If you need to modify their titles, permissions, or other attributes, you do it with Get Info in the Finder (⇨File⇨Get Info). Titles can be modified directly in the Finder.

If you're developing iOS apps, you may be tempted to skip over the references to OS X in this section: Don't. Remember that you use Xcode on a Mac to build apps for both iOS and OS X.

Working with Xcode project files and folders

When you create a project with Xcode, it places all of the files it creates for that project in a folder. You can specify the location for the project folder, but be careful about moving or renaming files inside a project. If you want to rename a file, select it in the Xcode project navigator and choose Edit⇨Refactor⇨Rename. By doing it this way, Xcode makes the necessary changes to keep all of the project files consistent.

When moving files around on a disk, it's best to move the entire project folder around so that the internal project links are properly preserved. If you have any issues with files in the project (perhaps after moving individual files around), remember that you can always select a file in the project navigator and fix its behavior.

Follow these steps to fix a file that is missing or that fails to appear in the project when you can see it on disk.

1. **Select the file in the project navigator as you see in Figure 14-1.**
2. **Choose the File inspector from the utilities area at the right of the workspace window.**
3. **Check the file's location.**

   When you do this, you can change files or view which file is being used, as follows:

   - Click the right-pointing arrow next to Full Path to see which file is being pointed to.
   - Change the file by using Full Path to see the file and then navigating in the Finder to the new file and double-clicking the new file.

4. **To prevent future problems, use the Location pop-up menu to choose how the location is interpreted.**

   See the following section for details.

Choosing location behavior

Xcode allows you to specify the location for each file in the project, and you can also choose how that location is managed as you move files around. This

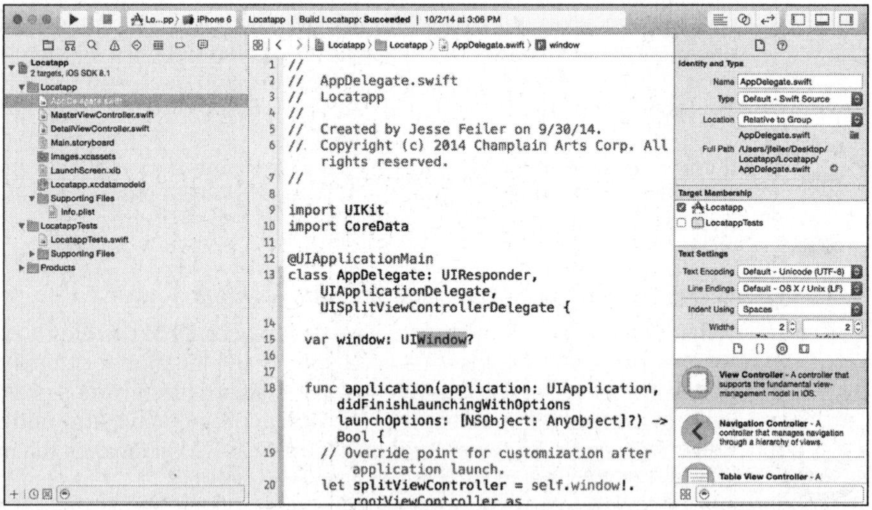

Figure 14-1: Using the File inspector to fix a missing file.

becomes important as you move project folders around — maybe even from one Mac to another. You use the Location pop-up menu at the top of the File inspector (shown in Figure 14-1) to change these settings.

Here are the common location behavior settings:

- **Absolute Path:** The path to this file is exactly as shown in Full Path. If you move the project to another Mac that doesn't have access to this path, you can't build your project. Use this setting to point to some file that you want to use in all cases — such as a corporate copyright notice file that must be included in every project on every Mac in an organization.
- **Relative to Group:** This is one of the most common settings for a project. Files are located relative to the group they're in within a project. Normally, however, the group itself is set to Relative to Project (see the next topic).
- **Relative to Project:** The project as a whole is used as the reference point. If you use this setting and move the entire Xcode project folder somewhere else, all the files inside the folder will move, and if the individual files are set to Relative to Project, all links and locations will be fine.

There are three additional settings — Relative to Developer Directory; Relative to Build Products; and Relative to SDK — but they aren't often used by most developers. As such, they're beyond the scope of this book.

Deleting derived data files

There are other files beyond those in your project folder. These files are generated by Xcode as you build your project (they are referred to as *derived files*). They contain data that the compiler has assembled as part of its processing; it reuses that derived data the next time you build your app.

If you want to change the locations of these files, you can do so with Xcode⇨Preferences You can see your projects in the Xcode Organizer (Window⇨Organizer), as shown in Figure 14-2. You normally don't need to worry about these files. If you move your project to another computer, the derived files will be created on that computer in accordance with the Xcode preferences on that computer.

You can delete the derived files using the Delete button shown in Figure 14-2. If you have made significant changes to a project, clean it; if you have mysterious build errors, delete the derived data files because you may be picking up old versions of the derived data. Normally this doesn't matter, but if you think it may be a problem, just use the Delete button in the Organizer for the project you're working on.

Often, people want to see where their app is placed after they build it. Most of the time, you don't have to worry about that: If you want to run it, run it using the Run button at the left of the Xcode toolbar. If you want to share it with someone else (or with the App Store), you must have built it for an actual device (not iOS Simulator). If you have an actual device chosen in

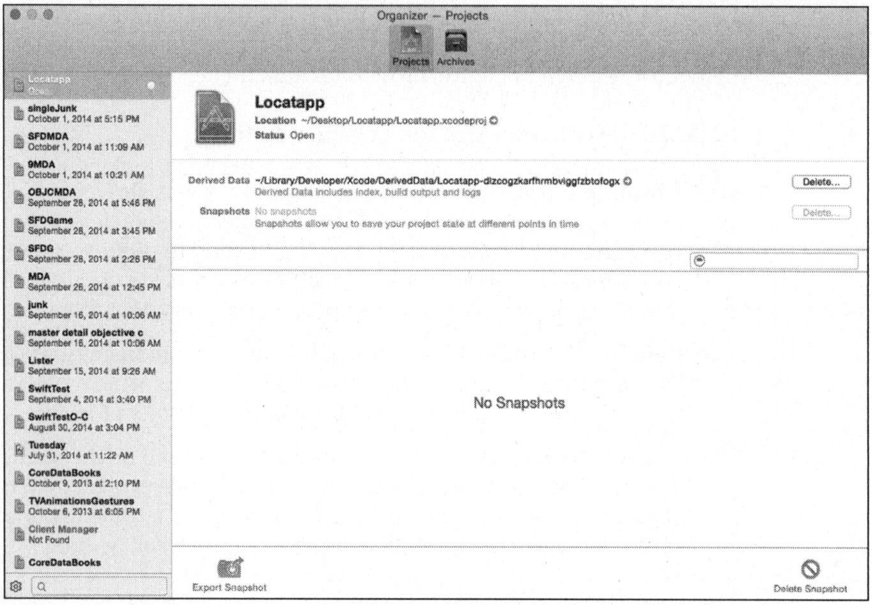

Figure 14-2: Managing the files in your project.

the Scheme pop-up menu at the left of the Xcode toolbar, you can choose Product➪Archive to start the process of creating an app to share. There is more on this at `developer.apple.com`.

Entities

Entities are the smallest units that can be managed with access control. In terms of access control, types (classes, structures, and enumerations), functions, properties, and the like are all entities.

You set the access level for an entity by using `public`, `internal`, or `private` in the entry's declaration. Remember that the default level is `internal`. When you are declaring types, the access control of the type itself interacts with its members. Here are the rules:

- If the type is `public`, its members are still `internal` unless otherwise specified as `public` or `private`.
- If the type (class, structure, or enumeration) is `internal` (or is not specified), its members are `internal` unless you specify that one or more is `private`. You cannot make a member of an `internal` or `private` class `public` because `public` access is impossible for a member of an `internal` or private class. How could people get to the public member if the class is not `public`?
- If the type is `private`, its members are automatically `private`.

Chapter 15

Building Classes, Structures, and Enumerations

In This Chapter

- Exploring a simple class, structure, or enumeration in Locatapp
- Declaring methods and functions
- Considering modifiers

Swift classes are very much like classes in other object-oriented languages. However, in Swift, classes aren't the only elements that exhibit so-called class behaviors. This is one of the things that makes Swift different from those other languages. Swift's structures and enumerations, for example, can contain properties and methods, just as classes do. This means that when you're structuring a Swift app, you may need to revisit some of your decisions about what should constitute the class objects. Sometimes a structure or enumeration may be more appropriate.

This chapter shows you the basics of how to build classes, structures, and enumerations. I've combined these together because they have more in common in Swift than they do in many other object-oriented languages.

Exploring Classes, Structures, and Enumerations

You've already seen a number of examples of classes, structures, and enumerations, but the emphasis has been on how you use them in specific parts of Locatapp and other templates. In this chapter, the focus is on those objects and how you (or the Xcode template builders) create them.

Putting classes, structures, and enumerations together reflects their common features in Swift, but there's one very important distinction: Enumerations and structures are *value types*. Instances of enumerations and structures are copied when they are passed to a function or assigned to a variable or constant. This means that you can have multiple copies of a structure or enumeration instance, each with its own values that are independent of the others.

On the other hands classes are reference types. When they are assigned to a variable or constant or when they are passed to a function, a *reference* to the instance is what is passed. Because there is a single instance underlying the references passed to functions or assigned to variables or constants, a change to the values of that underlying instance is reflected in all of the copies.

Take a look at Table 15-1, which shows you the features available in classes, structures, and enumerations. Most of these features are common to most object-oriented programming languages in one way or another, but if you need a refresher, I describe them in the text that follows the table. A few of them are slightly redefined for Swift. They are shown at the left of Table 15-1, and are briefly described here.

Table 15-1 Features in Classes, Structures, and Enumerations

Feature	*Classes*	*Structures*	*Enumerations*
Instances	X	X	X
Properties	X	X	computed properties only
Methods	X	X	X
Subscripts	X	X	X
Initializers	X	X	X
Extensions	X	X	X
Protocols	X	X	X
Inheritance	X		
Type casting	X		
Deinitializers	X		
ARC	X		

- **Instances:** An object which is an actual representation of a class in most object-oriented languages is called an *instance*. In some object-oriented languages, you can also use a class itself as an object (for example, this is true of Objective-C). For many languages, variables declared as `struct` or `enum`, are referred to by the `struct` or `enum` name. In Swift, it is an *instance* of a `struct` or `enum`, but people still often use the type name (as in "`myVar` is a `MyStruct`") rather than as an instance of a particular struct ("`myVar` is an instance of `MyStruct`"). Don't lose sleep over this.
- **Properties:** You can declare properties that may either be stored or computed as they are needed. (Enumerations only support computed properties.)
- **Methods:** You can declare methods that can be accessed through any instance of these objects.
- **Subscripts:** You can declare subscripts that let you access elements of a type instance based on the logic in the subscript. Examples include providing multiple indexing schemes for multi-dimensional objects that may sometimes be accessed as if they were one-dimensional arrays and sometimes using multiple dimensions. They also are useful in managing non-integer indexes.
- **Initializers:** Initializers let you set up the properties for a new instance. See Chapter 12.
- **Extensions:** Extensions let you add methods and properties without necessarily having the code for the object to which you are adding them. (Only computed properties can be used with enumerations.) See Chapter 13.
- **Protocols:** You can define methods in a protocol that must be implemented by any object that conforms to that protocol. See Chapter 18.
- **Inheritance:** Classes can inherit from one another forming a subclass/superclass structure. A class can have any number of subclasses but only one (or no) superclass.
- **Type casting:** You can treat one class as its sub- or superclass if conditions permit. This is basically a standard exercise in logic. `UILabel` is a subclass of `UIView`; therefore, all instances of `UILabel` are also instances of `UIView`. Not all instances of `UIView` are instances of `UILabel`.
- **Deinitializers:** Deinitializers let you clean up just before a class instance is about to be deallocated.
- **ARC:** *Automatic reference counting (ARC)* allows you to have multiple instances of a class. When you pass them around, they are passed by reference, so that, for example, if you have two instances of `UILabel`, setting the text for one `UILabel` doesn't have anything to do with setting the text for the other label.

Declaring a Simple Class

In previous chapters, you've seen classes, structures, and enumerations in several contexts, but I hadn't yet revealed the details of their syntax and structure. In this section, then, I finally explore the inner workings of Swift classes, structures, and enumerations (at least the inner workings that are common to all of them — refer to Table 15-1).

In Locatapp (actually the Master-Detail Application template) you can see two views at the same time when you run the app on an iPhone 6 Plus or any of the iPad models. When held horizontally (in *landscape* orientation), any iPad or an iPhone 6 Plus shows two views side by side as you see in Figure 15-1. (Note that this figure shows Locatapp as it is at the end of Chapter 9.)

On older iPhone models, however, you have a navigation interface: One view appears at a time. You navigate from view to view but only one view is visible at all times.

In the template, most of the code is in the master view controller (this is the view at the left in Figure 15-1). It's the view that lets you create events and delete events. The master view controller tells the detail view controller (shown at the right in Figure 15-1) the specific data to display — in fact, this is why it's called a *detail view controller*.

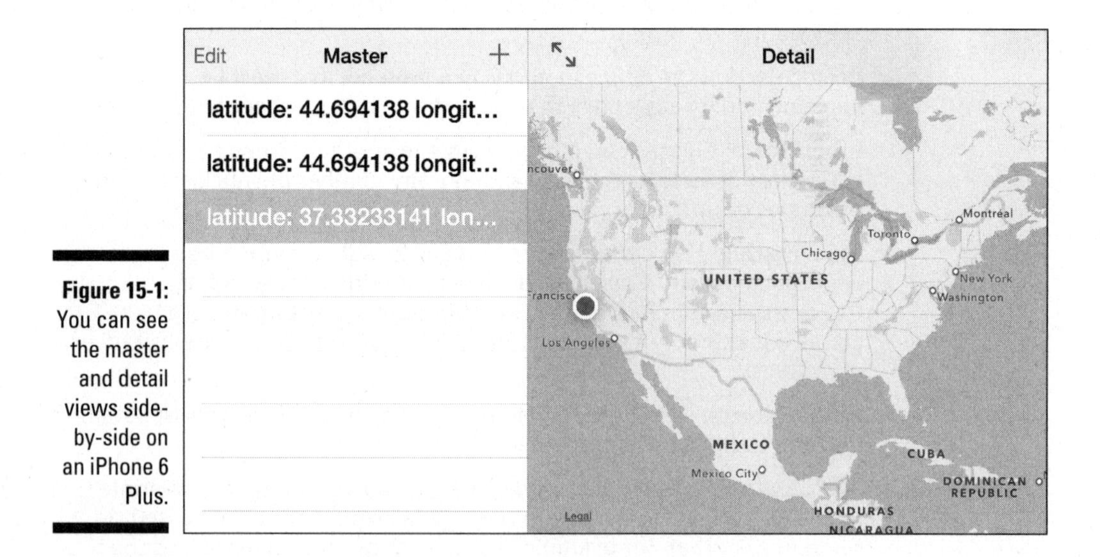

Figure 15-1: You can see the master and detail views side-by-side on an iPhone 6 Plus.

The detail view controller is implemented with a relatively simple class called `DetailViewController`. The simplicity of this class is why it's a good class to examine to get an idea of how classes work.

Listing 15-1 shows the code for `DetailViewController`. As you can see, there's not much code involved, so it's easy to explore the entire class. The comments in Listing 15-1 show the before and after syntax for the lines of code changed in Chapter 9 to implement the map.

Listing 15-1: DetailViewController from Master-Detail Application Template with Modifications

```
//
//  DetailViewController.swift
//  Locatapp
//
//  Created by Jesse Feiler on 10/23/14.
//  Copyright (c) 2014 Jesse Feiler. All rights reserved.
//

import UIKit
import MapKit

class DetailViewController: UIViewController {

  //@IBOutlet weak var detailDescriptionLabel: UILabel!
  @IBOutlet var mapView: MKMapView!


    var detailItem: AnyObject? {
        didSet {
            // Update the view.
            self.configureView()
        }
    }

    func configureView() {
        // Update the user interface for the detail item.
        /*if let detail: AnyObject = self.detailItem {
            if let label = self.detailDescriptionLabel {
                label.text =
           detail.valueForKey("timeStamp")!.description
            }
        }*/
    }

    override func viewDidLoad() {
        super.viewDidLoad()
```

(continued)

Listing 15-1: ***(continued)***

```
        // Do any additional setup after loading
           the view, typically from a nib.
        self.configureView()
    }

    override func didReceiveMemoryWarning() {
        super.didReceiveMemoryWarning()
        // Dispose of any resources that can be
           recreated.
    }
}
```

The following sections break down the code in Listing 15-1 into chunks from the top to the bottom of the file. Most Swift classes look like this one (except that many of them are bigger), so this discussion should give you an idea of class structure and syntax.

For more on the links between code and user interface elements in code or in storyboards, see Chapter 16.

Exploring a Swift Class, Structure, or Enumeration File

A Swift file typically contains the following elements. They can be in any order in most cases, but the comments and copyright notices and import declarations usually are at the top. Everything listed in this section is optional although some are interdependent. For example, if you have a class declaration like this

```
class DetailViewController: UIViewController {
```

you must have the matching } at the end of the class declaration.

Comments and copyrights

This section, generated by Xcode automatically, consists of comments. It picks up information from the environment (such as the date and your name) as well as the name of the file and the name of the class, structure, or enumeration. Most of this information comes from the options you set for creating a new class or file in Xcode.

- Because it consists of comments, you can modify this section as you see fit. You can add your own notes or even standard comment information for your employer, if that is the policy standard.
- This section contains information from your environment, so yours will look different from the code in this example, but its format and structure will probably be the same. (If the format and structure for your code is different, it may be because Xcode changes from time to time. However, this structure has been pretty consistent over the years.)

```
//
//  DetailViewController.swift
//  Locatapp
//
//  Created by Jesse Feiler on 10/23/14.
//  Copyright (c) 2014 Jesse Feiler. All rights
//  reserved.
//
```

You don't need any comment information at the top of a file, but most developers provide some standard information so that you don't just see a bunch of code when you open an unfamiliar file. Because this is a comment, you could actually delete it from the template file.

Import declarations

Next in a class file comes a section of `import` declarations, which import frameworks. When you create an Xcode class file for Swift, the following import declaration is included in your file by default for Cocoa:

```
import UIKit
```

For Cocoa Touch and Swift, this is what you get:

```
import Cocoa
```

If you're working on an Objective-C app, on the other hand, this statement is inserted in your file for OS X:

```
#import <Foundation/Foundation.h>
```

Notice that the syntax is different from Objective C: In Swift, `import` is a declaration, whereas in Objective-C it's a compiler directive. Also, with Swift you import the framework by its name; in OS X you import the framework by its name and interface file. In practice, you don't have to worry about details like these because the `import` statement is usually set up for you (in Swift); even if it isn't, you have a model or template you can use.

For ios, you always need `UIKit`. Depending on what you're building, you may need other frameworks as well. It's typically the case that you add frameworks as you add code to your app that relies on a specific framework. For example, in Chapter 9, when you needed to add a map, you had to add this line of code:

```
import MapKit
```

Thus, in the `import` statement, you'd have this code:

```
import UIKit
import MapKit
```

The first declaration was put there by Xcode when you created the class file, and the second one represents your input.

Class declaration

The class declaration takes up most of a class declaration file. (This is the case for all class declaration files.) Locate the first and last lines of the class declaration shown in Listing 15-1; they are shown in this code:

```
class DetailViewController: UIViewController {
}
```

Declaring a subclass

A class declaration begins with the keyword `class`, which is followed by the name of the class you are creating, then a colon, and then the name of the superclass. In this code, `DetailViewController` is the name of your class; it is a subclass of `UIViewController`. Remember, you can only have one superclass (or none).

Declaring a base class

If you are declaring a base class — that is, a class that doesn't have a superclass —, omit the colon and the superclass name. If `DetailViewController` were to be a base class, the class declaration would look like this:

```
class DetailViewController
```

Adopting a protocol

If your class adopts one or more protocols, they are listed following the superclass (if it exists). Otherwise, they just follow the colon.

Declaring a subclass and adopting a protocol

Here is a class and a superclass where the class adopts a protocol:

```
class DetailViewController: UIViewController, MyProtocol
```

Declaring a base class and adopting a protocol

Here is a base class that adopts the same protocol:

```
class DetailViewController: MyProtocol
```

You need the colon only if you have a superclass or a protocol. A base class with no protocol doesn't need a colon.

After the declaration of the class, the body of the class is placed in brackets. The class body is discussed in the next section.

Structure declaration

At this point, structure declarations are very simple: They are the same as class declarations except that they cannot have superclasses, so all that you specify are the protocols (if any) that the structure adopts.

Enumeration declaration

As with a class, an enumeration starts with a keyword — in this case, `enum`. That is followed by the name, a colon, and any adopted protocols. (So far, it's the same as for a class, except that there is no possibility of a superclass because enumerations don't inherit from one another.) Here is the beginning of a typical enumeration declaration:

```
enum MyEnum {
```

As is the case with classes and structures, by convention enumeration names begin with a capital letter.

The body of an enumeration consists of cases separated by commas. Each case has a name that is unique. It may also specify the type of values it stores.

```
enum MyAnimals {
  case dog, cat, horse, cow
}
```

Perhaps the most common use of Swift enumerations is with a `switch` statement. Both enumerations and `switch` statements are much more powerful in Swift than in other languages, and they work well together. Here's an example of a `switch` that uses the previous enumeration:

```
enum MyAnimal {
  case dog, cat, horse, cow
}

var myPet = MyAnimal.cat

switch myPet {
case .cow:
  println ("moo")
case .cat :
  println ("meow")
case .dog:
  println ("woof")
case .horse:
  println ("neigh")
default:
  println ("silence")
}
```

You can experiment with this code to see how the result changes when you modify the `var` statement. You'll notice that there's a `default` statement because Swift switch cases must be exhaustive. As an experiment, delete it: You'll see there's no error because you've covered all the possibilities.

Try adding `donkey` to the list of cases. This generates an error message because the cases are no longer exhaustive. You must either add `.donkey` (don't forget the dot) or a `default` case.

You can add raw integer values to the enumeration so that it looks a bit more like a traditional enumeration. Here's another way of writing the previous enumeration:

```
enum MyAnimal2:Int {
  case dog = 1, cat, horse = 3, cow
}
```

If you declare the type of the enumeration to be `Int`, you can access the raw values by using the `rawValue` function as in the following:

```
var myPet2 = MyAnimal2.cat.rawValue
```

Notice in these snippets that you don't have to have all of the values specified. Swift can infer that the value for `cat` would be 2.

For enumeration functions and methods, see the section later in this chapter.

Body

Inside the body of a class, structure, or enumeration, you typically have functions (called *methods* in this context), properties, and, sometimes instance variables. Functions, properties, and instance variables are defined in the same way for classes, structures, and enumerations.

In addition to functions, properties, and instance variables, classes often contain *actions* and *outlets*. These are properties that are designed to be linked to storyboard elements: The process of linking actions and outlets to storyboard elements is the glue that connects your code to the visible user interface objects. That is a topic for app development, but it's touched on in Chapter 16.

UI actions and outlets (classes only)

If they exist, they have this general format:

```
@IBOutlet var mapView: MKMapView!
```

This code was added in Chapter 9; it is a reference to the map that you added to the storyboard in that chapter. As is frequently the case with user interface objects, it is optional (hence the `!` after the type).

As a comparison, the code you replaced in Chapter 9 is left here as a comment. This is a reference to the label that shows the timestamp in the Master-Detail Application template. If you're modifying that template for your own app, this is the line you change or remove:

```
//@IBOutlet weak var detailDescriptionLabel: UILabel!
```

Variables and properties

Variables and properties are discussed in Chapter 16.

Functions and methods

Classes, structures, and enumerations can contain functions. There are three in `DetailViewController`. They are discussed from simplest to more complex (which happens to be the way they appear in the template):

Declaring a function with no parameters and no return value:

At its simplest, a function has no parameters and no return value. The `configureView` function is a good example of this. Here is the code:

```
func configureView() {
  // Update the user interface for the detail
  // item.
  /* if let detail: AnyObject = self.detailItem {
       if let label = self.detailDescriptionLabel {
         label.text =
         detail.valueForKey("timeStamp")!.description
       }
  }*/
}
```

This code includes the commented-out code that is replaced when you put the map in place in Chapter 9. With that code removed, here is the simplest bare-bones function:

```
func configureView() {
  // Update the user interface for the detail item.
}
```

Declaring an overridden function (classes only)

A function can override a function in its superclass (or in a superclass of its superclass — the override can go as far up the class hierarchy as necessary to find a function that is the basis of the overridden function).

An override function matches its base function in name, return value (if any), and parameters (if any). Very often, an override function calls its superclass's function as in the code in `DetailViewController` shown here:

```
override func viewDidLoad() {
  super.viewDidLoad()

  // Do any additional setup after loading the
  // view, typically from a nib.

  self.configureView()
}
```

This function calls its superclass and then it does its own processing. Calls to super are typically the first or last line of an override function.

Note that `super` doesn't need to be called at all. If a subclass relies on some processing of its superclass, then the superclass usually is called to do that processing. The subclass then performs its own processing after the superclass is finished (this process is reversed for deinitialization.) However, in the case where there is no superclass processing involved, the subclass typically does its own processing without regard to calling the function in the superclass. Sometimes, a function in a superclass is declared with a single `assert` statement or error message. This is used to ensure that subclasses *always* override the superclass method.

Special types of methods

In addition to the method modifier described in the previous section, there are two other modifiers commonly used with methods. These apply only to enumerations and structures:

- `mutating`: This modifies a method and indicates that it will modify `self`. Enumerations and methods are *value types* rather than *reference types*, so that means that mutating methods are written back to the original structure or enumeration. Mutating methods can reassign `self` — that is, they can change the instance to which an enumeration or structure refers.
- `class`: This modifier identifies methods of a class rather than instances of that class. In the case of enumerations and structures, the modifier `static` is used.

Chapter 16

Using Properties, Variables, Outlets, and Actions

In This Chapter

- Using properties to store values
- Adding interface outlets
- Connecting an action to a button

In Chapter 15, you see how to declare classes (and, along with them, the basics of enumerations and structures that share many of the class features except for inheritance). In this chapter, the focus is on properties and variables, which are where your data is stored, as well as on outlets and actions, which are the user interface elements of your app. (Most of the time, outlets and actions are created in storyboards and the links between the graphical user interface of a storyboard and your Swift code consist of outlets and actions.)

You've seen these elements in action in other chapters, but now it's time to focus on the details.

The code for this chapter can be downloaded as described in the Introduction. Just as a reminder, it's the Locatapp based on the Master-Detail Application template. Its basic functionality lets the user create new event locations with the + at the top right of the master detail view controller. The user's location is shown on the detail view controller. The screenshots in this chapter show the app running on an iPhone 6 Plus in landscape mode.

Figure 16-1 shows the basic app interface as it is at the end of Chapter 15. Starting from that image, this chapter explores the properties, variables, outlets, and actions that make it happen.

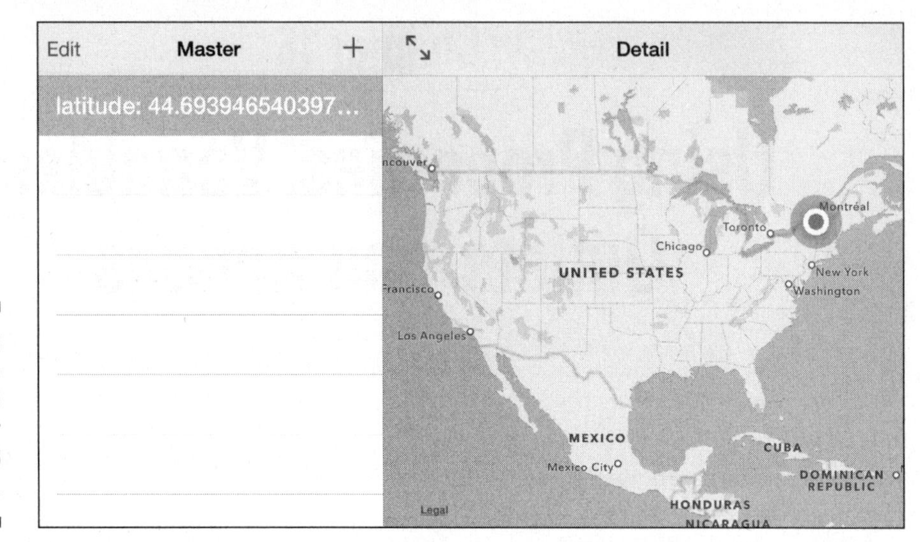

Figure 16-1: Locatapp on the iOS Simulator for iPhone 6 Plus.

Understanding Properties and Variables

The best way to understand properties and variables in Swift is to review a quick summary of the related topics in Objective-C. If you are familiar with Objective-C, you'll find that the Swift structure is much simpler. Certain aspects of the Swift syntax refer to Objective-C syntax, so that even if you are only using Swift, as long as you are using the Cocoa Touch or Cocoa framework (or the Xcode templates or the `developer.apple.com` examples), you should be aware of Objective-C's syntax, if only in order to see why the structure has evolved to what it is today.

The structure of properties and variables is powerful and flexible, and it reflects several stages in the evolution of object-oriented programming in general and Objective-C in particular.

Feel free to skip or skim the following section, but if anything confuses you about the structure of properties or variables in Swift, come back to it for a quick read to catch yourself up on the evolution of properties and variables that you deal with in Swift today.

Encapsulating Data for Good Design and Maintainability

Consider the concept of *encapsulation*, an important concept of object-oriented programming. The idea behind encapsulation is that objects should be opaque: You should not be able to tell what's inside an app's data, what functionality it contains, or what operations it carries out. Doing this makes your objects flexible and reusable.

This concept has proven its value over the years. The original architecture of Objective-C consisted of frameworks of objects (although the word "framework" was not used at the beginning). The objects were opaque so that software engineers couldn't look inside them (or, at least, they weren't supposed to). An object named (say) `myObject`, was assumed to have some data — perhaps called `data` – and this data itself was off-limits to developers. Instead of accessing the data directly, developers learned to send a message to `myObject` to obtain its data. By convention, the message would be named `objectData` and would cause `myObject` to return the data of `myObject`.

If you look closer at this design, `myObject` is the class; `objectData` is the name of the function or method that serves as a *getter*. Another method called (by default) `setObjectData` is the *setter*. The setter takes a single parameter (typically called (`newObjectData`). You would only access `objectData` using either `objectData` to get it or `setObjectData` to set or update it. One interesting and useful consequence of this design is that `objectData` (the data stored by `myObject`) need not exist at all. The accessors (`objectData` and `setObjectData`) can work with dynamic data that may never actually be stored. With encapsulation like this, you would never need to know whether or not the data is stored or calculated on the fly. All you need to know is that `myObject` gets data for you with `objectData` and takes data from you with `setObjectData`. As long as both accessors work, whether it's calculated on the fly, stored in a database, or even stored on the moon doesn't matter: `myObject` *encapsulates* its data.

Other languages would allow you to access the data directly using some syntax such as `myObject.objectData`, but because the actual reference to the data in this case would be `myObject.objectData()` — a method or function call (note the parentheses at the end) — encapsulation is complete.

REMEMBER

In this section, method and function are used synonymously.

The hypothetical syntax shown in the previous paragraphs is a generic version of modern syntax or "dot syntax" used in Objective-C from the late 1990s onward. Using the original style of Objective-C (sometimes called the *message format*) the way to send the `objectData` message to `myObject` would be with code like this: `[myObject objectData]`.

Creating and preserving encapsulation became an important part of Objective-C development. It is true that encapsulation preserves many of the powerful features of Objective-C and makes reusing code much easier, but in some cases, encapsulation can be a bit more complicated to write and sometimes takes more resources to execute.

Thus, although the structure isn't particularly complicated, storing, retrieving, and setting a variable's value requires three elements.

The components of this structure are:

- an actual variable or code to compute it (this is all invisible to you)
- a getter method to get the value of the variable (this is visible to you)
- a setter method to set the value of the variable (this is visible to you)

In Objective-C 2 (released in 2007), *named properties* were introduced. They provide a way of simplifying this structure, but they are totally compatible with it. A named property has a format such as this:

```
@property (strong, nonatomic) id detailItem;

@property (weak, nonatomic) IBOutlet
  UILabel *detailDescriptionLabel;
```

The property begins with the compiler directive `@property` followed by memory and usage attributes in parentheses, such as `strong`, `weak`, `readonly`, and `nonatomic` — the specific meanings don't matter at this point.

Following the parenthesized attributes are the type of the property and then its name. For object types, a pointer is used. The class type `id` is not a pointer. Again, the details don't matter at this point.

What does matter is that with a property declaration, the compiler is able to automatically declare and create a *backing variable,* which is the variable itself where the data is stored. It also is able to create a getter and a setter using the conventions described previously (the getter is the name of the variable and the setter is `setMyVariable`).

Several conventions come into play here. Variable names start with a lowercase letter. If the variable name consists of multiple words, words after the first begin with capital letters (this is called *camelCase*). Methods and functions start with lowercase letters; classes start with uppercase letters. The conventions meet up in the name of a setter. Consider a variable called `myVariable` whose setter is called `setMyVariable`. This conforms to the convention that methods start with lowercase letters, and it also conforms to the camelCase convention. However, because the meeting of these two conventions might suggest the name `setmyVariable`, camelCase overrides other conventions.

Thus, named properties reduce the amount of typing required to use properties by having the compiler do the work of creating the getter and setter accessors and of creating the backing variable.

In some cases, developers have needed more control over matters. The two most common cases of this were the following:

- When a developer needs a backing variable to have a certain name and needs to be able to access it directly.
- When the setter or the getter needs to do more than just set or get the value of a variable.

Here's where complexity starts to come in.

The automated property synthesizer synthesizes a backing variable with the property name preceded by an underscore. Thus, the default backing variable for `myProperty` is `_myProperty`. (You can set this as an option in the property declaration.)

You can also write your own accessors. It is common to have them perform additional tasks above and beyond their simple accessor roles. One of the most common of these tasks is establishing a database connection so that a getter can obtain a previously stored value for its property.

There are many other variations on this structure (including properties that have no backing variables but rely simply on a getter to compute or retrieve a value on as-needed basis). And, just to complete this part of the picture, you can mix and match properties with traditional variables (naked variables are not part of a declared property).

A lot of the arguments against the use of named properties (and they have been bitter) center around the fact that accessing a named properties value in the backing variable requires more machine resources than just accessing a memory location. With today's computers — even in mobile devices — this may seem like an extreme reaction, but it has been common in some circles.

This, then, is the world of properties and variables that Swift addresses. Whether all of its complexities and combinations are necessary is worth discussing: All have found uses in apps and even in the Apple frameworks that make up Cocoa and Cocoa Touch.

There is another layer of complexity with regard to the declarations of properties and variables. Most declarations in classes of Objective-C code are placed in a header file in the `@interface` section. (By convention, this file is named with a `.h` after the class name.)

Fairly recently (in the late 2000s) it became commonplace to add a second `@interface` section in the format of a class extension in the main body of the class file (the file with the `.m` extension). Declarations in the header file can be grouped into sections with various access — `public`, `private`, and `protected`. `public` and `private` interfaces are just that. `protected` interface elements are visible to the class itself and to any of its subclasses.

Finally, inside the main file (the `.m` extension file), you can access the backing variable by using its name, as in `_myBackingVariable`. This bypasses the use of the getter and saves a few machine cycles. It also can side-step any additional processing that the getter does; this convention can be very useful.

This is the background of properties and variables in Objective-C and now in Swift. You'll see pieces of this architecture in the Swift architecture that is described next.

Understanding Properties and Variables in Locatapp

Just as Chapter 15 focused on `DetailViewController` because its interface is brief, this chapter focuses on `MasterViewController` because its implementation is varied enough to demonstrate different aspects of properties and variables in Swift.

Figure 16-2 shows part of `MasterViewController.swift`. You'll notice that the jump bar's list of elements within the file has been expanded. It shows classes (prefixed by C), properties (prefixed by P) and methods (prefixed with M). They are shown in their order in the file.

The file itself is broken into sections which are shown in the list of properties and methods. This is done with comments such as:

```
// MARK: - Segues
```

It is a good idea to organize your files in this way. Note that how you categorize properties and methods is up to you — there often is more than one way of doing so. Don't let that deter you from organizing your methods and properties — almost any logical organization is better than none.

Here are the property declarations in sequence as shown in Figure 16-2. In the template, they tend to run from simpler to more complex. Properties in the drop-down list from the jump bar are italicized as well as being marked with a P.

First, there are two properties consisting of a variable (`var`). The first and second are optionals (note the `?` at the end of the type); because they are optionals, they can be initialized to `nil`, which is not a legal value for a

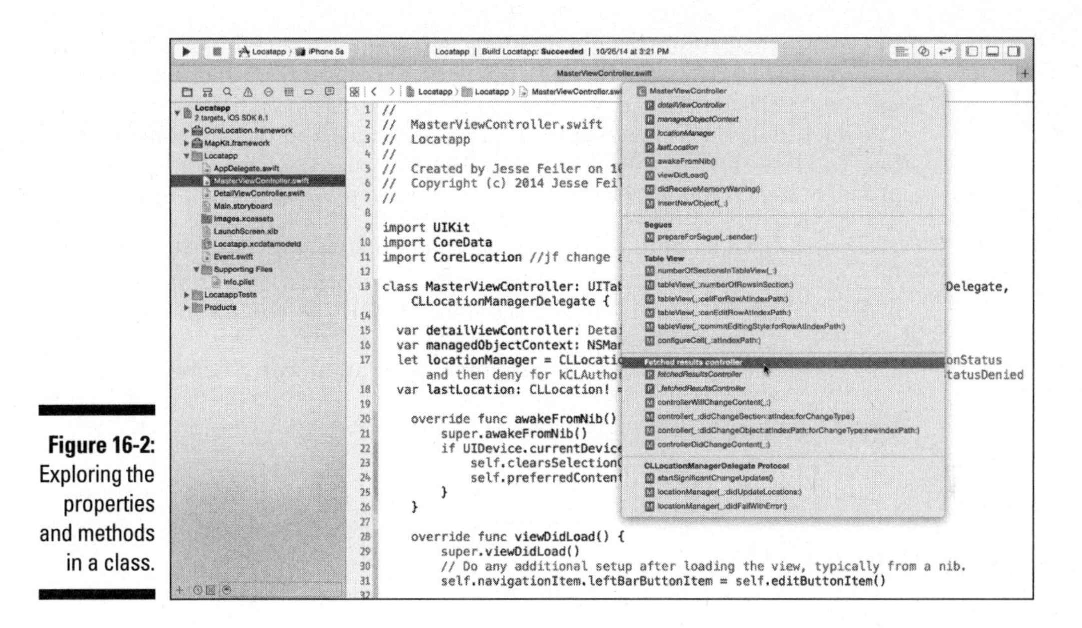

Figure 16-2: Exploring the properties and methods in a class.

non-optional type. The third is a constant (note `let` instead of `var`), and the fourth is a `var` that is forced to be unwrapped and set to `nil`.

```
var detailViewController: DetailViewController? = nil
var managedObjectContext: NSManagedObjectContext? = nil
let locationManager = CLLocationManager()
var lastLocation: CLLocation! = nil
```

Next there are four methods. The first three have no parameters, so they are listed like this:

```
awakeFromNib()
viewDidLoad()
didReceiveMemoryWarning()
```

The fourth has a single parameter. It is listed like this:

```
insertNewObject(_:)
```

Parameters in Swift (like their predecessors in Objective-C) have internal and external names. If you look at method in the actual header, the parameter looks like this:

```
func insertNewObject(sender: AnyObject) {
```

The internal name is required; in this case it is `sender`. There is no external name for the first parameter, so it is represented by an underscore in the list. The internal name is not for public use, so it's not shown in the list.

The rest of the properties and methods in the list use similar formatting and conventions until you get down to the fetched results controller section.

The relevant code is shown in Figure 16-3. Compare it to the list from the jump bar. You'll see that Figure 16-3 starts with a `fetchedResultsController` property and continues with a `_fetchedResultsController` property.

The first property is a property as declared in the Master-Detail Application template. The second is the backing variable. In Objective-C, it's part of the property. In Swift, however, it is a separate property as you see in Listing 16-1.

This code starts out as a simple property declaration with a name and a type.

```
var fetchedResultsController: NSFetchedResultsController
```

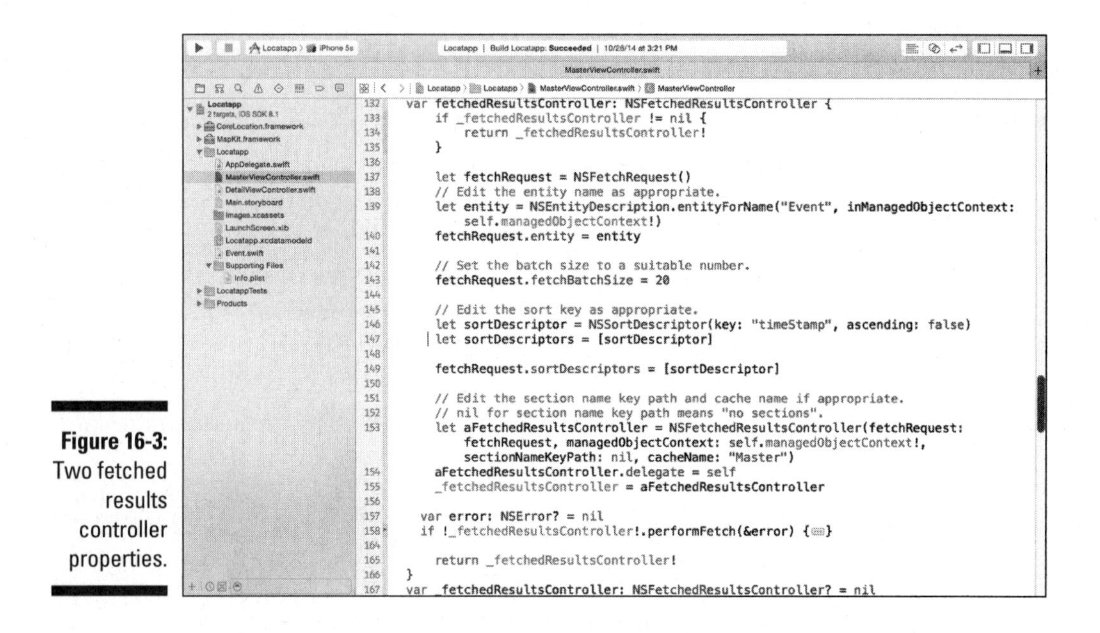

Figure 16-3: Two fetched results controller properties.

Listing 16-1: A Getter Property Declaration

```
// MARK: - Fetched results controller

  var fetchedResultsController: NSFetchedResultsController
    {
    if _fetchedResultsController != nil {
      return _fetchedResultsController!
    }
```

```
    let fetchRequest = NSFetchRequest()
    // Edit the entity name as appropriate.
    let entity =
      NSEntityDescription.entityForName("Event",
      inManagedObjectContext: self.managedObjectContext!)
      fetchRequest.entity = entity

    // Set the batch size to a suitable number.
    fetchRequest.fetchBatchSize = 20

    // Edit the sort key as appropriate.
    let sortDescriptor = NSSortDescriptor(key:
      "timeStamp", ascending: false)
    let sortDescriptors = [sortDescriptor]

    fetchRequest.sortDescriptors = [sortDescriptor]

    // Edit the section name key path and cache name if
          appropriate.
    // nil for section name key path means "no sections".
    let aFetchedResultsController =
      NSFetchedResultsController(fetchRequest:
        fetchRequest,
      managedObjectContext: self.managedObjectContext!,
      sectionNameKeyPath: nil, cacheName: "Master")

    aFetchedResultsController.delegate = self
    _fetchedResultsController = aFetchedResultsController

    var error: NSError? = nil
    if !_fetchedResultsController!.performFetch(&error) {
      // Replace this implementation with code to handle
      // the error appropriately.
      // abort() causes the application to generate a
      // crash log and terminate. You should not use this
      // function in a shipping application, although it
      // may be useful during development.
      println("Unresolved error \(error),
        \(error.userInfo)")
      abort()
    }

    return _fetchedResultsController!
  }

  var _fetchedResultsController:
    NSFetchedResultsController? = nil
```

What follows is a long block with a `return` statement (actually two — one is inside an `if` statement at the top). The code in this listing doesn't really matter. What matters here are the following points:

- In Swift, backing variables are explicitly declared if needed (usually in code converted from Objective-C).
- Getters need not use the `get` keyword.

Types of Swift properties

Swift properties can be variables or constants; each type can be either stored or computed, as follows:

- **Declaring a variable property:** A variable is introduced with the keyword var as in:

```
var _fetchedResultsController:
    NSFetchedResultsController? = nil
```

- **Declaring a constant property:** A constant (that is, a property that cannot be modified) is introduced with the keyword let. The previous declaration can be changed to declare a constant as follows:

```
let _fetchedResultsController:
    NSFetchedResultsController? = nil
```

- **Declaring a stored property:** The declaration of `_fetchedResultsController` shown in Listing 16-1 is a typical declaration of a *stored property*. A stored property is a property stored as part of an instance of the class, enumeration, or structure. The example in Listing 16-1 uses an Objective-C pattern for a backing variable: Swift stored properties don't need to begin with a special character such as an underscore; however, they do need to be initialized and given a type (perhaps inferred from the initialization) before they are used.

```
var _fetchedResultsController:
  NSFetchedResultsController? = nil
```

- **Declaring a computed property with a getter and a setter:** This point deserves a bit of elucidation. Listing 16-2 shows a basic getter and setter of a Swift property. You can see that `myVar` has a backing variable of `myInt`. The `get` and `set` keywords identify the getter and setter. By default, the variable passed into the setter is named `newValue`, and Swift uses the appropriate type for it.

  This is how you create a *computed property*.

Observing a property

In addition to the getters and setters shown in Figure 16-2, you can use observers as shown in Listing 16-3. This code is in the `DetailViewController.swift` file of Locatapp (from the Master-Detail Application template).

This is a good place to call a view updater (which is exactly what is done in the template). There are two observers you can use:

- **`didSet`:** This is called after the fact.
- **`willSet`:** This is called just before the setting happens.

Listing 16-2: Swift Property with Getter and Setter

```
var myInt:Int = 0

var myVar: Int {
  get {
    return myInt
  }

  set {
    myInt = newValue
  }
}
myVar = 20
```

Listing 16-3: Swift Property Observer in Action

```
var detailItem: AnyObject? {
  didSet {
    // Update the view.
    self.configureView()
  }
}
```

Declaring Outlets and Actions

Although building the interface is not strictly speaking a Swift process because Interface Builder builds the code for you, it's worthwhile taking a look at how you write code for outlets and actions using Xcode and Interface Builder (which is built into it).

In order to let people interact with social media from Locatapp, they need an action button which is typically placed at the right end of a navigation bar, as you will see in the following steps.

Here are the steps to add the action button — and to have Xcode write the code automatically while you're at it.

1. **Open `Main.storyboard` in Xcode.**

   This launches Interface Builder and displays the canvas for your interface. You may need to zoom the view in or out. Use Editor ➪ Canvas ➪ Zoom.

2. **Make sure you can see `MKMapView` in DetailViewController as shown in Figure 16-4.**
3. **Open the utilities area, if necessary.**
4. **Choose Bar Button Item from the library and drag it to the right of the navigation bar as shown in Figure 16-5.**
5. **In the Attributes inspector, choose Action from the Identifier pop-up menu as shown in Figure 16-6.**
6. **Choose the Assistant, as shown in Figure 16-7.**

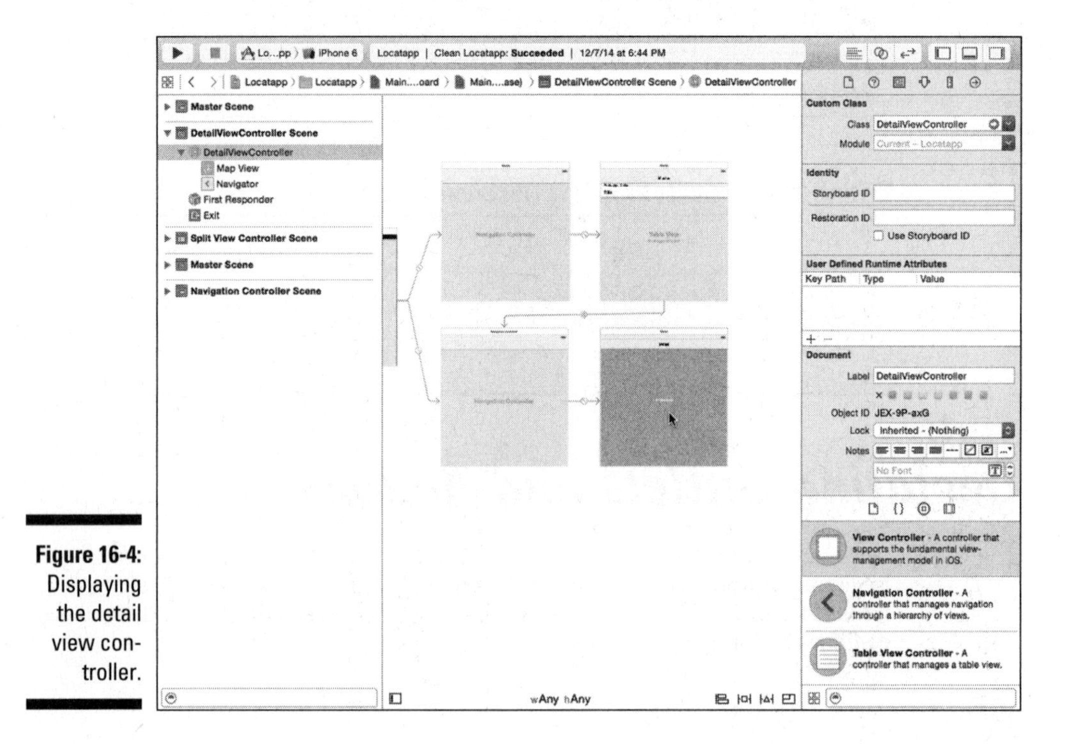

Figure 16-4: Displaying the detail view controller.

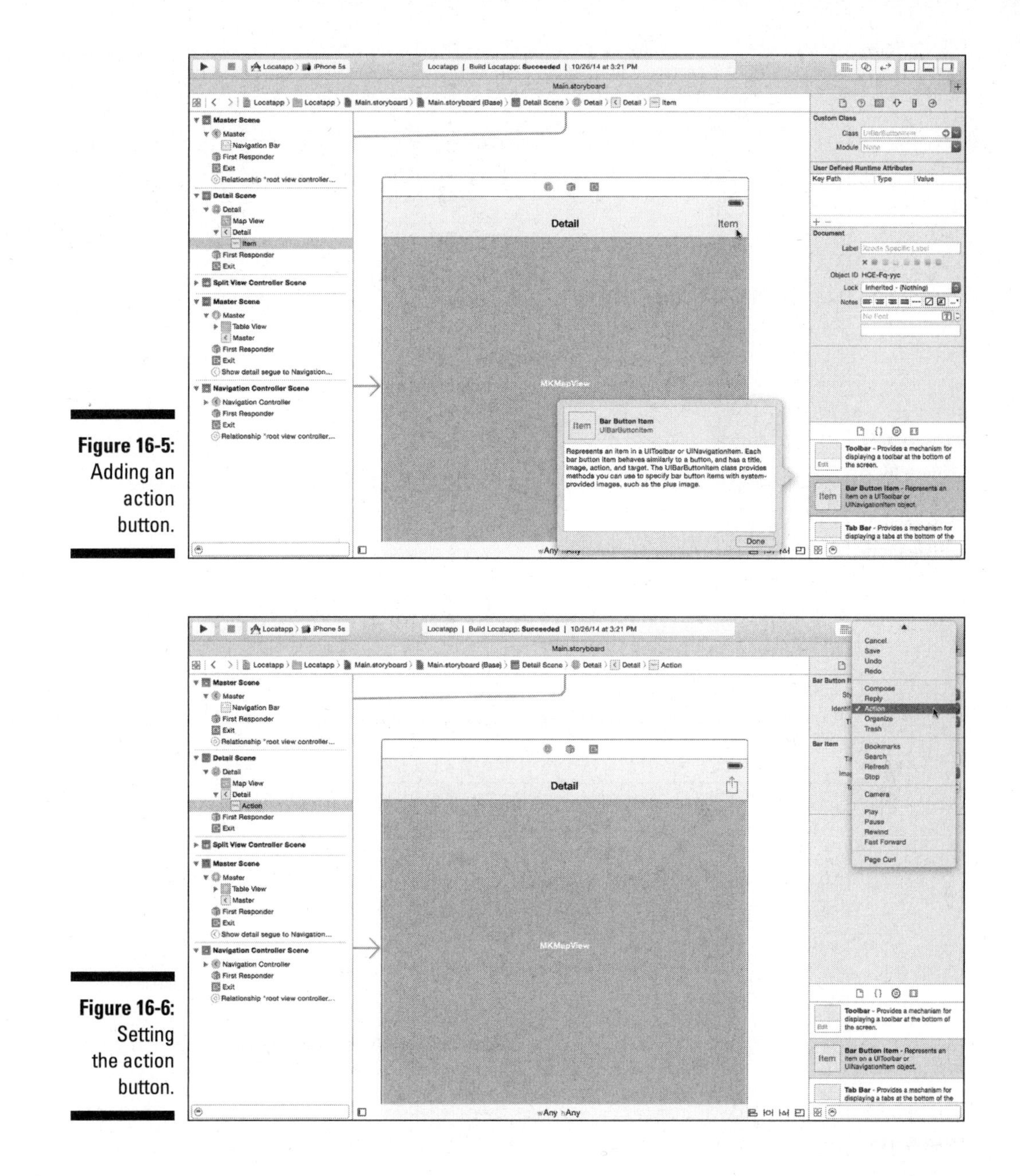

Figure 16-5: Adding an action button.

Figure 16-6: Setting the action button.

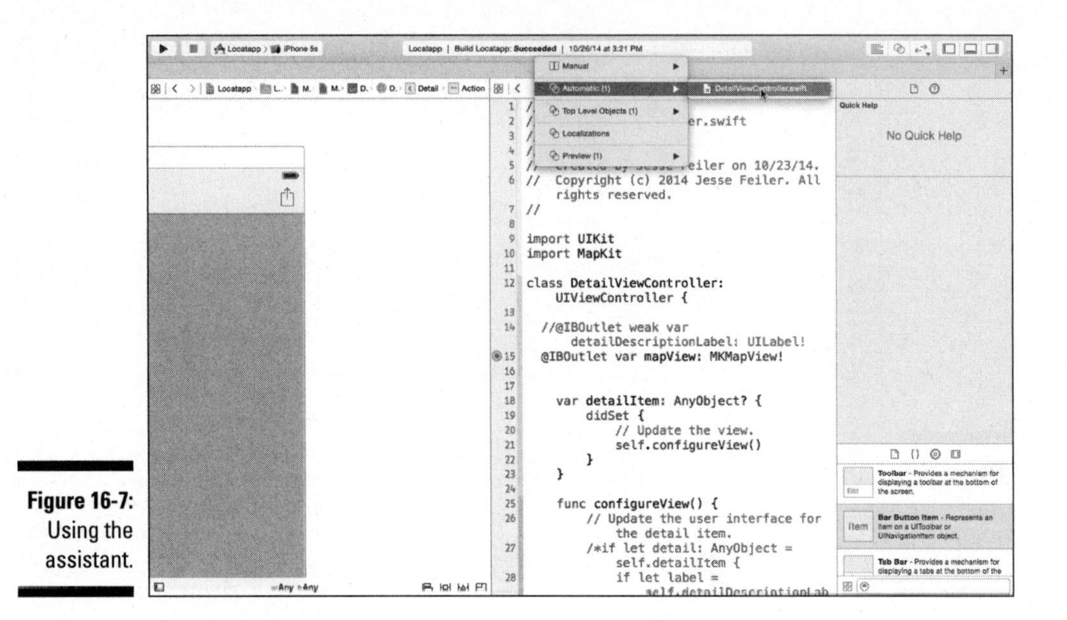

Figure 16-7: Using the assistant.

7. **Select `DetailViewController.swift` as the companion view, as shown in Figure 16-7.**
8. **Control-drag from the action button to the top of the `DetailViewController` class, as shown in Figure 16-8.**

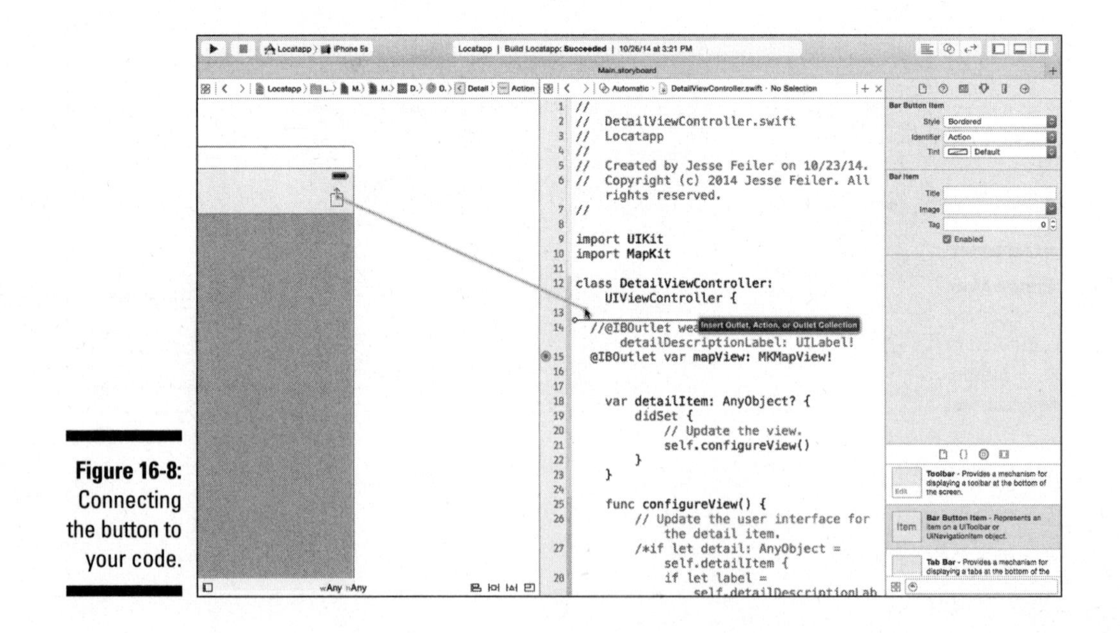

Figure 16-8: Connecting the button to your code.

9. **When you release the button, use the pop-up to set this connection to an action rather than an outlet or outlet connection. Name it `actionButton`, and leave the default type as `AnyObject` as you see in Figure 16-9.**

When you release the mouse button, you'll see that you've created an action like this:

```
@IBAction func actionButton(sender: AnyObject) {
}
```

Set a breakpoint in this method and run the app in iOS Simulator. The button causes the method to be called.

This technique of control-dragging from an interface element to a class interface in the Assistant in Xcode is the easiest way to create properties for interface elements such as view or buttons and actions for what happens when an interface element is clicked.

If you want to finish the app, add the code in Listing 16-4 to the app. Try out the new action button!

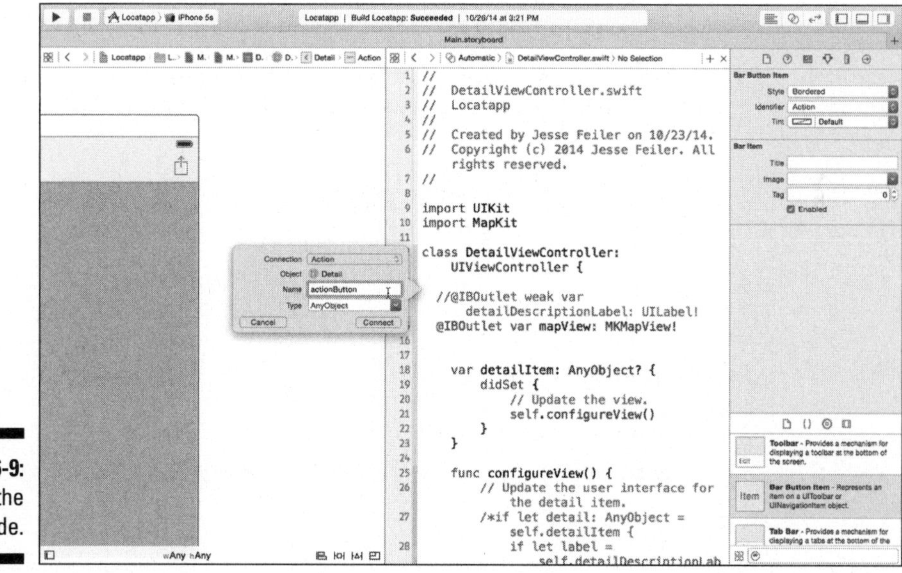

Figure 16-9: Finishing the action code.

Listing 16-4: Adding the actionButton Code

```
@IBAction func actionButton(sender: AnyObject) {
  var long:Double = detailItem!.longitude as Double
  var lat:Double = detailItem!.latitude as Double

  let socialString = "I'm using Locatapp at latitude
    String(format:"%f", lat) + " longitude " +
    String(format:"%f", lat)

  // fill in geocode location if you want

  if let activityURL =
    NSURL (string:"http://champlainarts.com") {
       //to make certain it's valid
      let activityItemsList = [socialString, activityURL]
      let activityViewController =
        UIActivityViewController (activityItems:
          activityItemsList, applicationActivities: nil)

      self.presentViewController(activityViewController,
          animated: true, completion: nil)
    }
}
```

Chapter 17

Working with Enumerations to Consolidate Values

In This Chapter

- Using raw values with enumerations
- Combining enumerations with switches
- Adding functions to enumerations

Swift takes structures and enumerations far beyond their roots in C and C-like languages. Structure, classes, and enumerations all can contain functions as well as data elements. They also can all adopt protocols.

This chapter shows you how to use Swift enumerations both in traditional ways and in ways that work alongside new Swift features such as embedded functions and raw values.

TIP

For more on structures, see Chapter 15 and Chapter 16.

Using Enumerations with Swift

In the world of Swift, you may want to rethink how you use enumerations.

Whereas in C, structures and enumerations are often used as simple types (that is, more or less as a way of saving keystrokes or organizing the code), structures, enumerations, and classes in Swift are all object-oriented first-class types. Accordingly, then, in the world of Swift, it is common to refer to *instances* of structures and enumerations, as well as instances of classes.

When an instance of a structure or enumeration is passed from one code component to another, it is passed by value, whereas instances of classes are passed by reference. Putting it another way, instances of structures and enumerations are placed on the stack, whereas instances of classes are placed on the heap.

For developers interested in what this means to them and their app, it means that when you pass a unique copy of a structure or enumeration around in your app, that instance is actually moved around, and each function or other segment of code that touches it touches the instance that moves. When one segment of code makes a change to the instance data, it doesn't affect other instances.

When you pass an instance of a class, that instance is shared among the sections of code to which it is passed (that's because typically behind the scenes you only pass a pointer to the instance). If you make a change to a property of a class instance, however, everyone who is using that instance sees that change.

Understanding Traditional C Structures and Enumerations

Before moving on to Swift, it's worthwhile reviewing some classic examples from C. Enumerations were not in the classic reference (*The C Programming Language* by Brian Kernighan and Dennis Ritchie), but they were added later on. They are also used in conjunction with a structure. Here is an example of an `enum` and a `structure` in C that uses it.

```
enum priority {
   urgent,
   medium,
   low,
   not assigned
};

enum priority myPriority;

myPriority = low;
```

The `enum priority` can take any of the four values. A variable like `myPriority` can be assigned any of those values. The values can have integer values assigned to them, and, in fact, integer values starting at zero are used by default.

Many developers are used to using an `enum` structure to declare constants so that related constants are all together.

Exploring Swift Enumerations

When you add Swift's features, enumerations become much more class-like. They are no longer just collections of constants because they can now have their own properties and functions.

Here's what a Swift enumeration can look like:

```
enum ParkPlace: Int {
    case park, pool, bars, track
}
```

With a bit of respacing, however, this can look very much like a classic C `enum`:

```
enum ParkPlace: Int {
    case park
    case pool
    case bars
    case track
}
```

You can assign an enumeration value to a variable in Swift using code like this:

```
let myPlace = ParkPlace.park
```

If you include this assignment and then try to print out `myPlace` in a playground, you'll see the value "Enum Value" at the right.

Refer to Figure 17-1 for examples of enumerations in playgrounds using variations on the code in this section.

You can reveal the underlying value of an enumeration using the intrinsic `rawValue`, as in this line of code:

```
println (myPlace.rawValue)
```

The result will be "0" because by default, enumeration raw values start at zero and the result of a `println` function is a string (hence the quotation marks).

You can assign your own raw values to enumeration cases. For example, you could arrange the declaration like this:

```
enum ParkPlace: Int {
    case park
    case pool = 25
    case bars
    case track
}
```

```
MyPlayground17.playground — Edited
MyPlayground17.playground
MyPlayground17.playground 〉 No Selection
1  // Playground - noun: a place where people can play
2
3  enum Place: String {
4    case
5      park = "park",
6      pool = "swimming pool",
7      bars = "climbing bars",
8      track1 = "running track",
9      track2 = "walking track"
10
11   static let facilities = [park, pool, bars, track1, track2]
12 }
13
14 let e = Place.pool.rawValue                          "swimming pool"
15
16 println (Place.pool)                                 "(Enum Value)"
17
18 for amenity in Place.facilities {
19   println (amenity)                                  (5 times)
20 }
21
22 var result: String = ""                              ""
23
24 for amenity in Place.facilities {
25   result = result + amenity.rawValue + ", "          (5 times)
26 }
27
28 println (result)                                     "park, swimming pool, climbing bars, running track, walki...
```

Figure 17-1: Using a playground to explore enumerations.

Here, `.park` will still be 0 by default. However, `.pool` is now set to 25, and the sequence continues from there. Thus, the following code snippet will print 26. If you were to set `bars` to 99, track would automatically become 100.

```
let myPlace = ParkPlace.bars
println (myPlace.rawValue)
```

It is common to use strings in an enumeration. Here is a sample in which the enumeration cases have strings assigned to them.

```
enum Place: String {
  case
    park = "park",
    pool = "swimming pool",
    bars = "climbing bars",
    track1 = "running track",
    track2 = "walking track"
}
```

Note in this and the previous examples that there is a distinction between the case elements which are not quoted strings and the associated values which are strings. Note also that in your code the case elements start with a period when you use them. The period is not used in the declaration.

`.track` would print 27.

Working with members of an enumeration

Inside an enumeration, you can declare variables or constants. As you can see in Figure 17-1 and Listing 17-1, the enumeration contains a static variable consisting of an array with the five cases of the enumeration. Work through the following steps to explore the code you see in Figure 17-1 and Listing 17-1.

1. **Declare the `Place` enumeration.**

   As discussed in the previous section, it has five cases.

2. **Declare a static member of the enumeration.**

   Its name is `facilities`, and it is an array consisting of the five enumeration cases.

   Note that the elements of the array are the enumeration cases: They are not strings and they are not quoted.

3. **Create a variable `e` and set it to the raw value of the `pool` case of the `Place` enumeration.**

   You are using the declaration and not an instance of the enumeration. As you see in Figure 17-1, it has the value "swimming pool" with the associated value of the case `pool`.

4. **If you print it, you'll see it identified only as an `Enum Value`.**

5. **Use fast enumeration to loop through the `facilities` array using `amenity` as the loop variable.**

   You'll see in the playground that the `println` statement executes five times.

Listing 17-1: Creating an Enumeration with a Member

```
enum Place: String {
  case
    park = "park",
    pool = "swimming pool",
    bars = "climbing bars",
    track1 = "running track",
    track2 = "walking track"

  static let facilities = [park, pool, bars, track1,
    track2]

}
```

6. **Create a `String` variable called `result` and set it to a blank string.**
7. **In another fast enumeration loop, add each raw value (string) to `result` along with a comma and a blank.**
8. **Print result.**

   This type of code could be used to create checkboxes for all the values of the enumeration.

That use of fast enumeration in Step 8 would be the reverse of what is often done when you draw the interface and then declare the variables behind checkboxes or other user interface elements. In this case, you define the enumeration and its cases and then write code to create the interface elements. Try it and you'll be convinced that it's faster.

Working with a function inside an enumeration

With the same basic code, you can add a function to the enumeration. This is something you haven't seen in C and perhaps not in other languages either. It's a new way of looking at enumerations.

Adding a simple function to an enumeration

Here is the function that's added to the enumeration. You can place it anywhere (except, of course, not in the middle of the `case`):

```
func enumFunction () -> Int {
  return -17
}
```

The function is named `enumFunction` and it returns an `Int` with the value of –17. You can access this function from any instance of the enumeration. Here's one example:

```
let i = Place.bars.enumFunction()
```

You may be thinking, "Wait a moment. That enumeration is typed as String and so it must return a String."

That's true, but you're not referring to the value returned by the enumeration. You are asking a member of the enumeration (not even an instance of the enumeration) to return the result of enumFunction, which is declared as Int.

Adding a switch statement to a function inside an enumeration

Swift enumerations are often used in conjunction with switch statements. Here is a function to place inside the enumeration that contains a switch statement. When you have an instance of an enumeration (or just the enumeration itself), you can call an internal function from an element just as you saw in the preceding code snippet. And, like the preceding code snippet, the result returned by the function need not be the same type as the type of the enumeration.

In the following code a function that returns a String is based on the result of a switch statement that uses the elements of the enumeration. Note that the elements of the switch are not strings (note the absence of quotation marks and the presence of the leading periods in the case names).

Experiment with this code, and you'll see that if you set the type of the enumeration to Int (or Double or anything other than String) the function will still return a String. That's the result of the function and not the type of the enumeration. This is a very useful technique to use, and many developers find that it dramatically reduces the code they have to write. (Those if-then-else-if statements inside switch case statements can be omitted, as can switch statements within case statements.)

```
func enumChoiceFunction () -> String {
    switch self {
    case .track1, track2:
      return "running or walking"
    case .park:
      return "Walking, sitting on a bench, feeding birds"
    default:
      return "enjoying nature"
    }
  }
```

Figure 17-2 shows the code described in this section. The code itself is provided in Listing 17-2 and Figure 17-3.

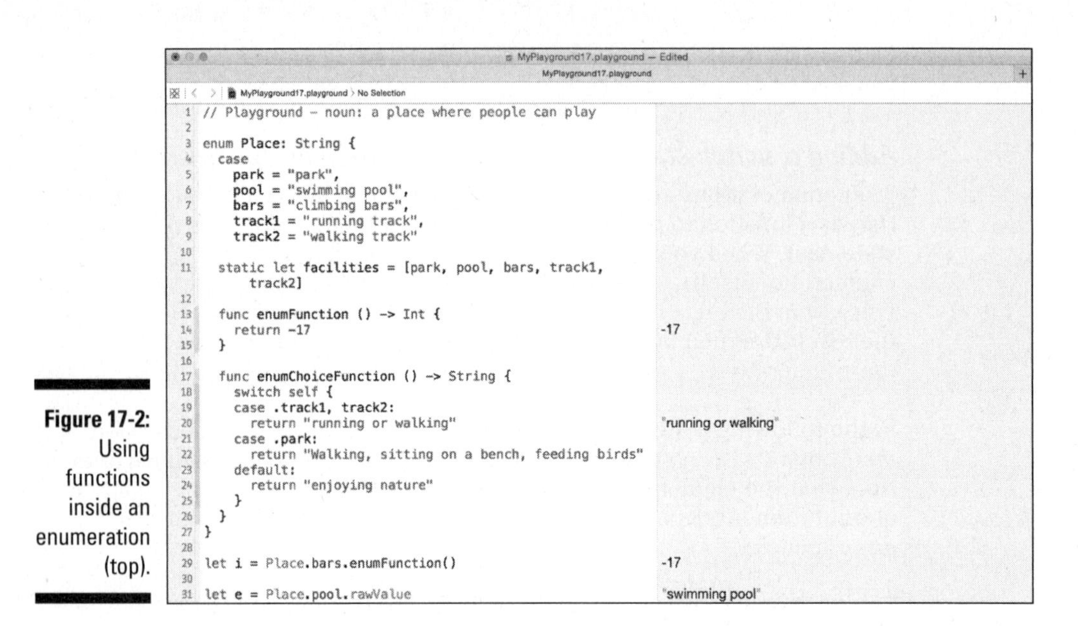

Figure 17-2: Using functions inside an enumeration (top).

Listing 17-2: Using a Simple and a Complex (switch) Function inside an Enumeration

```
enum Place: String {
  case
    park = "park",
    pool = "swimming pool",
    bars = "climbing bars",
    track1 = "running track",
    track2 = "walking track"

  static let facilities = [park, pool, bars, track1,
          track2]

  func enumFunction () -> Int {
    return -17
  }

  func enumChoiceFunction () -> String {
    switch self {
    case .track1, track2:
      return "running or walking"
    case .park:
      return "Walking, sitting on a bench, feeding
          birds"
    default:
      return "enjoying nature"
    }
```

```
  }
}
let i = Place.bars.enumFunction()

let e = Place.pool.rawValue

println (Place.pool)

let x = Place.track1.enumChoiceFunction()

var result: String = ""

for amenity in Place.facilities {
  result = result + amenity.rawValue + ", "
}

println (result)
```

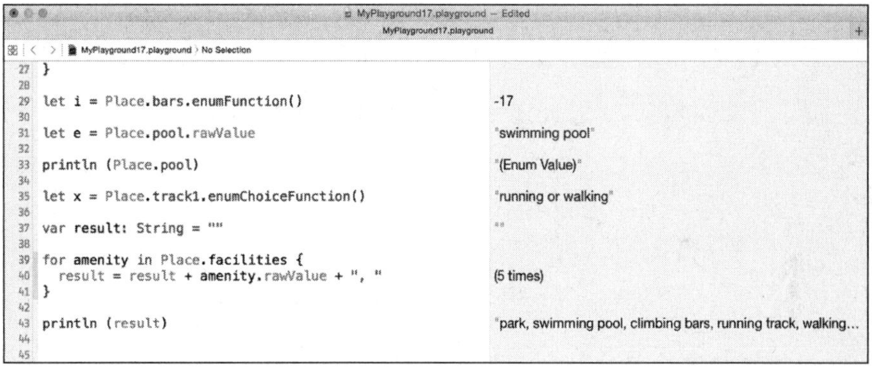

```
MyPlayground17.playground — Edited
MyPlayground17.playground
MyPlayground17.playground › No Selection
27 }
28
29 let i = Place.bars.enumFunction()                          -17
30
31 let e = Place.pool.rawValue                                "swimming pool"
32
33 println (Place.pool)                                       "(Enum Value)"
34
35 let x = Place.track1.enumChoiceFunction()                  "running or walking"
36
37 var result: String = ""                                    ""
38
39 for amenity in Place.facilities {
40   result = result + amenity.rawValue + ", "                (5 times)
41 }
42
43 println (result)                                           "park, swimming pool, climbing bars, running track, walking...
44
45
```

Figure 17-3: Results of functions within an enumeration (bottom).

Chapter 18

Using Protocols to Provide Templates for Functionality

In This Chapter

- Working with protocols
- Conforming classes, structures, and enumerations to a protocol
- Using protocols with a `UITableViewController`

In earlier chapters, when the subject of protocols came up, I promised to talk more about them later. This chapter, then, is the "later" I was referring to. It provides a formal description of protocols and *delegates* (the implementers of protocols) along with examples of their use — including perhaps the most common use of protocols and delegates you may encounter: table views with their data sources and delegate protocols.

You can find more details about protocols in the Swift documentation on `developer.apple.com`. Protocols can be used to implement complex architectures, but in and of themselves, they're quite simple, as you'll see in this chapter.

This chapter refers to the Locatapp example code shown in Chapter 4 and in more detail in Chapter 9.

Understanding Protocols

Protocols declare a set of methods and properties (as well as a few other syntax elements such as operators and subscripts) that are collected together and provided with a name. The structures of protocols and delegates allow you to implement additional functionality in classes without subclassing them; protocols also let you add functionality and properties to structures and enumerations. When a protocol exists, here's what can happen:

- **A protocol *declares* the methods and properties**: Protocols declare them, but they don't implement them. (Protocols and subscripts are not discussed in this chapter in order to focus on the more common properties and methods.)
- **A class, structure, or enumeration then *adopts* the protocol**: This means that a class/structure/enumeration must implement the methods and properties of the protocol.
- **A class, structure, or enumeration that adopts a protocol (or a class inherits from a class that adopts the protocol) *conforms* to the protocol:** The subclass that inherits from a class that adopts a protocol must implement the required methods and properties of that protocol unless the superclass which actually adopts the protocol already does so.

A protocol has no connection to the objects that adopt or conform to it.

In most cases, a protocol can be adopted by a number of different classes, structures, and enumerations.

The Cocoa and Cocoa Touch frameworks frequently use protocols and delegates. This use of protocols and delegates is called the *delegation* design pattern, and is one of a number of design patterns that occur frequently in Cocoa and Cocoa Touch (others include *key-value observing, target-action,* and *error reporting*).

In the delegation pattern, the instance of a class declares a property that is a delegate (and often it is named `delegate`, but this is not required). When messages are sent to the class (Objective-C) or when a function of the class is called (Swift), the class passes the message or call to its delegate which actually implements the code.

The syntax of protocols is different in Objective-C and Swift, but from here on, this chapter refers only to the Swift syntax. It's important to note, however, that protocols are inherently usable across both languages. The protocol declaration in Swift or Objective-C can be implemented in either language. Furthermore, in a single app, it's entirely possible for the same protocol to be implemented in different contexts by both Objective-C and Swift. Thus, protocols are one of the important elements in making the two languages work together.

Experimenting with Protocols

This section provides a brief example of a simple protocol and how you can use it with a class, structure, or enumeration. The example used here can be downloaded as described in the Introduction. The full code is shown in Listing 18-1 at the end of this section; it is shown in a playground in Figures 18-1 and 18-2.

Declaring a protocol

A protocol is introduced by the keyword `protocol`. It contains the declarations that must be implemented by the types that adopt the protocol. The most common elements of a protocol are methods and properties. The example shown in this section uses a single property, but multiple properties in a protocol are permitted. You can also have properties in protocols that are adopted by classes and structures. Functions (methods) can be adopted by all the types that can

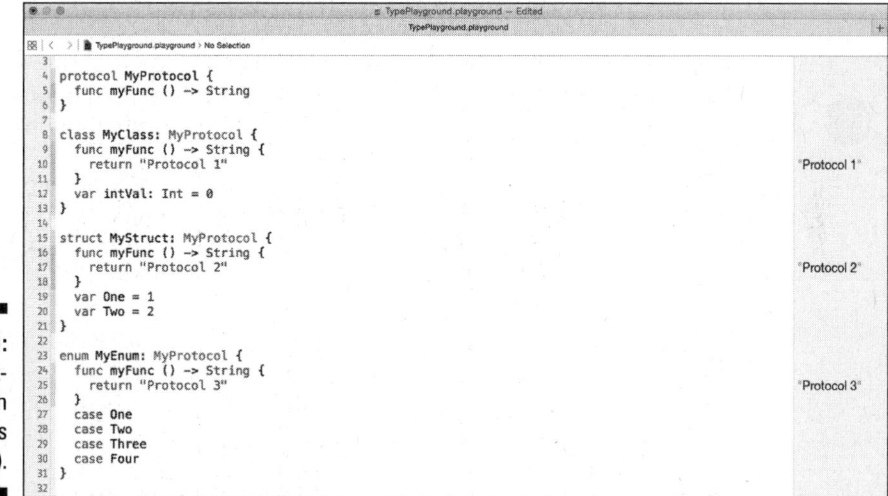

```
protocol MyProtocol {
  func myFunc () -> String
}

class MyClass: MyProtocol {
  func myFunc () -> String {
    return "Protocol 1"                         "Protocol 1"
  }
  var intVal: Int = 0
}

struct MyStruct: MyProtocol {
  func myFunc () -> String {
    return "Protocol 2"                         "Protocol 2"
  }
  var One = 1
  var Two = 2
}

enum MyEnum: MyProtocol {
  func myFunc () -> String {
    return "Protocol 3"                         "Protocol 3"
  }
  case One
  case Two
  case Three
  case Four
}
```

Figure 18-1: Experimenting with protocols (top).

```
var myClass: MyClass = MyClass()                {intVal 0}
myClass.intVal                                  0
myClass.myFunc()                                "Protocol 1"

var myStruct: MyStruct = MyStruct()             {One 1, Two 2}
myStruct.Two                                    2
myStruct.myFunc()                               "Protocol 2"

var myEnum: MyEnum = MyEnum.Two                 (Enum Value)
myEnum.myFunc ()                                "Protocol 3"
```

Figure 18-2: Experimenting with protocols (bottom).

adopt protocols (that is, by classes, structures, and enumerations), and I've included examples of each here so you can compare the usage.

A protocol is named just as other Swift elements are named. The basic protocol declaration looks like this:

```
protocol MyProtocol {
}
```

As with classes, structures, and enumerations, the name is capitalized. In fact, most Swift objects except for properties and functions are capitalized, and they use internal camelCase (capital letters for each of the embedded words except the first).

If the protocol contains a function that must be implemented by types that adopt it, the protocol declaration might look like this:

```
protocol MyProtocol {
  func myFunc () -> String
}
```

An object conforming to `MyProtocol` must implement `myFunc`.

In order to focus on the syntax of protocols, the examples in this section show *instance methods* rather than *type methods,* which are comparable to *class methods* in Objective-C. Instance methods are most commonly used.

Protocols can inherit from one another. Thus, you can declare a pair of protocols as follows:

```
protocol MyProtocol {
  func myFunc () -> String
}

protocol MyProtocol2: MyProtocol {
  func myFunc2 () -> String
}
```

An object conforming to `MyProtocol` must implement `myFunc`. An object conforming to `MyProtocol2` must implement `myFunc2`, but it must also implement `myFunc` because `MyProtocol2` inherits from `MyProtocol`. If `MyProtocol2` stands on its own (that is, if it does not inherit from `MyProtocol`), objects that conform to either `MyProtocol` or `MyProtocol2` must implement `myFunc` — but this is the same function in both protocols. This is okay. Just don't think you'd have to implement it twice.

The following sections allow you to experiment with protocols in order to show you the inheritance of protocols. Don't use a structure in which an identically-named function (or property) is used in multiple protocols unless you really mean it. (An `init` function would be a good example of the proper use of duplicate function names.)

Reference and value types

Structures and enumerations are value types, whereas classes are reference types. Although you may not have come across it before, this concept is used in languages other than Swift. A reference type is a reference (often a pointer) to an object that is allocated on the heap (an area of memory for the app to use). When you pass a reference to an instance of a class as a parameter to a function, behind the scenes you pass the pointer to the instance, and that single instance is what you access through the pointer. If you make a change in one context, it affects references to the instance in other contexts because there is only one instance with several references pointing to it.

When you use an enumeration or a structure, however, you pass it as a value in a parameter. The data is copied into a location on the stack rather than being shared from a common location in the heap. This means that changes you make to a structure or enumeration in a function are not applied to a shared instance.

If you want your protocol to be adopted only by classes, use the keyword class in the list, as in the following:

```
Protocol MyProtocol: class, MyProtocolToInheritFrom
```

Note that the class is the keyword you use: It's not the name of a class.

Adopting and conforming a class, structure, or enumeration to a protocol

Any of the major types (classes, structures, and enumerations) can adopt protocols. You can create a protocol that is adopted by any of them, or you can specify that it is adoptable only by a class. Here are examples of conforming to the basic protocol (`MyProtocol`) shown in the previous section.

Conforming a class to a protocol

Many of the protocols used in the Cocoa and Cocoa Touch frameworks are adopted by classes in the frameworks in part because in Objective-C, protocols are typically used only with classes. You'll be able to move beyond classes, but, when you're writing code that uses the frameworks, you'll frequently have to write code that conforms to protocols for classes.

Here are a few guidelines to conforming classes to protocols:

- You specify that a class adopts a protocol in its declaration, as in the following:

  ```
  class MyClass: MyProtocol {
  ```

- If you adopt more than one protocol, separate them with commas, as in the following:

  ```
  class MyClass: MyProtocol, MyProtocol2 {
  ```

- If your class is a subclass of another class, its superclass appears first in the list, as in the following:

  ```
  class MyClass: MySuperclass, MyProtocol2
  ```

  Remember that Swift does not support multiple inheritance, so there can only be one superclass (or none). You can add additional protocols to the list if necessary.

If your class is a subclass of a class that adopts a protocol, you must conform to that protocol in your own class unless the superclass already conforms to it. You don't specify this inherited adopted protocol in your own declaration. You'll see an example of this in the following section with `UITableView` and its protocols.

Having indicated that your class adopts a protocol, you must now implement all of the required properties and methods. (It's possible to signify that some methods and properties are optional, but the default setting is that they are all required.)

Here is an example of a class that conforms to a protocol. Note that `myFunc` is required by the protocol, whereas `intVal` is a class property that has nothing to do with the protocol:

```
class MyClass: MyProtocol {
  func myFunc () -> String {
    return "Protocol 1"
  }
  var intVal: Int = 0
}
```

You can create a variable (with `var`) or constant (with `let`) that contains an instance of the class with this code:

```
var myClass: MyClass = MyClass()
```

You can then access the class's `intVal` instance property as well as the protocol's required method `myFunc`:

```
myClass.intVal = 25
myClass.myFunc()
```

At this point, you make no distinction between the methods and properties required by the protocol and those that are simply part of the class.

Conforming a structure to a protocol

A structure (`struct`) adopts a protocol in the same way as a class does — with code like this:

```
struct MyStruct: MyProtocol {
  func myFunc () -> String {
    return "Protocol 2"
  }
  var intVal: Int = 0
  var One = 1
  var Two = 2
}
```

You can declare a variable that uses the structure. You can then access the members of the structure as well as the function that's required by the protocol:

```
var myStruct: MyStruct = MyStruct()
myStruct.intVal = 15
myStruct.myFunc()
```

Conforming an enumeration to a protocol

Enumerations follow the same basic design. You can declare an enumeration that adopts a protocol alongside its own data, as in the following code:

```
enum MyEnum: MyProtocol {
  func myFunc () -> String {
    return "Protocol 3"
  }
  case One
  case Two
  case Three
  case Four
}
```

Then, use the enumeration with a variable in your code:

```
var myEnum: MyEnum = MyEnum.Two
myEnum.myFunc ()
```

Listing 18-1 shows these samples put together. You can download the code as described in the Introduction and experiment with it in other ways.

Listing 18-1: Experimenting with Protocols

```
// Playground - noun: a place where people can play

protocol MyProtocol {
  func myFunc () -> String
}

class MyClass: MyProtocol {
  func myFunc () -> String {
    return "Protocol 1"
  }
  var intVal: Int = 0
}

var myClass: MyClass = MyClass()
myClass.intVal = 25
myClass.myFunc()

struct MyStruct: MyProtocol {
  func myFunc () -> String {
    return "Protocol 2"
  }
  var intVal: Int = 0
  var One = 1
  var Two = 2
}

enum MyEnum: MyProtocol {
  func myFunc () -> String {
    return "Protocol 3"
  }
  case One
  case Two
  case Three
  case Four
}

var myStruct: MyStruct = MyStruct()
myStruct.intVal = 15
myStruct.myFunc()

var myEnum: MyEnum = MyEnum.Two
myEnum.myFunc ()
```

Exploring Protocols and a UITableViewController

The Master-Detail Application template, and thus the Locatapp, uses a `UITableViewController` to display the master list of events. Table views are very common in Cocoa Touch and, on the Mac, in Cocoa. A great deal of the work is done for you already, and two protocols play a key role in the structure.

Table views on both OS X and iOS integrate very well with Core Data; the combination is frequently used as it is in Locatapp. This section explores the protocol side of things so that you'll see how to use `UITableViewController` in your own code.

This book focuses on Swift and not the frameworks, but this excursion into the frameworks helps to familiarize you with real-world uses of protocols and delegates.

The Master-Detail Application template contains the protocols that you need. They are already configured for you in the template, but you should examine what you have.

The basic architecture is that `UITableViewController` is designed to work together with two protocols: a data source (a class that adopts the `UITableViewDataSource`) and a delegate (a class that adopts the `UITableViewDelegate` protocol).

The data source provides the functionality involved with the table and its data. Its required methods specify the number of rows and sections in the table along with their titles and headers; its methods also manage editing of the table structure (moving and deleting rows).

The table view delegate protocol handles the appearance of the table: indentations, row heights, selection, editing table content (as opposed to the structure which is handled by the data source protocol), and taps in a cell, and the appearance of the contents of a cell.

Looking at delegation and protocols

The delegate protocol provides the user interface. Its methods manage selections and the editing of content.

Together, `UITableViewController` and its protocols (`UITableViewDataSource` and `UITableViewDelegate`) provide a powerful set of functionality that is easy for you to use and customize. This could all have been written as one gigantic class, but by splitting it into a main class and two protocols, it is easier to maintain (and, for many people, easier to understand).

The common implementation in many examples and Xcode templates basically reassembles the base class and the protocols into one large object.

Setting delegates in Interface Builder

You can assign an instance of a class to the `delegate` property in `UITableView`. You don't have to worry about that because first of all, that's a framework/interface issue and this book focuses on the Swift language, and second of all, it's already done for you in most of the templates and examples. Here's a review of how it's done.

1. **Open Main.storyboard in Xcode using Interface Builder (the default editor for that file).**
2. **Open the document outline if needed.**
3. **Open Master Scene, the Master controller (yellow circle), and then Table View.**

   There will be two Master Scene sections in the document outline. Open each one and then look at the Master controller in the yellow circle. One has a navigation arrow, and the other has a table list image. You want the table list image (which is shown in Figure 18-3.)

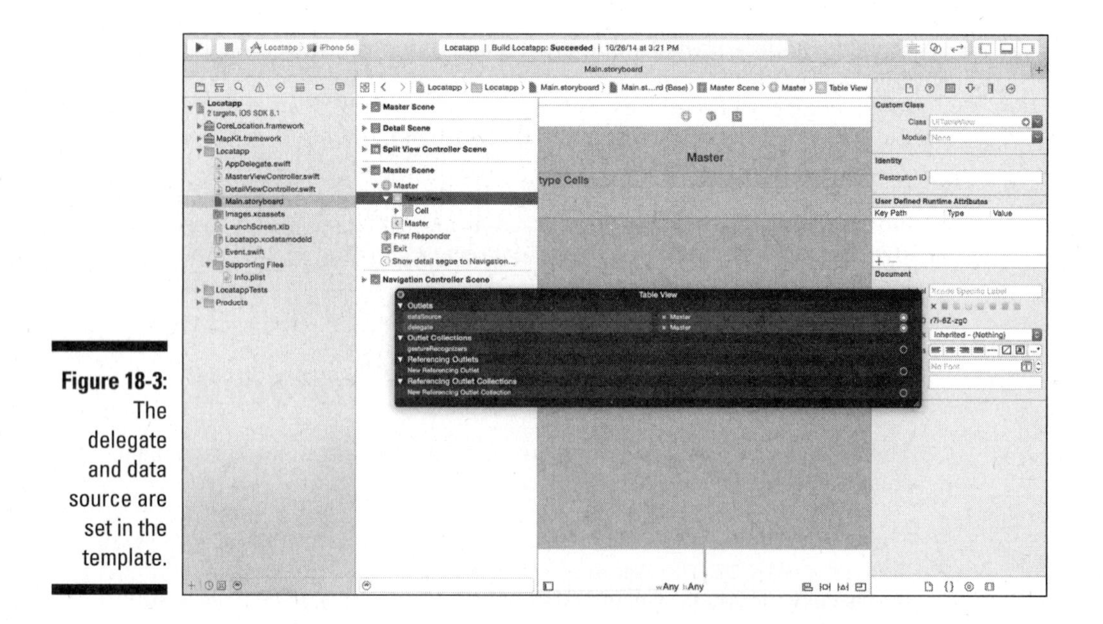

Figure 18-3: The delegate and data source are set in the template.

When you look at the `Table View` in `Main.storyboard` using Interface Builder in Xcode and shown in Figure 18-3, you'll see that the two declarations shown previously (`delegate` and `dataSource`) show up as outlets. They are connected to the `Master` object in the document outline rather than being connected in your code.

4. **Select Master (the yellow circle).**

   As you can see in Figure 18-4, when you select `Master` in the document outline of Interface Builder, you can see the other side of the connection: The two referencing outlets (`dataSource` and `delegate`) are connected to `Table View`. (Consult the detail windows shown in Figures 18-3 and 18-4 to see which one you're looking at.)

   When you make connections like these in Interface Builder, you can always look at it from both sides. It is this connection in the template that associates the table view with `Master`.

5. **With Master selected, look at the Identity inspector in the utilities area (shown at the back right of Figure 18-4).**

   As you see, `Master` is an instance of `MasterViewController`. You can see that by highlighting it and looking at Quick Help. There you'll see that `MasterViewController` is a subclass of `UITableViewController`.

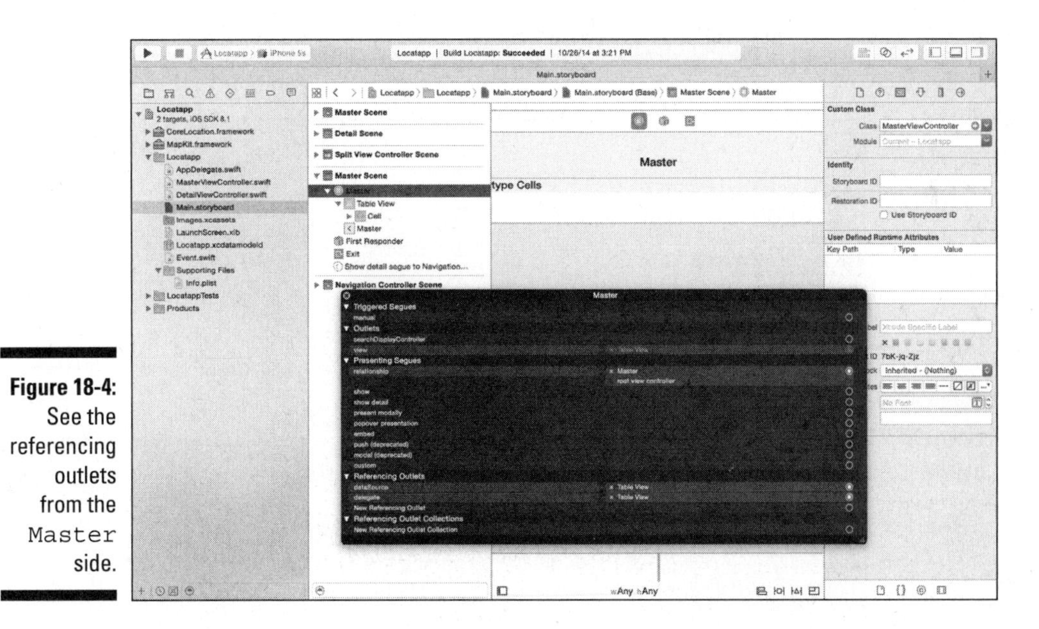

Figure 18-4: See the referencing outlets from the `Master` side.

6. **Look in `MasterViewController.swift` to see its declaration in the template (and, thus, in Locatapp).**

   Figure 18-5 shows the declaration.

   There's no reference to the protocols. How do they get into the code?

   The answer is that `MasterViewController` is a subclass of `UITableViewController` (you can see that in Figure 18-5).

7. **Highlight `UITableViewController` in the declaration shown in Figure 18-5 and open Quick Help.**

   There you can find a link to its reference.

8. **If you Click on the reference to the reference documentation for `UITableViewController`.**

   You'll see the documentation for `UITableViewController` as shown in Figure 18-6.

   The answer is at the top in the Conforms to section: `UITableView Controller` conforms to both `UITableViewDataSource` and to `UITableViewDelegate`. This means that it or subclasses of it must conform to those protocols. (It really doesn't matter whether it is the original class — `UITableViewController` in this case — or a subclass such as `MasterViewController` that conforms. The required methods and properties must be present when you build the project and run it.

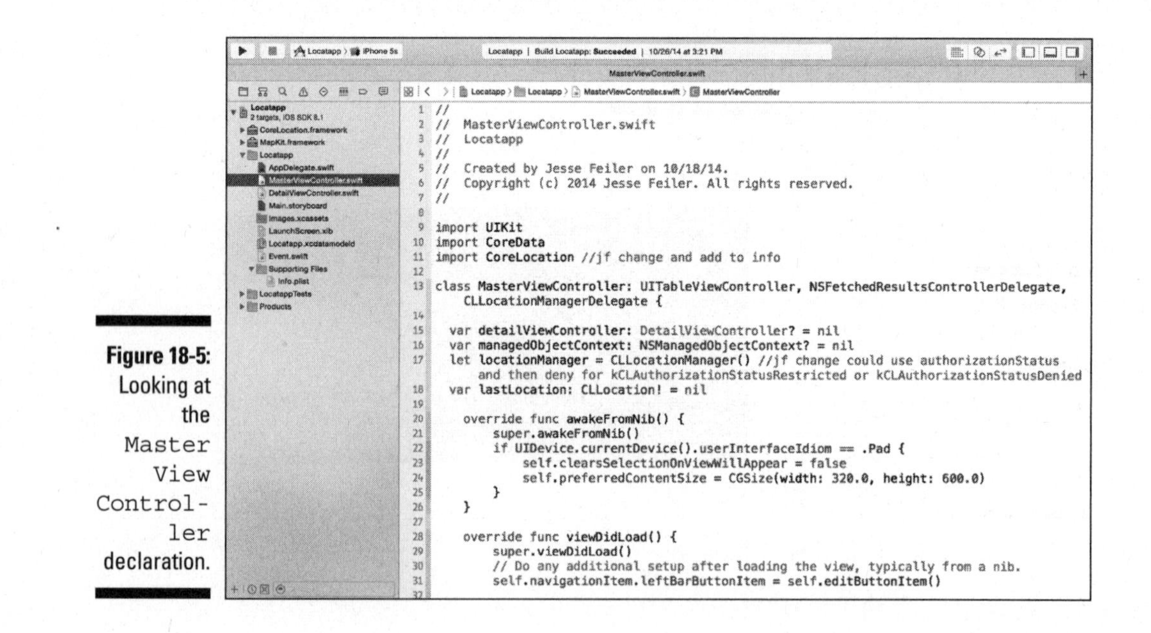

Figure 18-5: Looking at the `MasterViewController` declaration.

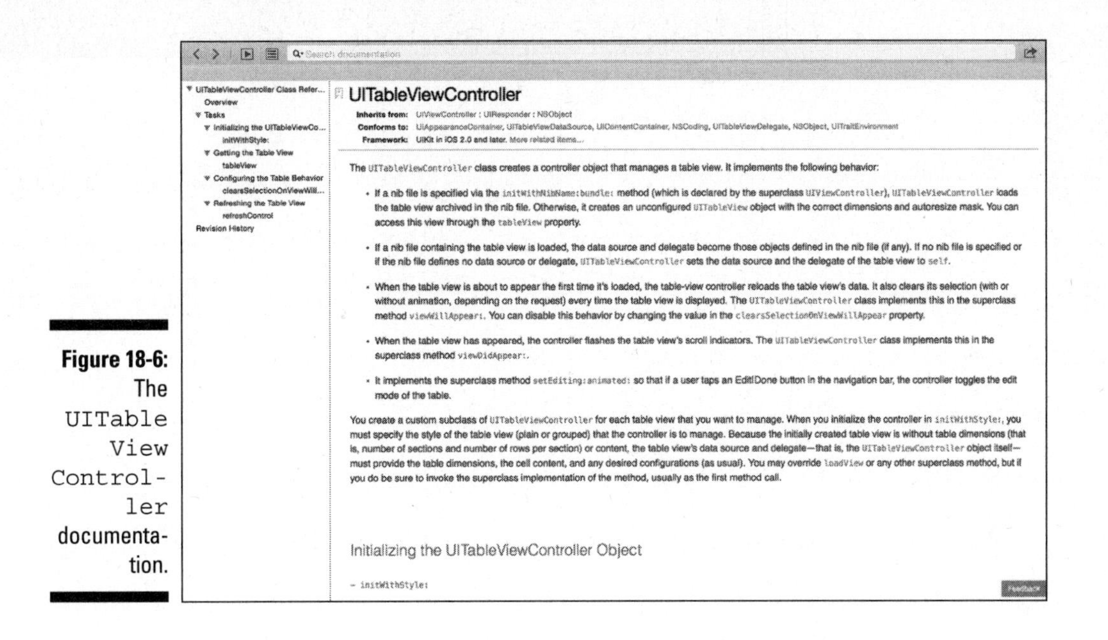

Figure 18-6: The `UITableViewController` documentation.

Chapter 19

Mixing Objective-C and Swift

In This Chapter

- Comparing frameworks in Objective-C and Swift
- Calling an Objective-C method in Swift

As this book is written in the beginning of 2015, the topic of mixing Objective-C and Swift isn't an *if*: it's a *now* (and, in this chapter, a *how*). The Cocoa and Cocoa Touch frameworks are written in Objective-C and have been since the first days of NeXTSTEP (and later OpenStep and still later Rhapsody; later still OS X and Cocoa, even later yet iPhone OS, and, most recently, iOS and Cocoa Touch). This is quite a long run for a programming language, but the languages of proven value in supporting operating systems do tend to stick around for a while. (These languages include Objective-C with the versions of our operating system just listed as well as C with UNIX and its offshoots.)

They stick around for several reasons — starting with the fact that they work. People have learned to work with them over the years, and they have proven (both the people and the languages) to be able to handle the problems that are thrown at them.

Additionally, these languages are the building blocks of major operating systems, but they're also the building blocks of many application programs. When used to build operating systems, languages like C and Objective-C have been able to support application programs written in a wide variety of languages.

The investment in these languages is enormous, and the benefits of using languages such as C and Objective-C are great.

With Swift, we have a new language that promises to make it easier for developers — particularly developers new to iOS and OS X — to write apps for Macs and iOS devices. These apps rely on the Cocoa and Cocoa Touch frameworks as well as C libraries, all of which have evolved over the years to meet changing needs of developers, users, and hardware designers.

When it comes to the libraries in C and the frameworks in Objective-C, there's little reason to undertake a massive conversion effort to Swift. In both cases (but more so in Objective-C) what happens inside a framework or library shouldn't matter to the software engineer who wants to use that framework or library: In fact, one of the main advantages of frameworks and software libraries is to generate code that can be used and reused by people who don't know the specifics of how that code works. These people only need to understand the interfaces to an unknown and maybe unknowable library or framework. Thus, we are looking at a composite world of both Swift and Objective-C.

That said, over the course of time it is likely that the Cocoa and Cocoa Touch frameworks will be converted to Swift. How long this will take isn't known. In fact, even if there is a schedule taped to the back of a door somewhere in Cupertino (Apple's headquarters), the transition to Swift will likely take several years and will be modified several times on the way to completion.

In the meantime, the tools we have from Apple and its engineers make it easy to mix and match Objective-C and Swift. Writing Objective-C apps is something that has been done for decades (albeit under the names of various operating systems). Writing a totally Swift app today isn't possible — if by "Swift" you mean to include the frameworks of Cocoa and/or Cocoa Touch rewritten in Swift. On the other hand, writing a Swift app today that builds on the opaque Cocoa and Cocoa Touch frameworks, which happen to be written in Objective-C, is an everyday occurrence.

Swift has been designed for the interoperability, and some tweaks to Objective-C in the last few years make that language more interoperable with Swift. (Whether that was done deliberately or not is unknown. It's probably a bit of both: part coincidence and part planned.)

I've already discussed some of the interoperable features of Swift (refer to the discussion of backing variables and properties in Chapter 16, for example).

This chapter is the final chapter in the main body of the book, so by now you should be pretty comfortable with Swift, and along the way you should have picked up a little bit about Objective-C. If you have followed along with the Locatapp example described in this book, you have an app that runs and that uses both Objective-C (in the frameworks) and Swift (in the Master-Detail Application iOS template in Xcode).

This chapter goes into the details of three interactions between Objective-C methods in frameworks and Swift in your own code. These interactions are good examples of similar interactions you'll do in your own apps.

Comparing Frameworks in Objective-C and Swift

The Master-Detail Application template uses a split-view controller in some cases and a navigation controller in others.

Originally (that is, with the launch of iPad), the split-view controller was intended for iPad, and the navigation controller was intended for iPhone. In 2014, with the advent of iPhone 6 Plus, the implementation changed. The split-view controller is now used for larger-screen devices and the navigation controller is used for smaller screen devices. The dividing line is no longer iPad vs. iPhone: It now starts with iPhone 6 Plus, which uses a split-view controller along with iPad. Other iPhone models use the navigation controller. This has caused a revision to the code, so even if you've used it for years, you should take a look at the code in this section in both languages.

The split view controller is set up in `AppDelegate` (`AppDelegate.swift` or the combination of `AppDelegate.h` and `AppDelegate.m` in Objective-C). This section shows you the declaration and the implementation in both Swift and Objective-C. As noted, you'll encounter this approach repeatedly with legacy Objective-C frameworks.

Identifying the key method

The key to the split-view controller is a protocol — `UISplitViewControllerDelegate`. Within that protocol, one of the most important methods is the one that manages collapsing the secondary view controller (the master list, in most cases). Even the name of this method differs in the two languages. In the jump bar, here is how it is identified in Swift:

```
splitViewController (_:collapseSecondaryViewController:
  ontoPrimaryViewController)
```

Here is how it is identified in the jump bar in Objective-C:

```
-splitViewController:collapseSecondaryViewController:
  ontoPrimaryViewController:
```

The first point to notice is that in Objective-C, the – at the beginning identifies this as an instance method as opposed to a class method. This can be done in Swift, but only in a different way. The name of the method in Swift doesn't reflect its class- or instance-ness.

Note that in the documentation, the Objective-C version is listed by the title. Following that, the Swift and Objective-C interfaces are shown (in that order). This pattern appears to be followed in all of the frameworks.

Comparing declarations

The actual declarations for these methods are shown here. First Swift:

```
optional func splitViewController(
  _ splitViewController: UISplitViewController,
  collapseSecondaryViewController
    secondaryViewController: UIViewController!,
  ontoPrimaryViewController primaryViewController:
    UIViewController!)
  -> Bool
```

Next, the Objective-C declaration:

```
- (BOOL)splitViewController:
    (UISplitViewController *)splitViewController
  collapseSecondaryViewController:
    (UIViewController *)secondaryViewController
  ontoPrimaryViewController:
    (UIViewController *) primaryViewController
```

Now that you're looking at the actual code, you can see there are more differences than just the – that marks this as an instance method in Objective-C. Here are the major differences:

- In Objective-C, the return result is shown in parentheses at the beginning of the function, as in

  ```
  - (BOOL)splitViewController:
  ```

- In Swift, the return result is shown at the end of the function, as in

  ```
  -> Bool
  ```

- In Objective-C, the parameters (except the first) are shown in this order: external name, colon, type (in parenthesis and asterisk), internal name, as in

  ```
  collapseSecondaryViewController:(UIViewController *)
    secondaryViewController
  ```

- In Swift, the parameters (including the first) are shown in a different order: external name, internal name, colon, type, as in

  ```
    collapseSecondaryViewController
          secondaryViewController:
     UIViewController!
  ```

- Types in Swift can include `!` and `?` as postfix operators to indicate unwrapping or optional status. In addition, the external name can be missing and replaced by an underscore, as in

```
_ splitViewController: UISplitViewController
```

Calling an Objective-C Method in Objective-C within Swift to Set a Pin on the Map

If you have followed along with the changes to Locatapp, you know that adding stored locations to the map is very simple. The code you have already written does the job of storing the locations. All you need to do is to add a pin for the selected location.

The code that follows uses Swift, but it uses the MapKit and Core Location frameworks even more than the Swift language.

The first change is in `MasterViewController.swift`. It's in `prepareForSegue (_:sender:)` Here are the steps:

1. **Locate the following line.**

```
let object =
  self.fetchedResultsController.
    objectAtIndexPath(indexPath)
    as NSManagedObject
```

2. **Change it to this:**

```
let object =
  self.fetchedResultsController.
    objectAtIndexPath(indexPath)
    as Event
```

The other changes need to take place in the `DetailViewController` class. Listing 19-1 shows the new version. Previous deletions are commented out in that listing.

Listing 19-1: Updating `DetailViewController`

```
class DetailViewController: UIViewController {

  //@IBOutlet weak var detailDescriptionLabel: UILabel!
  @IBOutlet var mapView: MKMapView!
  @IBAction func actionButton(sender: AnyObject) {
  }

    var detailItem: Event? = nil { //AnyObject? {
      didSet {
        // Update the view.
        self.configureView()
      }
    }

    func configureView() {
      // Update the user interface for the detail item.

      var pin = MKPointAnnotation ()

      var long:Double = detailItem!.longitude as Double
      var lat:Double = detailItem!.latitude as Double

      var myCoordinate:CLLocationCoordinate2D = CLLocation
           Coordinate2D(latitude: lat as CLLocationDegrees,
           longitude: long as CLLocationDegrees)

      pin.coordinate = myCoordinate
      pin.title = "Test Title";
      pin.subtitle = "Test Subtitle";

      if var myMapView = self.mapView {
        myMapView.addAnnotation(pin)
      }
    }

    override func viewDidLoad() {
      super.viewDidLoad()
      // Do any additional setup after loading the view,
           typically from a nib.
      self.configureView()
    }

    override func didReceiveMemoryWarning() {
      super.didReceiveMemoryWarning()
      // Dispose of any resources that can be recreated.
    }
}
```

Here are the steps to take to update the existing code in `configureView` from the version you have at the end of Chapter 16:

1. **Change `detailItem` to type `Event`.**

   That's how it's described in the data model, but until now it's been used as a generic `NSManagedObject` or `AnyObject`. Change the declaration as shown here (the previous code is commented out).

   ```
   var detailItem: Event? = nil { //AnyObject? {
   ```

2. **Change the `configureView` function to add a map pin.**

   This has several steps. The first is to create a `pin` variable of type `MKPointAnnotation` (part of the `MapKit` framework).

   ```
   var pin = MKPointAnnotation ()
   ```

3. **Create a `Double` from the stored `longitude` value which is an `NSNumber` at this point.**

   You do that in Chapter 9, "Functioning Successfully."

   ```
   var long:Double = detailItem!.longitude as Double
   ```

4. **Do the same with the stored `latitude` value.**

   ```
   var lat:Double = detailItem!.latitude as Double
   ```

5. **Create a `CLLocationCoordinate2D` called `myCoordinate`.**

   This combines the latitude and longitude.

   ```
   var myCoordinate:CLLocationCoordinate2D =
     CLLocationCoordinate2D(
       latitude: lat as CLLocationDegrees,
       longitude: long as CLLocationDegrees)
   ```

6. **Set the `coordinate` property of `pin` to `myCoordinate`.**

   ```
   pin.coordinate = myCoordinate
   ```

7. **Set the `title` property to a title.**

   ```
   pin.title = "Test Title";
   ```

8. **Set the `subtitle` property to a subtitle.**

   ```
   pin.subtitle = "Test Subtitle";
   ```

9. **Convert `self.mapView` to a `var` called `myMapView`, if possible.**

10. **If successful, call `addAnnotation` with `pin`.**

    ```
    myMapView.addAnnotation(pin)
    ```

Your app now lets you select a location and see it on the map. The updated code appears in Listing 19-1.

In the declarations and in the method/function calls in Listing 19-1, most of what you've done is directly translated from Objective-C code to Swift. In both languages, the syntax that you use is repeated over and over. There are differences between the two languages, but you get used to the patterns you need to use to work with both languages over time.

Bridging between Objective-C and Swift

There are cases where you need to mix and match code between the two languages. When it comes to the frameworks, the engineers at Apple are working through the interfaces to provide Swift interfaces alongside the Objective-C versions so that you can use either one to get to the framework in your own app.

Sometimes you need to use a bridge to get to code that you need. A typical example occurs when you use Core Data with relationships. Given a data model for Core Data (often provided as part of a template), you can use Editor➪Create NSManagedObject Subclass to create files to add to your project. Choose the option to create Objective-C files. At the bottom of the .h file that's created you'll find declarations of methods for members of relationships such as these:

```
@interface WhereCategory (CoreDataGeneratedAccessors)

- (void)addNecklaceObject:(Necklace *)value;
- (void)removeNecklaceObject:( Necklace *)value;
- (void)addNecklaces:(NSSet *)values;
- (void)removNecklaceses:(NSSet *)values;

@end
```

This code lets you add or remove individual related objects or the whole set of related objects. When you try to create the files, you'll see an alert asking you if you'd like to create a bridging header.

The file that is created will be named MyProject-Bridging-Header.h. Simply add import statements to that file for the Objective-C .h files, as shown here, and you'll be ready to build your mix-and-match project.

```
//  Use this file to import your target's public headers
//  that you would like to expose to Swift.

#import "Bracelet.h"
#import "Pendant.h"
```

Part V
The Part of Tens

Enjoy an additional Part of Tens list online at www.dummies.com/extras/swift.

In this part . . .

- Remember these ten Swift features that aren't in Objective-C.
- Check out ten Swift features that aren't in C.
- Take a look at ten Objective-C features that aren't in Swift.

Chapter 20

Ten Swift Features That Aren't in Objective-C

Objective-C dates back to the 1980s — quite a long time ago by computer technology standards. In the decades since its first release, Objective-C's influence on programming language technologies and best practices (along with hardware and operating system changes) has demonstrated that the Objective-C design is robust and flexible. With the dawn of a new century, Apple's engineers embarked on the development of a new language for the technology world in which we live today.

As of this writing, Objective-C and Swift are both available to developers. Both let you work with the Cocoa and Cocoa Touch frameworks. In all likelihood, Objective-C one day will be replaced by Swift, but this won't happen quickly. Even with Swift's shorter learning curve, the transition from Objective-C to Swift will be measured in years.

For now, developers can work in either language. Most of the frameworks are still written in Objective-C, so even if you write your code in Swift, you will need to interact with Objective-C frameworks. Fortunately, this isn't difficult.

This chapter covers ten Swift features that aren't available in Objective-C. As you switch back and forth between the two languages, this chapter may help you distinguish between the features available in each language. In general, of course, you can rely on Swift to follow one overall theme: With Swift, you'll frequently write less code. This is because the Swift language is designed to handle a number of Objective-C's common situations all by itself.

Before getting to Swift features that aren't in Objective-C, let me point out three terms common to both languages that have slightly different meanings in Swift:

- **closure:** In Swift, a *closure* is a section of code that can be executed non-sequentially. It's declared with its own variables (and references variables available in the scope in which it's created), and it's executed when needed. Closures are frequently used as completion handlers for asynchronous processes, so whenever that process completes (even if completion is a failure), the closure will run. Swift considers a function to be a special case of a closure. Closures in Swift are similar to blocks in Objective-C.

- **type:** In Swift, a *type* can be a class, structure, or enumeration. Any of these can contain methods. functions, and members.
- **pass by reference/pass by value:** Passing variable back and forth is a classic issue in object-oriented programming. In Swift, structures and enumerations are passed back and forth by value (or by copying — the same thing). This means that the same value can be passed to several places, and in each place, it can be used and modified without affecting any of the other occurrences. Class instances in Swift are passed by reference so that a single version of the instance is referenced by all clients. If there are multiple instances of a class, each of those instances is passed around by reference. Objective-C deals with these issues in different ways such as by referring to `strong` and `weak` references.

Using Playgrounds to Explore Code and Syntax

Playgrounds are a new feature of Xcode 6 that let you test code easily. They can make writing your code very much like writing code for an interpreted language because you see the results immediately. Many of the examples in Part II of this book use playgrounds to demonstrate how code snippets work. You can do the same with your code — you don't have to get a clean compile and build to get down to testing how a single line of code works (or doesn't work).

See Chapter 2, "Playing in the Playground."

Using Tuples

Tuples let you group individual values into a single unit. In Objective-C, this is often done with dictionaries that organize multiple values together. When the multiple values have a logical organizing principle, consider using tuples for cleaner and more easily understood code.

See Chapter 6, "Using Swift Types."

Using Ranges to Save Code

Like tuples, ranges let you create reusable constructs that can be used in creating and using functions. They generally replace small sections of code. By naming and reusing them, you can avoid the typographical errors often introduced by retyping the same code several times.

See Chapter 8, "Controlling the Flow."

Taking Advantage of Strict Typing and Type Safety

Unlike other languages, including Objective-C, Swift makes you handle type conversion and casting explicitly. Among other things, this gets rid of pesky errors that arise when the compiler and operating system convert a value from one type to another (and you were thinking that the conversion would not take place or would be a different type of conversion). Now, you are responsible for the conversions, and the compiler and operating system do your bidding instead of sometimes surprising you.

See Chapter 6, "Using Swift Types."

Initializing Your Variables and Constants

Although you may not always realize it, Swift requires that each property be initialized either with an explicit value and an explicit type annotation, or with an inferred type based on an explicit value.

See Chapter 12, "Initializing and Deinitializing Data."

Understanding Optional Types

Swift requires that you type properties explicitly or by providing a value whose type Swift can infer. Swift gives you a number of tools that can type a property as optional. Optional types let Swift know that you have thought about a type, but you haven't yet reached a final conclusion about it. With an optional type, you provide enough information for Swift to keep going.

See Chapter 6, "Using Swift Types."

Looking at Frameworks for Your Own Code

When developing apps, you'll constantly use Cocoa and Cocoa Touch frameworks. The frameworks that we use tend to be very large — `UIKit` is an example — but with Swift, Apple provides sample code that takes advantage of a number of very small custom frameworks. By combining the framework architecture and Swift's simplicity, you have a convenient way to construct your own apps and reuse code. When you start to explore Swift beyond this book, make frameworks one of your first stops.

Including Annotations and Attributes in Declarations

The format of declarations has changed significantly in Swift. The original format of declarations consisted of two parts:

```
<type>variableName
```

This style dates back to the early days of FORTRAN. Over the years, additions and decorators were added. Now, with Swift, this core syntax has been replaced with annotations and attributes that are more flexible.

See Chapter 6, "Using Swift Types."

Deinitializing Variables Where Necessary

Swift manages memory and you can rely on it to clean up as needed when you (or the system) deallocates an instance. You can write a deinitializer (named `deinit`) to do anything other than simple memory releasing. Among the tasks a deinitializer might do are closing a file and placing a data structure in a known state for its next use, among similar tasks.

See Chapter 12, "Initializing and Deinitializing Data."

Use Patterns to Simplify Your Code

You can specify cases inside a `switch` statement that consist of patterns. This can get rid of a good deal of code because in addition to switching on values, you can switch on ranges of data as well as conditions and characteristics of data that go beyond individual values.

See Chapter 11, "Declaring the Symbols."

Chapter 21

Ten Swift Features That Are Not in C

Considering that Swift is a newly developed, object-oriented language, and that C was developed almost half a century ago (by Dennis Ritchie in 1969-1973), when the object-oriented paradigm wasn't even in widespread use, you might think that comparing these two languages would be difficult and, in many ways, unfair to both languages.

That's one way of looking at things, but another way is to look at C's impact on modern languages. C is still taught in computer-science courses in a variety of programs from primary schools to post-graduate courses. C is still being taught because it is still one of the most widely used languages. C may not be cutting-edge, but it has served a major role in the development of today's software and the people who design and develop it.

For those who are familiar with C and now learning Swift, this chapter explains the major distinctions between the two languages. I take for granted that you know that Swift has been developed for an environment that includes large and small computers (that is, Macs and mobile iOS devices) whereas C was developed for minicomputers and mainframes.

With that out of the way, here are ten Swift features that are not in C.

Strong Typing

Swift is much more strongly typed than C. If you want to cast a value to another type, you have to do it rather than rely on it being done for you automatically. For example, consider this code:

```
var x = 4
var y = 4.0
var z = x + y
```

The last line produces an error because you can't add an `Int` and a `Double`.

However, either of the following two lines will work:

```
var z = x + Int(y)
var z = Double (x) + y
```

Swift's typing is so strict, that even the following line will not work:

```
var z = Float(x) + y
```

Swift infers the type `Double` for the value 4.0 unless you explicitly assign it the `Float` type when using it in an operation or when declaring it, as in the following line of code:

```
var y :Float = 4
```

If you're not used to a strongly typed language, this can take some getting used to.

Libraries Extend C

Libraries are the primary way of extending C, but you can extend Swift with libraries (in addition to the built-in Swift standard library) as well as with frameworks, classes and subclasses, extensions to classes, structures, and enumerations.

Switch Statements Fall through Cases in C

You can sometimes tell C programmers are writing Swift code by their `switch` statements. In C, a `switch` statement consists of `case` elements, as in the following:

```
switch(choice) {
  case choice1:
    break;
  case choice2:
    break;
}
```

Without the `break` statements, control passes through to the next `case`. This doesn't happen in Swift. There is some C-style code that takes advantage of the fact that without `break` statements, control passes to the next `case` statement(s). That has always been considered dubious programming style, but now it won't happen in Swift.

C Is an International Standard

C is an international standard (specifically ISO/IEC 9899:201x), and Swift is not. Whether or not this matters is up to you. A number of people (including the author) think that this is pretty much irrelevant at this time. Languages that aren't governed by international standards organizations can sometimes evolve more quickly, and, if such standards become necessary, they can be added later. International standards don't have much of a role to play in the initial development process of a language, when it's more important to get as many people as possible to use the language. This is the stage Swift is in now.

Swift Is Tightly Linked to the Cocoa and Cocoa Touch Frameworks

In fact, it's hard to tell where Swift leaves off and the frameworks take over. Even though this book focuses on the language, I've included examples that use the Cocoa and Cocoa Touch frameworks because certain language features can't be described without reference to these frameworks.

Obviously, this is not the case with C.

Swift Includes Memory Management

Automatic Reference Counting (ARC) is built into Swift. In C, memory management is the developer's task.

Swift Is Designed to Function in a Multi-Threaded Environment

In Swift, certain language features, such as closures, are designed to support multi-threaded environments in which a number of different tasks may be executed simultaneously on several multiple-cored processors. Language features such as closures are specifically designed for the multi-threaded environment found on Macs and iOS devices.

Types Can Be Created Easily in Swift

Even in comparison with Objective-C, which in many ways is Swift's closest predecessor, Swift's ability to create new types (sometimes alongside or instead of custom classes) distinguishes it from all other languages, including C.

Swift Has Its Own IDE and Compiler

Swift is designed to be used with its own IDE (Xcode 6 or later) and its own compiler (LLVM). There is no apparent reason why another IDE couldn't be used and another compiler written, but at the moment, neither of these appear to be in the works, and developers seem to be generally content with the existing tools. (I say "generally" because developers are developers and envisioning different futures is part of the job description.) C and other languages are not tightly integrated with an IDE and compiler.

Types Can Be Classes, Structures, or Enumerations

In Swift, types can be classes, structures, or enumerations, and each of them can have properties and methods. Swift's properties and methods are not just for classes. This sure isn't the case in C!

Chapter 22

Ten Objective-C Features That Aren't in Swift

If you are an experienced Objective-C developer, this chapter reminds you of some features you may be used to that aren't available in Swift. In each case, I show you workarounds and strategies for replacing your old tried-and-true Objective-C friends. And don't worry: In most cases, you'll end up writing less code and your code will be more robust.

Saying Goodbye to Header (.h) Files

In Swift, the header (`.h`) files are gone. The `.h` and `.m` files for headers and bodies (originally called messages) of a class are consolidated into a single `.swift` file.

Saying Farewell to Dangling Pointers (Almost Always)

It's hard (but not impossible) to reference a dangling pointer in Swift. Over the last few years, Objective-C has also made such references more difficult, but they remain distinctly possible. You can avoid issues with these references if you make certain that pointers to instances are always set before they are used, and that they're set to `nil` before the instance is deallocated. Swift uses very few pointers, so they can't dangle.

Forgetting About Uninitialized Variables and Properties

Swift requires initialization of declared properties, variables, and constants. This immediately removes a whole set of problems that can occur when you reference uninitialized variables and may either crash or cause unexpected (and frequently unrepeatable) errors.

Exploiting a Common Superclass Like NSObject

Most objects in Objective-C are subclasses of `NSObject`; almost all of them conform to the `NSObject` protocol. Thus, collections such as `NSArray` and `NSDictionary` can contain objects of any kind as long as they are subclasses of `NSObject`. In Swift, the elements of an array or dictionary do not have a common superclass, but they do have to have a common type so that they can be manipulated. This is now your responsibility.

Managing Type Casting

Objective-C manages type casting where it can, but if your assumption about the correct cast differs from Objective-C's, your code may crash. With Swift, you have to do the casting explicitly. However, Swift can infer a type from initial values of variables or constants, so, on balance, your code is more robust and you may actually need less of it because you can let Swift infer types for you.

Preferring Closures to Blocks

Blocks in Objective-C are like closures in other languages. In Swift, that function is provided by closures, and the documentation reflects this use.

Getting Rid of Legacy Memory Management

Although manual memory management with `alloc` and `dealloc` has been deprecated in Swift, much code still exists that either uses it or refers to it in comments and commented-out lines of code. If you are converting old code rather than writing new Swift code from scratch, it's worthwhile to remove these vestiges of manual memory management. It's very unlikely they will return.

Replacing Property Decorators

Instead of Objective-C's property decorators, Swift has annotations in declarations. The mixture of attributes, such as `readonly`, `strong`, `weak`, and the like, is gone with Swift. The necessary information is encompassed in types.

Using Swift Style to Access Class Properties

Swift style uses dot syntax to reference objects within a class, structure, or enumeration. Remove any left-over bracket-based syntax.

Clarifying Swift Access Control

The privacy directives in Objective-C are handled differently in Swift. In Objective-C you use the following directives:

- `@private`
- `@protected`
- `@public`

Declarations of methods and properties can also be placed both in the `.h` file or in a class extension of a `.m` file. This provides two disjoint ways of specifying visibility.

Swift has no `.h` or `.m` files and therefore no class extensions with hidden declarations. It has a single access control model using

- `public`
- `private`
- `internal`

These are part of the language itself rather than being compiler directives.

TIP

The Swift access control structure is described in Chapter 14.

Index

• Symbols •

• A •

• E •

• F •

• G •

• H •

• I •

• M •

• N •

• O •

• P •

• T •

• U •

• V •

• W •

• X •

• Z •

About the Author

Jesse Feiler is a developer, consultant, and author specializing in Apple technologies. He is the creator of Minutes Machine for iPad (a meeting management app) and Saranac River Trail app (a guide to the trail that includes location-based updates as well as social media tools). His apps are available in the App Store and are published by Champlain Arts Corp. (champlainarts.com).

As a consultant, he has worked with small businesses and nonprofits on projects that address such topics as production control, publishing, and project management, often involving FileMaker.

His books include *iOS App Development For Dummies* (Wiley, 2014), *iOS 6 Foundations* (Wiley, 2013), and *iWork For Dummies* (Wiley, 2012).

He is heard regularly on WAMC Public Radio for the Northeast's The Roundtable. He is president of the Plattsburgh Public Library board and founder of Friends of Saranac River Trail, Inc. He is a recipient of the Velma K. Moore award for exemplary service and dedication to libraries from the New York State Association of Library Boards. A native of Washington, DC, he has lived in New York City and currently in Plattsburgh, NY.

He can be reached at `www.northcountryconsulting.com` (consulting) and `www.champlainarts.com` (app development).

Author's Acknowledgments

This project couldn't have succeeded without the help and support of many people.

This book would not have been possible without the wonderful help of Chris Morris, the project editor, and Aaron Crabtree, the technical editor. They have provided invaluable advice and suggestions to make the book clearer and more useful to readers.

As always, Carole Jelen at Waterside Productions has been a stalwart supporter and guide through the world of publishers and publishing.

Publisher's Acknowledgments

Acquisitions Editor: Andy Cummings
Senior Project Editor: Christopher Morris
Copy Editor: Christopher Morris
Technical Editor: Aaron Crabtree
Editorial Assistant: Claire Johnson
Sr. Editorial Assistant: Cherie Case

Project Coordinator: Melissa Cossell
Cover Image: ©iStock.com/nadla

le & Mac

For Dummies,
:dition
1-118-72306-7

ne For Dummies,
:dition
1-118-69083-3

s All-in-One
)ummies, 4th Edition
1-118-82210-4

: Mavericks
)ummies
1-118-69188-5

gging & Social Media

book For Dummies,
:dition
1-118-63312-0

al Media Engagement
)ummies
1-118-53019-1

dPress For Dummies,
:dition
1-118-79161-5

iness

k Investing
)ummies, 4th Edition
1-118-37678-2

sting For Dummies,
:dition
0-470-90545-6

Personal Finance
For Dummies, 7th Edition
978-1-118-11785-9

QuickBooks 2014
For Dummies
978-1-118-72005-9

Small Business Marketing
Kit For Dummies,
3rd Edition
978-1-118-31183-7

Careers

Job Interviews
For Dummies, 4th Edition
978-1-118-11290-8

Job Searching with Social
Media For Dummies,
2nd Edition
978-1-118-67856-5

Personal Branding
For Dummies
978-1-118-11792-7

Resumes For Dummies,
6th Edition
978-0-470-87361-8

Starting an Etsy Business
For Dummies, 2nd Edition
978-1-118-59024-9

Diet & Nutrition

Belly Fat Diet For Dummies
978-1-118-34585-6

Mediterranean Diet
For Dummies
978-1-118-71525-3

Nutrition For Dummies,
5th Edition
978-0-470-93231-5

Digital Photography

Digital SLR Photography
All-in-One For Dummies,
2nd Edition
978-1-118-59082-9

Digital SLR Video &
Filmmaking For Dummies
978-1-118-36598-4

Photoshop Elements 12
For Dummies
978-1-118-72714-0

Gardening

Herb Gardening
For Dummies, 2nd Edition
978-0-470-61778-6

Gardening with Free-Range
Chickens For Dummies
978-1-118-54754-0

Health

Boosting Your Immunity
For Dummies
978-1-118-40200-9

Diabetes For Dummies,
4th Edition
978-1-118-29447-5

Living Paleo For Dummies
978-1-118-29405-5

Big Data

Big Data For Dummies
978-1-118-50422-2

Data Visualization
For Dummies
978-1-118-50289-1

Hadoop For Dummies
978-1-118-60755-8

Language & Foreign Language

500 Spanish Verbs
For Dummies
978-1-118-02382-2

English Grammar
For Dummies, 2nd Edition
978-0-470-54664-2

French All-in-One
For Dummies
978-1-118-22815-9

German Essentials
For Dummies
978-1-118-18422-6

Italian For Dummies,
2nd Edition
978-1-118-00465-4

Available in print and e-book formats.

Available wherever books are sold. **For more information or to order direct visit www.dummies.com**

Math & Science

Algebra I For Dummies, 2nd Edition
978-0-470-55964-2

Anatomy and Physiology For Dummies, 2nd Edition
978-0-470-92326-9

Astronomy For Dummies, 3rd Edition
978-1-118-37697-3

Biology For Dummies, 2nd Edition
978-0-470-59875-7

Chemistry For Dummies, 2nd Edition
978-1-118-00730-3

1001 Algebra II Practice Problems For Dummies
978-1-118-44662-1

Microsoft Office

Excel 2013 For Dummies
978-1-118-51012-4

Office 2013 All-in-One For Dummies
978-1-118-51636-2

PowerPoint 2013 For Dummies
978-1-118-50253-2

Word 2013 For Dummies
978-1-118-49123-2

Music

Blues Harmonica For Dummies
978-1-118-25269-7

Guitar For Dummies, 3rd Edition
978-1-118-11554-1

iPod & iTunes For Dummies, 10th Edition
978-1-118-50864-0

Programming

Beginning Programming with C For Dummies
978-1-118-73763-7

Excel VBA Programming For Dummies, 3rd Edition
978-1-118-49037-2

Java For Dummies, 6th Edition
978-1-118-40780-6

Religion & Inspiration

The Bible For Dummies
978-0-7645-5296-0

Buddhism For Dummies, 2nd Edition
978-1-118-02379-2

Catholicism For Dummies, 2nd Edition
978-1-118-07778-8

Self-Help & Relationships

Beating Sugar Addiction For Dummies
978-1-118-54645-1

Meditation For Dummies, 3rd Edition
978-1-118-29144-3

Seniors

Laptops For Seniors For Dummies, 3rd Edition
978-1-118-71105-7

Computers For Seniors For Dummies, 3rd Edition
978-1-118-11553-4

iPad For Seniors For Dummies, 6th Edition
978-1-118-72826-0

Social Security For Dummies
978-1-118-20573-0

Smartphones & Tablets

Android Phones For Dummies, 2nd Edition
978-1-118-72030-1

Nexus Tablets For Dummies
978-1-118-77243-0

Samsung Galaxy S 4 For Dummies
978-1-118-64222-1

Samsung Galaxy Tabs For Dummies
978-1-118-77294-2

Test Prep

ACT For Dummies, 5th Edition
978-1-118-01259-8

ASVAB For Dummies, 3rd Edition
978-0-470-63760-9

GRE For Dummies, 7th Edition
978-0-470-88921-3

Officer Candidate Tests For Dummies
978-0-470-59876-4

Physician's Assistant Exam For Dummies
978-1-118-11556-5

Series 7 Exam For Dummie
978-0-470-09932-2

Windows 8

Windows 8.1 All-in-One For Dummies
978-1-118-82087-2

Windows 8.1 For Dummie
978-1-118-82121-3

Windows 8.1 For Dummie Book + DVD Bundle
978-1-118-82107-7

Available in print and e-book formats.

Available wherever books are sold. **For more information or to order direct visit www.dummies.com**

Take Dummies with you everywhere you go!

Whether you are excited about e-books, want more from the web, must have your mobile apps, or are swept up in social media, Dummies makes everything easier.

Leverage the Power

For Dummies is the global leader in the reference category and one of the most trusted and highly regarded brands in the world. No longer just focused on books, customers now have access to the For Dummies content they need in the format they want. Let us help you develop a solution that will fit your brand and help you connect with your customers.

Advertising & Sponsorships

Connect with an engaged audience on a powerful multimedia site, and position your message alongside expert how-to content.

Targeted ads • Video • Email marketing • Microsites • Sweepstakes sponsorship

For Dummies is a registered trademark of John Wiley & Sons, Inc.